Polish Popular Music on Screen

"Insightful, informative, clearly written and thoroughly engaging, Mazierska's book explores Polish musicals, biopics, music documentaries and music videos bringing to light a fascinating history unknown to non-natives, and under-researched in Poland. While explicitly national in its focus, the observations and points of analysis introduced call for further studies and comparative approaches of popular cinemas and music in other European and World contexts. Thoroughly recommended both for its illuminating breadth and depth, and for the invitation to comparisons that it inspires."

—Dr. Lydia Papadimitriou, *Reader in Film Studies, Liverpool John Moores University*

Ewa Mazierska

Polish Popular Music on Screen

Ewa Mazierska
School of Arts and Media
University of Central Lancashire
Preston, Lancashire, UK

ISBN 978-3-030-42781-8   ISBN 978-3-030-42779-5 (eBook)
https://doi.org/10.1007/978-3-030-42779-5

© The Editor(s) (if applicable) and The Author(s), under exclusive license to Springer Nature Switzerland AG 2020
This work is subject to copyright. All rights are solely and exclusively licensed by the Publisher, whether the whole or part of the material is concerned, specifically the rights of translation, reprinting, reuse of illustrations, recitation, broadcasting, reproduction on microfilms or in any other physical way, and transmission or information storage and retrieval, electronic adaptation, computer software, or by similar or dissimilar methodology now known or hereafter developed.
The use of general descriptive names, registered names, trademarks, service marks, etc. in this publication does not imply, even in the absence of a specific statement, that such names are exempt from the relevant protective laws and regulations and therefore free for general use.
The publisher, the authors and the editors are safe to assume that the advice and information in this book are believed to be true and accurate at the date of publication. Neither the publisher nor the authors or the editors give a warranty, expressed or implied, with respect to the material contained herein or for any errors or omissions that may have been made. The publisher remains neutral with regard to jurisdictional claims in published maps and institutional affiliations.

Cover design by eStudioCalamar
Cover image: A scene from Piętro wyżej (Upstairs, 1937), directed by Leon Trystan

This Palgrave Macmillan imprint is published by the registered company Springer Nature Switzerland AG
The registered company address is: Gewerbestrasse 11, 6330 Cham, Switzerland

Acknowledgements

Many people helped me to write this book. I am grateful to them for meeting me, helping me to get hold of films and books and reading parts of this book. They include colleagues from the National Film Archive in Warsaw, Adam Wyżyński, Grażyna Grabowska and Michał Pieńkowski, fellow academics Elżbieta Ostrowska, who gave me the idea to embark on this project, Mariusz Gradowski, Sylwia Kołos, Leonardo Masi, Grzegorz Piotrowski, Artur Szarecki and Zsolt Győri, with whom I worked on other publications, concerning popular music in Eastern Europe. I am also indebted to film director Józef Gębski, who provided me with material concerning his work, as well as a wealth of information about Polish television of state socialist period and Jerzy Skrzypczyk from the band Czerwone Gitary, who shared with me information about documentary films and videos of this band.

I am also grateful to my employer, University of Central Lancashire, for financially supporting several of my trips to Poland and my family, Gifford, Kamila and Daniel for enduring for many years my indulgence in music and films which were not particularly to their taste and helping me with proofreading the manuscript.

Contents

1	**Introduction**	1
	Popular Cinema in Poland and Its Critical Appraisal	2
	The Boundaries of Popular Music	7
	What Popular Music Offers Screen Media; How Screen Media Serve Popular Music?	11
	Structure and Chapter Description	14
	Works Cited	17

Part I Polish Musicals: Themes, Styles, Ideologies

2	**Music and Dance in the Service of Modern Poland: Interwar Musicals**	23
	Hollywood and European Musicals	23
	Polish Politics, Industry and Cinema Between the World Wars	27
	Radio Days	31
	Songs in the Service of Industry	38
	Spying, Loving, Singing	40
	From an Aristocrat to a Popular Musician	43
	Dancer's Musical	46
	Conclusions	51
	Works Cited	52

3	**From Popular Songs to Manufactured Entertainment: Musicals of the State Socialist Period**	57
	Polish Politics, Economy and Cinema Under State Socialism	58
	The Beginnings: Remembering War Songs	62
	Dancing to the Rhythm of Mass Songs	66
	Stabilising Small Stabilisation	70
	A Gentle Beat of Big Beat	83
	Escapism of 'Gierek' and Martial Law Musicals	91
	Rock Films with Real Rock Stars	101
	Conclusions	107
	Works Cited	108
4	**Recycling Without Nostalgia: Postcommunist Musicals**	113
	Poland After the Fall of the Berlin Wall	115
	From Documenting to Erasing Culture: Disco Polo Musicals	117
	Satire Without a Vantage Point	126
	Female-Friendly Musicals for the YouTube Generation	129
	Cold War Forever	137
	Conclusions	145
	Works Cited	146

Part II Biopics on Large and Small Screen

5	**From Socio to Psycho-Biographies: Biographical Films About Popular Musicians**	151
	Western and Eastern European Biopics	152
	Biopics in Quotation Marks	157
	Destined for Blues *or* Condemned to Drugs?	168
	A Synthesis of Psycho and Socio-Biography	172
	The Last Cult Music Journalist	176
	Conclusions	181
	Works Cited	181
6	**Epic Biopics: Biographies of Polish Music Stars on Television**	185
	Authenticity and Suffering	186

Living as a Pole, Dying as a Swiss 194
Works Cited 205

Part III   Music Documentaries

7   From Reporting to Analysing: Documentaries About
    Musical Events and Phenomena 209
    Polish Documentaries About Popular Music 212
    From Festival Reportages to Festival Impressions 213
    All You Need Is Rock 217
    Beats of Freedom *When There Was No Freedom* 222
    The Soundtracks to Life Among the Concrete Blocks 225
    *Disco Polo and Techno Through the Lens of Maria
    Zmarz-Koczanowicz* 227
    Polish Music Business as Szołbiznes 234
    Conclusions 236
    Works Cited 237

8   Victims of the System? Documentaries About Popular
    Musicians 241
    Whose Life Gets Documented? 241
    Two 'Shots' at Czesław Niemen 243
    When a Band Is Still a Band 252
    The Ultimate Polish Diva 256
    A Bitter Self-Made Hero 261
    Conclusions 262
    Works Cited 263

Part IV   Music Videos

9   Singing and Dancing Without the Audience: Music
    Videos of the Interbellum and State Socialist Period 267
    Art, Not Commerce 270
    Polish Music Videos Before Music Videos 271
    Music Video 'Combines' 277

| | Music Videos in the Polish Top of the Pops | 282 |
| | Works Cited | 284 |

10 **The Power of YouTube: Music Videos After the Fall of the Iron Curtain** — 287
    Celebrating Parochialism — 289
    OjDADAna — 293
    Rocking Intelligently — 296
    Striving for Universalism — 298
    From Slums to Pleasure Boats — 300
    Between Music Video and Computer Game — 304
    Conclusions — 306
    Works Cited — 307

Index — 309

List of Figures

Fig. 2.1	Playing together jazz and classical music in *Piętro wyżej* (*Upstairs*, 1937), directed by Leon Trystan. Henryk Wars plays the piano	34
Fig. 2.2	Julian (Eugeniusz Bodo) demonstrates how to be become a successful singer in *Pieśniarz Warszawy* (*Singing Fool of Warsaw*, 1934), directed by Michał Waszyński	44
Fig. 2.3	Young ballet dancers (played by Tacjanki) in *Strachy* (*The Ghosts*, 1938), directed by Eugeniusz Cękalski and Karol Szołowski	48
Fig. 3.1	Hanka Ruczajówna on her first visit to Warsaw in *Przygoda na Mariensztacie* (*An Adventure at Marienstadt*, 1954), directed by Leonard Buczkowski	68
Fig. 3.2	Joanna (Elżbieta Czyżewska) with her suitors in *Małżeństwo z rozsądku* (*Marriage of Convenience*, 1966), directed by Stanisław Bareja	78
Fig. 3.3	Szpicbródka (Piotr Fronczewski) falling in love with Anita (Gabriela Kownacka) in *Halo Szpicbródka* (*Hello, Fred the Beard*, 1978), directed by Janusz Rzeszewski and Mieczysław Jahoda	95
Fig. 3.4	Old cars brought on stage in the finale of *Lata dwudzieste, lata trzydzieste* (*The Twenties, the Thirties*, 1984), directed by Janusz Rzeszewski	98
Fig. 4.1	Tomek (Dawid Ogrodnik) and Gensonina (Joanna Kulig) perform 'Because All Poles Are One Family' at the end of *Disco Polo* (2015), directed by Maciej Bochniak	125

Fig. 4.2 Zosia (Eliza Rycembel) sings 'Joy in the Morning' in #WszystkoGra (*Game On*, 2016), directed by Agnieszka Glińska 131
Fig. 4.3 Krysia (Kinga Preis) and the mermaids (Michalina Olszańska and Marta Mazurek) perform 'You Were the Beat of My Heart' in *Córki dancingu* (*The Lure*, 2015), directed by Agnieszka Smoczyńska 136
Fig. 4.4 Mazurek's performance in *Zimna wojna* (*Cold War*, 2018), directed by Paweł Pawlikowski 140
Fig. 5.1 Dorota Stalińska as Hanka Ordonówna with her penchant to luxurious clothes in *Miłość ci wszystko wybaczy* (*Love Can Take Everything*, 1981), directed by Janusz Rzeszewski 162
Fig. 5.2 Riedel's wife Gola with her drugged husband in *Skazany na bluesa* (*Destined for Blues*, 2004), directed by Jan Kidawa-Błoński 171
Fig. 5.3 Marcin Kowalczyk as Magik in *Jesteś Bogiem* (*You Are God*, 2012), directed by Leszek Dawid 176
Fig. 6.1 Italian hosts try to sexualise Anna German's image in *Anna German* (2013), directed by Waldemar Krzystek 192
Fig. 6.2 Anna German (Joanna Moro) performs for the grateful audience in *Anna German* (2013), directed by Waldemar Krzystek 193
Fig. 6.3 Eugeniusz Bodo (Tomasz Schuchardt) with Reri (Patricia Kazadi) in *Bodo* (2016), directed by Michał Rosa and Michał Kwieciński 200
Fig. 7.1 Ewa Demarczyk performing in *Sopot 70* (1970), directed by Józef Gębski and Antoni Halor 216
Fig. 7.2 Shazza recording in *Bara bara* (*Hanky Panky*, 1996), directed by Maria Zmarz-Koczanowicz 228
Fig. 8.1 Niemen drinking water from the soda stream in *Sukces* (*Success*, 1968) by Marek Piwowski 246
Fig. 8.2 The unique dressing style of Czesław Niemen in *Sen o Warszawie* (*Dream about Warsaw*, 2014), directed by Krzysztof Magowski 249
Fig. 8.3 Violetta Villas performing in *Violetta Villas* (1988), directed by Zbigniew Kowalewski 259

CHAPTER 1

Introduction

Music and film epitomise the most popular of arts and forms of entertainment. Bringing them together was always seen as a way to add to their attractiveness. This is a reason that the first Hollywood sound film, *The Jazz Singer*, released in 1927, was a musical and it was followed by many imitations, in the USA and elsewhere.

An awareness that showing popular music on screen would add to the mass appeal of both film and music was not lost on Polish filmmakers, as demonstrated by the fact that (if we include in this category music videos), there are thousands of films with and about popular music and about the people who create them. This book is devoted to several types of such films: musicals, biographical films of popular music stars, music documentaries and music videos. This list is by no means exhaustive, as there are some types of moving image, in which music is important, that I left out, such as advertisements, video games, non-fiction experimental films and even some fiction films which are memorable only thanks to their soundtrack. Yet, in this book I focus on diegetic music, which, speaking figuratively, is not only heard, but also seen. Moreover, even without addressing these other types of film, this is the most comprehensive publication covering the interface between Polish popular music and film. However, before moving to analysing films, let's briefly map the area which I intend to cover and explain the crucial terms.

© The Author(s) 2020
E. Mazierska, *Polish Popular Music on Screen*,
https://doi.org/10.1007/978-3-030-42779-5_1

Popular Cinema in Poland and Its Critical Appraisal

Why is material about popular music on Polish screen so scarce? One reason is the traditional low prestige of popular cinema in Polish film studies, where most of the popular music can be found. This is detectable in reviews published in the Polish press in the period between the two world wars (interbellum), and even more, after the Second World War, during the period of state socialism. What is significant is that the object of neglect and scorn has not been popular cinema as such, but that produced in Poland. By contrast, American popular cinema has been treated with respect, as measured by a large number of books published in Polish devoted to this topic. The tacit and on occasion overt assumption is that Poles are not able to produce popular cinema matching American products or even that they fall behind popular films produced in some European countries such as France and Great Britain.

During the interbellum, the explanation lay in the poverty and adhocism of the Polish film industry, being geared towards quick profit, which resulted in cutting corners and repeating formulas, to the overall detriment of the quality of the films (Madej 1994; Lubelski 2009: 79–80). Such a model, described as 'professional cinema' (*kino branżowe* or *branża*), albeit with an added scorn, served the production of a large quantity of popular films, but arguably not their quality, leading to negative reviews by critics exasperated by seeing on screen the same characters in the same situations over and over again. One of the fiercest critics of *branża*, Karol Irzykowski, described it as 'mafia, which will bungle and fudge films for a hundred years, and prevent anybody intelligent to intervene in its operations, out of fear and shame' (Irzykowski 1982: 505).

In the postwar period, under so-called communist rule (which I prefer to label 'state socialism'), the inhospitable climate for popular cinema allegedly resulted yet, again, from the economic model and organisation of the Polish film industry. According to this model, fulfilling ideological objectives was a higher priority than making profit. At the beginning of this period, it was also assumed that socialist film is by definition popular, because it is addressed to the whole society and represents the interests of its avant-garde: the working class. This was even largely the case during the first years of Polish postwar cinema, which saw the production of a number of comedies, including musical comedies. They were meant to inculcate in their viewers a positive attitude towards the socialist state, according to the rule identified by Antonio Gramsci that popular culture plays a crucial role in making the masses to adapt to the goals of the state (Gramsci 1992: 136–162; see also Stuart Hall 1986: 22–23). Gramsci referred to the capitalist state, but his assessment is at least as applicable to the socialist state.

Subsequently, however, setting up semi-autonomous film units in Poland, the socialist equivalents of Hollywood studios, permanently subsidised by the state, resulted in production of a large number of 'auteurist films', in which conveying the vision of the director was the ultimate goal of filmmaking. In such circumstances making intentionally popular films by employing genre conventions made little sense from the perspective of a director, because it still required him or her to adhere to ideological principles, while it did not bring the perks related to making auteurist films, such as being regarded as somebody who produces autonomous and authentic art. Many film critics of the state socialist period assumed that Polish genre cinema must be bad and condemned it even before the films were made. For example, Bolesław Michałek, probably the most respected critic of this period, stated that Poland had no chance to compete not only with Hollywood, but even with European producers of popular cinema, such as France, therefore it is in its interest to stick to what it does best: auteurist films (Michałek 2002: 125–132).

Maybe all Polish filmmakers would take to their hearts Michałek's directive, if not for the fact that Polish cinema's main sponsor, the state, upon discovering that when left to their own devices the directors tend to favour dark films which neither praise the state nor appeal to the mass audience, demanded from them to make popular films (as if to follow Gramsci's rule) both as a more effective way of instilling in viewers the right attitudes and helping the financial condition of the Polish film industry. In the early 1960s the Party published a document, which encouraged filmmakers to make films about everyday life, which will be truthful, yet optimistic and praising the socialist status quo (Uchwała 1994). The remainder of the state socialist period did not bring a repeat of such documents, but some informal pressure was put on filmmakers to make intentionally popular films. This pressure resulted in the perception of the existence of two tiers of filmmakers in Poland—those who could afford to be artistically independent, despite and in reality largely thanks to working under the state socialist system, the *auteurs*, and those who had to compromise because they had not enough clout to force their personal visions on their sponsors and the censors. The first type was represented by such directors as Andrzej Wajda, Jerzy Kawalerowicz, Wojciech Jerzy Has, Krzysztof Kieślowski, Agnieszka Holland and Andrzej Zanussi; the second by the rest. Of course, these were ideal types; the boundary between then was not rigid and it was possible to move up or down on this cultural ladder. The position of the auteurs was strengthened by the fact that the films of some of them, especially Andrzej Wajda, such as *Człowiek z marmuru* (*Man of Marble*, 1976) were watched by millions of viewers, despite rejecting genre conventions. However, it is fair to say that filmmakers who were working in television belonged to the second tier. Due to the mass character of this medium, they were expected to produce films geared towards the general public.

In the light of the situation sketched out above it is not surprising that we can identify two principal meanings of 'popular cinema' in Poland. One concerns films which tried to be popular by conforming to genre conventions and showing a positive attitude to the state. The early films of Stanisław Bareja represent this type well. Films of the second type tried to achieve popularity by engaging with problems regarded as important for the society and often showed a critical attitude towards state socialism. Here the films of Andrzej Wajda fit the bill.

There are filmmakers who bucked these trends, most importantly Juliusz Machulski, whose *Vabank* (1981) and *Seksmisja* (*Sex Mission*, 1984) were genre, popular, politically subversive (or at least read by the audience this way) and yet praised by the critics. However, it should be emphasised that Machulski started his career in the 1980s, when the Polish film industry attempted to reform itself by becoming more market-oriented. Although these early attempts at neoliberalisation were only modestly successful, they instilled in filmmakers and critics the idea that commercial success matters and there is a correlation between the film's adherence to genre and its popularity. Inevitably, Machulski became not only a successful filmmaker throughout the 1980s and the following decades, but inspiration for the younger generations of Polish filmmakers.

As a result of the privileged position of arthouse film in Poland, the vast majority of studies of Polish cinema conducted before 1990 are concerned with this type of cinema, while omitting or marginalising popular cinema. For example, there are at least twenty volumes, published in Poland about different aspects of the work of Andrzej Wajda, but none devoted to Polish science fiction films or musicals. This reluctance to tackle popular genres and films reflects an assumption, which I frequently encountered when meeting Polish colleagues, that writing about such films would undermine their own position by suggesting that they are themselves fans of such low-brow productions.

If we look at the literature available in English, the situation is even worse (from the perspective of discussing popular cinema), with auteurist cinema having the almost undivided attention of scholars. Not only are there few studies of Polish genre cinema, but what is also missing is a consideration of the work of famous authors from the perspective of genre, for example locating the work of Andrzej Wajda in the tradition of war film or melodrama or considering reasons why certain auteurist endeavours were hits among Polish and international audiences, while others flopped.

The situation started to change after the fall of the Iron Curtain. The effective privatisation of the film industry in Poland forced filmmakers to move away from the auteurist paradigm towards the production of genre films. After 1989 we see an upsurge of heritage films, police dramas, comedies and, finally, musicals (Mazierska 2007a). The change in the economic model of Polish cinema coincided with a shift in film studies, marked by moving away from (pure) textual analysis towards paying greater attention to production context and reception of films, and from seeing film directors as sole authors of films to acknowledging the input of other filmmakers, including composers. Another change in film studies concerns paying increased attention to shorter and more ephemeral forms of moving image than full-length fiction films, such as documentaries, amateur films, trailers and adverts, as documented in numerous volumes on film theory published after 2000 (for example Gledhill and Williams 2000).

These two changes also affected film studies in Poland. Polish film historians turned to popular films, including those produced during the period of state socialism. Hence after 1990 we find volumes about Polish popular cinema at large (Zwierzchowski and Mazur 2011), as well as about specific genres (Skotarczak 2004; Talarczyk-Gubała 2007) and popular film directors, such as Juliusz Machulski (Majer 2014) and Stanisław Bareja (Łuczak 2007; Replewicz 2009). There is also a greater interest in popular cinema in Eastern Europe, as testified by edited collections (Ostrowska et al. 2017; Mazierska and Gyori 2018), and themed issues of the *Studies in Eastern European Cinema*, devoted to genres such as science fiction and musical. The number of such publications is still small, but given that till recently there were none, the increase is immense.

One can also observe a move away from the condescending tone about popular films, which dominated in the previous histories of Polish cinema towards their more positive reappraisal. Yet, in these new histories music-centred films still play a relatively minor part. Similarly, in the histories of music on screen, covering a wider area, such as global cinema or European cinema, Polish and Eastern European films and music videos are omitted.

Why has the interface between Polish screen media and popular music has attracted so little attention? To answer this question I shall mention that I have never met a film scholar who admitted of not being able to write about comedies or melodramas on the grounds of not being versed in humour or not being familiar with unrequited love. It is assumed that researching these topics require little specialist knowledge. By contrast, it is assumed that to write about music in film one needs to have in-depth knowledge about 'music as music', which only musicians and musicologists possess. I do not deny that such knowledge is useful and feel myself hampered by its lack, but do not regard it as necessary. This is because music can be studied from many perspectives, including cultural, similarly as film can be approached from different angles. Nevertheless, this opinion might be one reason that studies of popular music in Polish screen media are scarce and the only monograph on film music, *Polska muzyka filmowa 1945–1968* (2006), is written by film historian with a musicologist background, Iwona Sowińska.

There is no shortage of musicologists and popular music scholars in Poland, but it is difficult to find those whose attention is directed to the moving image; they prefer to study 'music as music'. That said, recent years have seen the publication of a volume *Media jako przestrzenie muzyki (The Media as Spaces of Music)* (Parus and Trudzik 2016), with some chapters devoted to music and documentary film, as well as Mariusz Gradowski's monograph *Big Beat* (2018), which includes a short, but competent chapter about big beat in film and television. Nevertheless, overall the body of research devoted to popular music on screen is modest.

This book is meant to fill this gap and true to the word 'popular' used its title, I want to focus here on films which were intended to be popular and which featured music and musicians which were popular. This brings me to the next question: what is popular music?

The Boundaries of Popular Music

Popular music is a notoriously slippery concept (more than popular film), in part because it can be approached from different perspectives (history, musicology, sociology, economy) and in part because it arouses strong emotions, because of its entanglement with the concept of taste. As Pierre Bourdieu noted, 'nothing more clearly affirms one's "class", nothing more infallibly classifies, than tastes in music' (Bourdieu 2010: 10).

In one of the first and most influential essays on popular music, titled 'On Popular Music' and originally published in 1941, its author, Theodor Adorno argues that the main characteristics of popular music are standardisation and the primacy of its parts over the whole (Adorno 1990: 302–303). From that derive other aspects of popular music, all negative, in Adorno's view, most importantly, that popular music is inauthentic (pre-digested) and does not demand from the listener any true involvement. As he puts it: 'The composition hears for the listener. This is how popular music divests the listener of his spontaneity and promotes conditioned reflexes' (ibid.: 306).

In subsequent years western scholars moved away from the moralistic tone applied by Adorno, yet retained some insights from his examination, most importantly the idea of standardisation of popular music. Richard Middleton defines popular music as music with wide appeal, distributed through the music industry and which can be performed and enjoyed by people with little or no musical training (Middleton 1990: 3–7). Critics also agree that a privileged form of popular music is song, with its verse, chorus and bridge structure. Songwriters favour such pleasurable devices as tonality, melody and simpler rhythms, which serious musicians tend to shun (Goodwin 2000: 223). Simon Frith treats popular music, which he labels 'commercial', as one of three main categories of music; the two remaining ones being art and folk (Frith 1996: 21–46).

These definitions and categorisations are useful in the Polish context, but Poland, in this respect, has its specificity, resulting from a different political and cultural history than the West. As Leonardo Masi observes, the famous essay by Adorno was translated into Polish only in the 2010s and probably his work remained unknown to the majority of Polish cultural historians, making them come up with their own ideas (Masi 2020). Masi points to the pioneering work of Czesław Hernas, historian of baroque literature, who in 1975 published an essay 'Potrzeby i metody badania literatury brukowej' (On the necessity of popular literature studies and about its methodology), in which, anticipating western authors critical of Adorno, such as Frith, he divides the literature into official (serious), folk and popular (*brukowa*), likening the last one to song. Hernas also defends such literature (and by extension) music, stating, 'Let's stop the presumption that [commercial literature] is awkward, literary wannabe, non-fulfilling the requirements of certain poetics. This kind of reproach comes from the cultured classes, which refer to its own values and tastes and don't approve as a whole the immanent poetics which rules that kind of literature' (quoted in Masi 2020). Subsequently many more Polish cultural, literary historians and musicians engaged in a debate about the character, boundary and value of popular music. Space constraints prevent me from summarising their discoveries, but it is fair to say, that the minority followed Hernas's approach, while the majority proved to be more Adornian in their outlook, namely judging the value of popular music using high-art criteria. A milestone in these debates is a book by Grzegorz Piotrowski, published in 2016. Its author succinctly presents the debates concerning the character of popular music, in western (principally Anglo-Saxon and German) context and the Polish one and attempts to pinpoint the specificity of popular music by looking at its external and internal aspects. One of his important insights is noting a dynamic character of popular music, which Adorno purposefully ignores. This means that what is regarded as 'popular' in one period, is often considered as 'serious' in a different period. For example, before the Second World War many Polish singers were regarded as 'popular' by film audience, for example Jan Kiepura and Lucyna Szczepańska, although by today's standards they will be seen as serious, thanks to, for example, performing in opera houses.

Polish take on popular music was affected by its history, most importantly two periods: Romanticism and the postwar period, especially the time when socialist realism dominated art production. To understand this, it is worth noting that music composed by Mozart and Chopin was very popular in their time. Yet, in Poland the work of Polish classical composers such as Chopin and Stanisław Moniuszko tend to be presented as 'people's music', namely music inspired by folk culture and serving people by, for example, encouraging them to stand up to their enemies (Panek 1986: 275; Mazierska 2004). After the Second World War the state attempted to erase the divisions between serious, folk and commercial art, including music, by rendering all these types of music as 'popular'. This resulted in 'serious' composers embarking on a task to compose 'mass songs' (Malinowski 1993: 54–55; Tompkins 2013: 2) and folk music being featured in mass media, such as radio. However, ultimately the project of making all types of music popular failed in Poland and, although some artists and works fit into more than one category, Poles openly or tacitly accepted that serious, folk and popular musics are different, as in the scheme described by Frith.

For this reason, in this book I focus on filmic representations of what was regarded as popular music at the time of productions of specific films. I will thus omit classical music and folk music, except in the situations when it is 'repackaged' for commercial consumption. Also, while I examine some examples of jazz music in popular films from the interwar period, I omit films devoted to jazz, which were produced after the Second World War. This is because, although jazz was extensively used in Polish soundtracks of the 1960s, a phenomenon which I examined elsewhere (Mazierska 2007a: 91–114; Mazierska 2010: 147–170), the 'jazz crave' was hardly documented in cinema when it happened[1]; the best known film about jazz fever in Poland, *Był jazz* (*And All That Jazz*, 1984), directed by Feliks Falk, looks at it retrospectively, tacitly assuming that the status of this genre had changed, from popular to elitist. Moreover, most jazz music is instrumental, while my preoccupation here are songs.

There are various types of songs considered in this book. First, there are humorous and love songs, performed with the accompaniment of a small number of instruments, typically piano and violin, which dominated in Polish interwar cinema, as precursors of genres which were later described as 'cabaret songs'. Next I cover 'folklorist' songs, written by professional composers and lyricists in a style which evoked folk songs. We find plenty of examples of this type of music in the films produced during the period of state socialism, as folk music (*muzyka ludowa*) was regarded as a manifestation of the authentic culture of simple people, especially peasants, who were oppressed by higher classes and their descendants, living in a liberated Poland.

Another type of songs which is of interest to me are estrada songs (*piosenki estradowe*). This term has many meanings, but of specific importance is the type of performance in which singers were accompanied by huge orchestras dominated by wind instruments (Ventsel 2016: 73–74). Such music ruled in the Polish media of state socialism; it filled radio and television programmes and was privileged at music festivals, which used large orchestras to give an 'estrada feel' to the songs performed there, even if they were rock or folklorist songs. Estrada music was projected as music addressed to the entire society and especially to families. Hence certain (implicit) restrictions were imposed on its producers and performers, such as avoiding political themes, swearing, overt eroticism, anything which could be regarded as unsuitable for children or critical of the state socialist regime. The boundaries of estrada music were porous—it overlapped with folklorist and cabaret productions, actors' songs, jazz and, finally, pop and rock, which were born in the late 1950s.

The dominance of estrada music in the postwar landscape of popular music was reflected in using this term to describe semi-autonomous institutions, set up in the 1950s, whose purpose was to organise live performances all over Poland, both on its own initiative, and on request by other institutions.[2] However, 'Estradas' did not limit itself to estrada music; from the 1960s a large proportion of its activities was dedicated to rock music. To differentiate between estrada as a genre and Estrada as an institution, the first I write using lower case, while the second I capitalise.

A large proportion of my investigation is devoted to what Motti Regev labels 'pop-rock' (Regev 2002: 251) and what is also known as 'youth music'. The creative processes pertaining to 'pop-rock' include 'extensive use of electric and electronic instruments, sophisticated studio techniques of sound manipulation, and certain techniques of vocal delivery, mostly those signifying immediacy of expression and spontaneity' (ibid.: 253). I use the term 'pop-rock' with an awareness that it is problematic, due to widespread opposition against putting rock and pop in one category. Regev himself refers to several distinctions between 'rock' and 'pop', of which the most widely accepted is that between rock as a more authentic and artistic sector of popular music and 'pop' as its more commercial, 'inauthentic' and watered-down version (on the division between pop and rock see also Frith 2001: 94–95; Keightley 2001: 109). I'm not against such division and will refer to it on many occasions, but argue that what connects these categories is more important than what differentiates them, and during a large part of Polish history it was very difficult to discern between pop and rock. The book also covers the representation of disco music and hip hop, which I consider as subgenres of pop-rock but which are often seen as phenomena in their own right.

While in the West the problem of the division between popular and serious/academic music and between pop and rock is mostly academic and cultural, in the socialist East, as I already hinted, it was also political. This reflected the fact that, as Gregory Kveberg argues in relation to the Soviet Union, but which is also valid in the rest of Eastern Europe, including Poland, in the absence of other markers of distinction, status in this geographical region became very closely tied to the acquisition of culture and the Soviet model of culture demanded that cultural activity fostered personal growth, rather than being merely a form of entertainment (Kveberg 2015: 213). This required maintaining a strict hierarchy of cultural products. In this hierarchy 'classical music was the most culturally valued, followed by political and agitational songs, with love songs, dance music and [estrada] music at the bottom' (ibid.: 213). Although this hierarchy was imposed from above, some of its aspects were accepted and internalised by the producers and consumers of popular music in Eastern Europe. As Kveberg observes, a belief in the need to spread culture and raise the cultural level of the audience linked conservative Soviet officials and many key figures of the underground (ibid.: 217). These hierarchies are reflected in the production of films about different types of music and musicians, especially documentaries. In particular, although estrada music dominated on the radio, television and at music festivals, Polish documentarists preferred to make films about serious musicians or 'serious' rockers, such as Czesław Niemen.

What interests me are different facets of these genres: the music itself, their producers and consumers and the culture created around them. However, it is not always possible to achieve such a full picture, because in different films popular music fulfils different functions and receives varied amounts of attention; an issue which I examine in the next section.

WHAT POPULAR MUSIC OFFERS SCREEN MEDIA; HOW SCREEN MEDIA SERVE POPULAR MUSIC?

In this book, as much as possible, I treat popular music and screen media as equal partners, while at the same time recognising the fact that in different genres music receive unequal attention. In Polish musicals popular songs are typically used to beautify the represented reality, help to understand plots and characters, especially their inner lives, and strengthen the messages conveyed by other elements of the diegesis. Producers of musicals also take advantage of the popularity of certain artists and phenomena and document them and their impact on society, as well as the state of society at the time when the film is set. As Mike

Lang, the co-producer of Woodstock Festival said, music is 'about what's happening now' and 'if you listen to the music and the lyrics, then you'll know what's going on in the culture' (quoted in Grant 2012: 118). Music in such films is subservient to the plot and the majority of films examined here would survive, even if only in a truncated form, if musical numbers were cut out from them, especially as in many of these films they do not exceed ten per cent of the duration of the film. Not only does film take advantage of music and musicians in such films, but also films help music, acting as their adverts and adding to the popularity of those actors who are able to sing and dance and singers and dancers who are able to act.

Music and musicians receive more autonomy in biographical films, because these films cover the lives of musicians. However, even in such films the requirement to tell the story effectively means that music is sidelined because the life of X as an unhappy lover or a disturbed young man is more important than his or her life as a musician. Equally, music tends to be literally or metaphorically silenced in such films, to give way to drama and when it is used, it had little autonomy within the film, being used to dramatise the story.

In contrast to musicals and biopics, in music documentaries music and music culture is their raison d'être. Plots not connected with music do not distract the audience from concentrating on the music and its context. Such films are made to immortalise specific music events and phenomena and offer their more complete account. Indeed, we know best these events and stars, who were captured on camera. Elvis Presley, the Beatles, the Rolling Stones, Bob Dylan, Woodstock and Monterey festivals do not cease to be objects of critics and historians' attention largely because they were objects of innovative and accomplished documentaries.

In common with music documentaries, music videos exist solely of and for music; they are seen as adverts for records, boosting their sales. The music in them is even more dominant than in music documentaries because not only is music the topic of the film but the length of an individual song featured in the film determines its length and affects its style, preventing extended plots and encouraging fluidity of characters and the spaces they occupy (Vernallis 2004). As in the case of music documentaries, music videos considerably prolong the length of songs. Today, when we think about famous songs, we often think about their videos.

Popular music not only affected the production and afterlife of individual films and filmmakers, but the history of specific media: cinema, television and the internet. Musicals in Poland, as elsewhere in the world, belong to the age of cinema. When film acquired diegetic sound in the end of the 1920s, a large proportion of Polish films included songs, and musical comedies became the most popular genre in the country. Biographical films about musicians were made both for cinema and, in the form of series, for television. Music documentaries and music videos were made initially for television; their length and intimate format lent itself to the medium of 'home cinema' and the ethos of providing light entertainment. Finally, internet platforms, such as YouTube, are a perfect place to present music videos. YouTube also affected the way other forms of screen media, where music holds a privileged position, such as musicals, are currently produced and consumed (Vernallis 2011).

To examine these different forms in which the moving image and popular music come together, I draw on several strands of research. One is the political, economic and social history of Poland, to reflect on the Marxist and Gramscian idea, that base affects superstructure. I also draw on Martin Cloonan argument (which can be regarded as a refinement of Gramscian ideas) that there are three types of relationship between the nation state and popular music: authoritarian, benign and promotional. Whereas the authoritarian state strongly controls record production, licensing of live music, and music imports, the benign state leaves popular music to free markets, acts as tax-collector and a referee between competing interests. Finally, the promotional state treats popular music as an asset and devises national policies to combat the dominance of Anglo-American music (Cloonan 1999: 203–204). I argue that these three models can be used to examine the relationship not only between music, but also between cinema and state and they can be mapped onto three periods of Polish history: after the First World War till the end of the Second World War, the state socialist period and the post-communist one. The benign model dominated in cinema and popular music in the period between the two world wars; the authoritarian during state socialism, although there were aspects of promotional model as well (Mazierska 2020: 202–208). Finally, the benign model returned to popular music after the fall of the Iron Curtain, but promotional model has dominated in Polish cinema, especially after setting up the Polish Film Institute.

For example, the wealth of Polish musical comedies in the 1930s can be attributed to the fact that Polish cinema had to make a profit to survive by making films attractive to an 'average' viewer, as the state did little to help film industry. Their decline after the Second World War, on the other hand, can be largely attributed to the diminished requirements for films to be profitable.

I also use the existing histories of Polish cinema and popular music, to account for whether there is a fit between them, in particular, whether the development of music-centred forms of moving image reflect the trajectories of Polish popular music. For example, do we find films about the greatest Polish stars of popular music and the status they hold in the histories of Polish cinema? Further, I will draw on the existing histories and theories of music-centred films, musicals, music biopics, music documentaries and videos, to assess how their Polish makers remade certain pre-existing formulas to suit local circumstances. Finally, I pay attention to technological developments as a factor shaping the relationship between popular music and the moving image. I also use additional methods, to reflect the fact that each example brings a unique set of issues.

Structure and Chapter Description

My book is divided into four parts. The first of them concerns musicals. There, in three chapters, I cover, respectively interwar, postwar and post-communist musicals against the background of the history of musicals in Hollywood and Europe, Polish political and economic history and the history of Polish cinema. For this reason, at the beginning of each chapter I include some information about Polish history and Polish cinema in a specific period.

When I move to film analysis, I introduce the type of music featured in them and their stars. Such information helps to understand why music was used and why this rather than that genre or artist received centre stage. I also attempt to account for meaningful gaps, namely music genres and artists who were ignored in Polish films, despite their high profile in the national arena. In my analysis I try to establish what music does in specific films to the characters, narratives and the audiences—what is its function and purpose. From this perspective it is useful to refer to the categorisation, proposed by Anahid Kassabian, who writes that 'any instance of music [in film] has various relationships: to other music, both within the same film and more generally; to the narrative and the world it creates, and to other tracks of the films' (visual images, dialogue, sound effects) (Kassabian 2001: 11). When discussing musicals I draw attention to all of these aspects, but the most important is the narrative. This is because in Polish musicals songs and dances were typically subservient to the narrative and ideology of the films. They were put there not to create an autonomous world, sealed off from the everyday reality, but to convince the audience that the reality is more attractive than they otherwise might think and encourage the viewers to work towards improving it. This function is most visible in musicals from the interwar period and socialist realism. Only in musicals from the last decade do singing numbers receive more autonomy; on occasions they even dominate the narrative. This drive towards autonomy can be attributed to the changing media landscape and modes of watching films, with YouTube being the main platform for listening to songs. The first part is the only part in this book where I cover extensively interwar cinema. This is because other types of music-centred films, such as biopics and documentaries about popular music were not produced during this period.

In the second part of the book I write about biographical films, which in practice are a subgenre of musicals. However, the difference is that their protagonists are real musicians and their life is at the centre of the narrative. This part is divided into two chapters: one considers biographical films, produced for theatrical release; the other television series. On this occasion I treat the works as adaptations, or hypertexts in relation to the artists lives, their hypotexts[3] and present reasons why these artists were chosen and specific aspects of their lives were played up, while others were omitted. As in the previous part, the relationship of music to the narrative is here of paramount importance, but I also discuss the relationship of the world created on screen with extradiegetic reality. I emphasise the effect of using different media, respectively film and television, on the way musicians are portrayed.

In the third part I examine music documentaries. This part also consists of two chapters. On this occasion the dividing criterion is the topic of documentaries; the first concerns documentaries about events and phenomena; the second about specific musicians. In this part I am particularly interested in the relation of films to other histories of Polish music. This part sheds light on the two previous parts, because many musicals represent specific events and phenomena and biopics depict musicians, as do music documentaries, albeit using different means. Again, the positive choices made by directors are as interesting for me as their omissions. I point to the fact that the majority of documentaries about musicians in the post-communist period concern stars of state socialist era.

The last part of the book is devoted to the youngest form of the musical film—music video, a genre which, as Timothy Warner put it, 'reverse the traditional cinematic convention; it is the images that "accompany" the music' (Warner 2006: 168). This part, again, has two chapters. The first is devoted to early music clips, which we find as early as interwar cinema, as well as Polish television. The focus of the second chapter is on music videos, produced after the fall of state socialism, whose main home is YouTube. In this part my main question is how does music video serve specific music genres, by looking at how music is related to other aspects of the films, most importantly, images.

Due to space limitations, which requires making hard choices of material, my book privileges Polish popular music and musicians in Polish films, rather what can be described as transnational Polish popular music and cinema. For this reason, I omit here, for example, films featuring Jan Kiepura, as those in which he appeared were practically all foreign (German, British, French, Austrian), as well as Polish films, such as *Yesterday* (1985), directed by Radosław Piwowarski, which are about Polish fascination with Anglo-Saxon rock or music videos of Polish musicians, such as Basia Trzetrzelewska, produced abroad. Films like those deserve special treatment and I wish this book inspire some scholars to fill the gaps in my investigation.

I believe that readers of this book will gain a fuller picture of Polish screen media by learning about poorly known or forgotten works, which were targeted at local audiences, often television viewers, hence exist outside the critical canon of national and international cinema. I also hope that they will see how screen media reflect and shape the hierarchies of Polish popular music and hence the book will be of value to both Polish film and popular music scholars and fans. In a wider sense, I wish for this book to be a valuable addition to the scholarship about screen media produced and consumed at the periphery. The importance of such study lies not only in the fact that it gives us as a fuller picture of national, regional and global cinema, but also because province is where most of global population lives.

Notes

1. The most successful film from the perspective of depicting Polish jazz fever is *Niewinni czarodzieje* (*Innocent Sorcerers*, 1960), directed by Andrzej Wajda.
2. Probably the first was Warsaw Estrada (Stołeczna Estrada), founded in 1955.

3. When using such terms I draw on Robert Stam work on adaptation. Stam proposes to treat adaptation as a relation between the 'hypertext' to an anterior text, the 'hypotext', which the hypertext transforms, modifies, elaborates and extends (Stam 2000: 65–66).

WORKS CITED

Adorno, Theodor W. [1941] 1990. On Popular Music. In *On Record: Rock, Pop, and the Written Word*, ed. Simon Frith and Andrew Goodwin, 301–314. London: Routledge.
Bourdieu, Pierre. [1984] 2010. *Distinction: A Social Critique of the Judgement of Taste*. London: Routledge.
Cloonan, Martin. 1999. Pop and the Nation-State: Towards a Theorisation. *Popular Music* 2: 193–207.
Frith, Simon. 1996. *Performing Rites: On the Value of Popular Music*. Oxford: Oxford University Press.
Frith, Simon. 2001. Pop Music. In *The Cambridge Companion to Pop and Rock*, ed. Simon Frith, Will Straw and John Street, 93–108. Cambridge: Cambridge University Press.
Gledhill, Christine, and Linda Williams (eds.). 2000. *Reinventing Film Studies*. London: Arnold.
Goodwin, Andrew. 2000. On Popular Music and Postmodernism. In *Music: Culture and Society: A Reader*, ed. Derek B. Scott, 221–224. Oxford: Oxford University Press.
Gramsci, Antonio. 1992. *Prison Notebooks*, vol. 1, trans. Joseph A. Buttigieg and Antonio Callari. New York: Columbia University Press.
Grant, Barry Keith. 2012. *The Hollywood Film Musical*. Southern Gate, Chichester: Wiley.
Hall, Stuart. 1986. Popular Culture and the State. In *Popular Culture and Social Relations*, ed. Tony Bennett, Colin Mercer, and Janet Woollacott, 22–49. Milton Keynes: Open University Press.
Irzykowski, Karol. 1982. *Dziesiąta Muza oraz Pomniejsze pisma filmowe*. Kraków: Wydawnictwo Literackie.
Kassabian, Anahid. 2001. *Hearing Film: Tracking Identifications in Contemporary Hollywood Film Music*. London: Routledge.
Keightley, Keir. 2001. Reconsidering Rock. In *The Cambridge Companion to Pop and Rock*, ed. Simon Frith, Will Straw and John Street, 109–142. Cambridge: Cambridge University Press.
Kveberg, Gregory. 2015. Shostakovich Versus Boney M.: Culture, Status, and History in the Debate over Soviet *Diskoteki*. In *Youth and Rock in the Soviet Bloc: Youth Cultures, Music, and the State in Russia and Eastern Europe*, ed. William Jay Risch, 211–227. Lanham: Lexington Books.

Lubelski, Tadeusz. 2009. *Historia kina polskiego: Twórcy, filmy, konteksty*. Katowice: Videograf II.
Łuczak, Maciej. 2007. *Miś, czyli świat według Barei*. Warszawa: Prószyński i Spólka.
Madej, Alina. 1994. *Mitologie i konwencje. O polskim kinie fabularnym dwudziestolecia międzywojennego*. Kraków: Universitas.
Majer, Artur. 2014. *Kino Juliusza Machulskiego*. Bielsko Biała: Wydawnictwo Kwieciński.
Malinowski, Władysław. 1993. O socjalistycznym realizmie w muzyce. *Twórczość* 1: 50–68.
Masi, Leonardo. 2020. The Beginnings of Popular Music Studies in Poland. *Załącznik Kulturoznawczy*, 7 (forthcoming).
Mazierska, Ewa. 2004. Multifunctional Chopin: The Representation of Fryderyk Chopin in Polish Films. *Historical Journal of Film Radio and Television* 2: 253–268.
Mazierska, Ewa. 2007a. *Polish Postcommunist Cinema: From Pavement Level*. Oxford: Peter Lang.
Mazierska, Ewa. 2007b. *The Cinema of a Cultural Traveller*. London: I.B. Tauris.
Mazierska, Ewa. 2010. *Jerzy Skolimowski: The Cinema of a Nonconformist*. Oxford: Berghahn.
Mazierska, Ewa. 2020. Polish Popular Music Beyond the Borders of Poland. In *Made in Poland*, ed. Patryk Galuszka, 201–211. London: Routledge.
Mazierska, Ewa, and Zsolt Győri (eds.). 2018. *Popular Music and the Moving Image in Eastern Europe*. New York: Bloomsbury.
Michałek, Bolesław. 2002. *Bolesław Michałek ambasador polskiego kina: Wspomnienia i artykuły*. Kraków: Rabid.
Middleton, Richard. 1990. *Studying Popular Music*. Buckingham: Open University Press.
Ostrowska, Dorota, Francesco Pitassio, and Zsuzsanna Varga (eds.). 2017. *Popular Cinemas in East Central Europe: Film Cultures and Histories*. London: I.B. Tauris.
Panek, Wacław. 1986. *Mały słownik muzyki rozrywkowej*. Warszawa: ZAKR.
Parus, Magdalena, and Artur Trudzik (eds.). 2016. *Media jako przestrzenie muzyki*. Gdańsk: Wydawnictwo Naukowe Katedra.
Piotrowski, Grzegorz. 2016. *Muzyka Popularna: Nasłuchy i namysły*. Warszawa: Państwowy Instytut Wydawniczy.
Regev, Motti. 2002. The Pop-Rockization of Popular Music. In *Popular Music Studies*, ed. David Hesmondhalgh and Keith Negus, 251–264. London: Arnold.
Replewicz, Maciej. 2009. *Stanisław Bareja: Król Krzywego Zwierciadła*. Poznań: Zysk i Spółka.

Skotarczak, Dorota. 2004. *Obraz społeczeństwa PRL w komedii filmowej*. Poznań: Wydawnictwo Naukowe UAM.
Sowińska, Iwona. 2006. *Polska muzyka filmowa 1945–1968*. Katowice: Wydawnictwo Uniwersytetu Śląskiego.
Stam, Robert. 2000. Beyond Fidelity: The Dialogics of Adaptation. In *Film Adaptation*, ed. James Naremore, 54–76. London: Athlone Press.
Tompkins, David G. 2013. *Composing the Party Line: Music and Politics in Early Cold War Poland and East Germany*. West Lafayette: Purdue University Press.
'Uchwała Sekretariatu KC w sprawie kinematografii'. 1994. In *Syndrom konformizmu: Kino polskie lat sześćdziesiątych*, ed. Tadeusz Miczka and Alina Madej, 27–34. Katowice: Wydawnictwo Uniwersytetu Śląskiego.
Ventsel, Aimar. 2016. Estonian Invasion as Western Ersatz-Pop. In *Popular Music in Eastern Europe: Breaking the Cold War Paradigm*, ed. Ewa Mazierska, 69–88. London: Palgrave.
Vernallis, Carol. 2004. *Music Video: Aesthetics and Cultural Context*. New York: Columbia University Press.
Warner, Timothy. 2006. Narrating Sound: The Pop Video in the Age of Sampler. In *Changing Tunes: The Use of Pre-Existing Music in Film*, ed. Phil Powrie and Robynn Stilwell, 167–179. Aldershot: Ashgate.
Zwierzchowski, Piotr, and Daria Mazur (eds.). 2011. *Polskie kino popularne*. Bydgoszcz: Wydawnictwo Uniwersytetu Kazimierza Wielkiego.

PART I

Polish Musicals: Themes, Styles, Ideologies

CHAPTER 2

Music and Dance in the Service of Modern Poland: Interwar Musicals

HOLLYWOOD AND EUROPEAN MUSICALS

The first part of this book is devoted to Polish musicals. This raises the question of which films to include in the analysis and how to structure the material. One possibility is to apply an existing definition as a criterion to choose musicals from the multitude of Polish films produced since the beginning of its history or, more precisely, from the time it acquired sound. The second is to propose a definition which captures the specificity of the Polish situation, which I embrace here. I follow the existing approach, but adapt it to local circumstances, recognising the fact that genres are not stable, but constantly develop and reflect cultural specificities of given countries and regions, as argued in the seminal work by Rick Altman (1981a, 1987, 1996, 1999).

Of course, in order to delineate the object of study, we need to define 'musical'. Unfortunately, in academic books such definitions are rare—'musicals' are typically defined through an analysis of specific films and if definitions appear, this happens in the context of Hollywood rather than European cinema. For my purpose, however, it is worth using Altman's divisions of musicals into musicals 'proper' and what he describes as 'musical films'. As he puts it:

> The term 'musical' is used in several different senses. In its weakest sense, 'musical' means simply a film with a significant amount of diegetic music (music made by onscreen characters). In this sense, the term designates an

extremely diverse international genre, with important examples from every decade since the 1920s and from every continent.

Such films will be referred to here as 'musical films', while the standalone term 'musical' will be reserved for films featuring not only the presence of music, but also a shared configuration of plot patterns, character types, and social structures associated with that music. In this stricter sense, the musical is not an international genre, but one of the most characteristic creations of the Hollywood film industry. To study the musical is thus primarily to analyse the history of Hollywood's 1,500 or so musical films. (Altman 1996: 294)

According to this definition, Polish films cannot be more than 'musical films'. This opinion is indirectly confirmed by the fact that the majority of publications about musicals are devoted to American musicals (Altman 1981a, 1987, 1996; Feuer 1993; Langford 2005: 82–104; Grant 2012; Friedman et al. 2014: 200–241).[1] However, since Altman made this claim new studies have appeared which use the term 'musical' in relation to non-Hollywood films, such as Lydia Papadimitriou's monograph, examining Greek musicals (2006) and a volume edited by Corey Creekmur and Linda Mokdad, titled *The International Film Musical* (2012). The fact that they have 'film musical', rather than 'musical film' in their titles, suggests that their authors defy Altman's claim that there are no musicals outside Hollywood, even though many authors admit to their national cinemas suffering from an inferiority complex. My study follows in their footsteps, therefore I also decided to employ the term 'musical' in this part, even though I will deal here mostly with films which are musicals according to what Altman terms a 'weak definition'.

However, even this weak definition, which captures a common-sense approach to musicals, raises some questions. For example, how many songs there should be in a diegesis to qualify a film a musical? Does their mere presence render the film a musical or do they need to play a specific role in the narrative? Does embarking on the production of musicals require the filmmakers to make a film in a specific mode (comic or tragical) and employ a specific structure and style? Do Polish musicals render themselves to a particular ideology? What is the relationship between Polish musicals and national identity? Finally, are there any substantial differences between Hollywood and Polish musicals?

In order to answer these questions, it is worth recapitulating what was discovered about Hollywood musicals and European musicals. One important characteristic of the former is that they are meta-cinematic.

They not only show singing and dancing, but are *about* singing and dancing as a form of entertainment, most importantly in the type of musical known as 'show' or 'backstage' musical (Feuer 1981, 1993: 23–65; Altman 1987: 200–250). Moreover, Hollywood musicals tend to have a dual structure: underscoring parallels between characters and settings is more important than advancing their narratives (Altman 1987: 16–27). This also means that 'whereas the traditional approach to narrative assumes that structure grows out of *plot*, the dual-focus structure of the American film musical derives from *character*' (ibid.: 21). Due to its huge potential to attract a mass audience, American musicals were often lavish films, with a high budget and production values and tried to be consensual, appealing to the audience irrespective of their economic standing or political views. As Feuer puts it, 'the Hollywood musical becomes a mass art which aspires to the condition of a folk art, produced and consumed by the same integrated community' (Feuer 1993: 3). Hollywood musicals typically stayed away from controversial issues and their ideology tended to be conservative by presenting and normalising patriarchal reality, typically by including in the narrative a male master and a female pupil, who flourishes under his guidance and tutelage. There is, moreover, an ideological duality in them, with one protagonist representing the work ethic characteristic of American Puritan heritage, while the other, liberating countercultural values (Altman 1981c: 197).

From the literature about European musicals we can distil several important points about musicals themselves and the state of research on this topic. First, there is a tendency to make in Europe what Altman would describe as 'musical films', as opposed to 'proper musicals'. This is the case of, for example, French and Italian musicals (Conway 2012: 31; Marlow-Mann 2012: 80). Second, European musicals are often employed to engage in debates about national identity, as was the case of Greek musicals of the 1960s (Papadimitriou 2006: 1); hence the reason to focus on the 'national' in studies of European musicals. Third, European musicals frequently break the rules established by American musicals. Rather than mixing music and comedy, they often merge music and dance with tragedy, as in *Une Femme est une femme* (1961), by Jean-Luc Godard or *Dancer in the Dark* (2010) by Lars von Trier, even becoming anti-musicals (Carroll 2017). Even if they are not tragic or anti-musical, they tend to be 'less optimistic, less energetic, less abundant and fulsome', as John Mundy argues in relation to British musicals (Mundy 2012: 17). Moreover, while in Hollywood a high demand for musicals led to the specialisation of actors, directors and studios, in Europe, especially after the Second World War, it was less the case. This, on one hand, makes European musicals perfect material to investigate the boundaries between different genres and the interface between arthouse and popular cinema. On the other hand, however, this renders this phenomenon less distinct. While an average cine-file is able to list at least half a dozen performers and directors who excelled in musicals, such as Busby Berkeley, Maurice Chevalier, Gene Kelly, Fred Astaire and Ginger Rogers, and knows about Warner Brothers and Metro-Goldwyn-Mayer musicals, most likely s/he would not be able to compile a list of European directors specialising in this genre, perhaps with the exception of Jacques Demy, or list any studios producing musicals. European musicals, not unlike many other European genre films, are thus seen as parochial productions, appealing almost exclusively to local audiences. However, even if European musicals do not break new ground, often they come across as highly accomplished and popular films. For example, Alain Resnais' musical *On connait la chanson* (1997) was commercially his most successful film, which the director himself described as a film which 'finally everybody likes' (Wilson 2006: 171).

Much of what was written about Greek, Italian, Spanish or German musicals and the state of their research can be repeated in relation to Polish cinema. In particular, like Papadimitriou, who observes that despite their popularity, Greek musicals received little attention in existing studies of Greek cinema and their critical evaluation has been predominantly negative because they were considered to be no more than an imitation of Hollywood (Papadimitriou 2006: 1), I can say that this rule also applies to Polish musicals.

There are additional reasons why Polish musicals received a bad press or were just omitted from national histories. One of them has to do with the fact that the majority of studies of Polish cinema were conducted after the war or even from the 1960s onwards. At the time the dominant paradigm was auteurism (Michałek and Turaj 1998: xi); films were assessed from the perspective of their aesthetic and high cultural value. Much less importance was paid to box office results or even the popularity of films was often treated as a sign of their inferiority. For example, in the reviews of musicals published between the 1960s and the 1980s we frequently find an opinion, evoking Adorno's thinking about popular culture, that people went to see such films because they appealed to their low instincts and there was nothing else to see in a given category. Arguably the best Polish study of the interwar cinema, Alina Madej's *Mitologie i konwencje. O polskim kinie fabularnym dwudziestolecia międzywojennego* (1994), is written from the perspective of patronising sympathy towards filmmakers of this period, who had to bend over backwards to attract viewers and make their movies pay. Such a condescending attitude, inevitably, precludes seeing Polish musicals as a phenomenon with a specific tradition, which contributes both to the national cinema and to transnational and global cinema.

Polish musicals were indeed parochial affairs, confined to the local market. but they were often a product of international collaboration or were international in their setting, showing Polish characters travelling abroad, to places such as Vienna and Paris. They expressed an ambition to overcome the boundaries of Polish culture and Polish cinema. Some Polish musicals reworked famous hypotexts, such as foreign operettas. For example, the plot of the interwar comedy *Ada to nie wypada!* (*Ada, Don't Do It!*, 1936), directed by Konrad Tom, was taken from the famous French operetta, *Mam'zelle Nitouche* by Hervé, with the libretto by Henri Meilhac and Albert Millaud, which was also used in French, Italian, Hungarian, Swedish, Soviet and other films. I will risk the statement that Polish musicals are the most international of Polish genres, and deserve to be looked at closely from this perspective. Here, however, I will privilege their Polishness, beginning with those musicals which were made between the two world wars, locating them within a wider Polish history.

Polish Politics, Industry and Cinema Between the World Wars

In 1918 the First World War ended and Russia, Prussia and the Habsburg Empire, who had ruled Poland since the end of the eighteenth century, ceased to exist. In this way the great Polish dream of living again in one independent country could be fulfilled. For Poles, the regaining of statehood was a great cause for celebration. Other aspects of their situation, however, provided grounds for concern. The borders of Poland were fragile, due to conflicts with its neighbours about regions with mixed populations (Ukrainian, Czech, Lithuanian and German) and Soviet Russia's initial ambition to export communism to the whole of Europe. Transportation, communication and administration were difficult because of the legacy of Poland being divided between three states.

A good measure of the problems facing Poland after the War was the fact that over four-fifths of industrial workers were unemployed in 1918. Politically Poland was divided too, with several centres of power favouring competing visions of Poland. In summary, Poland between the two world wars (the interbellum) was a poor country suffering from many political and economic crises, including the global crisis at the end of the 1920s–early 1930s and a drive towards totalitarianism under Marshall Józef Piłsudski in the mid-1920s. That said, the economic and political situation improved in the second half of the 1930s; the last four or five of prewar Poland can be regarded as the period of a speedy march towards prosperity and stability—a march, which was halted by the outbreak of the Second World War.

Although the economic and political situation in Poland in the interwar years oscillated between bad and mediocre, this was not reflected in a simple way either in the state of the Polish film industry or in the images projected by films of this period. As in other capitalist countries, the bulk of Polish films were produced and distributed by private companies, and exhibited in privately owned cinemas. In existing literature the Polish interwar film industry is presented as a cottage industry, but also as a somewhat speculative, even wild enterprise. With few professionally equipped studios, the majority of film companies were starved of capital and were geared towards making immediate profit (Banaszkiewicz 1966: 124; Madej 1994: 22–23; Hendrykowska 2009: 12; Lubelski 2009: 41). A third of them managed to produce only one film and there were few studios flourishing during the entire interwar period, such as Sfinks, set up by Aleksander Hertz in 1908, which lasted till 1936 (Stradomski 1988: 21; Maśnicki and Stepan 2007: 24–26). An important player in the film industry were cinema owners. They received much state subsidy and had a major influence on the choice of themes, actors and songs used in the films (Zajiček 1992: 11).

The authorities intervened in the operations of the Polish film business indirectly, introducing specific customs and tax regulations applied to film production and distribution. In the years 1919–1920, imported films were classified as luxury products, next to cognac, champagne, caviar, diamonds and silk (Banaszkiewicz 1966: 120). The autarkic character of the Polish economy had an even greater effect on film production in the 1930s. During this period which is of specific interest here, to spare foreign currency, the government limited the import of foreign films and introduced tax relief for cinemas showing Polish movies (Stradomski

1988: 20). Given that cinema-going belonged to the cheapest forms of entertainment (Madej 1994: 62) and cinemas were centres of cultural life, the Polish film industry in the interwar period flourished. In total, during the two decades of its existence, Poland produced 321 full-length films, of which 166 were sound films.

The filmmakers' main objective in this period was to attract viewers. Polish films had to repay their costs for the film producers, distributors and exhibitors to survive. This fact accounts for conservatism in the film fare, most importantly its adherence to the rules of genre cinema and favouring those genres, which have an immediate effect on viewers, by causing bodily reactions: melodrama (tears) and comedy (laughter). Linda Williams describes such films as 'films of excess' or 'jerkers' (Williams 2000: 207). An additional advantage of such genres, as opposed to war cinema, science fiction or proper musicals with hundreds of extras, was their relative cheapness. Other consequences of operating in a market economy included a reliance on stars (Madej 1994: 58–62), adaptation of the most popular books and a predilection to certain settings, such as music hall, cabaret, ballroom and high-class restaurant, which can be seen as a way of offering the film audience expensive entertainment in an ersatz form. By the same token, this cinema lent itself to music, as these were places where music was played and consumed communally. This was especially the case once Polish cinema acquired sound, which happened in 1930. Initially Polish films were scored by serious composers, such Ludomir Różycki and Grzegorz Fitelberg, but subsequently this task was given to specialists in popular music (Milewska and Wyżyński 2003).

The majority of Polish films from the 1930s include song and dance sequences. It is difficult to find a comedy without songs, but there are also many songs in melodramas. On some occasions such musical episode was added, to present singing and dancing skills of a specific star. For example, in *Kłamstwo Krystyny* (*Krystyna's Lie*, 1939), directed by Henryk Szaro, the characters go to a *dancing* (a restaurant with live music and a dancing hall), which allows to show the performance of Loda Halama. On other occasions the film included only a melody or a leitmotif, which became a proper song outside of the film. This was the case of 'Ja wiem, że nie byłam dla ciebie' (I Know That I Wasn't For You), which in *Trędowata* (*The Leper*, 1936), directed by Juliusz Gardan, is merely a melody composed by Władysław Eiger, but on the record was a proper song, with words by Zenon Friedwald and performed by Janina Paszkowska. By having singing and dancing numbers in a film, viewers got three forms of entertainment (music, dance and film) in one package. Naturally, the stars of these films had to be good dancers and singers. Many actors, who became stars in the 1930s, moved to the movies from the music hall and divided their time between playing in films and performing on stage, singing and dancing. Such a musical heritage applies to Eugeniusz Bodo, Adolf Dymsza, Loda Halama, Tola Mankiewiczówna and Helena Grossówna, some of the greatest stars of Polish 1930s cinema. The scripts of the films in which they played and songs which they performed were often written by authors working for Polish music and revue theatres, especially the Warsaw's 'Qui Pro Quo' and its successor 'Banda', such as Konrad Tom. Barbara and Leszek Armatysowie talk about a symbiosis of Polish cinema of the 1930s with light theatre (Armatysowie 1988: 213). There was also a symbiosis of cinema, recording industry and radio (Milewska and Wyżyński 2003). Polish cinema and popular music represented in this period an integrated system, in which the fortunes of one part of the industry depended on and strengthened the success of the other. This was conveyed, for example, by announcing in the initial film titles that the songs performed in the film are available on a specific record. We can compare this system to Tin Pan Alley of song production, which was a Fordist, 'factory-type' institution, with standardised song form and strict division of labour between professional songwriters, musicians and star singers (Wall 2003: 22–24). Such an image emerges, for example, from Ryszard Wolański's biography of Eugeniusz Bodo (Wolański 2012) and Dariusz Michalski's biography of Mieczysław Fogg (Michalski 2015), and from an interview given by Helena Grossówna, included in one of the newsreels from the 1980s, in which she mentions that in the 1930s popular actors played in seven or eight films per year; a film was typically made in a month. Contemporary directors (those working under state socialist system), she added, 'waste money'. In favouring singing and dancing actors Polish cinema was no different from other European cinemas of this period, such as British, where some of the greatest stars, Gracie Fields and George Formby (Mundy 2012: 20–21), were also known for their singing and dancing talent and French, where 'Arletty, Raimu, Jules Berry and Fernandel, began their career in the music hall, vaudeville or *boulevard* theatre' (Conway 2012: 31).

The critics of Polish interwar cinema (quoted in Gierszewska 2012), in common with those writing about interwar cinema from a postwar perspective (Madej 1994; Lubelski 2009: 73–108) chastise films of the

1930s for being exaggerated or formulaic. Such an assessment goes hand in hand with criticising the dominant commercial mode of producing films of this period and the group of filmmakers who succeeded in this mode. As I mentioned in the introduction, they were described as 'professionals' (*branża*). In a different (especially Hollywood) context the label might have positive connotations, emphasising professionalism, but in Poland, it was a derogatory term. It stood for producing kitsch and the domination of the film industry not by creative people but by businessmen: producers, distributors and owners of cinema theatres (Starski, quoted in Lubelski 2009: 79). I agree with the opinion that Polish films of the 1930s and romantic comedies especially, lack believable narratives. An example of that is the frequent use of the motif of mistaken identities, when it is obvious to everybody except the central character, what is the true identity of the person s/he mistakes for somebody else. However, the use of sound and music, and the discourse about the recording industry make up for this deficiency, at least for the viewers who value the acoustic aspect of the film as much as its visual dimension.

Radio Days

Almost all Polish comedies from the 1930s include songs and dances. Describing them will require many more pages than the size of this publication allows. Hence, my priority is to present the most distinct films from the perspective of the use of music and sound. I decided to begin with films in which the music and dance numbers are related to narratives about the emergence of a 'new Poland'—a country many citizens aspired to: urban, dominated by the middle class, deriving its wealth from new industries and connected by modern technology, most importantly radio. Nowhere is this shown more clearly than in two films with the most popular Polish actor of the 1930s, Eugeniusz Bodo, in the main parts, playing a man who makes his living in the 'radio industry': *Piętro wyżej* (*Upstairs*, 1937), directed by Leon Trystan and *Paweł i Gaweł* (*Poe and Joe*, 1938), directed by Mieczysław Krawicz. The action of the first film, as the very title suggests, is set on two levels: the ground floor and the first floor. The ground floor is occupied by the owner of the house, an elderly Mr. Hipolit Pączek. Above him lives, somewhat improbably, another man of the same surname, a much younger Henryk Pączek (Eugeniusz Bodo), who is his tenant. The owner tries to get rid of Henryk due to clashes of habits of these two men. The older Pączek is a fan of classical music. When he is not quarrelling with the young Mr. Pączek, we see him playing classical pieces with his friends on instruments such as a flute, a violin and a cello. By contrast, the young Pączek, who works as a radio presenter, prefers to play jazz with his friends, who use instruments such as a piano, a saxophone and a rattle. Often the two bands play at the same time and the old Pączek tries at all costs to stop the music of the young Pączek. He calls the police or encourages his friends to play louder, so that the jazz from upstairs is drowned by the sounds of classical music from downstairs. The performances of the two bands can be interpreted not only as contests between two types of music, but also between different lifestyles and visions of Poland. Hipolit Pączek represents the old, quasi-feudal Poland, in which income comes predominantly from renting land or property. Henryk Pączek, with his jazz combo, stands for the modern Poland of young professionals working in new industries, such as radio. The title of the film, *Upstairs*, suggests that the vision of Poland which the young Pączek encapsulates is superior. This is also confirmed by the development of the narrative—all battles between the Pączeks are ultimately won by Henryk. In the end he even manages to gain the love of Hipolit's beautiful niece, Lodzia (Helena Grossówna), who is meant to inherit Hipolit's estate.

In *Upstairs* radio is presented as a source of good income and prestige, even the celebrity of Henryk Pączek. At some point he says that he does not need to chase girls with dowries because he earns 600 zloties per month; a good salary at the time. We also see two female fans trying to meet him in his flat but, as is the case in comedies based on the motif of mistaken identities, instead they bump into Hipolit Pączek. The film also includes an episode of Henryk singing to the microphone about his enchantment with Lodzia (although by this point he does not know that she is Hipolit's niece) and we can observe how his listeners are moved by his warm voice. Perhaps the greatest proof of the importance of the radio is that even Hipolit wants to perform there, playing classical music with his friends.

The film projects radio as a spontaneous and intimate form of communication. Although Henryk is meant to read what somebody else has written, he constantly diverts from the script and instead of reading the news, sings his love songs. However, rather than being punished for such transgressions, he is rewarded, as his spontaneity attracts more listeners, who are glued to the radio when he performs, as if it was a fetish, replacing the true object of their dreams. The peak of Henryk's spontaneous performance is at the end of the film, when, due to a misunderstanding, two teams of players perform at the same time—Hipolit's classical quartet and Henryk's jazz band. Contrary to the expectation of a cacophony, the performance of what is in reality one of Antonín Dvořák's *Humoresques*, is a perfect fusion of classical music and jazz (Milewska and Wyżyński 2003), anticipating such practices after the Second World War. Not surprisingly, Henryk is congratulated by his boss who regards the impromptu concert as a great success. It shall be emphasised that in this performance Henryk rather than Hipolit leads, being the conductor of the small orchestra. By the same token, the film demonstrates the domination of jazz music, epitomising modern times, over classical music, symbolising the past. This idea is also conveyed by the use of nondiegetic music in the film—the score is mainly jazz or, at any rate, music which feels contemporary to the narrative, written by Henryk Wars, the leading composer of Polish film music from this period, who also plays the pianist in Henryk's band (Fig. 2.1).

Musicals are associated with creating a utopian world: a reality which is meant to take us away from the hardship of everyday life. Richard Dyer says: 'Musicals were predominantly conceived of, by producers and audiences alike, as "pure entertainment" - the *idea* of entertainment was a prime determinant of them' (Dyer 1992: 17) and adds 'Two of the taken-for-granted descriptions of entertainment, as "escape" and as "wish-fulfilment", point to its central thrust, namely utopianism. Entertainment offers the image of "something better" to escape into, or something we want deeply that our day-to-day lives don't provide' (ibid.: 18). In a similar vein Barry Langford maintains that of all genres the musical is the most 'unencumbered by any ongoing commitments to social realism, historical authenticity or for that matter any suggestion of performative naturalism. The musical creates a hermetically enclosed generic world whose conventions and verisimilitudes are purely and peculiarly its own, and whose function is to enable and situate the musical performances that define the form' (Langford 2005: 83). Such a reading is also offered by historians of Polish interwar cinema, who linked the emergence of Polish musical comedies in the early 1930s to the economic crisis (Armatysowie 1988: 213).

Upstairs also offers the viewers a fair dose of utopianism, complete with a fairy tale romance and the end of a feud between two tenants, which can be read as a metaphor of reaching national harmony through overcoming class and generational divisions. However, it is realistic in its recognition

Fig. 2.1 Playing together jazz and classical music in *Piętro wyżej* (*Upstairs*, 1937), directed by Leon Trystan. Henryk Wars plays the piano

of the importance of radio in the lives of Poles. As historians of the interbellum notice, the ownership of radios increased from 120,000 in 1927 to 246,000 in 1930 (Lukowski and Zawadzki 2001: 214). Moreover, it is not utopian in the sense that a traditional utopian dream of marrying somebody much richer than oneself, for the sake of freeing oneself from financial problems, is not fulfilled on this occasion. Henryk's friend, Kulka Kulkiewicz, who dreams about marrying a rich girl so that his debts can be written off, has his dream quashed.

Upstairs also deserves to be discussed in the context of music because it is probably the most acoustic Polish film made in the 1930s, with a plethora of different sounds filling its soundscape. Apart from classical and jazz music, there is also a goose cackling, brushes moving on the floor and on the ceiling, radios and microphones malfunctioning and so on. All these sounds come across as very musical, somewhat reflecting on the earlier decade when the borders of music expanded by including ordinary noises, as pronounced in Russolo's 'The Art of Noises' (2004). Milewska and Wyżyński draw attention to a large variety of instruments used in the films of the 1930s, which, apart from classical instruments, include mouth organ, accordion, banjo, zither, guitar, harpsichord, church bells, hunting horns and barrel organ, with some instruments used for humorous effects (Milewska and Wyżyński 2003).

Poe and Joe is based on a similar premise to *Upstairs*: the feud of two men living on different floors in the same tenement block.[2] This time, however, the men are living somewhere in the province and are renting office and shop space from an elderly lady; Poe (Eugeniusz Bodo) downstairs and Joe (Adolf Dymsza) upstairs. Both sell electrical equipment, which suggests modernity, given that electrification could not be taken for granted in Poland in this period. Poe sells radios and is himself the inventor of a small, transistor radio, which he tries to sell to his customers. This proves difficult, as some of the people who visit his shop are not into miniaturisation; they prefer bulky radios which look like proper furniture. Moreover, for his radios to perform well, the electricity line in his building cannot be overloaded. In practice, it means that Joe cannot switch on the electrical gear in his shop, when Poe is playing his radios. This does not work, in part because Joe has to show his customers how the equipment works and in part because he is a prankster, who gains pleasure from causing mischief to his neighbour.

To get greater exposure for his invention, Poe travels to Warsaw. He visits the offices of various newspapers, hoping to be interviewed by journalists working there. Initially there is no interest, but thanks to Joe's intervention, eventually all newspapers cover the story of Poe's radio. In Warsaw, he also falls in love with a young woman, Violetta (Helena Grossówna), who is nineteen, but pretends to be a thirteen-year-old violin virtuoso. The reason for this deception is an assumption that more people will attend her concerts not knowing her real age and she desperately needs the extra tickets sold because she has to pay the debts of her father to the man who is now her manager. Due to a series of coincidences, Poe is taken for Violetta's Italian father and she subsequently follows him to his home town. Unbelievably, till the end of the film Poe fails to notice Violetta's true identity. This, of course, proves the point of the critics of Polish interwar cinema, that its narratives lacked realism. However, the use of music makes up for this shortcoming. What is particularly remarkable is the variety of music genres and dance styles used in this film, which one might associate more with the transgressive films of Jean-Luc Godard than interwar commercial Polish cinema. One of them is classical music, performed by Violetta in a concert hall, to the accompaniment of a symphony orchestra. Next there is popular music (popular in this period), of a Schlager type. In such style is a song, in which Poe confesses his love to the girl. Such music is also played in a dance hall in the hotel, where a large part of the film is set. Another type of music is a lullaby, which Poe and Joe sing to Violetta to send her to sleep. Finally, we get a several-minute long sequence set in a Gypsy camp, where the Gypsies play ethnic instruments, sing and dance, together with Violetta. This part, more than that set in the hotel, allows Grossówna, who graduated from ballet school, before launching an acting career, to show her dancing skills. The heterogeneity of music can be regarded as a reflection of different musical and ethnic cultures flourishing in interwar Poland and the eclectic musical taste of the audience, assumed by the makers of such films.

As in *Upstairs*, *Poe and Joe* pictures a utopian world, in which those who love each other, are eventually united in hope that they will live happily ever after. Also, as in *Upstairs*, this happiness is bestowed on 'modern' people, such as Poe, who is both an inventor and rejects the advances of the daughter of his landlady, who tries to win him with her cuisine. She is 'crossed out' because she represents 'old money' and an old way of attracting a man, associated with patriarchy. By contrast, Violetta wins, because she has talent for music and dance, rather than cooking, and because she does not wait passively for man to choose her, but follows him and fights for him. By contrast, those who make their money on the back of somebody else's work, such as Violetta's manager, lose.

The soundtrack for *Poe and Joe*, as for *Upstairs*, was composed by Henryk Wars (Henryk Warszawski), a musician of Jewish origin, who was the most successful film composer of the interwar period, as his contemporary, Władysław Szpilman, stated (quoted in Michalski 2007: 716). Wars was involved in a third of Polish film production of the entire interwar period and collaborated with the best Polish lyricists of the era, on occasions being compared to Isaak Dunayevsky (Michalski 2007: 702–728; Wolański 2012: 301). His strengths were tunefulness and rich instrumentation, with the use of unusual instruments being his personal signature (Michalski 2007: 718). He was particularly important in films which cast Eugeniusz Bodo. According to Bodo's biographer, Ryszard Wolański, about half of the films with this actor had a soundtrack composed by Wars; in total Wars scored 53 films (Wolański 2012: 301–302). Although films made in Poland of the interbellum has a reputation for being produced in haste, Wars was a meticulous composer, who put a lot of effort into producing a soundtrack suitable to the narrative and include hits in his films (ibid.: 303-4). Apart from writing film music, he was also the artistic director of the recording company, 'Syrena Record', to which I return in due course.

Songs from these two films, such as 'Umówiłem się z nią na dziewiątą' (I Have a Date with Her at Nine), 'Sex Appeal' and the lullaby 'Ach, śpij kochanie' (Oh, Sleep, My Darling) are popular to this day, as demonstrated by the fact that they are frequently heard on radio and are covered by younger Polish artists. Some of them received a second life thanks to appearing in postwar films about Poland of the 1930s and 1940s, such as *The Pianist* (2002) by Roman Polański, where we can hear 'I Have a Date with Her at Nine' and *Bodo* (2016), Bodo's biopic, directed by Michał Kwieciński and Michał Rosa, which I will examine in Chapter 6.

After serving in the Polish Army during the Second World War, Wars emigrated to the USA, where he managed to resume his career as Henry Vars, writing songs and scoring films, including for *Flipper* (1963) by James B. Clark. However, in the American film industry he never achieved a comparable status to what he enjoyed in Poland. A much worse fate was met by the lyricist of some of Wars's hits, Emanuel Schlechter (written also Szlechter, in a Polonised version), another author of Jewish origin of great importance for Polish interwar cinema, who ended up in the Lviv ghetto and later concentration camp, where he perished in 1942 or 1943. Another lyricist of Jewish origin, collaborating with Wars, Ludwik Starski, who wrote lyrics for 'Oh, Sleep, My Darling' survived the war and continued to work and thrive in the nationalised Polish film industry (see next chapter).[3] Indeed, there were so many composers of Jewish descent in the interwar Poland, who produced film and cabaret hits, that Mikołaj Gliński states that 'this group of artists invented popular culture in Poland' (Gliński 2015).[4] However, as the same author notes, drawing on the work of Elżbieta Janicka, 'while Jewish artists created the Polish entertainment culture, they were invisible on its various scenes: film screen, theatre and cabaret stage, concert halls. Janicka describes this situation as an example of the "ob-scenity" principle, which defines what qualifies for stage and what doesn't'. Another sign of their ob-scenity was hiding their Jewish identity behind their Polonised or exotic names (ibid.).

Songs in the Service of Industry

In *Zapomniana melodia* (*Forgotten Melody*, 1938) by Konrad Tom and Jan Fethke and *Będzie lepiej* (*Happy Days*, 1936), directed by Michał Waszyński, both scored, again, by Henryk Wars, songs not only convey the feelings of the characters, as it is the case in musical comedies, but play an important narrative function—they are key to a successful enterprise.

The first film casts in the main role Helenka Roliczówna (Helena Grossówna), a pupil in an all-girls school and the young daughter of a cosmetics tycoon, whose firm is on the verge of releasing his new product—a soap named 'Fenomen', which looks and tastes like chocolate, but is as efficient as a normal soap. The main concern of Mr. Rolicz is not to pass the secret of his new product to his main competitor, the cosmetic firm Roxy. For this reason he attempts to memorise the recipe for the production of the soap. He only manages to do it, when he listens to a melody, played by Helenka, which says 'You Will not Forget Me', to which he invents the words about how to produce the soap. The melody was in fact composed by a man who fell for Helenka and introduced himself as Stefan Roxy (Aleksander Żabczyński), to conceal the fact that he is a nephew of her music teacher, Professor Frankiewicz. Consequently, he is taken for a spy sent by Roxy, trying to steal the recipe of the magic soap. The narrative revolves around a forgotten melody, due to the fact that the piece of paper where the recipe was written was misplaced and destroyed by chance and Rolicz forgets the melody for the 'soap song'. The story finishes happily, as is expected in a romantic comedy: the recipe is retrieved and Stefan and Helenka embrace each other in the final shot.

Song on this occasion not only brings the couple together, but helps a Polish company to be successful. Although this does not happen in the narrative, we can believe that the 'soap song' will also work perfectly as advertising for the said chocolate soap. Throughout the film the point is made that songs have multiple functions: they can serve love and business, reflecting the capitalist approach taken by Polish film, music and theatre industries. Another use of songs, to which *Forgotten Melody* refers is in sport and leisure. The film begins with an episode of schoolgirls canoeing on the Vistula river, while singing 'Ach jak przyjemnie' (Oh, How Pleasant), with a chorus 'Oh, how pleasant it is to sway in the waves'. This song and 'You Will Not Forget Me' belong to the most popular Polish songs of all time, not only in the sense of being played on the radio, but also accompanying Poles in their ordinary lives. I remember singing 'Oh, How Pleasant' at summer camps in my school days in state socialist Poland. At the time I was not aware that the composer of this song was Henryk Wars; I assumed that it was a 'folk song'.

Although the conflict between the old, semi-feudal and modern Poland does not feature as prominently in the narrative of *Forgotten Melody* as in the films discussed in the previous section, it is conveyed through the discourse of music. The first dialogue we hear in the film is between the music teacher, Professor Frankiewicz, and the headmistress of an all-girls school. He complains that the girls indulge in new musical fashions, 'African jazz bands' with 'wild, Negro rhythms', which brings the risk of moral corruption. He, for his part, during the music lessons, tortures the girls by making them repeat the Polish version of the French nursery rhyme, 'Frère Jacques' (Panie Janie). The competition between 'Panie Janie' and jazz music can be interpreted as that between French and Anglo-Saxon culture as the principal source of Polish self-colonisation. Leaning towards the latter is presented in the film as a sign of modernity, which would also be the case of postwar Poland. In Poland of the 1950s and 1960s jazz, and later rock, would be condemned for their bad influence on the morality of young people. Eventually all the songs we hear in the film, including 'Panie Janie', get rearranged in a jazzy style, thanks to Professor Frankiewicz's nephew. At one point we also see the girls engaging in an energetic tap dance, which allows us to admire Grossówna's dancing skills. This is not the first time when this actress was tapping on-screen; the first time this happened in 1935, in the film *Kochaj tylko mnie* (*Love Only Me*), directed by Marta Flantz; this was also first tap dance in a Polish film (Mamontowicz-Łojek 1972: 84). In *Forgotten Melody* Grossówna's character is surrounded by other dancing girls: her friends from the school. In reality they were played by members of the most popular interwar dancing ensemble, led by Tacjanna Wysocka, so-called Tacjanki. They appeared in several other interwar films, including *The Ghosts*, which I will discuss in due course. By now, *Forgotten Melody* is largely forgotten; only its catchy songs survived the passage of time.

Happy Days features a popular comedy duo from Lviv, Szczepko and Tońko (Kazimierz Wajda and Henryk Vogelfänger), a kind of Polish Laurel and Hardy, who gained great popularity thanks to their radio programme, *Na wesołej lwowskiej fali* (*On the Cheerful Lviv's Wave*), broadcast under different titles, from 1932, which in due course became the most popular radio programme in Poland, making the Lviv dialect easily recognised all over Poland (Pieńkowski 2014). In *Happy Days* the couple begin their adventure when working in a factory producing toys, such as singing dolls and miniature musical instruments. The factory is owned by Julian Dalewicz (Aleksander Żabczyński), a man obsessively focused on his work. His motto is 'Work and silence, silence and work' and he expects everybody who works for him, to follow this rule. Yet, there is a contradiction between the commodity, produced in Dalewicz's plant, which is noisy, and the demands to respect the boss's need for peace and privacy; this being one of the sources of humour in the film. In contrast to the most famous cinematic rendering of factory work of the interwar period, *Modern Times* (1936) by Charles Chaplin, where the movement of the objects down the conveyor belt is frantic, the belt in *Happy Days* moves slowly, indeed too slowly, making the workers lethargic. This difference points not only to Chaplin's left-wing leanings, which he was not shy to reveal in his films, contrasting with Michał Waszyński's unwillingness to reveal his *Weltanschauung*, but also to the different position of capitalism in the United States and Poland. In the first country, where it ruled for a long time, it was taken for granted, while in backward Poland it was seen as a progressive order. The point made in the film is that Poland needs to speed up, to catch up with the more developed West and songs can help in this transition.

Szczepko and Tońko, after noticing that one of the dolls which they assemble, does not sound as it should, break the rule of silence (which also means working slowly) and start singing. Their singing proves contagious and soon the whole hall is taken up by their singing, holding dolls in their hands, playing miniature instruments and dancing. Such a scene can be regarded as a perfect advert for the factory, but Dalewicz, alerted by the noise, enters the hall, and is outraged by the behaviour of the workers. He sacks Szczepko and Tońko, despite their protesting that they acted in good faith.

The songs were again, composed by Henryk Wars, and lyrics were written by Emanuel Schlechter. On this occasion, however, the most memorable sound is that of the voices of Szczepko and Tońko, whose Lviv's dialect practically disappeared after the Second World War.

Spying, Loving, Singing

The rule of the Polish interwar musicals was that they were comedy-musical hybrids. There were, however, a few exceptions. One of them was *Szpieg w masce* (*The Spy*, 1933), directed by Mieczysław Krawicz, which is a hybrid of musical, melodrama, spy and science fiction film. It is one of several films in which played Hanka Ordonówna (1902–1950), the greatest Polish star of cabaret and music theatre. *The Spy* is, however, the only film in which she fully displayed her versatile talents.

The film draws on early Hitchcock films, such as *Blackmail* (1929) and *The Lady Vanishes* (1938), as well as *Mata Hari* (1931) by George Fitzmaurice with Greta Garbo. Like Hitchcock, Krawicz casts as his main character somebody who is essentially good, but due to adverse circumstances commits crimes. On this occasion this is a cabaret singer Rita Holm (played by Ordonówna) who works as a spy for a foreign regime. Given her foreign name, we can assume that she works for the German state and against Poland, but the film avoids naming any country and presents a universal situation, perhaps in a bid to receive international distribution and make it feel more futuristic. Rita and her superiors are tasked with stealing military secrets from a lab, where an older engineer Skalski works with his pilot son Jerzy to construct a remote controller, able to stop the motion of cars and planes. This device, according to the engineer, will save the world from a war, because it will be able to stop any dangerous machines before they launch an attack. Rita's job is to lure Jerzy in order to steal the keys to the lab from him. However, she falls in love with a dashing pilot and tries to disentangle herself from her job, but without success. The story finishes with the chase of the spies in which Jerzy shoots and injures a spy in a gas mask, who turns out to be Rita.

The plot, although different from the films previously discussed, can be regarded as a means to showcase Polish modernity. There are two places when the advancement of technology is displayed: the lab where Skalski works with his son and the musical shop 'Do Re Mi', where Rita holds meetings with fellow spies. The first has advanced machinery; the second soundproof cabins, where one can listen to records and overhear what happens in a neighbouring cabin. This technological power might be regarded as a warning against starting a war, addressed to Poland's western neighbour, given that Krawicz's film was made in the same year as Hitler seized power in Germany and launched a programme of Germany's remilitarisation. The record shop, like the radio studio in *Poe and Joe*, shows the importance of technological mediation in Polish musical culture of the interbellum. It also tacitly recognises the fact that Ordonówna's popularity was based, in a large part, on her records.

The romantic plot allows to show Ordonówna sing her most popular songs, 'Na pierwszy znak' (At the First Sign) and 'Miłość ci wszystko wybaczy' (Love Can Take Everything). The lyrics for both of them were written by Julian Tuwim and music by the previously mentioned Henryk Wars. Tuwim, another author of Jewish origin, is in fact better known as a serious poet, a leading representative of the poetic group 'Skamander'. Wars, as I earlier mentioned, was the artistic head of the recording firm 'Syrena Record'. This firm, with headquarters on Piękna Street 33 in Warsaw, was the largest recording firm in Poland. Here such Polish stars as Zula Pogorzelska, Tola Mankiewiczówna, Eugeniusz Bodo and Ordonówna made their records. In total, by September 1939 it released about 20,000 records which means almost one thousand per year (Michalski 2007: 209–210), testifying to the dominance of the Fordist model in Polish popular music business. A perceptive viewer could notice that the film acts as a subtle advert for this enterprise, as the wall of the shop 'Do RE Mi' is decorated with a poster of 'Syrena Record' and the songs. sung by Ordonówna, came also from 'Syrena's' records, confirming the previously made point about the film and music industries being in a symbiotic relation.

Performed at the different points of the story, Ordonówna's songs capture the different stages of the relationship between Rita and the dashing pilot. 'At the First Sign' refers to falling in love; 'Love Can Take Everything' to love as redemption. After Phil Powrie, I will describe these songs as crystal-songs; songs which mark important shifts in the narrative and emotional tone and deeply affect both performers and the audience (Powrie 2017: 1–2). The second song is played in different versions. First we hear Rita singing it in front of a large audience; then it is played from the record in 'Do Re Mi' shop and performed by Rita privately for her lover. The melody of the song is also used in the soundtrack as non-diegetic music. The music has a foreboding character—it foretells the heroine's doom and her redemption. In terms of integrating a song in the narrative, 'Love Can Take Everything' is probably the best-integrated song in Polish cinema of this period. However, in a review from this film Tadeusz Miciukiewicz criticised the use of songs, claiming that they slowed down the film, while praising the quality of the sound (Miciukiewicz 2012: 183–184).

The modernity of *The Spy* is also conveyed by its costumes and décor. Ordonówna wears 'asymmetrical' dresses in Art Deco style and on one occasion hides herself behind a fan made of peacock feathers. The interiors where she lives are also populated with Art Deco artefacts. Ordonówna's performance in the 'speaking parts' is understated, demonstrating that she could be one of the greatest film stars of the Polish interwar cinema. Yet, the previously quoted reviewer criticised Ordonówna's acting, describing it as 'theatrical' (Miciukiewicz 2012: 184) and after this performance she practically ceased to play in Polish films, which most likely reflects the fact that her career as a live performer and recording artist was more profitable to her than playing in the movies.

The Spy is prophetic not only in alluding to the approaching war, but also to the problem of spying in the community of Polish artists. One of the actors in the film, Igo Sym, who played a chief of the 'Polish' counter-intelligence, whose mother was Austrian, in due course became a Nazi collaborator and betrayed fellow Polish artists, including Ordonówna. I will return to this motif in Chapter 5, when discussing Ordonówna's biopic, directed by Janusz Rzeszewski.

From an Aristocrat to a Popular Musician

Pieśniarz Warszawy (*Singing Fool of Warsaw*, aka *Le chanteur de Varsovie*, 1934), directed by Michał Waszyński, is another film which connects songs and dances with the issue of social advancement. It is, however, different from those discussed previously, as it is not so much about songs which convey progressive ideology, but about the social progress of a man who performs songs. The novelty of this film lies in the fact that, rather than offering a 'rags to riches' narrative, it presents 'aristocrat to artist' narrative. Its main character, Julian, played by Eugeniusz Bodo, is the black sheep in an aristocratic family. This is demonstrated by a row of portraits of his ancestors, at which Julian shoots in the opening scene, to demonstrate his desire to go his own way rather than conform to the family's plans. What exactly these plans are, we never learn, although his uncle wants him to become a 'professional', which suggests that even the Polish aristocracy tried to modernise themselves in the interbellum. Nevertheless, the overall impression is that Julian and his relatives lead an idle life on borrowed money and have no desire to change it. This eventually gets on the nerves of Julian's relatives and Julian himself. A solution appears when he sees a street musician with a guitar. The man is passed by indifferent people because he sings a sad song. Julian borrows his guitar and tells him how to perform to attract attention (Fig. 2.2).

Suddenly he is surrounded by a crowd of people who cheer his performance. This gives him an idea to become a street performer and he turns out to be very popular because his songs are melodic, cheerful and simple.

Fig. 2.2 Julian (Eugeniusz Bodo) demonstrates how to be become a successful singer in *Pieśniarz Warszawy* (*Singing Fool of Warsaw*, 1934), directed by Michał Waszyński

One, in particular, grants him a status of the 'Warsaw singer' (which is the literal translation of the film's title)—'Już taki jestem zimny drań' (I'm Such a Cold Cad). The success of this song has, of course, much to do with the quality of the song, one of the greatest hits, composed by Henryk Wars with lyrics by Jerzy Nel and Ludwik Starski. Another reason is that it perfectly reflects the character of the singer, who does not take himself too seriously. It also captures the mischievous character of a Warsavian, that of a fixer, who had to be selfish and smart in his dealings with the Russian occupier during the times of partitions, because the foreign authorities were hostile to his plight. The synergy between 'I'm Such a Cold Cad' and the 'Warsaw character' is presented in the manner the song is performed: Julian starts singing it and then it is taken up by different people in different places, using different instruments, which gives the impression that the whole of Warsaw is singing the song. As I will argue in due course, the same device would be used in the first postwar musical, *Forbidden Songs*, for the same purpose—to show how 'forbidden songs' (forbidden by the German occupier) brought the inhabitants of Warsaw together. That such a device was used, can be explained by the fact that both films were scripted by Ludwik Starski.

The next stage of Julian's career is playing in a revue theatre, thanks to him meeting by accident the actress, who is its star. This brings him success because in the theatre Julian again performs his hit—'I'm Such a Cold Cad'. Being a street musician and revue actor makes Julian famous, but deepens his conflict with his family, who regards his status as not commensurate with his aristocratic roots. His opposition is greater since he falls in love with a woman of a lower class: a girl selling cigarettes. To frustrate Julian's plan his uncle hires a private detective whose task is to break Julian's engagement with the cigarette girl, but in the end his plot is revealed and the uncle accepts his nephew's profession. Besides, he himself falls in love with the actress who facilitated Julian's career. The story thus finishes with a happy end: that of the marriages of people of different social classes. It might be seen as a call to overcome class conflict, which marred Poland after the First World War.

Singing Fool of Warsaw can also be read as a metaphor of what I described in the introduction as an integrated system of Polish popular music and cinema, with its seamless transfer of personnel and products between its different sectors and selling the same product, such as a song, in different incarnations: in a revue theatre, on a record, in a film and during a recital. The film can also be regarded as an autobiography of sorts of its star and co-author of the script, Eugeniusz Bodo. Bodo, from his mother's side, also belonged to the Polish gentry, but was not interested in and possibly had no means to indulge in the aristocratic lifestyle or even become a 'professional', for example a lawyer or an officer. Instead, he wanted to be a performer and managed to climb the professional ladder, starting in provincial revue theatres, to progress to the most prestigious theatres and cinema. Bodo's recipe for success was largely that which Julian uses in the film—avoid sad songs (and stories) and give people laughter and joy. There is also a certain fit between the lyrics of the song 'I'm Such a Cold Cad' and Bodo's character, which includes a verse:

Moja mama nad kołyską
Tak śpiewała mi co dzień,

> Że zdobędę w życiu wszystko
> I usunę wszystkich w cień.
> (My mother over my cradle
> Sung to me every day
> That I achieve everything in my life
> And put everybody in a shadow)

Indeed, Bodo proved to be very successful and had the reputation of a cad towards women, whom he charmed and quickly abandoned. Significantly, one of his biographies has a title, taken from this song—*Już taki jestem zimny drań* (Wolański 2012).

Paradoxically, *Singing Fool of Warsaw* was lambasted for its use of music. The leading Polish critic, Stefania Zahorska, described it as 'barbarically unmusical', adding that 'Bodo has a wooden voice, without timbre' and 'melodies have no charms' (Zahorska 2012a: 195). For me, however, such an opinion reflects on the harshness of critics, rather than the quality of music used in this film.

Dancer's Musical

The directors of *Strachy* (*The Ghosts* aka *Terror*, 1938), Eugeniusz Cękalski and Karol Szołowski, and the cinematographer Stanisław Wohl, before they started making films, belonged to START (Society of the Devotees of Artistic Film), a left-leaning cine-club, which criticised the commercialism and naivete of Polish cinema and advocated producing films which were socially conscious and aesthetically challenging. In 1935 they set up their own studio: the Cooperative of Film Authors (SAF) with the intention of putting their ideas into practice. *The Ghosts* was one of two films produced by the SAF, which had its premiere before the war broke out and it was both commercially successful and critically acclaimed. The previously mentioned Zahorska described it as the most accomplished Polish film of the 1930s (Zahorska 2012b: 303).

This success had much to do with the fact that, given the reality of film production and distribution of the interwar Poland, even the STARTers had to find a compromise between arthouse ambitions and a need to recuperate the costs of production by respecting the interests and values of mainstream audiences and using tricks of the trade. They included basing the film on a popular book and casting stars in the main parts. The literary source is a novel of the same title written by Maria Ukniewska, published in 1938, which gained great popularity thanks to being set in the milieu of music theatres and cabarets, an environment the author knew first-hand, being a revue dancer herself. Ukniewska's *The Ghosts* can be compared to the works of Jean Rhys, with both authors drawing heavily on their own life stories. Such a choice of a literary hypotext can be seen as a way to offer exciting spectacles and narratives of love and betrayal on one hand, and to denounce the many social problems of interwar Poland, such as poverty, the lack of prospects for young people, corruption, patriarchy and the harsh abortion law, on the other. On this occasion Eugeniusz Bodo is cast in the main male role of an ageing artiste Modecki.

The main female character, Teresa Sikorzanka, is a chorus girl trying to make a career in the unstable world of the Warsaw show business. Teresa's origin is working class; she is the main breadwinner in a family consisting of her parents and younger sister. Given that her father is an ill-tempered alcoholic, she seems to have only two options in life: either to work in a music theatre or cabaret or to become an apprentice with a hairdresser. One can also think of a third option, prostitution, which here is not included, perhaps because at the time a career in show business was regarded as a cover for or a gateway to prostitution. Teresa chooses the music theatre not because it pays better or because it offers more stable employment than hairdressing, as the opposite is the case, but because she has a vocation. She loves theatre and would like to be famous. Although she is ambitious, she is also a realist, as shown in an episode when she writes on a piece of paper in one row her expected income and another her expenses, to make sure that her work provides her a 'surplus value' in the material sense (Fig. 2.3).

Following Ukniewska, Cękalski and Szołowski present the music hall as a patriarchal world, where men occupy positions of power, acting as the theatre's directors, producers and solo singers and dancers, while women are ordinary employees labouring in a Fordist way, as chorus girls, rarely entrusted with solo parts. This professional order along gender lines is underscored by the division of space. Men have their own offices; women have to share a common dressing room. Men earn enough to afford elegant apartments; Teresa returns after work to a room which she shares with her parents and sister. In the music hall the boundary between the professional and private lives of the dancers is blurred, because men control women's sexuality, by luring them to bed with promises of promotion. Both Teresa and her best friend, Linka, have such liaisons with senior men in the theatre, respectively the leading singer and

Fig. 2.3 Young ballet dancers (played by Tacjanki) in *Strachy* (*The Ghosts*, 1938), directed by Eugeniusz Cękalski and Karol Szołowski

dancer Modecki and the producer Radziszewski, and become pregnant by them. Their fate, however, could not be more different. Linka is not only abandoned by her lover, but has an abortion and is blackmailed by him. Modecki enjoys the prospect of becoming a father and proposes to Teresa. The film thus finishes with a happy ending. And yet, the ending is not entirely happy, because Teresa does not see marriage as a proper career for her. She prefers working in theatre.

While in other Polish musicals singing is foregrounded, in *The Ghosts* dancing gets the centre stage, hence I will describe it as a 'dancer's musical' (Altman 1981b: 2) or 'dance film' (Vize 2003: 24). It is the dancing, not the singing, which creates magical spectacles, such as illusions of a train moving, a man flying in the sky, or a gigantic black and white ball made of moving legs. The dancing scenes are performed by the previously mentioned Tacjanki, the dancing ensemble, led by Tacjanna Wysocka who, according to Bożena Mamontowicz-Łojek was also the main choreographer of the dancing scenes in the film (Mamontowicz-Łojek 1972: 84). The main female roles of Teresa was played by Hanka Karwowska, who was by then the pupil of a dance school (ibid.: 84). In the male roles, apart from Bodo, who had a great talent for dancing, was also cast the German dancer Georg Groke, who played the dancer Dubenko in the dancing episodes, most importantly in the dance 'Devil'. The dances are in varied styles, reflecting some international fashions and a wide range of dancing skills of Tacjanki, such as the dance of shadows, acrobatic, 'African' and constructivist dance (ibid.: 84). Although over 80 years passed since *The Ghosts*' premiere, I will argue that it has remained the most accomplished dance film in the Polish history.

Cękalski and Szołowski's representations of female dancers bring association with Busby Berkeley's films, such as *Footlight Parade* (1933) and *Dames* (1934), with which the Polish directors might be familiar, given that *The Ghosts* was made several years after their premiere. Berkeley's films are criticised by feminist authors, because of their narratives which represent and normalise patriarchal order and because they de-individualise women and reduce them to images. Lucy Fischer writes: 'What happens in most Berkeley numbers (and quintessentially in *Dames*) is that the women lose their individuation in a more profound sense than through the similarity of their physical appearance. Rather, their identities are completely consumed in the creation of an overall abstract design' (Fischer 1981: 75).[5] I agree with Fischer that women in dance numbers in Berkeley's films are de-individualised and the same happens in *The Ghosts*. However, Fischer condemns such arrangements from the perspective of individualism, which constitutes a crucial part of American ideology and through tacitly assuming that women in Berkeley's and other backstage musicals are reduced to stereotypes and cogs in the entertainment machine, while men remain individuals. One can argue that production in which an artist is subsumed by the collective is not necessarily inferior to the work of an artist-author or harmful to his or her dignity of a performer. Such a principle operates also in orchestras, which are rarely criticised for not allowing individual performers to shine. Consequently, I argue that Fischer's criticism is not valid. Moreover, *The Ghosts* are different from Berkeley's musicals because the film plays down the role of (male) stars and directors, suggesting that the chorus girls essentially direct themselves due to male absence or incompetence. It might seem far-fetched, but in my opinion this elevation of the community of workers over the stars reflects the ethos of START, which was also communal. The group perceived its strength not so much in creating excellent films, as in offering an alternative programme for the

Polish cinema and working together for the common good. This ethos is reflected in the production of *The Ghosts*, which has, unusually for Polish films, not one, but two directors.

Cękalski and Szołowski are not only preoccupied with dance, but also with the culture of professional dancers. Much of the film is set in the dressing and rehearsal rooms and in a room the dancers rent when working in the province, and the camera draws attention to the props used by them, such as shoes, clothes and mirrors, which play a double function: they allow the dancers to assess their appearance and also attach the photos of their idols to the glass. The atmosphere of the dressing-rooms is heated, due to overcrowding and hurry, as the girls have little time and space to prepare. In such places it is easy to lose temper, start quarrelling and fighting, especially for the attention of the male 'master', and it sometimes happens, but overall solidarity prevails over competition. The primacy of dancing is also conveyed in some episodes, which ostensibly have nothing to do with dancing, such as when Hanka and Modecki go on a merry-go-round, which creates an impression that the couple is dancing some euphoric dance, in which they lose their minds.

To add magic to the spectacle the then young cinematographer, Stanisław Wohl (who after the war became a successful director and scriptwriter, while continuing working as a director), followed the aesthetics of German Expressionism, employing chiaroscuro lighting and shooting from unusual angles. Normally, one would expect that such techniques would break the film's realism, but here it accentuates it by pointing to the difference between the material world and that created on stage.

Cękalski and Szołowski's success in representing dance can be explained by the former's experience in documenting dances. In 1935, Cękalski made three films about Polish folk dances, respectively from the Kraków, the mountains, Silesia and Kujawy and *Trzy etiudy Chopina* (*Three Chopin's Etudes*, 1936), in which one of the etudes is represented through the dance of Olga Sławska. *Three Chopin's Etudes* is regarded as the best representation of artistic dance in Poland of the interbellum and received awards at the Venice Biennale (Mamontowicz-Łojek 1972: 85). Unfortunately, after the Second World War Cękalski abandoned his passion for filming dance and devoted his energy to making overtly propagandist films, such as *Jasne łany* (*Fair Cornfields*, 1947) about the fight with rich farmers (*kułacy*) in the Polish countryside and a documentary about Feliks Dzierżyński (Felix Dzerzhinsky) (1951), a communist revolutionary and founder of the first Soviet secret service, the Cheka. From the perspective of music and dance cinema, Cękalski's talent was thus wasted. Ukniewska's novel, however, fared better. It was republished in postwar Poland and I even read it as a teenager. Its continuing popularity and relevance resulted in its adaptation as a four-part television series of the same title, directed by Stanisław Lenartowicz, in 1979, with the popular singer and actress Izabela Trojanowska, in the main part.

Conclusions

In this chapter I argued that music and songs in Polish films from the 1930s were multifunctional. They were shown to help development of Polish industry and smooth Poland's transition from a semi-feudal to a modern, capitalist state in which talent and hard work matters more than class origin. For this reason, rather than describing their use as 'utopian', as argued by Richard Dyer, it is better to describe them as 'aspirational', as they do not advocate leaving everyday reality for a place which does not exist, but staying in this place and trying to improve it. It is also worth emphasising the boldness and inventiveness of the scores and dance sequences, as demonstrated by mixing in one film music and dances from different traditions, rearranging old songs in contemporary style and making music out of everyday noises. Subsequently, music saved these films and many other Polish 1930s films, especially musical comedies, from oblivion. Songs in the 1930s films are typically more important than dances, but often in one film we can enjoy singing and dancing talents of the leading actors, such as Eugeniusz Bodo, Helena Grossówna and Hanka Ordonówna. Moreover, in *The Ghosts*, one of the most original and accomplished Polish films of the interbellum, dancing gets centre stage, producing spectacles, whose magic would be difficult to match in Polish postwar films. Unfortunately, this cinema has practically no continuation in postwar Poland, and not only because of the change of the political system, but because of the loss of its talent, due to death, emigration or discarding the old singers–actors as conduits of the 'wrong' ideology and work ethics.[6] Polish fiction cinema thus never became 'musical' again, only had films with popular music.

Notes

1. At the same time some of these publications use a liberal concept of a 'musical'. In particular, in his book Grant covers *Woodstock*, widely regarded as a music documentary, rather than musical.
2. *Poe and Joe* has two more hypotexts. The first is a humorous poem 'Paweł i Gaweł', written by a famous Polish nineteenth century poet and playwright, Aleksander Fredro; the second is a film *Robert and Bertrand*, directed in 1938, about two salesmen who end up in jail. It also cast Bodo, Dymsza and Grossówna in the main parts.
3. A comprehensive account of Starski's life and career is presented by Barbara Milewski in her essay about *Forbidden Songs* (Milewski 2020).
4. Gliński provides an extensive list of the most important song authors of Jewish descent and describes their mostly tragic fate during the Second World War (Gliński 2015).
5. Not all feminist authors condemn Berkeley for the way he treats female bodies. Molly Haskell writes: 'The Busby Berkeley numbers, which are not only more spectacular and indigenous to Hollywood than the important follies of Ziegfeld, are also more celebratory and less degrading of the female image. Maintaining a careful balance between abstraction and personalization, between the symmetrical and the erotic, Berkeley pays tribute to both the whole and the parts of a woman in a way that none of the fetishists of later decades and decadence have seemed able to do' (Haskell 1987: 146).
6. Those of the actors of the interbellum who survived and tried to continue their careers, found a safe haven in the Warsaw theatre Syrena, which continued the tradition of Polish musical theatres. This was the case of, for example, Adold Dymsza, Jadwiga Andrzejewska, Helena Grossówna and Loda Halama.

Works Cited

Altman, Rick (ed.). 1981a. *Genre: The Musical: A Reader*. London: Routledge and Kegan Paul.

Altman, Rick. 1981b. Introduction. In *Genre: The Musical. A Reader*, ed. Rick Altman, 1–7. London: Routledge and Kegan Paul.

Altman, Rick. 1981c. The American Film Musical: Paradigmatic Structure and Mediatory Function. In *Genre: The Musical. A Reader*, ed. Rick Altman, 197–207. London: Routledge and Kegan Paul.

Altman, Rick. 1987. *The American Film Musical*. Bloomington and Indianapolis: Indiana University Press.

Altman, Rick. 1996. The Musical. In *The Oxford History of World Cinema*. ed. Geoffrey Nowell Smith, 294–303. Oxford: Oxford University Press.
Altman, Rick. 1999. *Film/Genre*. London: British Film Institute.
Armatysowie, Barbara and Leszek. 1988. Film fabularny w latach 1930–1934. In *Historia Filmu Polskiego*, vol. 2., ed. Barbara Armatys, Leszek Armatys, Wiesław Stradomski, 207–265. Warszawa: Wydawnictwa Artystyczne i Filmowe.
Banaszkiewicz, Władysław. 1966. Pierwsze lata niepodległości. In *Historia Filmu Polskiego*, vol. 1. Warszawa: Wydawnictwa Artystyczne i Filmowe, 117–178.
Carroll, Beth. 2017. The Anti-Musical or Generic Affinity: Is There Anything Left to Say? In *Contemporary Musical Film*, ed. K.J. Donnelly and Beth Carroll, 58–71. Edinburgh: Edinburgh University Press.
Conway, Kelley. 2012. France. In *The International Film Musical*, ed. Corey K. Creekmur and Linda Y. Mokdad, 29–44. Edinburgh: Edinburgh University Press.
Creekmur, Corey K., and Linda Y. Mokdad (eds.). 2012. *The International Film Musical*. Edinburgh: Edinburgh University Press.
Dyer, Richard. 1992. *Only Entertainment*. London: Routledge.
Feuer, Jane. 1981. The Self-Reflective Musical and the Myth of Entertainment. In *Genre: The Musical. A Reader*, ed. Rick Altman, 159–174. London: Routledge and Kegan Paul.
Feuer, Jane. 1993. *The Hollywood Musical*, 2nd ed. Houndmills: Macmillan Press.
Fischer, Lucy. 1981. The Image of Woman as Image: The Optical Politics of *Dames*. In *Genre: The Musical*, ed. Rick Altman, 70–84. London: Routledge and British Film Institute.
Fischer, Lucy. 1989. *Shot/Countershot: Film Tradition and Women's Cinema*. London: British Film Institute.
Friedman, Lester, David Desser, Sarah Kozloff, Martha P. Nochimson, and Stephen Prince. 2014. *An Introduction to Film Genres*. New York: W. W. Norton & Company.
Gierszewska, Barbara Lena (ed.). 2012. *Polski Film Fabularny 1918–1939: Recenzje*. Kraków: Księgarnia Akademicka.
Gliński, Mikołaj. 2015. The Rise & Fall of Polish Song. *Culture.pl*, March 24. https://culture.pl/en/article/the-rise-and-fall-of-polish-song. Accessed 12 October 2019.
Grant, Barry Keith. 2012. *The Hollywood Film Musical*. Southern Gate, Chichester: Wiley-Blackwell.
Haskell, Molly. 1987. *From Reverence to Rape: The Treatment of Women in the Movies*, 2nd ed. Chicago: University of Chicago Press.
Hendrykowska, Małgorzata. 2009. Pomiędzy Wielką Wojną a przełomem dźwiękowym: kinematografia polska w latach 1914–1930. In *Sto lat polskiego*

filmu. Kino wielkiego niemowy. Część Druga: Od Wielkiej Wojny po erę dźwięku, ed. Grażyna M. Grabowska, 9–43. Warsaw: Filmoteka Narodowa.

Langford, Barry. 2005. *Film Genre: Hollywood and Beyond*. Edinburgh: Edinburgh University Press.

Lubelski, Tadeusz. 2009. *Historia kina polskiego: Twórcy, filmy, konteksty*. Katowice: Videograf II.

Lukowski, Jerzy, and Hubert Zawadzki. 2001. *A Concise History of Poland*. Cambridge: Cambridge University Press.

Madej, Alina. 1994. *Mitologie i konwencje. O polskim kinie fabularnym dwudziestolecia międzywojennego*. Kraków: Universitas.

Mamontowicz-Łojek, Bożena. 1972. *Terpsychora i lekkie muzy: Taniec widowiskowy w Polsce w okresie międzywojennym (1918–1939)*. Kraków: Polskie Wydawnictwo Muzyczne.

Marlow-Mann, Alex. 2012. Italy. In *The International Film Musical*, ed. Corey K. Creekmur and Linda Y. Mokdad, 80–91. Edinburgh: Edinburgh University Press.

Maśnicki, Jerzy, and Kamil Stepan. 2007. Aleksander Hertz obchodzi. In *Historia kina polskiego*, ed. Tadeusz Lubelski and Konrad J. Zarębski, 24–26. Warsaw: Fundacja Kino.

Michałek, Bolesław, and Frank Turaj. 1988. *The Modern Cinema of Poland*. Bloomington and Indianapolis: Indiana University Press.

Michalski, Dariusz. 2007. *Powróćmy jak za dawnych lat: Historia polskiej muzyki rozrywkowej, lata 1900–1939*. Warszawa: Iskry.

Michalski, Dariusz. 2015. *Poletko pana Fogga*. Kraków: MG.

Milewski, Barbara. 2020. Hidden in Plain View: The Music of Holocaust Survival in Poland's First Post-War Film. In *Music, Collective Memory, Trauma and Nostalgia in European Cinema After the Second World War*, ed. Michael Baumgarten and Ewelina Boczkowska, 111–137. London: Routledge.

Miciukiewicz, Tadeusz. 2012 [1933]. Szpieg w masce. In *Polski Film Fabularny 1918–1939: Recenzje*, ed. Barbara Lena Gierszewska, 183–184. Kraków: Księgarnia Akademicka.

Milewska, Hanna, and Adam Wyżyński. 2003. *Leksykon Polskiej Muzyki Filmowej 1930–1939. CD Rom*. Warszawa: Fundacja Promocji Muzyki Polskiej.

Mundy, John. 2012. Britain. In *The International Film Musical*, ed. Corey K. Creekmur and Linda Y. Mokdad, 15–28. Edinburgh: Edinburgh University Press.

Papadimitriou, Lydia. 2006. *Greek Film Musical: A Critical and Cultural History*. Jefferson, NC: McFarland.

Pieńkowski, Michał. 2014. Będzie lepiej – pierwszy film lwowski. *Nitroblog*. http://blog.nitrofilm.pl/2014/04/bedzie-lepiej-pierwszy-film-lwowski/. Accessed 30 May 2019.

Powrie, Phil. 2017. *Music in Contemporary French Cinema: The Crystal Song*. London: Palgrave.
Russolo, Luigi. 2004 [2013]. The Art of Noises: Futurist Manifesto. In *Audio Culture: Readings in Modern Music*, ed. Christoph Cox and Daniel Warner, 10–14. London: Continuum.
Stradomski, Wiesław. 1988. Drugi oddech polskiego kina. In *Historia Filmu Polskiego*, vol. 2, ed. Barbara Armatys, Leszek Armatys, and Wiesław Stradomski, 13–107. Warsaw: Wydawnictwa Artystyczne i Filmowe.
Vize, Lesley. 2003. Music and the Body in Dance Film. In *Popular Music and Film*, ed. Ian Inglis, 22–38. London: Wallflower.
Wall, Tim. 2003. *Studying Popular Music Culture*. London: Hodder Arnold.
Williams, Linda. 2000. Film Bodies: Gender, Genre, and Excess. In *Film and Theory: An Anthology*, ed. Robert Stam and Toby Miller, 207–221. Oxford: Blackwell.
Wilson, Emma. 2006. *Alain Resnais*. Manchester: Manchester University Press.
Wolański, Ryszard. 2012. *Eugeniusz Bodo: 'Już taki jestem zimny drań'*. Poznań: Rebis.
Zahorska, Stefania. 2012a [1934]. Pieśniarz Warszawy. In *Polski Film Fabularny 1918–1939: Recencje*, ed. Barbara Lena Gierszewska, 195. Kraków: Księgarnia Akademicka.
Zahorska, Stefania. 2012b [1938]. Nareszcie polski film. Strachy. In *Polski Film Fabularny 1918–1939: Recencje*, ed. Barbara Lena Gierszewska, 303–304. Kraków: Księgarnia Akademicka.
Zajiček, Edward. 1992. *Poza ekranem: Kinematografia Polska 1918–1991*. Warsaw: Filmoteka Narodowa.

CHAPTER 3

From Popular Songs to Manufactured Entertainment: Musicals of the State Socialist Period

One of the early articles about Polish musicals of the postwar era has the title 'A quarter way towards the musical'. This phrase was later embraced by Piotr Fortuna in a piece offering a bird's eye view of Polish musicals of this period, 'Muzykol – a cultural metaphor of the Polish People's Republic' (Fortuna 2015). The term 'muzykol' is, as one can easily guess, a Polonised version of 'musical'. This it is also a derogatory word on account of its associations with such offensive terms as 'robol' (a vulgar description of a manual worker). Fortuna also observes that many authors before him announced the production of the first (postwar) Polish musical, tacitly acknowledging that any films which beforehand might wear this label, in reality did not deserve it (ibid.: 121). Although upon reading his article a reader realises that Fortuna himself does not wholeheartedly embrace contempt for Polish ambition to produce musicals, his approach reflects the prevailing way of seeing Polish postwar musical as an ersatz of a 'real' Hollywood musical (on this take see also Talarczyk-Gubała 2007: 85–92; Otto 2011; Zwierzchowski 2017). Much less attention is paid to how the authors of 'muzykole' tried to negotiate different musical and cultural traditions and how Polish musicals changed over the decades, reflecting political pressures exerted on filmmakers on the one hand and musical and cinematic fashions and tastes of the audiences on the other. Finding answers to these questions is the goal of this chapter. First, however, let's locate Polish postwar musicals in the history of Poland of this period.

© The Author(s) 2020
E. Mazierska, *Polish Popular Music on Screen*,
https://doi.org/10.1007/978-3-030-42779-5_3

Polish Politics, Economy and Cinema Under State Socialism

In 1945 the Second World War ended. Its effect on Poland was in many ways similar to that of the First World War: the country was again destroyed. Poland was at the time the most devastated country in Europe; it lost about 38% of its wealth, which was many times more than Germany's loss. Poland also lost the bulk of its intelligentsia. To exist, it had to rebuild its infrastructure, the factories, the housing stock, the roads and railway lines and its cultural capital. Poland also entered this period from a position of economic backwardness, with the vast majority of its citizens living in the countryside, lacking basic facilities. Its borders changed, moving westward. Poland gained a large part of what previously belonged to Germany, but lost a large chunk of its eastern part, which was incorporated into the Soviet Union. In total, its size was reduced by 20%, but it acquired a 300-mile-long Baltic coastline and the part it regained was economically more developed than what it lost, to some degree making up for the losses inflicted on it by the German occupier (Landau and Tomaszewski 1985: 184).

Around the same time Poland underwent a profound political change: from capitalism to state socialism. This was the consequence of a new global political order, imposed at the Yalta conference in February 1945 by the victorious powers: Britain, the USA and the Soviet Union, which agreed to incorporate part of Poland directly into the Soviet Union and the rest into the Soviet sphere of influence. The Polish state had to cede a large part of its sovereignty to Moscow and follow the Soviet economic model. Political power in Poland was to be concentrated in the hands of the Polish communist party (the PZPR).

This system lasted till 1989. During this period the main tenets of state socialist politics and economy survived. Among them was the doctrine of friendship between Poland and the Soviet Union, the state ownership of the most important branches of the industry and privileging heavy industry. Under state socialism, strategic decisions had to conform to grand ideological designs and the Party was determined to keep all power within its own control.

Although after 1989 it is easier to find a negative assessment of Polish industry than positive, in many ways it was a success story. Industrial production of the postwar period increased 38 times (Ciborowski and Konat 2010: 29–31) and in some periods grew faster than in the West.

The geography of industry also changed, being more balanced at the end of the state socialist period than before the Second World War thanks to building many industrial centres in regions which were previously underdeveloped.

At the same time, the politics and economy kept transforming, reflecting changes in the Soviet Union and to some extent in the world, as well as specific priorities and personal characteristics of the subsequent First Secretaries of the PZPR. It is a custom to regard every change at the top of the PZPR as an announcement of the new area not only in Polish politics and economy, but in culture at large. Due to space constraints, I will not go into details of these changes. Suffice to say that the rule of Bolesław Bierut (1948–1956) was marked by the greatest zeal in implementing the principles of the socialist ideology, such as fighting any attempts at developing a private economy. Władysław Gomułka's rule (1956–1970) meant lessening the hard grip of the Party, although with variable speed. Edward Gierek's (1970–1980) ascent to power meant not only moving further from the totalitarian tendencies of his predecessors, but also introducing some elements of the capitalist economy. Each of these rulers left in a moment of acute economic and political crisis, of which the sign was widespread strikes. In the end of the 1970s the dissatisfaction was so widespread and the state so weak, that it led to the dismantling of state socialism in the end of the next decade and the introduction of market capitalism.

The situation of Polish cinema after the Second World War was not much better than that of Polish industry at large. The interwar film industry was practically destroyed by the occupier. All film studios were in ruins, together with film labs and distribution offices. Poland also lost a large proportion of its filmmakers. Many perished in the fight against the Nazis, others died in camps or emigrated. In 1947, when the first union of filmmakers was created, it comprised only 28 people (Zajiček 1992: 42–43). Without nationalisation the film industry would not survive and the state took upon itself the responsibility to rebuild it, and support it by financing and distributing films. Polish cinema of the period of state socialism is widely seen as a success story, both in terms of quantity and quality. With the exception of the first years after the Second World War and Stalinism, Poland produced on average thirty to thirty five films per year, ranking it close to that of France. In the Eastern European context Poland was seen as a mini-cinematic 'empire' and its films penetrated this region quite deeply: a fact which could be appreciated only after 1989, when the country lost this position (Mazierska and Goddard 2014: 6–10). Some Polish directors, such as Wanda Jakubowska, Andrzej Wajda, Jerzy Kawalerowicz, Andrzej Munk, Wojciech Has, Krzysztof Kieślowski, Krzysztof Zanussi, Agnieszka Holland, achieved worldwide fame, setting the standards of arthouse cinema in Europe at large.

As the state paid for films, it was only natural that it also sought to influence the products it paid for through overt and covert censorship, the character and severity of which kept changing, usually following the larger political conjunctures, which brought with them either liberalisation or tightening the belt of filmmakers. In general, it was a two-tiered process. First, scripts were pre-approved by industry internal censors and then the completed films were assessed by Party representatives (Michałek and Turaj 1988: xiii; Iordanova 2003: 33–36; Adamczak 2012: 178–179). It was difficult to stop a film once it was approved for production. This allowed the filmmakers to depart from the script by including politically 'unsafe' material during shooting (Adamczak 2012: 79).

The filmmakers themselves knew that in order to pass the final examination by Party officials, a certain degree of self-censorship was necessary. In combination, the censors' fluctuating tolerance and the filmmakers' calculated compromises make it impossible to draw a clear line between 'conformist' and 'dissident' films and filmmakers, although some filmmakers at a certain point of their career were so unhappy the way the film industry operated in Poland, that they emigrated.

The changes in Polish cinema after 1945 mirrored the political junctures, such as the end of Stalinism and the ascent of Władysław Gomułka in 1956, the fall of Gomułka and his replacement by Edward Gierek in 1970, Gierek's fall in 1980, the first victory of Solidarity in 1980–1981, the imposition of martial law in 1981 and, finally, the fall of state socialism in 1989. However, there was some delay till a new political situation was reflected in cinema. This particularly affected full-length fiction films, whose production is lengthy, especially under the socialist system, when the script and the film required acceptance by the political authorities.

Political events not only affected the type of films made in Poland, but also the organisation of the film industry and the number of films produced. Political liberalisation used to bring more autonomy for the film industry, reflected in setting up semi-autonomous film units, with prominent directors as their heads. Over the course of time directors such as Wanda Jakubowska, Aleksander Ford, Jerzy Kawalerowicz, Andrzej Wajda, Krzysztof Zanussi and Juliusz Machulski, to list just a few, were their heads. Some of these artists, such as Wanda Jakubowska, were put in their positions because they were seen as both accomplished filmmakers and loyal to the regime. Others, like Wajda or Machulski, received this role mostly due to their artistic achievements and, albeit more rarely, the popularity of their films. Liberalisation also went hand in hand with the increase in film production and Polish successes in the international arena, which was also an important goal for Polish filmmakers. Centralisation, by contrast, meant fewer films of mostly lower quality. Such organisation affected the status of film directors in Poland. As Bolesław Michałek and Frank Turaj maintain, under state socialism

> the creative position of a director is considerably enhanced. [He] is no mere manipulator of mise-en-scène, nor simply an executor of a producer's projects, nor yet a combination technician-businessman-organizer (a paradigm familiar to Americans). He is nothing less than an exponent of universal aspirations and concerns, a creator who has gained the status heretofore reserved for poets, writers, and artists. (Michałek and Turaj 1988: xi)

Given such circumstances, Polish cinema under state socialism was dominated by auteurism. Another specificity of the state industry was that, as Michałek and Turaj put it, 'the threat of unprofitability was of no concern' (ibid.: xii; see also Adamczak 2012). This explains why at times Poland embarked on super-productions which could compete in their lavishness with the Hollywood product, as exemplified by *Rękopis znaleziony w Saragossie* (*The Saragossa Manuscript*, 1965), directed by Wojciech Has, *Faraon* (*Pharaoh*, 1966) by Jerzy Kawalerowicz or *Ziemia obiecana* (*The Promised Land*, 1974) by Andrzej Wajda (Adamczak 2010: 229–235). On many occasions, the more expensive the film, the higher the bonus for its director. By contrast, the profit made by the film had little impact on the financial or critical standing of their makers. Box office hits were routinely derided by critics as conformist and pandering to the low taste of the audience. The relative neglect of profit also affected the star system. Polish postwar cinema had many stars, such as Zbigniew Cybulski, Daniel Olbrychski, Elżbieta Czyżewska and Krystyna Janda, but it lacked a 'star system' of the type operating in Hollywood or even Western Europe (Skwara 1992), because the value of a star as a creator of extra profit was of little relevance to the film producers.

The focus on directors-auteurs, as opposed to stars and a blasé attitude to commercial success explains why Polish cinema and popular music in the state socialist period failed to create an 'integrated system', whose purpose was to maximise revenue, which pertained to the interbellum. In Polish cinema after 1945 song and dancing numbers were no longer needed to sell films to the public, because selling films ceased to be the main objective of filmmaking, being superseded by the requirement to fulfil political goals imposed on filmmakers by the authorities and their desire to express themselves. Box office successes were even looked on with distrust, because they suggested a lack of artistic integrity.

The Beginnings: Remembering War Songs

The history of musical film in the Poland liberated from German occupation began very early and successfully. The first Polish postwar fiction film, *Zakazane piosenki* (*Forbidden Songs*, 1947), directed by Leonard Buczkowski and scripted by Ludwik Starski, was a musical. It also proved to be one of the most popular films in Polish history; more than 10.8 million people watched it in the following three years (Haltof 2002: 50) and till 1960, when the first Polish super production *Krzyżacy* (*Teutenic Knights*, 1960), directed by Aleksander Ford, appeared on Polish screens, it was the most watched Polish film (Lubelski 2009: 136).

The key to its success was the skilful interweaving of popular songs in a simple narrative. Such talent, as I argued in the previous chapter, was not uncommon among the directors working in the 1930s and Leonard Buczkowski belonged to the most successful directors of this period, although his specialism was not romantic comedies, where songs appeared most often, but patriotic films, focusing on Poles maintaining their national identity during the times of partitions, as in *Florian* (1938) or defending their borders after the end of the First World War, as in *Gwiaździsta eskadra* (*Stormy Squadron*, 1930). As *Forbidden Songs* was meant to be a patriotic film, Buczkowski was well placed to direct it. Starski, whose birth name was Ludwik Kałuszyner, also proved himself in the interwar period to be very apt in working at the interface between music and other media, being a talented lyricist, sound engineer and scriptwriter, as I mentioned in the previous chapter. Due to being Jewish, he spent war years in hiding, but luckily managed to avoid being sent to a ghetto and concentration camp (Milewski 2020: 113–117). The third important creator of the film's success was Roman Palester, whom

Starski commissioned to create the film score (ibid.: 117). Palester started his career before the war, composing classical music and in due course gained a reputation of Karol Szymanowski's successor and one of the most eminent Polish composers. In the first years after the war (1945–1947) he composed the music or served as a musical director for several Polish films (ibid.: 118). In 1947 he moved to Paris and settled there, due to his disapproval of socialist realism. From 1952 to 1972 he lived in Munich, where he headed the cultural department of the Polish section of Radio Free Europe.

The product of these artists' collaboration was intended to be a documentary, whose purpose was to preserve the songs sung in the occupied Warsaw. However, when the film was finished, during its vetting procedure (*kolaudacja*)[1] it was suggested to extend it to full-length and so a new version was created which was subsequently changed, to keep pace with the changing political situation, most importantly the requirement to present the Soviet Union and especially the Soviet Army in a positive light. The new version entered Polish cinemas in 1948. *Forbidden Songs* is skilfully integrated into a story of people living in the same tenement block. All of them seem to be of middle-class background, as suggested by their spacious and tastefully furnished apartments and manners. Such a choice of characters most likely reflects the prewar, 'bourgeois' interests of Buczkowski and Starski, as well as the fact that the film was made before socialist realism was properly introduced into Polish cinema.

Despite the changes made during re-shooting of the film, much of the documentary character survived in the final version, beginning with the introductory subtitle: 'The main protagonist of this film is a song: naïve, simple, but true. During the greatest hardship of the German occupation, it was able to ridicule the enemy, raise people's spirits and therefore it deserves to have a film made about it'. Such a statement suggests the continuation of a utilitarian approach to songs in Polish cinema, dominating in the 1930s, in Polish postwar cinema. Songs in 1930s films were meant to promote the development of Polish industry; on this occasion they are in the service of the war effort. This is demonstrated by their lyrics and mode of performance. The songs have simple melodies and lyrics, often describing everyday life under Nazi rule, but behind their simplicity, lies sophistication. The most famous of them is 'Siekiera, motyka' (Axe, Hoe), probably the most popular Polish war song, with lyrics written by Anna Jachnina. Every verse begins with the words 'axe, hoe', which are the names of simple farming tools, but also can be regarded as weapons which Poles are prepared to use to fight the hated Nazis. The early verses outline the cruelty and damage caused by the occupiers; the later, with the phrase 'The stupid painter lost the war' express the hope that the Germans would lose the war.

These 'forbidden songs' are sung mainly by street, unprofessional or semi-professional singers, including children. Their mass character is underscored by numerous scenes when we see somebody starting to perform a song which is then taken over by another person and then another. Sometimes this impromptu choir is in close physical proximity, on other occasions the singers are located in different places, which strengthens the effect of the whole capital or even the whole country singing the same song. Such a device brings to mind *Singing Fool of Warsaw*, discussed in the previous chapter, where Bodo's song 'I'm Such a Cold Cad' was sung by the whole of Warsaw. Given that Starski wrote scripts for both films, it is only natural that we find this device in *Forbidden Songs*. The manner of performing Polish street songs is contrasted with the way the Germans sing their songs: by soldiers during marches. Such comparison renders Polish performance superior, as it is presented as a voluntary, spontaneous and truly communal activity. Moreover, while Poles sing a variety of songs, the German soldiers appear to know only one song, which they repeat. This oppressive refrain 'Heili heilo' was extracted from the popular Nazi *Marshlied*, 'Ein Heller und ein Batzen' (Milewski 2020: 119). In this way, Polish popular culture comes across as richer than the culture of their enemies. Buczkowski's film includes popular songs not only in the sense of being written to gain popularity, but by belonging to the whole nation. If I am not mistaken, it is the only Polish postwar musical which offers us songs popular in this sense. In later Polish musicals we only find songs which are manufactured to be popular.

During the course of the film the voice-over informs us that Germans were averse to Polish songs not only because of their lyrics, but also their melodies, based on Polonaise, Mazurka and Kujawiak. Most of all they hated Chopin's music. Precisely for this reason, during the occupation Poles assembled to listen to it, as demonstrated in the scenes of people gathered around a piano on which somebody (in reality a future famous composer and conductor Jan Krenz) plays Chopin's compositions. By juxtaposing street-level protest songs *Forbidden Songs* offers a certain model of Polish popular music and culture for the postwar period: folk music and classics. Again, this model is contrasted with what the Germans wanted Poles to consume: jazz music and cabaret entertainment (which in fact were popular in Poland of the interbellum, as the films of this period attest). Significantly, in the 1950s music belonging to these genres would be forbidden or strongly discouraged in Poland, on account of being either imperialist or of low quality and harking back to the interwar entertainment, deemed trivial and vulgar.

The vast majority of diegetic music in *Forbidden Songs* is performed live, with the accompaniment of a large variety of instruments, such as accordion, violin, trumpet, saxophone, harmonica, drums and piano. The last instrument plays the most important role, as it is always used in a domestic setting. The focus on the piano adds to the sense that the film is set among the middle classes. As Adrian Daub observes 'The standardisation and industrialisation of piano manufacturing in the first half of the nineteenth century made the instrument a "sonic hearth" of the middle-class homes of Europe and America (Daub 2014: 37). In the aristocratic and bourgeoise homes, the auditorium had become 'not only a musical but also a social and political space' (Müller 2010: 836). This is what we observe in *Forbidden Songs*: Poles gathered around a piano playing Chopin's compositions or patriotic songs become a political force, eager to fight the occupier. The power of collective listening to music is proven by the fact that the majority of characters engage in anti-Nazi conspiracy, most importantly by taking part in the Warsaw Uprising. This even refers to a musician who by nature is cowardly, but in the end gives into the atmosphere of patriotism and decides to fight against the occupier.

Although the piano is important as a playback device, the film alludes to the fact that it lost its privileged function after the war, being replaced by a phonograph and the radio. The film is framed by the main character, Roman Tokarski (whom we can regard as stand-in for Starski), visiting the radio in response to the newspaper advert looking for people knowing the war's 'forbidden songs'. The frame suggests that although the songs were performed live during the occupation, the only way to preserve them and make them live again is through recording them and their stories. The radio is thus presented as an ethnomusicologist, collecting Polish musical heritage. The narrative frame is unobtrusive, yet very effective. It allows the viewer to immerse him/herself in the on-screen world as if it happened here and now, while at the same time being aware that it belongs to the past.

Dancing to the Rhythm of Mass Songs

If we could predict the development of Polish postwar cinema on the basis of its beginnings, we could conjecture that musicals would play a prominent role in them. This would be especially the case during the period of Stalinism, when socialist realism became the dominant style in art. As David Tompkins argues in relation to Poland and East Germany, music

> served a peculiarly important function in the legitimation strategies of these communist regimes in their early phase from 1945 to the late 1950s… The ruling parties sought to influence musical production to saturate the public space with politically effective ideas and symbols that furthered the project to construct their version of a socialist society. Music helped the parties establish legitimacy; both extensive state support for musical life and messages in the music itself encouraged musical elites and ordinary citizens in the audience to accept the political elite's dominant position and political mission. (Tompkins 2013: 2)

Given that film was also a very important art form, even the 'most important art' for communist ideologues, as Lenin himself stated, one would expect that the end of the 1940s and the first half of the 1950s would see the production of many Polish musicals. However, this was not the case. Between *Forbidden Songs* and the end of Stalinism in Poland in the mid-1950s, following the deaths of Stalin and Bolesław Bierut, the Polish Stalinist leader of the PZPR and political thaw, which started with Władysław Gomułka's ascent to power in 1956, only one musical *Przygoda na Mariensztacie* (*An Adventure at Marienstadt*, 1954), was produced in Poland and it was again directed by Leonard Buczkowski and scripted by Leon Starski. This scarcity can be attributed to three factors. One of them was the low number of films produced during this period overall, which was a trend observed across the Soviet Union and the entire Eastern bloc during the period when socialist realism dominated (Kenez 2001: 121). The second was the scarcity of filmmakers able and willing to shoot musicals. The prewar 'professionals' (*branża*) were dying out and a new cadre of Polish cinema was unwilling to engage in cinema of this type, preferring to shoot more serious films, of which the model of this period was Wanda Jakubowska's *Ostatni etap* (*The Last Stage*, 1947). Thirdly, except for 'folklorist' music, as it was labelled in Poland or 'newly composed folk music', as it was more aptly described in

Yugoslavia, Poland had little new popular music to showcase in films and especially of the type which could appeal to a young audience.

It is thus worth devoting some attention to this music, because it would re-appear in different times in the history of the Polish musical, up to *Zimna wojna* (*Cold War*, 2018) by Paweł Pawlikowski. By 'folklorist music' I mean music based on folklore, but adjusted to the taste of wider audiences, particularly those living in the cities. Such music was promoted in all state socialist countries as an expression of the authentic 'spirit of the people' and an antidote to supposedly poisonous western influences. However, Poland seemed to take the task of preserving its musical folklore more seriously than the rest of the bloc, as demonstrated by the nationwide action of collecting Polish folk music (Akcja Zbierania Folkloru Muzycznego) in the years 1949–1954, by recording and transcribing it. In subsequent decades this action was scaled down, by limiting it only to certain regions. Nevertheless, it resulted in the collection and cataloguing of over 40,000 items. According to Ryszard Krawczyk, who was himself engaged in this initiative, it was probably the most comprehensive collection in Europe (Krawczyk 1980: 4).

There also existed numerous state institutions, including a special department of the Ministry of Culture, devoted to this type of music. Although such actions did not have any direct effect on the development of Polish popular music, they sent a signal to the music and the film establishment that it pays to be 'folklore-friendly'. One consequence was the setting up of large singing and dancing ensembles, Mazowsze and Śląsk, respectively in 1948 and 1953, whose names were based on the names of the most important regions in Poland, Mazovia and Silesia. The purpose of these ensembles was promoting Polish folk music nationally and internationally. Mazowsze plays in *An Adventure at Marienstadt* and one of its members, Lidia Korsakówna, is cast in the main role of Hanka Ruczajówna, a country girl who upon visiting Warsaw for the first time falls in love with the capital and one of its shock worker builders and decides to return there, to become a bricklayer herself (Fig. 3.1).

The band in which Hanka plays, however, does not perform under its true name 'Mazowsze', but is presented as a supposedly amateur 'band from Złocień', one of many existing in Poland, set up by a factory or a state farm. However, this band is presented as performing for the city audience, it thus comes across not as folk but folklorist, in the same way Mazowsze was a folklorist ensemble.

Fig. 3.1 Hanka Ruczajówna on her first visit to Warsaw in *Przygoda na Mariensztacie* (*An Adventure at Marienstadt*, 1954), directed by Leonard Buczkowski

In common with *Forbidden Songs*, *An Adventure at Marienstadt* did well in the box office. Commercially it was the most successful Polish socialist realist film, still very popular with Polish audiences (Lubelski 2009: 149). The story presented in Buczkowski's film has much in common with a formula previously tested in Soviet art, especially the musical comedies of the 1930s, as it is utopian, rather than realistic, a 'flight into the future' (Lunacharsky, quoted in Taylor 2012: 106). Moreover, it concerns the emancipation of women; a topic of great importance for communist ideologues due to their goal of achieving gender equality (Mazierska 2017: 114–115). At the same time, it can be regarded as a typical romantic comedy, in which 'boy meets the girl, boy loses the girl and the boy regains the girl'.

However, the love between the boy and the girl, Janek and Hanka, is of a peculiar socialist realist type, as 'it is not "tainted" by sexual or erotic impulses; rather it is a "pure" romantic love based on its object's labour proficiency' (Taylor 2012: 108). Critics who analysed the film, most importantly Piotr Zwierzchowski and Paul Coates, point to the perfect balance between these two strands of the film: 'ideological' (women's emancipation) and 'popular/romantic', which ensured the commercial success of the film and its longevity (Zwierzchowski 2000: 3–38; Coates 2005: 67–90).

This perfect balance is augmented by the three types of songs used in the film, each representing a different musical tradition. One is 'To idzie młodość' (The Youth Is Marching), a socialist realist song with music by Tadeusz Sygietyński and lyrics by Ludwik Starski. Songs of this type were promoted by the Party ideologues and the music establishment, such as the Marxist musicologist Zofia Lissa, during the state socialist period. They are described as 'mass songs', although they were not written by the masses, but by professional composers and lyricists, who typically, after Stalinism had ended in Poland, were ashamed of them. According to Dariusz Michalski, the most prolific composers of such fare were Edward Olearczyk and Władysław Szpilman (the protagonist of *The Pianist* by Polanski), followed by Alfred Gradstein, Witold Lutosławski (often using the pseudonym Derwid), Jan Maklakiewicz, Henryk Swolkień and Zbigniew Turski. The most prolific authors of their lyrics were Jacek Bocheński, Stanisław Chruślicki, Stanisław Ryszard Dobrowolski, Henryk Gaworski, Krzysztof Gruszczyński, Helena Kołaczkowska, Tadeusz Kubiak, Kazimierz Wajda and Witold Woroszylski (Michalski 2009: 485–486).

'The Youth Is Marching' is sung by members of the 'band from Złocień' (in reality Mazowsze), when travelling through the Warsaw streets on the back of a lorry, adding to the song's dynamism. The fact that it is the first song we hear in the films suggests that the ideas it represents have priority over other cultures. The authors of *An Adventure at Marienstadt* borrowed such a way of presenting a mass song from the Soviet musicals of Alexandrov and Pyriev. As Richard Taylor observes, following Trudy Anderson, in these musicals the 'scores made widespread use of choral singing, which helped to universalise the characters and situations in which they found themselves. Furthermore, the combination of catchy tunes and ideologically loaded texts… meant that, when the audience left the cinema humming the tune, it also carried with it a message of reel reality into the real world outside' (Taylor 2012: 108).

The second song, 'Cyraneczka' (Teal), is a real folk song from the region of Kurpie; it is again sung by a whole choir during its public performance, hence fulfilling a similar function to 'The Youth Is Marching'. Finally, we hear the waltz 'Jak przygoda, to tylko w Warszawie' (If an Adventure, Then Only in Warsaw) sung by Hanka (in reality Irena Santor) and Janek. They perform it in the evening, in an empty square, surrounded by tall residential buildings, whose inhabitants applaud them, which gives the impression that Hanka and Janek are performing on stage. This type of singing and dancing recollects the type of petit-bourgeois culture which flourished before the Second World War and was frequently represented in the interwar cinema.

Judging by its music, *An Adventure at Marienstadt* was conceived as a 'conciliatory' film, which tried to bring together different strands of Polish popular culture, suggesting that not only they can exist next to each other, but also enrich each other. The songs and accompanying dances and dance-like movements feel like an organic part of the narrative, while at the same time fulfilling an important ideological function: promoting socialism and emphasising the importance of folklore in Polish culture. This ideal of rendering songs integral to the narrative and vice versa, was in my opinion never again achieved in Polish postwar cinema, although some films by Janusz Rzeszewski approached this ideal.

Given the success of *Forbidden Songs*, one would expect Polish critics to be enthusiastic about filmmakers using songs in their films. However, the opposite happened. The presence of songs was seen by them as an encouragement to lambast the film. The rule was that the more songs, the worse the film in the eyes of the critics. Symptomatic of this perspective was a piece entitled 'Inflation of a Song', published in 1953 by Jerzy Płażewski, one of the most influential Polish critics, active for over half a century. In it, Płażewski advocates using only one song in a film on the grounds that one song has a better chance to be remembered by the viewer than two or more and fulfils the role song should play in the film: to underscore the emotional tone of the movie (Płażewski 53: 18). Fortunately, Polish filmmakers did not follow Płażewski's advice, even if it presumably put many off from making musicals.

Stabilising Small Stabilisation

During the hegemony of socialist realism, the role of the director-auteur was played down and cinema addressed the whole of society. A split of cinema into popular and auteurist strands occurred with the advent of the

Polish School in the second half of the 1950s, whose creators were seen as auteurs, conveying their own vision rather than one coming from above (Michałek and Turaj 1988: xi–xii). The next split happened in the 1960s, the period labelled 'small stabilisation', marked by abandoning the ideological zeal characterising the 1950s and encouraging citizens to focus on minding their own business, even being politically passive (Mazierska 2017: 146–148). In 1960 a distinction between 'engaged cinema' and 'popular cinema', especially comedies and *filmy obyczajowe* (which can be translated as 'films about the everyday'), addressed to mass audiences was officially made by the state at the resolution of the Central Committee of the Party (Uchwała 1994: 33). Both types of films were meant to be socialist in spirit, but in due course it was assumed by the critics that popular cinema, being the natural heir of socialist realist cinema, is conformist, while auteurist cinema is 'ideologically engaged'. Such a reading of Polish cinema is simplistic, as in both types of films and often even in one film we find examples of conformism and opposition to the dominant ideology, but it reflects well the behaviour of critics and micropolitics in the Polish film industry of the 1960s and 1970s, namely the fact that those filmmakers with significant cultural capital avoided making comedies and *filmy obyczajowe*, leaving this task to the less well-known and powerful directors who received fewer resources than their more established colleagues. This led to a kind of vicious circle—the lack of investment and negative selection of directors was disadvantageous to producing high-quality popular films, especially comedies and musicals, and the expectation of being lambasted by critics further discouraged directors-auteurs from trying their hands in these genres. Consequently, Polish musical films of the 1960s, 1970s and 1980s were made predominantly by less well-known filmmakers. An exception are the musical comedies of Stanisław Bareja, perhaps the only filmmaker in the Polish cinema of state socialism, who gained the status of an auteur, despite making films addressed to the mass audience.[2] Polish critics themselves often admitted that they were unfair towards popular cinema, being snobbish and lacking training, skills and criteria in assessing popular cinema, and having little understanding of the taste of the average movie-goer (B.J. 1970), hence suffering from some of the shortcomings which they attributed to the lambasted popular films. Nevertheless, they carried on regardless, treating Bareja's musical films with particular hostility (Klejsa 2007: 82; Talarczyk-Gubała 2011: 86).

Before I move to specific films, it is worth emphasising that the Party directive to make popular films resulted in an increase in the production of genre films in the 1960s, and some specialisation of Polish filmmakers. The best known example is Bareja, who in this decade made three comedies in which popular music plays a major role: *Żona dla Australijczyka* (*Wife for an Australian*, 1964), *Małżeństwo z rozsądku* (*Marriage of Convenience*, 1966) and *Przygoda z piosenką* (*Adventure with a Song*, 1968). Popular music and musicians also entered the popular television series, *Wojna domowa* (*Domestic War*, 1965–1966), about two families living in the same tenement block. It included, for example, an episode about a teenage son who tries to get to the concert of a youth music star, played by Magda Zawadzka.

Some authors explain the popularity of music and musicians in the cinema of the 1960s by a 'negative selection' of available characters. Given that film scripts were vetted by a special committee, the filmmakers assumed that it was better to avoid certain types of characters, such as the members of the Party, higher functionaries of the police (Polish *milicja*) and state security, the Catholic Church and even workers (Otto 2011: 70). Representing them was particularly risky in comedies, as by their very nature comedies are critical of people and institutions. Poking fun at the operation of the Party could lead if not to imprisonment, then at least problems with completing the next project. This left the filmmakers with a limited choice of professions to make fun of. Artists, including popular musicians, were among those who could be laughed at with impunity, along with peasants, the remnants of the prewar aristocracy and criminals (ibid.: 71). Another reason why filmmakers turned to popular musicians was the fact that in the 1960s popular music was flourishing in Poland. Especially popular were three genres: estrada songs, actors' songs and rock (big beat) music. These three types of music are also used in the 1960s musicals, often more than one type in a film, yet with big beat receiving most attention, because at the time it was a novelty and was most popular among the young audiences, whom the filmmakers in Poland tried to woo, as elsewhere in Europe.

Bareja's musical comedies deserve special attention. Being three of them, they create a cycle and one can regard them as a document of sorts about popular music in Poland in the 1960s, together with institutions which promoted and supported it. Second, they act as a litmus test of the changing hierarchy of different types of popular music in Poland. Finally, they testify to Bareja's maturation as a specialist in musicals. Despite the critics of the period dismissing Bareja as lacking in talent and taste, I will argue that his films demonstrate his growing ability in using music on screen, by learning from the masters, such as Busby Berkeley and Jacques Demy, yet also being sensitive to local circumstances and able to balance between the authorities' demands to make constructive, pro-socialism and optimistic films and pleasing ordinary viewers.

As the critics observed, Bareja's 1960s films show us Poland opening itself to the world, which in practice means to the West (Klejsa 2007: 117). However, in reality this opening was not unproblematic due to the Cold War and representing it was also ridden with problems. As Piotr Zwierzchowski observes,

> Władysław Gomułka treated the western world with suspicion and never understood it. The western mass culture that he considered in general terms and did not know at all, was seen by him as a threat to socialism, Polish national culture, and to formation of the young generation. He spoke about artists that some of them were forgetting about these social duties, forgetting their own nation and its needs, look only at the West for artistic inspiration. This wish to catch up with Paris or New York, these snobbish attempts to keep up with various art movements, that appeared in the West and soon disappeared, would be funny if they had not entailed concrete ideological, cultural, and moral damages. (Zwierzchowski 2017: 199)

In order to avoid problems with censorship, the West in the films of the 1960s had to come across as less attractive than Poland and this is what happens in Bareja's films. The director shows characters travelling abroad or engaging with foreigners on their own soil, but ultimately returning home. In *Wife for an Australian* and *Adventure with a Song* the sojourning characters are musicians, which suggests that this was a privileged profession, as the majority of Poles were not able to cross the Iron Curtain.

In *Wife for an Australian* the lucky travellers are members of the ensemble Mazowsze, the most famous Polish folklorist band, as previously mentioned. In reality the band travelled widely, performing mostly for members of the Polish diaspora, but also for the foreigners. In the film we find it on the most prestigious ship, an ocean liner MS Batory. The plot, as the title indicates, concerns an Australian, who travels to Poland to find a wife. One shall add that he, Robert, is a Polish Australian, speaking Polish throughout the film and played by well-known

Polish actor and Bareja's regular, Wiesław Gołas. Upon confessing to his acquaintance from Gdansk that he would like to find a wife in Poland, he is taken to Mazowsze's performance and falls in love with its leading singer, Hanka Rębowska, whose very name looks similar to that of the female protagonist of *An Adventure at Marienstadt*, Hanka Ruczajówna. The plot is about bringing Robert and Hanka together; in this sense *Wife for an Australian* follows a pattern typical for Hollywood musicals (Altman 1981: 198–201), as well as Polish interwar films. The visual strategy used by Bareja is that of a tourist guide. The director presents Poland in the best possible light, using strategies of selection (only certain sites, buildings and people are chosen for tourist brochures and excursions), homogenisation (features of an area and its people are stereotyped according to some dominant cultural model), beautification and decontextualisation (ethnic subjects appear in settings that lack some concrete lived-in, historical referent') (Albers and James 1988: 154–155). As Ning Wang summarizes, 'tourists usually see only tourist sights and attractions and the social context in which these sights appear is usually ignored' (Wang 2000: 141).

To make his film touristy, it is set in one of the most picturesque cities in Poland, Gdansk, among its main tourist attractions. The people walking the streets are shown dressed up and the cars on the streets are mostly western. The place where Robert brings the kidnapped Hanka is not an ordinary flat in the apartment block or a hotel room, but a mansion, with a porch and a balcony supported by marble columns and whose interiors are adorned with exotic furniture, an open fire and a tiger skin lying on the floor. Consequently, the film gives the impression that Poland is a kind of picturesque consumer paradise, which is at odds with that of most Poles living in this decade, who remember it mostly for low quality of consumers goods. The music and dances for the film were chosen according to the same strategy. As I mentioned earlier, Mazowsze was the Polish 'postcard band'—it repackaged Polish folklore for the tourist consumption, choosing its most attractive elements: the most melodic and catchy songs, arranged by the best composers. Although the name of the band was Mazowsze (Mazovia), it had in its repertoire songs and dances from different parts of Poland, including from the Polish mountain region, in this way decontextualising them. In reality, no true folk band would have such a wide repertoire. The touristy approach was also reflected in the attractiveness of singers and dancers, who were not ordinary boys and girls from the countryside, but highly trained performers.

They were, moreover, performing in very colourful matching clothes. In the film they are put against attractive background, such as the Town Hall in Gdansk, whose interior appears to be covered in gold. Mazowsze is shown from different angles, so that we can appreciate the band as an ensemble and look at the singers and dancers from a close distance, to appreciate their beauty and acrobatics, for example, men clad in mountain costumes jumping over their canes. Of specific interest are shots from above which render the dancers creating abstract arabesques with their moving skirts, in a way reminiscent of the choreography of Busby Berkeley. On occasions the camera also zooms in and singles out Hanka from the group and brings her closer to Robert. Such selection happens when Robert is daydreaming while watching Mazowsze's performance. In this way Bareja's film adheres to the rule, pertaining to Hollywood musicals that no matter how idealised is the 'real world', it will be contrasted with a more idealised dreamworld (Feuer 1993: 67–85). In the dreamworld, created in *Wife for an Australian*, Robert and Hanka are together, dancing on the idyllic meadow and getting married.

At the end of the film the couple decide to marry. This is not surprising, given the title of the film. What is unexpected is that Robert decides to stay in Poland, charmed by its landscape and music. In this way the film acts as a perfect advert for state socialist Poland, without engaging with the ideology of state socialism, unlike *An Adventure at Marienstadt*, to which this film is a figurative heir. At the same time the film papers over the misogynist behaviour of the main male characters, Robert and the matchmaker Żelazkiewicz, who initially treat Polish women as chattel, which can be bought, sold and transported without their consent. One can gather that this would not be possible in films made during the hegemony of socialist realism, when work was more important than marriage and women were supposed to compete with men. Instead, it points to the return to more traditional, even Catholic values during Gomułka's rule, which put family at the centre. This shift is also indicated by the songs, which picture a traditional division of gender roles. This is only natural, given that the film uses folk and folklorist songs. However, in *An Adventure at Marienstadt* they were balanced by songs of different types. In Bareja's film, on the other hand, there are only songs evoking folk culture. Not only they are used diegetically, but folk melodies also provide extradiegetic music. Folklorist elements also dominate the visual side of the film. Even when Hanka is not performing, we see her in a dress which is based on the traditional style of clothes from the Łowicz region. The folk motifs of cockerels and multi-coloured stripes used in dresses worn by the members of Mazowsze are also used in the film's initial titles.

Following the film's premiere, the eminent Polish critic, Aleksander Jackiewicz, observed that Bareja does not pretend to show us the real Poland, in the same way Mazowsze does not pretend to show us the real Polish countryside (Jackiewicz 1964: 12) and the critic praised Bareja for being consistent in this approach. Piotr Fortuna, writing about this film a half century later, agreed with this assessment, maintaining that the film was compensatory—its idyllic images and songs compensated for the shortages of consumer goods in the 1960s (Fortuna 2015: 127).

The subsequent musicals by Bareja still show us Poland of the 1960s seen through rose-tinted glasses, but they are more engaged with the absurdities of the state socialist economy. This is reflected in the songs they use; rather than having the characters perform folk or folklorist songs, they sing songs which are contemporary and reflect the specific situation of the characters. *Marriage of Convenience* begins with a song performed by a band of street musicians, with the singer of satirical songs, Tadeusz Chyła, as its leader. The band would reappear later, like the chorus in a Greek play, commenting on the events unfolding in front of our eyes. The song *Mr. Kwiatkowski, Mr. Kowalski*, with music by Jerzy Matuszkiewicz (who was also the author of the film's entire score) and lyrics by Agnieszka Osiecka, the most renowned song lyricist of state socialist period, includes the well-known motifs of socialist realism, such as rebuilding Warsaw, which is now full of schools and kindergartens and announcing that they are constructed for the benefit of ordinary people, who are well cared for. The song also says that it does not matter whether one lives in a villa with a garden or a small, cramped place, because statistically it is getting better in Poland and everything Poles possess is a common good. It is worth recollecting here that the socialist project consisted of the nationalisation of the country, namely taking away what belonged to private citizens to put to communal use. But the characters presented by Bareja base their actions on the opposite premise: if under socialism everything is common, appropriating it for private use is acceptable, because in this way the citizens take only what belongs to them anyway.

The plot of *Marriage of Convenience* revolves around the relationship of Joanna, pretty daughter of semi-legal traders from Różycki bazaar, trading in *ciuchy*, privately produced or imported clothes, and her two suitors: a slacker aristocrat Edzio and Andrzej, an artist, whom Joanna prefers. The film oscillates between denouncing socialist absurdities and presenting the main couple overcoming their differences, as is the case in classical musical. Song and dance show them coming together by embracing socialist reality, most importantly in a musical number performed in a furniture shop, where they praise the system of instalments which allows young couples to furnish their apartment all at once, as opposed to the older generations who acquired their furniture over a long period of time. In reality this system, as much as helping people to acquire consumer goods, laid bare the poverty of ordinary Poles, who couldn't even afford to buy a table or wardrobe in one go, as well as alluding to the crampness of 'Gomułka's apartments'. While the song has Polish lyrics and refers to Polish specificity, the music and dancing evokes the Charleston—a dance popularised in the USA in the 1920s, somewhat confirming Zwierzchowski's thesis that Polish musicals of the 1960s had Polish content, yet Hollywood form (Zwierzchowski 2017).

The last song and dance in the film, titled 'Byłem kiedyś' (I Was Once), again a product of collaboration between Osiecka and Matuszkiewicz, is performed during the wedding of the main couple. It tells the story of various people who failed, but got a second chance, such as a man performing in opera, whose braces broke, causing a scandal, so that he got fired and became a street musician. They might be regarded as an ironic take on the change of elites during state socialism, yet with acknowledgement that under this system the losers got a second chance. The style of singing and dancing merges several traditions. One is a folk wedding song, in which each new person who joins in, humorously engages with what was sung by his or her predecessor, a formal dance in the French tradition, which could be seen in films set in some castles, which is, however, modernised and at times brings to mind a dance of single women in Milos Forman's *A Blonde in Love* (1965). Finally, it includes a short solo of the then popular modern dancer Gerard Wilk. Despite merging so many traditions, the song and dance numbers work well and do not draw attention to their heterogeneity. It could be regarded as an epitome of Bareja's effort to overcome differences between his characters and Gomułka's attempts to unify his country in the face of growing disunity and competing demands of different section of the society. These efforts were successful till the years 1968–1970, when a major crisis erupted, leading Gomułka first to denounce the Polish Jewish minority and then workers as acting against the welfare of their country.

In both films the main female role is played by Elżbieta Czyżewska, who was one of the most popular Polish actresses of the 1960s, to a large extent thanks to her roles in Bareja's films. She was a perfect choice for these films because, unlike some other Polish actresses of her generation, such as Beata Tyszkiewicz, Teresa Tuszyńska or Barbara Brylska, she transcended class. She looked good in folk attire, was convincing as a daughter of the traders from Różycki bazaar and could be plausibly taken for a progeny of diplomates. She was just a 'girl for all seasons' and could be regarded as a symbol of a classless society which the political authorities purported to engineer (Fig. 3.2).

If *Wife for an Australian* suggested that there is only one right melody in Poland (a folk melody), suitable for every occasion, *Marriage of Convenience* tried to seamlessly merge different tunes and dances, *Adventure with a Song* is less successful in unifying different narratives and musical traditions Perhaps, its very point is that the differences cannot be smoothed over. Of the three films by Bareja, *Adventure with a Song*

Fig. 3.2 Joanna (Elżbieta Czyżewska) with her suitors in *Małżeństwo z rozsądku* (*Marriage of Convenience*, 1966), directed by Stanisław Bareja

is also the most saturated with songs, squeezing twelve of them into 93 minutes, It is also the most topical or even realistic, by making reference to the Opole Festival of Polish Songs, set up in the 1960s, and to the fact that doing well in this festival was used as a platform to perform abroad, especially in Paris, whose famous Olympia concert venue hosted many artists from Poland, such as Czesław Niemen, Ewa Demarczyk and Urszula Sipińska. Pola Raksa, who plays Mariola, the winner of the festival, looks like a cross between Poland's two main blonde estrada stars, who both did very well at the Opole festival: Urszula Sipińska and Maryla Rodowicz; even her name looks like a cross between Maryla and Urszula. In a way, reminiscent of the style of Rodowicz, who at the beginning of her career was compared to Joan Baez, Mariola's song which wins the festival, 'Osiołkowi w żłoby dano' (Food was put in the donkey's manger), draws on folklore, yet is sung in a modern style.

More than in his previous films, on this occasion Bareja presents Poland in awe of foreign (French) culture. This fascination is revealed most conspicuously in an early scene showing signs and display windows of famous Parisian cafés and clubs such as Moulin Rouge. However, Bareja's ultimate goal is to demonstrate that this charming veneer of Paris covers a less appealing core. This is done by presenting Mariola's travails in Paris. She goes there, taking up an offer from a dodgy impresario, who promises her to make career in France's capital. Yet she fails to achieve success and eventually returns to Poland. The fault is, however, not on Mariola's side, but on Paris itself. One reason is the envy of an older singer of Polish origin, Susanne, who does not want competition from a younger colleague, which can be regarded as a metaphor of the West's hostility to Eastern European products. Another is the lack of any idealism on the part of French show business. This is reflected in the fact that deprived of any means to support herself, Mariola is reduced to performing striptease in a seedy night club. At some point she confesses to her landlady: 'I didn't know that it is so hard [to achieve success] in Paris', to which the older woman replies: 'Because [in Poland] you were in your own place'. 'Not only that', says Mariola. 'In Poland, what matters is art, while here only money matters.' 'Well, in your place art is subsidised', responds the landlady with a note of sarcasm, probably reflecting the position of Bareja, whose films, regarded as merely entertainment, not only failed to receive state subsidy, but had to subsidise the less successful auteurist films.

Mariola's adventure is contrasted with that of her boyfriend, composer Piotr, who follows her to Paris. There he fares much better, both financially and artistically. This is because he receives a scholarship from the Polish Ministry of Culture, which allows him to live comfortably. Moreover, as one reviewer observes, there seems to be no strings attached to this scholarship, no programme of activities to fulfil, so he can spend his time in Paris on writing songs for Susanne, while at the same time courting his girlfriend (Lech 1970: 9). In the end Mariola and Piotr return to Poland, giving up on the mirage of the West, as if experience taught them to embrace the scornful attitude to the West, espoused by Gomułka. The return is rational, because, as one reviewer asked rhetorically, 'where would the characters find another country as generous and idealistic as Poland?' (Lech 1970: 9).

Zwierzchowski summarises Polish musicals of the 1960s with the phrase 'socialist content, Hollywood form', but the origin and character of *Adventure with a Song* is more complicated. The plot, based on numerous misunderstandings and missed opportunities, brings to mind prewar musical comedies, as examined in the previous chapter. This link is not accidental, given that the script was co-written by Bareja and Jerzy Jurandot, who started his career in the 1930s, writing songs and sketches for musical theatres, as well as dialogues for interwar films such as *Manewry miłosne* (*Love Manouvres*, 1935) and *Ada! To nie wypada!* (*Ada, Don't Do That!*, 1936), both directed by Konrad Tom. The songs are mostly about love and homesickness, drawing on the traditional notion that a woman cannot survive, even less find happiness, without a man. Another non-Hollywood origin of *Adventure with a Song* is *Kabaret Starszych Panów* (*Elderly Gentlemen's Cabaret*, 1958–1966), a television programme with music. The *Cabaret* was renowned for its gentle and absurd humour and, as the name suggests, adulation of all things old-fashioned. One of its stars was Barbara Krafftówna, who played a warm and whimsical woman on the verge of middle-age, who takes care of lost souls. In Bareja's film she plays Mariola's landlady, who iterates this character and sings in a similar style as in *Cabaret*. The futuristic costumes worn by the actors and dancers in many musical numbers, often made of transparent material, and cartoon captions and animated images at the beginning of the film in the style of pop-art, bear similarity to *Przekładaniec* (*Rolly-Polly*, 1968) a television science fiction film by Andrzej Wajda, which had its premiere the same year as Bareja's film.

They play a double function: announce that we will be watching a fictitious, two-dimensional world and underscore the modernity of Bareja's production. Another sign of the film's attempt not to lag behind are modern-style dances, performed by two leading dancers of the 1960s, the previously mentioned Gerard Wilk and Krystyna Mazurówna, and setting several episodes at airports.

The film was influenced by both American and European musicals, but the latter prevail. The scene where the character walks on the wall is a borrowing from *Royal Wedding* (1951), directed by Stanley Donen, where Fred Astaire defies gravity, but this is really the only quote from Hollywood cinema in the entire film. Pola Raksa looks more similar to a subdued Catherine Deneuve from *Les Demoiselles de Rochefort* (*The Young Ladies of Rochefort*, 1967) by Jacques Demy than Hollywood stars and the scenes in which she auditions and performs striptease in a seedy club might even be regarded as a reference to Jean-Luc Godard's *Une femme est une femme* (*A Woman Is a Woman*, 1961), Godard's dystopian musical. The songs performed in the film are also more in the style of French *chansons* than American songs popular at the time.

Most songs are sung by Susanne, played by Irena Santor, then the first lady of Polish estrada music, Mariola, played by Raksa and Piotr, played by Bohdan Łazuka. Of them Łazuka's part is the most memorable. He can be regarded as an heir of the Polish 1930s stars of musical theatre and cinema, such as Eugeniusz Bodo, due to being equally comfortable in singing/dancing numbers and spoken parts. There was a grace and elegance to his performance which was not matched by his screen partners who lacked either acting (Santor) or singing (Raksa) skills. As Monika Talarczyk-Gubała observes, Łazuka was the only actor of the 1960s, whose songs, such as 'Miłość złe humory ma' (Love Tends to Have Bad Moods) became hits and he had a recital in the prestigious venue of the Congress Hall of the Palace of Culture in 1964 (Talarczyk-Gubała 2007: 90).

The 1960s was also a period of rapid development of Polish television, where popular music was treated with greater care than in Polish cinema, as demonstrated by introducing programmes devoted to it, such as *Muzyka łatwa, lekka i przyjemna* (*Easy, Light and Pleasant Music*), directed by Janusz Rzeszewski and the previously mentioned *Elderly Gentlemen's Cabaret* (Kończak 2007: 70). This programme, which consisted of gags or sketches, woven together by a thin narrative and songs, started to be broadcast in 1958, during Gomułka's thaw.

It would be difficult to imagine a programme like that to be looked at favourably by the authorities during Polish Stalinism. This was because it represented a poignantly different ethos. In socialist realist works people had to act with a clearly defined purpose and focus on the future. There was no place for ambiguity and gentleness, while the characters in *Elderly Gentlemen's Cabaret*, especially the titular gentlemen, played by Jerzy Wasowski (the composer of songs presented in the *Cabaret*) and Jeremi Przybora (the lyricist and scriptwriter) seemed to wander aimlessly, their actions driven more by accident than a plan. Moreover, they looked back, rather than into the future, as stated by the very title of the programme, which included the word 'gentlemen' (*panowie*), which was a dirty word in the socialist realist vocabulary. Similarly, their appearance, marked by cylinder hats, ties, jackets and flowers in the buttonholes, signified bourgeois elegance, rather than the socialist fashion, marked by waders and work uniforms. For this reason, an eminent Polish writer and film critic, compared the two elderly gentlemen to Chaplin's tramp, as all characters signified anachronism and alienation from the reality in which they found themselves (Woroszylski 1964: 4). The difference between Chaplin's creation and those of Wasowski and Przybora lies in the fact that the elderly gentlemen try to rise to any challenge which the world places on them. In the end, they miraculously triumph, because the world around them, surreally, adheres to their perceptions and actions (ibid.). This logic is perfectly captured by one of their most popular songs, 'Piosenka jest dobra na wszystko' (Song Is Good For Everything) which, as Woroszylski explains in his perceptive analysis, proclaims that a (good) song can help to deal with such problems as low social status and unrequited love.

Elderly Gentlemen's Cabaret became the most popular entertainment programme of the 1960s (Kończak 2007: 70) and it could be described as a 'cult' programme, given that people on the streets were quoting fragments from its dialogues (a practice existing till now, especially among the older generation). Not surprisingly, the creation of Przybora and Wasowski attracted the interest of other media. The *Cabaret* had its radio franchise and in 1964 its cine-version, under the title *Upał* (*Heat*, 1964), directed by Kazimierz Kutz and scripted by Jeremi Przybora and Jadwiga Berens. The thin narrative concerns the two elderly gentlemen, played by Przybora and Wasowski, entrusted by the prime minister with the task of looking after the country when he leaves the capital due to the unbearable heat. Despite having no political experience, they agree and try to rise to the challenge, which includes averting the rage of a foreign diplomat, offended by not seeing anybody greeting him on his arrival and dealing with the narcoleptic employee of an elegant fashion shop. In their efforts to govern the country they are assisted by a woman working in a milk bar (Barbara Krafftówna) and members of an anti-sunstroke squad, led by Zuzanna, played by another of *Cabaret*'s regulars, Kalina Jędrusik. The film is essentially made of sketches, joined by songs. Although it was shot in Warsaw, it bears little resemblance to the real Warsaw. There are no real passers-by on the streets and the only car we see is a limousine carrying a foreign diplomat.

The film divided critics. Some, like Zygmunt Kałużyński, regarded it as one of the best Polish comedies, thanks to its surrealism, whimsicality and fragmentation (Kałużyński 1964; see also Woroszylski 1964). Others, on the other hand, complained that the director was not able to translate the television format of *Elderly Gentlemen's Cabaret* onto the wide screen: the film looks like a television programme, but just longer and boring at times (Drozdowski 1964; Kochański 1964; Kydryński 1964), an opinion with which I agree. One difference between the televised *Cabaret* and *Heat* concerns the use of songs. In *Heat* they are sparse in comparison with their television counterparts and chopped into small pieces, as if the director did not trust the power of the song to move the plot forward or make up for the shortcomings of the script. Most likely this was the case, as demonstrated by the fact that for Kutz it was his only foray into musical comedy.[3] After *Heat* there were no more attempts to make films based on *Elderly Gentlemen's Cabaret*, despite the fact that the programme got a second lease of life in the late 1970s under the title *Cabaret of Even More Elderly Gentlemen*.

A Gentle Beat of Big Beat

The type of songs Bareja and Kutz presented in their films were popular in Poland throughout the whole period of the Polish People's Republic. However, they did not capture the musical Zeitgeist of the decade, in which big beat (or bigbeat, bigbit, big-beat),[4] the Polish version of rock music, was born. This task was taken by other directors, such as Jerzy Passendorfer, who directed *Mocne uderzenie* (*Big Beat*, 1966), Jan Rutkiewicz, who directed *Kochajmy Syrenki* (*Let's Love Mermaids*, 1967) and Hieronim Przybył, who directed *Milion za Laurę* (*Million for Laura*, 1971).

According to historians of Polish popular music, the symbolic date of the birth of big beat is the first concert of the band Rhythm and Blues, which took place on 24 March 1959 (Zieliński 2005: 15). Inevitably, as everywhere in Europe, big beat reflected western influences, as conveyed by the foreign name of the band Rhythm and Blues. However, its creators and promoters, most importantly Franciszek Walicki, the manager of several early Polish rock bands, tried to ensure it flourished by convincing the authorities that it is not a hostile force, coming from the West, but a phenomenon which is rooted in Polish culture. This was necessary, given the previously mentioned opposition of Gomłka to all things western. Walicki did so by coining the slogan 'Polish Youth Sings Polish Songs' which encouraged Polish would be rockers to switch from English (or any other language) to Polish (Walicki 1995: 132; Gradowski 2018: 89–90). Such a move also reflected the wider trend of Polonisation of state socialism during the 1960s. As a result, the 1960s saw a mushrooming of bands, influenced by western rock, but singing in Polish, such as Niebiesko-Czarni, Czerwono-Czarni, Czerwone Gitary, Skaldowie and Trubadurzy. Of them, Niebiesko-Czarni, founded by Walicki, deserves special attention, as it marked a transition of Polish rock from simple imitation of the Anglo-Saxon idiom to its Polonisation (Gradowski 2018: 87) and was a super-band, with a number of distinctive personalities of singers, such as Michaj Burano, Wojciech Korda, Czesław Niemen, Andrzej Nebeski, Helena Majdaniec and Ada Rusowicz, appearing on stage one after another. The idea behind it was to create an incubator for new talent. It was assumed that after proving their skill and getting some experience, the more creative members would set up their own bands with their own styles, which, indeed, happened. Several of these bands, such as Skaldowie, No To Co and Trubaurzy, were folk-rock or folk-pop bands, singing songs derived from folklore of specific regions and frequently performing in folk clothes. As I mentioned earlier, folk music was strongly promoted by the political authorities. Hence, it is difficult to say to what extent this folkisation of Polish rock was a result of political calculation and to what extent it reflected the background and interest of specific musicians, such the brothers Andrzej and Jacek Zieliński from Skaldowie, who came from Podhale and rendered their roots conspicuous in their work. However, it is certain that showing a positive attitude to Polish folk music was conducive to making a rock career in Poland (Zielinski 2005: 148; Gradowski 2018: 135). This was reflected in making records, touring abroad, as well as appearing on screen. Skaldowie and

No To Co proved to be the favourites of Polish filmmakers of this period, even though the most popular Polish band of the 1960s was Czerwone Gitary.

The small cycle of big beat films can be regarded as the Polish response to the 'rock musical', flourishing in Britain and the USA from the mid-1950s and exemplified by films such as *Rock Around the Clock* (1956), directed by Fred Sears and *Jail House Rock* (1957), directed by Richard Thorpe. David James argues that these films responded to the loss of cinema's dominant position as mass medium. 'Cinema was forced to compete, sometimes to attack or attempt to contain or take revenge upon upstart rock "n" roll, but more often to incorporate, enhance, or celebrate it in the creation of hybrid audio-visual forms' (James 2016: 2). These films also responded to a need to target particular audience demographic, that of young people, in the light of the dwindling cinema audience, and served as vehicles for their real-life stars, such as Elvis Presley. As Roy Shuker observes, 'teenage musicals placed youth in opposition to adult authority and for conservatives confirmed the "folk devil" image of fans of the new genre associating them with juvenile delinquency, a major concern internationally through the 1950s' (Shuker 2016: 1447).

Polish big beat films in some ways followed in the footsteps of Anglo-Saxon rock musicals, but there were also differences. One was a time lag; Polish films were made over a decade after the trend for rock musicals started in the USA. Second, they were never vehicles for real-life music stars, as such stars appeared only in the background. Third, they were not necessarily addressed to young people; rather they tried to explain big beat culture to the society at large, and they underplayed the generational conflict or presented it in a simplified manner. Finally, they did not reflect the interlocking of business arrangements between film and popular music (Smith 2003), but rather the scarcity or even the lack of shared interest, reflected in the absence of any attempt to market films by music and vice versa.

Big Beat, as its very title suggests, was meant to capture the new phenomenon of the fascination of young Poles for big beat music. The plot concerns Kuba, who on his wedding day is slapped in the face by a young woman, his alleged girlfriend, who accuses him of leaving her without saying goodbye. It turns out she had mistaken him for Johnny Tomala, a rock star who looked exactly like Kuba. Inevitably, Kuba's fiancée Majka is taken aback by this discovery and the wedding is called off. To prove to her that he is not Johnny, Kuba first tries to find his double and when this does not work, temporarily adopts his identity, to perform on television, so that Majka can see the difference between Kuba and Johnny. Indeed, Majka notices the difference, but ultimately falls for the more flamboyant Johnny, and Lola, the girl who assaulted Kuba at the day of his wedding, falls for Kuba. In-between these romantic trials and tribulations we see Johnny performing with the then popular band Skaldowie, yet not live, but in a television studio, because on television the producers are able to conceal Kuba's true identity thanks to using playback. The director of the television music programme states that, in part thanks to this great invention, one does not need to sing or play guitar to become a big beat star. Such a patronising attitude, which can be attributed also to the director and scriptwriter of *Big Beat*, can be explained by the generation gap between themselves and the rock performers and their fans, they purported to depict. The scriptwriter, Ludwik Starski, was 66, when the film had its premiere and the director, Jerzy Passendorfer, was 43 and both were known for being dismissive of rock music (Wachowicz 1966: 16). Both were hired to do the film due to their previous experience with musicals, with Passendorfer working as an assistant to Buczkowski *Adventure at Marienstadt*, while Starski (who in the end withdrew his name from the project) was a scriptwriter of many Polish musical comedies, including to *Marienstadt*. Not surprisingly, little attention was paid to render Kuba/Johnny Tomala as a real rock star. Jerzy Turek, cast in this double role, did not have the physical appearance to make his character plausible, being a 'character actor', cast in comedies in supporting roles. Similarly, the process of creating a music star, which in Hollywood cinema is treated with utmost care, showing great effort which to-be-stars and their managers and collaborators have to put in, in order to succeed, is here reduced to putting Kuba in shiny clothes, a wig and giving him some alcohol before pushing him on stage, so that he has the courage to perform. It is possible to regard the dismissive attitude of the director to the rock stars, as Piotr Fortuna does, as a reflection of the low Polish ethic of work. As he puts it, 'although the action of the majority of the [Polish musicals] takes place in the world of show business, … this is not a pretext to show work as the dominant value, unlike in the American musicals' (Fortuna 2015: 123). This, according to Fortuna, also demonstrates that Polish show business did not need to work hard to win the viewer; the more important objective was to please the authorities and the artists themselves (ibid.).

There are several songs of Skaldowie featured in *Big Beat*, most of them written especially for the occasion, but the band's presence is subdued. It is only shown playing with Kuba; the members have no speaking parts and come across as a faceless group. On some occasions, the band members are mixed with the actors, further obscuring the real identity of the band and revealing the careless attitude to what is supposedly the main topic of the film: the rise of big beat culture. Near the end of the film there is also an extended episode showing the concert of another well-known band of this period, Niebiesko-Czarni, which comes across as a filler: stretching the medium-length production to the size of a full-length fiction film. The presence of these bands is decontextualised; we never learn anything about them, only see their show. The unwillingness to show big beat as a phenomenon rooted in a specific culture, is also conveyed by the dancing scenes. Their choreographer was Conrad Drzewiecki, a ballet dancer and subsequently one of the most renowned Polish choreographers. However, Drzewiecki's natural milieu was ballet and opera, and this is reflected in the scenes of people dancing on the streets, who do not perform rock dance, but the type of dance which recollects *West Side Story* (1961), directed by Robert Wise and Jerome Robbins. They do so to the accompaniment of jazz music, rather than big beat, suggesting that the choreographer and director felt more comfortable with this type of music, which by the late 1960s started to be associated with high-taste rather than rock.

During the film we hear various people talking about big beat, including a presenter, opening a television programme, who defends big beat, using pseudo-Marxist jargon. He says that in the past songs were the property of the bourgeoisie, while now they belong to and serve the whole country. Although his tirade is meant to be humorous, it reflects well the Polish authorities' attitude to popular music and cinema in the 1960s—these forms were legitimised by their appeal to the masses. At the same time, the mocking of a defender of popular culture could be interpreted as self-irony, pointing to the fact that the majority of genre directors preferred to make arthouse films, given their higher prestige. They directed comedies because they lost in the race for getting funds for more serious productions.

Million for Laura to a large extent repeats the formula, used for the first time in *Big Beat*. Again, there are mistaken identities, of people and objects, most importantly of the eponymous Laura, a baroque Italian guitar which by accident finds itself in the house of Mr. Bulak, a trader at the Różycki bazaar and eventually is offered as the main award in a competition for the best big beat band. The competition takes place in the remote mountain region of Bieszczady, forcing the characters to travel there, either in search of the lost guitar, as is the case of Bulak or to take part in the competition. Such a setting can be explained by seeking the best scenery to showcase the work of the band Łobuzy, played by No To Co, one of the leading folk-rock bands. Once the band moves to Bieszczady, we hear them singing about the pleasures of rural life against performing such tasks as raking hay. The film finishes with a festival, in which No To Co take part along with performers representing estrada music and other genres, suggesting that big beat can easily be integrated into Polish popular music at large. This in fact reflects well the time when the film was made. As with *Big Beat*, songs from *Million for Laura* are not memorable, testifying to the lack of economic synergy between film and popular music in Poland of the 1960s.

Let's Love Mermaids, in common with *Million for Laura*, places big beat alongside another type of music: estrada music. This time, however, the filmmakers are less interested in music and its fans, and more in the Polish popular music business, of which big beat constituted only a small part. The script for this film was written by Jacek Fedorowicz, a satirist and media personality, who knew Polish show business first-hand and based the script largely on his own experience of touring Poland in the capacity of a professional entertainer. It is worth recollecting here that the institution which was in charge of organising live entertainment in Poland was also called 'Estrada', suggesting that the music promoted by it would also belong to light entertainment. The film revolves around two men who, stripped of cash, caused by the purchase of a second-hand car, the eponymous Syrenka (Mermaid), accept the job of travelling agents for the Estrada events. They cover the region of Mazury and their strategy is to target large state companies, whose managers buy tickets for Estrada events in bulk. *Let's Love Mermaids* shows that, unlike the recording industry, the live music sector in Poland was competitive and market-oriented. This meant that Estrada agents had to work hard, using various tricks, to fill the spaces of performance and make enough money. This included threatening intervention by the minister if tickets are not purchased, covering posters of the competition and even kidnapping a rival. It appears that the birth of big beat disturbed the monopoly of 'softer genres' of popular music in the provinces, making it more difficult for its promoters to sell their events to the public.

As with the two films previously discussed, *Let's Love Mermaids* shows little interest in, and understanding of, Polish rock as a distinct phenomenon. There is a big beat band Żywioły (Elements), played by the real band Tajfuny, but we have few opportunities to admire their talent (or lack thereof) and we never see them on stage; its role is to support a pretty pop singer. By contrast, a large part of the film is devoted to presenting a typical Estrada performance, with its revue-like format, which, apart from singers, also includes a man who offers parodies and imitations of sounds. The main star of this show is a singer named Seweryn Patera. Most likely this character was based on the real estrada star of the 1960s, Mieczysław Wojnicki (Otto 2011: 72). Contrary to the idea that under state socialism popular musicians were labourers rather than stars, Patera demands star treatment.

We get snippets of Patera's performances and some other singers, accompanied by a band. On each occasion the presenter announces that the song will be 'funny' or 'lyrical'. This is one of several occasions betraying the patronising attitude of the Estrada people to their customers from the provinces. However, the person with most singing and dancing numbers is Marek, one of the agents and co-owner of the second-hand Syrenka, played by the previously mentioned Bohdan Łazuka. He displays his dancing skills, dancing on the pier with a small girl and tap dancing on a desk in the office. Looking at him confirms the view that he was the most talented singing and dancing actor of postwar period and it is a pity he did not have more opportunities to show his talents.

One aspect of the big beat film, which resurfaced in Polish rock films of the 1980s, most importantly *To tylko Rock* (*This Is Only Rock*, 1984), directed by Paweł Karpiński is the importance of television in promoting popular music. We get the sense that no band or performer really existed in Poland unless it existed on television. This was indeed the case at the beginning of the big beat movement, when this music was shown in various programmes addressed to young people, such as *Proton* (1963–1965), *Po Szóstej* (*After Six*, 1965–1968) and *Telewizyjny Ekran Młodych* (*Youth Television Screen*, 1969) (Gradowski 2018: 98). However, later this music developed naturally and largely in other spaces, most importantly at concerts. Such representation creates the impression of big beat as something managed top-down. This is also reflected in the way the music impresarios are represented—they are always older men who seem to know little about youth culture. Such representation speaks truth to the overall structure of governing in Poland, in the Party, the factories and cultural institutions. Big beat also developed and gained legitimacy this way, being a child of the manager Franciszek Walicki, who was one generation removed from the talent which he nurtured.

Comparing Bareja's films with the big beat films we can see an important difference in the way songs and artists are treated in them. In the former, the story is foregrounded, songs are performed by the main characters who are usually not played by professional singers and they serve to illuminate the story and describe the characters. They are thus close to proper musicals. By contrast, in the big beat films, the connection between the main story and the songs performed is tenuous or nonexistent. In a nutshell, they are there because the bands and big beat at large were popular at the time. What all these films have in common, is their setting in a petit-bourgeois milieu, normally treated with disdain by both the Party ideologues and intellectuals. Such a choice can be explained by the fact that these films were comedies and it was easier to make fun of people trading fake designer clothes or chewing gum at the Różycki bazaar than of factory workers and policemen.

The musical comedies of the 1960s generally have bad press. Most often the reviewers lambasted them for naïve and fragmented narratives, claiming that songs break thin plots, instead of keeping them together (Skąpski 1967: 14). They also pointed to the lack of humour or their humour being of the lowest rank (ZeD 1971). Another common criticism was the poor choice of songs, especially in the big beat films (Skąpski 1967: 14). While I disagree with the first two arguments, I sympathise with the last one. Given that in the 1960s bands like Skaldowie and No To Co had plenty of hits, one wonders why they were not included in the films. The same reviewers, however, admitted that producing a successful musical is a difficult task, as it requires a high budget, among other things, for extended period of rehearsals of song and dance numbers (ZeD 1971). Instead, Polish musicals of this period were made on the cheap, no doubt because they were directed by less-known directors. Although this was not presented as a criticism, some authors noted that the music featured in the films were on the 'softer side' of big beat (Wachowicz 1966: 16), most likely reflecting the generational gap between those who made the films and their characters. It should be added, however, that such 'softening' or 'taming' of rock and rock stars on screen was not only a specificity of Polish rock films, but concerned also Anglo-American screen representations. For example, Paul Shore criticised Elvis Presley films as the 'pinnacle of show-biz exploitation, the adulteration of rock rebellion (Shore 1984: 43). Writing about big beat films from a distance of half a century, Mariusz Gradowski reiterates opinions of the original reviewers of these films, comparing the big beat comedies negatively with Polish films about jazz culture such as *Niewinni czarodzieje* (*Innocent Sorcerers*, 1960), directed by Andrzej Wajda. He explains the low quality by the prevailing attitude to big beat as a passing fad, not worthy serious examination (Gradowski 2018: 99).

Escapism of 'Gierek' and Martial Law Musicals

The difficulty of producing musical comedies, against the background of a system which favoured arthouse cinema, did not help its production or critical standing in the next two decades. Moreover, the leading director of musical films in the 1960s, Stanisław Bareja, changed his interests and moved away from films affirming Polish social reality towards more critical works. Another factor in thwarting musical cinema in Poland was the development of television, which was more sympathetic towards popular music due to being more of a mass medium than cinema. Especially from 1972, when Maciej Szczepański became the Chairman of the Television and Radio Committee (de facto the CEO and almost an absolute ruler of these institutions), there was plenty of popular music on Polish television and the mode of its representation changed thanks to huge investment in equipment, such as cameras and lighting. Szczepański's rule, which ended in 1980, is best known for programmes with estrada stars in shiny clothes, descending from high stairs, as if they were semi-gods entering the humble apartments of their viewers. Szczepański was also remembered for his efforts to internationalise Polish show business by inviting many foreign stars to Poland, to take part in television shows, especially its flagship *Studio 2*, as well as co-producing the Sopot International Music Festival.

Yet musicals did not disappear from the Polish movie theatres in the 1970s, as the authorities, not unlike in the 1960s, recognised their commercial potential. In fact, in the 1970s, when Edward Gierek was the Party leader, there was a particular drive to show Poland as happy, colourful and successful, and musicals and television entertainment programmes were particularly suitable to project such an image. What had changed, however, was the recognition that in order to make successful musical films, investment in their production and specialisation was needed. Consequently, the musical films of the 1970s look more lavish than their predecessors. Most of them are directed by one artist, Janusz Rzeszewski (1930–2007). Of all Polish directors who made their debut after the Second World War, he is the one who was closest to the Hollywood model of a director. Thrown out from the Lodz Film School on the grounds of having little talent, he ended up in television, where he fulfilled various minor functions, till he gained recognition as a specialist in entertainment. He was involved in many film music genres, such as musicals, music documentaries, including transmissions from the most important Polish festivals in Opole and Sopot, and early music videos (see subsequent chapters). They all proved very professional, even elegant, despite the fact that many of them were produced under conditions of scarcity. He was also an originator and director of one of the most popular television programmes of the 1970s, *Bajki dla dorosłych* (*Fairy Tales for Adults*). One would expect that he would also direct television series about music stars, if such request appeared. However, for that he died too early—Polish television turned to biographical series only in the 2010s. His bad luck was operating in an environment, where the type of work in which he excelled was not valued highly. Consequently, to this day there is no monograph devoted to his work and most of the details about his life one can learn from the 20-minute long documentary *Janusz Rzeszewski -Król Musicalu* (*Janusz Rzeszewski: The King of Musical*, 2015), directed by Adam Wyżyński.

Rzeszewski can also be regarded as the only true scion of Polish interwar cinema in the postwar period. This is demonstrated by his interest in Poland of the interbellum, which is the setting of all his full-length fiction films, his attraction to pomp and romance, reliance on stars and ability to organically interweave film and music. He directed three musical films in the years 1978–1983: *Halo Szpicbródka* (*Hello, Fred the Beard*, 1978), co-directed with Mieczysław Jahoda, *Miłość ci wszystko wybaczy* (*Love Can Take Everything*, 1981) and *Lata dwudzieste, lata trzydzieste* (*The Twenties, the Thirties*, 1984). All of them are set in interwar Poland, but they are also children of their times. They are apolitical and entertaining, in response to the authorities' expectations that cinema should provide entertainment and repay their costs. Second, in foregrounding the spaces of entertainment, such as revue theatres, music halls, night clubs, restaurants with live music, they testify to an increase in such spaces in Poland of the 1970s. In a wider sense, they point to a shift of the Polish economy from industrial production to production of consumer goods and Polish society from one focused on production to a consumer society. Finally, they capture well the state of Polish popular music in the 1970s, which was dominated by estrada music rather than rock, as demonstrated by the fact that the 'Golden Records' for best chart results, were awarded mostly to estrada singers such as Maryla Rodowicz, Mieczysław Fogg, Zdzisława Sośnicka, Halina Kunicka and Duet Framer (Jotem 1989: 22). By contrast, in this decade rock music was in decline, with only a handful of bands, such as Breakout and Budka Suflera defending its position.

Two of Rzeszewski's musicals, *Hello, Fred the Beard* and *The Twenties, the Thirties* represent the subgenre of musical which Rick Altman describes as 'the show musical', also known as 'the backstage musical' (Altman 1987: 200–271). Films of this type 'construct their plot around the creation of a show (Broadway play, fashion magazine, high school revue, Hollywood film), with the making of a romantic couple both symbolically and causally related to the success of the show' (ibid.: 200). Rzeszewski's films do not centre on shows of this type, but they also present production of the spectacle—in his case shows in musical theatres. The premise of the films is similar—the protagonist takes over a declining theatre for reasons which have nothing to do with art, but becomes involved in running it and makes it a success, finding love on the way.

In *Hello, Fred the Beard*, set in the 1920s, a gentleman burglar who introduces himself as Fred Kampinos and who is known among the Warsaw police as Szpicbródka decides to buy a failing theatre in Warsaw called Czerwony Młyn (the Red Mill) and becomes its co-director. The actors and other staff who weren't paid for a long time are happy about the change, as is the director of the theatre, who in this way is saved from bankruptcy. Fred visits the theatre the same day as the bailiff, who is trying to strip the actors and dancers of their costumes as a way to pay the debt. The theatre's employees are unaware that the true reason for Fred's interest is the proximity of the Red Mill to the largest bank in Warsaw, which he plans to reach through building a tunnel under the theatre. Fred pretends that this underground work is needed to make improvements to the theatre. However, he falls in love with one of the dancers and the theatre itself and prolongs the work on the tunnel in order to attend the first premiere under his directorship, which is, ironically, a play about Szpicbródka.

Such a plot allows the viewer to learn about the internal dynamics of the musical theatre. This dynamic is filled with clichés, which can be found in many backstage musicals, such as an older star trying to thwart an upcoming star. Yet, these clichés work, in part because of the precision of the script, impeccable acting and the meticulous way of interweaving song and dance into the narrative. The script was written by a veteran of Polish cinema, Ludwik Starski, who by this point was in his mid-seventies; it was the last film in his career. No doubt he brought to the film his memory of prewar cinema. But there are also new elements, as far as Polish cinema is concerned, testifying to Rzeszewski's talent for staging musical numbers. This talent shines best in the last part of the film, which shows the premiere of the play taking place the same evening as the police chase Szpicbródka. What happens in the tunnel below the theatre is juxtaposed with a play about Szpicbródka's exploits. To add dynamism and drama to this part, songs are cut into small pieces to be edited with matching action. *Hello, Fred the Beard* stood out from the bulk of Polish postwar musicals also thanks to inclusion of a wider variety of musical styles than one might expect from a film set in the interwar period. This was a consequence of employing several composers, such as Wojciech Trzciński, Adam Skorupka and Andrzej Korzyński, suggesting a more generous budget than was the case with musicals of the previous decade. We can hear some 'revue' songs, played during the performance, intimate romantic songs, shared by Szpicbródka and his beloved Anita and a humorous song performed by the old Makowska, once a famous dancer, nowadays a barrista. Near the end of the film the music goes electronic. Pulsating rhythm of the electronic instruments, accompanying images of dancers opening safe deposits with fire, adds to the alluring spectacle. Another sign of an investment into Rzeszewski's film and a reason for its success was the star-studded cast. Fred is played by Piotr Fronczewski, an actor with a distinct voice, who was then at the peak of his artistic form.[5] On this occasion Fronczewski perfectly adopts the character of Pygmalion (often used in Hollywood musicals), who shapes his Galatea-Anita, a chorus girl who progresses to become a star and 'upon whose untested and slender shoulders the success of the show may ultimately rest' (Friedman et al. 2014: 225). Anita is played by Gabriela Kownacka, for whom it was the role of her life (Fig. 3.3).

Kownacka had neither a distinct voice nor dancing talent, but was very pretty and likeable, hence perfectly suited to her character of a hapless chorus girl. Moreover, a certain clumsiness in her dance rendered her believable. There were also stars in supporting roles, such as Ewa Wiśniewska in the role of Anita's rival, Vera Patroni and Irena Kwiatkowska, playing Makowska. All these investments: in the script,

Fig. 3.3 Szpicbródka (Piotr Fronczewski) falling in love with Anita (Gabriela Kownacka) in *Halo Szpicbródka* (*Hello, Fred the Beard*, 1978), directed by Janusz Rzeszewski and Mieczysław Jahoda

music, visual effects and cast, paid off, as proved by the fact that *Hello, Fred the Beard* received the 'Viewer's Chair' for the Polish film which had the biggest box office in the first year after its release. Critics of the film were generally positive, albeit in a lukewarm, patronising and dismissive way, as epitomised by the title of one of the reviews: 'Ramotka ma wdzięk', which can be translated as 'This old-fashioned second-class pic has some charm'. The premise of this and similar reviews was that Rzeszewski's film was nothing special, but should be appreciated in the context of the lack of Polish tradition of musical cinema. The commercial success of *Hello, Fred the Beard* led to the discussion in the editorial office of *Film* magazine about a need to produce musicals and especially musical comedies in Poland. The discutants included directors (Rzeszewski and Jahoda), composers (Andrzej Korzyński and Katarzyna Gaertner) and a lyricist (Ernest Bryll) (Wojnach 1979: 8–9). In nutshell, they listed numerous problems with embarking on such task, including the scarcity of actors able to dance and sing and ballet ensembles, the lack of costumes (which on occasion of *Hello, Fred the Beard* were imported from East Germany), low honoraria for the authors writing songs for musicals (as opposed to those working for the theatre and Estrada). The creators of the musical side of musicals also mentioned the lack of recognition of their work, against that enjoyed by directors and stars of musical films. And yet, the conclusion was that it is worth to make musical comedies, because the audience loves them (ibid.: 9).

Rzeszewski's next foray into musical was a biopic about Hanka Ordonówna, Polish interwar singer and dancer, which I will discuss in the next part of this book. The last instalment in 'Rzeszewski's trilogy of entertainment ' is *Lata dwudzieste,..., lata trzydzieste* (*The Twenties, the Thirties*). The film had its premiere in 1984, hence belongs to the next decade, but in its topic and style, it fits well the earlier films made by Rzeszewski and the spirit of extravagance which was transferred from 'Szczepański television' into cinema.

The film's title reflects Rzeszewski's interest in the 1920s and 1930s, where song and dance were so much more important to the condition of Polish theatre and cinema than after the Second World War. It also suggests that he looks at the period from a distance, acknowledging that it had passed, as it is unlikely for a filmmaker who lives in a specific decade to make a film named after this decade. Also, given that films set in the past are also about the present, we can conjecture that *The Twenties, the Thirties* offer some insight into the 1970s from the perspective of the political and economic crisis of the 1980s, which was attributed, at least by the Solidarity opposition, to the ineptitude of Gierek's government. The film captures well the ambitions of the political authorities of the 1970s to change Poland from a backward country, whose wealth was based on the extraction of crude material to a modern one, whose success relied on the production of modern fare, such as entertainment. This idea is conveyed by a narrative centred on an engineer named Adam Dereń, who is searching for oil in southern Poland and tries to convince his partners from Warsaw to invest in his enterprise by buying American drills. It is not difficult to see this situation as paralleling that of Poland in the 1970s, when the state bought many western licences in order to modernise its industries. Such a strategy was opposed by a more conservative faction of the Party, which regarded it as bringing a distinct risk of heavy debt and losing economic and politic independence.

Adam's partners refuse to invest in his project. Angry with them, he goes to Warsaw to withdraw all their money in order to invest in a venture which guarantees failure, choosing to buy a struggling musical theatre named Mirage. However, to his surprise, the theatre, not unlike in *Hello, Fred the Beard*, turns out to be a success. Consequently, instead of bankrupting his partners, Adam multiplies their investment and in the end he returns to the South of Poland, to his old girlfriend, the owner of the fields, where oil was found after all, thanks to her purchasing American drills. This can be seen as a reference to the unfinished 'Gierek's revolution', when funds for modernising Polish industry were cut in the second half of the 1970s, resulting in many enterprises, such as new roads, remaining unfinished. If money was poured into them, maybe they will be successful in the end, the film suggests.

Adam's effort to spend lavishly on the theatre gives the film's authors an opportunity to present rehearsals and in the finale, the completed spectacle, as in the scheme of a 'show' musical described by Altman, and as it was tested in *Hello, Fred the Beard*. However, on this occasion the film focuses on the preparation for the spectacle, a revue also titled *The Twenties, the Thirties*, undertaken by just one person, a provincial singer and dancer from Rzeszów named Liza, whom Adam meets on the way to Warsaw. In Warsaw Liza secretly visits an old dancer and a retired opera singer, asking them to give her dancing and singing lesson. She succeeds, and receives the main part in the revue.

Despite using the same formula and in part because of repeating it, *The Twenties, the Thirties* is a less successful film than *Hello, Fred the Beard*. Firstly, it has a less dramatic story, especially in the finale. Adam's anguish about the success of the spectacle couldn't be compared to Fred-Szpicbródka's attempt to escape the police with his beloved woman. Similarly, the romance at the centre of the film is not very convincing, as both Liza and Adam are involved with other people—Adam with his old girlfriend and Liza with Fryderyk, the director in charge of the revue. There are love triangles and a touch of melodrama, but it is not developed because neither of the characters seems to be convincingly in love. The film's scriptwriters, Ryszard Marek Groński and Michał Komar, were experienced writers and scriptwriters, but musicals were not their specialism. Indeed, after the death of Ludwik Starski in 1984, Polish cinema lacked writers, specialising in this genre.

The singing and dancing scenes also lack the dynamism of those in Rzeszewski's first musical, and ultimately the dances of actors are upstaged by 'dances' of old cars which are brought on stage in the film's finale (Fig. 3.4).

Fig. 3.4 Old cars brought on stage in the finale of *Lata dwudzieste, lata trzydzieste* (*The Twenties, the Thirties*, 1984), directed by Janusz Rzeszewski

Liza, played by Grażyna Szapołowska, who most likely was offered this role because in the early 1980s she was one of the greatest female stars in Polish cinema, known mostly from her roles in the films of Krzysztof Kieślowski, disappoints as a star in the musical. She has limited dancing skills and lacks the cuteness and warmth of Kownacka, who played Anita in *Hello, Fred the Beard*. Moreover, there are no sparks between her and her screen partners, Adam and the theatre director. Piotr Fronczewski cast as the theatre director appears to be tired of his role of Pygmalion, and Irena Kwiatkowska, again in the role of an old actress who is trying to squeeze into the revue, is less funny than in the previous film.

While in terms of its structure Rzeszewski's films are closest to the Hollywood model, as described by Altman, in terms of their cultural references they are closer to Europe. The Red Mill in *Hello, Fred the Beard* is obviously a reference to Moulin Rouge and the characters talk about their trips to Vienna, which are also nods to Polish interwar cinema, because rich people travelled there frequently, often to visit theatres.

The Twenties, the Thirties was produced in the Perspektywa Film Studio, one of the most commercially minded of Polish film studios, which also produced science fiction films, comedies and historical series. When searching for reviews from Polish musicals I found information about a plan to set up there a special unit devoted to producing musical comedies, but in the end it did not happen, perhaps due to the deep economic crisis in the late 1970s, followed by imposition of martial law. Nevertheless, the very fact that such an idea was considered points to the recognition of the advantages of investing in musicals and in the difficulty of producing them without a sufficient base.

Another musical which reflects well the spirit of Gierek's Poland is *Alicja* (*Alice*, produced in 1980, premiered in 1982). In many ways this is an oddity in Polish cinema, yet reflecting well the period when it was made. It was a film made for television, which, however, looked like a cine-film and eventually received theatre distribution, most likely because its completion coincided with the upheaval in Polish politics which led to the introduction of martial law in December 1981. This resulted in a crisis in film production, which translated itself into a shortage of films to be distributed in the cinema. 'Sending' *Alice* to Polish cinemas was meant to alleviate this problem of scarcity (Kołodyński 1982: 16).

Alice is a Polish-Belgian-British co-production, whose budget was about 5,000,000 USD, half of which covered by the Polish side. This was a high budget for a Polish film of this period, especially given that it was a television production. However, it highlights that Polish television, under Maciej Szczepański's rule, tried to modernise by investing in its infrastructure and increasing the budgets of the entertainment programmes, as previously mentioned. On this occasion, as with other investments with foreign partners in the 1970s, shooting *Alice* was based on the assumption that foreign investment would result in a production attractive to both Polish and western consumers. However, it turned out to be a flop and today is known mainly as topping the lists of the worst Polish films ever made. The film also reflects the dominant approach to internationalisation of Polish culture and, to some extent, other areas of the Polish economy of the 1970s, by assigning the Polish side a less creative, secondary role in comparison with the foreign side. Except for the film directors, the crucial roles were on this occasion taken by foreigners. The composer of songs was Henri Seroka, a Belgian whose father was

Polish, and the cast was dominated by foreign actors. Alice was played by the Belgian actress Sophie Barjac, who looked like Catherine Deneuve when she played in Jacques Demy's musicals *The Umbrellas of Cherbourg* (1964) and *The Young Girls of Rochefort* (1967). In the role of Rabbit was cast French actor Jean-Pierre Cassell. The casting strategy was typical of the way Polish cultural managers approached the foreign market—they tended either to invite young and upcoming artists in the hope that they would become stars or invited stars who had passed their prime, yet had recognisable faces and most likely agreed to be paid less than the hottest stars. By contrast, Wiesław Gołas, a Polish star specialising in comedies, is given a very small and almost mute role of one of Rabbit's assassins. The Polish directors of the film were Jerzy Gruza and Jacek Bromski. Gruza (1932–2020), was one of the most recognised directors of television programmes centred on music, including directing broadcasts from the principal Polish music festivals. He was also behind popular television series, such as *Wojna domowa* (*Domestic War*, 1965–1966) and *Czterdziestolatek* (*Being Forty*, 1975–1978). Bromski (b. 1946), for whom it was one of his first assignments, in due course became a prolific director of cine-films, yet without significant achievements. Gruza and Bromski also scripted *Alice*. It is worth mentioning that a large proportion of Polish musicals have two directors and two or more scriptwriters. This is an unusual situation for Polish cinema, where the norm is that the film has only one director and scriptwriter and it is the same person. This fact points to the difficulty of making musicals, everywhere and particularly in Poland of the state socialism period, where professionalism was valued less than originality.

Unlike Rzeszewski, who was careful to furnish *Hello, Fred the Beard* and *The Twenties, the Thirties* with coherent narratives, the narrative of *Alice* is episodic. Its plot concerns a young woman, who works as a quality controller in an unspecified factory and a man called or nicknamed Rabbit, who owes somebody a large sum of money and is chased by two assassins, hired by the Queen of Hearts. Alice and Rabbit fall in love with each other and throughout the film chase each other, although one is not sure how much of this chase takes place in reality and how much in a dream. When Rabbit learns that he is in mortal danger, he abandons Alice, which breaks her heart and most likely leads to a suicide attempt and a spell in a psychiatric asylum. This story is largely conveyed through and, to some extent obscured by, song and dance numbers. It is through song that Alice and Rabbit declare their love for each other.

The majority of songs are pop songs which Polish critics described as catchy, yet not exactly hits (Cybulski 1982: 16). A likely inspiration of them were songs written by Michel Legrand for Demy musicals. However, at some stage we see Alice descending into a discotheque, presented as an inferno. From there Alicja is taken to be executed at the scaffold and is rescued by a helicopter. Inevitably, in the disco sequence, we hear disco music. The style of dancing changes too—from Fred Astaire's numbers to disco dances. The patchwork approach to music is also reflected in the design. It is difficult to pinpoint the film to a specific location. Its action begins in a large park where Rabbit takes his daily run, kids talk in English and the Queen of Hearts takes her three Afghan hounds for a walk, which recollects Hyde Park. Subsequently, however, the film sheds its English look and we see the characters in some nondescript locations. In reality, for the outdoor episodes Polish locations were used and the objective seemed to be to de-Polonise the exteriors, rendering them western. Such a way of constructing space can also be found in another widely derided film of this period, *Test pilota Pirxa* (*The Test of Pilot Pirx*, 1979) by Marek Piestrak. However, Piestrak's film succeeded in constructing a futuristic look; Gruza and Bromski merely cleansed it of any national culture. There is also no consistency in colour schemes and lighting. Realistically shot episodes are followed by some which are brightly lit. By the time the film had its premiere, *Alice* was by a large margin the most incoherent and fragmented musical in Polish cinema.

There are no box office numbers for *Alice*, but the reviewers admitted that in Warsaw the film was watched in full cinema theatres. Such interest can be attributed to the lack of competition and a greater than normal desire to escape from reality on the part of the viewers, reflecting the period of martial law.

Rock Films with Real Rock Stars

When the last films of Rzeszewski and *Alice* went into production, there were several films under way which used a different type of music: Polish rock, which was no longer known as big beat, but simply rock or 'music of the young generation' (Muzyka Młodej Generacji). Most of them were documentaries and I will examine them in the part of my study, dedicated to this genre. However, there were also some fiction films which afforded rock music a privileged place, such as *Wielka majówka* (*The Big Picnic*,

1981), directed by Krzysztof Rogulski and *To tylko rock* (*This Is Only Rock*, 1984), directed by Paweł Karpiński, which I will consider in this section.

There was an explosion of rock in Poland in the 1980s. This can be explained by several factors, such as better access to western music, an increase of outlets where fans could listen to their favourite bands, of which the Jarocin Festival had a privileged position and the specific political climate of the 1980s, marked by the successes of Solidarity at the beginning of the decade and after the end of the martial law, in the years 1983–1984 (Zieliński 2005: 72). There was a sense that Polish rock music caught the spirit of the time: it was an important vehicle for the population to express its political views, being denied other means of expression (Patton 2011). Rock was regarded as either an area of resistance against the authoritarian, yet weak state or a safety valve, allowing the state to channel the opposition into activities it saw as innocuous. As in the 1960s, one can observe the setting up of hundreds of new bands, with many of them of European standards. Among them the best known were Maanam, Perfect, Lady Pank and Republika. They failed to achieve European-wide popularity, but this was in part due to their privileging Polish rather than the international market. The vast majority of bands belonging to the Polish 1980s 'super-league' were all-male. An exception was Maanam, having a female singer and lyricist Kora. Kora's true name was Olga Jackowska and she was the wife of Marek Jackowski, who composed the vast majority of Maanam's songs. Kora's unique place as the only girl in a male world, and her charisma, which I will consider when discussing a biopic devoted to the band (see Chapter 5), rendered Maanam a great asset to the 1980 Polish cinema. This was exploited by Krzysztof Rogulski, the director of *The Big Picnic*.

Rogulski does not easily fit into any recognisable paradigm of Polish cinema and his trajectory is somewhat atypical, because rather than moving from documentary to fiction cinema, he started with documentary films, made two fiction films, of which the second was *The Big Picnic*, to return to documentary filmmaking and occasionally to what is known in Poland as 'television theatre': a hybrid between a television production and a theatre play. Post-*The Big Picnic* Rogulski's profile was low, despite his film being an instant hit. Why it failed to launch his career might be explained by the period in which it was made, shortly before the imposition of martial law in Poland. After this event many Polish filmmakers moved abroad or stopped making films altogether. Rogulski belonged to the first category. He tried to continue his career in France, but with moderate success. *The Big Picnic* has remained his greatest achievement.

The film is based on a true story of the adventures of two young men of modest background. Sixteen-year old Rysiek runs away from a borstal-cum-orphanage to his father who rejects him on the grounds of being unable to support him financially. Hungry, yet adamant not to return to a place where he was bullied, Rysiek breaks into a villa somewhere in the provinces and finds there, hidden in a fridge, a million Polish Zloties. With this huge amount of money Rysiek travels to Warsaw where he meets Julek, a man in his twenties, who pretends to be a sailor, although in reality is a drifter, living in a provincial town without any stable occupation. The young men decide to spend their money on making their dreams come true, and they have their titular 'big picnic'. They buy expensive clothes, a large convertible car and stay in Victoria, at the time the most luxurious hotel in Warsaw. The exploits of the two friends allows Rogulski to create a specific image of Polish society in the final stages of state socialism as built on economic and social contrasts. On one hand, there is an impoverished province, where parents cannot support their children and there is nothing to do. On the other hand, we find an affluent and cosmopolitan Warsaw, with foreign guests served by high-class prostitutes. However, money rules everywhere. Almost everybody wants to do business and the unofficial economy thrives. Foreign currency has an almost magical value and some places are reserved only for foreign guests, rendering Poles second-class citizens in their own country.

The adventures of Rysiek and Julek take place in the close proximity of Maanam and to the accompaniment of its music, both extradiegetic and diegetic. Wherever they go, they encounter the band playing or just appearing as if out of nowhere. For example, when they run through the centre of Warsaw, Maanam has a concert opposite the Central Department Store (Domy Centrum), observed by crowds of people. Rysiek also attends Maanam's recording session and dances when listening to their song 'Oddech szczura' (Rat's Breath), which was one of Maanam's greatest hits and became even bigger thanks to being featured in *The Big Picnic*. That such song is included in the film, points to Rogulski's different strategy of using rock music in comparison with big beat films, namely capitalise on its popularity. There is a particular rapport between Rysiek, who is the more idealistic and naïve character of the two and Kora. She is like a good fairy, appearing when he is in trouble. For example, when Rysiek meets Julek with his posh girlfriend Agnieszka, embarrassing Julek, who pretends to be wealthier than he actually is, Kora approaches Rysiek, giving the impression that they know each other well. Their encounter changes the dynamic of the situation by suggesting that Rysiek, who has such stunning friends as Kora must be 'somebody'. The fairy tale character of Maanam is most obvious in the last scene of the film, when Rysiek and Julek are tried in court for theft. When the prosecutors present a long list of crimes committed by the two young men, they leave the court to find Maanam again, this time travelling in the back of a lorry with their instruments. They board a vehicle which is followed by another one, carrying a giraffe, seeing which fulfilled Rysiek's greatest dream.

By linking Maanam with the two provincial fugitives, Rogulski underscores the utopian character of Maanam's music, which is also conveyed by inclusion in a film of the paintings of Henri Rousseau. In Rogulski's film Maanam stands for a pure world, which cannot be corrupted by money and lies, in which the 'adult world' indulges, rather than any specific political option or ideology. This is also revealed by the songs included in it, such as 'Moja miłość jest szalona' (My Love Is Mad), played several times and 'Rat's Breath'. These songs point to the band's ideology of living for the present, yet being removed from everyday reality, as if existing in a parallel world. This is also the way Rysiek wants to live. For this reason, it is difficult to imagine any of the two other most popular rock bands of the 1980s, Perfect and Republika, in the role in which Rogulski cast Maanam, because the other two were too anchored in Polish reality. Although Maanam in *The Big Picnic* is so close to ordinary people, its magic is preserved. This is achieved by making the band communicate almost exclusively through music rather than dialogue. One of the reviewers compared the role played by Kora to that of a mime (Dolińska 1981).[6] Moreover, the band is located outside the course of action; not unlike the chorus in an ancient play, which affords it special dignity.

This Is Only Rock, despite having a happy ending, comes across as the opposite of *The Big Picnic*, as it paints the world of rock music not as an antidote to the corruption of the real world, but its extension. It was directed by Paweł Karpiński, who, not unlike Rogulski, was a versatile, yet unremarkable director, whose films are largely forgotten by this point and who in the last two decades worked mostly as a director of television soap operas. Around the time he made *This Is Only Rock* he also produced two documentaries about Polish rock music, *Jarocin 82* (1982) and *Śmierć kliniczna* (*Clinical Death*, 1983), the latter about the punk band of this name. *This Is Only Rock* was evidently an attempt to spin up the material registered by his crew in Jarocin by adding a story to it. At the same time, this film probably reflects Karpiński's career in television. While it appears that he might have known television from an insider's position, his knowledge about the world of Polish rock was limited.

This Is Only Rock follows the formula, frequently tested in American films, of a struggling musician trying to achieve a breakthrough and finally succeeding. On this occasion the story concerns a talented singer Sylwia, from the provincial band Krzyk (Cry or Shout). Her progress, in a fashion typical for musicals, is juxtaposed with the journey in the opposite direction of an older singer, Majka. While Sylwia secures the interest and support of top musicians, Majka is treated by them as an expired product. While Sylwia is invited to play in a large rock festival, Majka's new clip is taken out of a television programme. While Majka is winning the festival, a bitter and drunken Majka kills herself in a car accident. Throughout the film insiders from the popular music business suggest to Sylwia that the only way to make a career in popular music is through immoral means: betraying one's friends and going to bed with people who hold power in the show business. The social reality sketched in the film is thus very similar to that dominating in the Cinema of Moral Concern of the second half of the 1970s. The closest relative of *This Is Only Rock* is *Wodzirej* (*Top Dog*, 1977) by Feliks Falk (Winiarczyk 1987: 12), which showed corruption among employees in the provincial Estrada. The connection is strengthened by casting Bogusław Sobczuk in both films in the role of a prominent person working in Polish television. Other actors who at the time specialised in portraying 'television animals', such as Janusz Rewiński, were also cast in the film. Sylwia ultimately resists the sexual advances of an older lyricist-cum-composer-cum-manager, rejects the award at the festival on the grounds that her song was plagiarised and rather than singing solo her new, bland song, performs a rock song with her old band, a proof that she chose authenticity over success.

Putting aside the clichéd and unconvincing meanders of the narrative, the authors of *This Is Only Rock* betrayed a lack of familiarity with the development of Polish rock in the 1980s, namely the fact that its cultural currency was based on its distance from the official channels of promotion, most importantly television. Polish rockers wanted to present themselves as counter-cultural and politically oppositional (Patton 2011); winning in television-sponsored rock competition would not help their careers in 1983; namely after the martial law, when television was strongly linked to this political event (Mazierska 2009).

Presenting female stars in the proximity of rockers might be seen as a sign that the filmmakers tried to reflect the fact that many female singers who started as estrada performers in this decade collaborated with rock bands. The most significant in this respect was Budka Suflera, one of the most popular Polish bands in the 1970s, which in the 1980s recorded many hits with Zdzisława Sośnicka, Izabela Trojanowska and Urszula. However, rather than showing the mutual benefit between the estrada singers and rockers, Karpiński and his co-scripters underscored the distance and discord between them. This happens when Sylwia is asked to leave her rock band in order to make a career as a solo singer and, most likely, became a bland estrada star, which would be a bad step in the 1980s. The entire approach to gender relations, suggesting that women in Polish popular music just sing, while men compose and write lyrics for them, as well as control their entire careers, was far from the truth even in the 1970s, when singers such as Maryla Rodowicz proved very skilful in managing their careers, but even more so in the 1980s when the previously mentioned Kora became the greatest Polish rock star of the decade.

The long sequence at the rock festival, somewhere in Poland's province, a clear allusion to Jarocin festival, betrays misunderstanding of its purpose. For the bands playing in Jarocin, in common with the majority of rock festivals and in contrast to estrada festivals, such as Opole or Sopot, what was at stake was the approval of the audience, not an award given by the official jury, made up of aged members of the popular music and television establishment. It would also be an unlikely event for a woman singing a dramatic song to play at such a festival.

This ignorance about the state of Polish rock is also revealed through different ways the film represents foreign and Polish music. A concert of the English new wave band Classix Nouveaux is presented as a polished, professional show, stirring awe in the audience, including in Sylwia and her musician boyfriend. By contrast, Polish music comes across as amateurish. Sylwia's colleagues from Krzyk admit that they don't know how to perform on stage. The makers of *This Is Only Rock* even managed to spoil the performance of Lady Pank, at the time one of the most popular bands in Poland, reducing it to the background to a business talk between two television employees. At some point it is also suggested that touring with Classix Nouveaux as the supporting band is a great honour for the Polish band. In reality, however, the 1980s was the time when Polish rock lost its inferiority complex. Bands such as Maanam, Republika or Perfect felt that they better cater for Polish audiences than any foreign bands and did not regard a career abroad as their ultimate goal. By denouncing Polish popular music, including rock, as an area of manufactured, even manipulated entertainment, Karpiński grossly misread the position of this genre, which in this period was regarded as a pinnacle of authenticity and the antidote to the fake and exhausted official cultural sphere.

Conclusions

In comparison with the interwar period, musicals and especially musical comedies, after the end of the Second World War lost their privileged position in Polish cinema. This is reflected in their scarcity, their cold critical reception and the fact that few songs from postwar musicals enjoyed an extensive after-life, unlike the songs from interwar musicals which are remembered till the present day. This decline can be explained by the fact that under the system in which artistic prestige mattered more than box office results, the filmmakers did not have much incentive to make genre films and especially musicals, which required high budgets and actors with singing and dancing skills. The dozen or so musical films which were produced during this period were thus an exception to the rule. From the 1960s the relative infrequency of musicals can also be explained by the development of television, which freed cinema from its duty to be a mass medium.

Many musicals of this period, such as Bareja's films and Rzeszewski's *Hello, Fred the Beard*, borrow from classical Hollywood musicals, but even more they refer to the European tradition of this genre. The main point of reference for their characters are Vienna and Paris. They are thus not only Polish but (trans)European.

While many motifs in Polish musicals are constant, for example practically all of them include a heterosexual romance, there are also developments. The most important concerns the diminishing role of folk music and ordinary people as creators of music. While folk music was very important till the end of the 1960s, from the 1970s it disappears from the picture and *muzykole* show us manufactured entertainment, produced by specialists, for the audiences who enjoy it passively. Most likely, this situation reflects the fact that in the last period of state socialism Polish folk music stopped being an inspiration for popular musicians. The situation would change again in the 1990s, the decade of disco polo. Another change consists of moving from musical comedies, which prevailed in the 1960s and the 1970s, to musical films more serious in tone in the 1980s. It appears that while in the 1960s one could easily laugh at big beat, this was no longer the case with 1980s rock. Yet, paradoxically, in the 1980s Polish cinema had finally a popular director, Juliusz Machulski, whose films, most importantly *Vabank* (1981) and *Seksmisja* (*Sex Mission*, 1983) were not only watched by millions of viewers, but also were praised by critics as being of a Hollywood standard. Machulski, however, preferred other genres than the musical, perhaps aware of the thankless task of producing musicals in Poland.

Notes

1. A good description of the films' vetting system can be found in Coates (2005: 74–80).
2. However, Bareja's musical comedies are studied chiefly because of his later, 'oppositional' and iconoclastic comedies and television series rather than due to their independent significance.
3. Kutz is remembered as an author of films presenting important moments from the history of Silesia, the region he comes from.
4. I am using 'big beat', due to the fact that this is the most recent literature, such as Gradowski (2018).
5. In due course Fronczewski created a singing character 'Franek Kimono', arguably the first Polish rapper.
6. At the same time the lack of speaking parts for Maanan in *Great Picnic* can be explained by the lack of trust of Polish directors in the acting skills of Polish rock stars.

Works Cited

Adamczak, Marcin. 2010. *Globalne Hollywood, filmowa Europa i polskie kino po 1989 roku: Przeobrażenia kultury audiowizualnej przełomu stuleci*. Gdańsk: Słowo/Obraz Terytoria.

Adamczak, Marcin. 2012. Rashomon: Kinematografia okresu PRL. *Człowiek I Społeczeństwo* 34: 177–195.

Albers, Patricia C., and William R. James. 1988. Travel Photography: A Methodological Approach. *Annals of Tourism Research* 15: 134–158.

Altman, Rick. 1981. The American Film Musical: Paradigmatic Structure and Mediatory Function. In *Genre: The Musical*, ed. Rick Altman, 197–207. London: Routledge & Kegan Paul.
Altman, Rick. 1987. *The American Film Musical*. Bloomington and Indianapolis: Indiana University Press.
B.J. [Bożena Janicka]. 1970. Krytycy i film popularny. *Film* 7: 6–11.
Ciborowski, Tomasz, and Grzegorz Konat. 2010. Między II a III RP. Gospodarka Polski Ludowej. In *PRL bez uprzedzeń*, ed. Jakub Majmurek and Piotr Szumlewicz, 17–49. Warsaw: Książka i Prasa.
Coates, Paul. 2005. *The Red and the White: The Cinema of People's Poland*. London: Wallflower.
Cybulski, Władysław. 1982. Alicja. *Film* 41: 16.
Daub, Adrian. 2014. *Four-Handed Monsters: Four-Handed Piano Playing and Nineteenth Century Culture*. Oxford: Oxford University Press.
Dolińska, Elżbieta. 1981. Konsumowanie cudzego nawisu. *Film* 48: 12.
Drozdowski, Bogumił. 1964. Kompromis. *Ekran* 41: 6.
Feuer, Jane. 1993. *The Hollywood Musical*, 2nd ed. Houndmills: The Macmillan Press.
Fortuna, Piotr. 2015. Muzykol – kulturowa metafora PRL. *Kwartalnik Filmowy* 91: 121–140.
Friedman, Lester, David Desser, Sarah Kozloff, Martha P. Nochimson, and Stephen Prince. 2014. *An Introduction to Film Genres*. New York: W. W. Norton & Company.
Gradowski, Mariusz. 2018. *Big Beat: Style i gatunki polskiej muzyki młodzieżowej (1957–1973)*. Warszawa: Oficyna Wydawnicza ASPRA-JR.
Haltof, Marek. 2002. *Polish National Cinema*. Oxford: Berghahn.
Iordanova, Dina. 2003. *Cinema of the Other Europe: The Industry and Artistry of East Central European Film*. London: Wallflower.
Jackiewicz, Aleksander. 1964. Żona z Cepelii. *Życie Literackie* 25: 12.
James, David E. 2016. *Rock 'N' Film: Cinema's Dance with Popular Music*. Oxford: Oxford University Press.
Jotem. 1989. Kilogram złota. *Magazyn Muzyczny* 1: 22.
Kałużyński, Zygmunt. 1964. O! Piękne! *Polityka* 41: 10.
Kenez, Peter. 2001. *Cinema and Soviet Society: From the Revolution to the Death of Stalin*. London: I.B. Tauris.
Klejsa, Konrad. 2007. Stanisław Bareja – nadrealizm socjalistyczny. In *Autorzy kina polskiego*, vol. 2, ed. Grażyna Stachówna and Bogusław Zmudziński, 79–128. Kraków: Wydawnictwo Uniwersytetu Jagiellońskiego.
Kochański, Kazimierz. 1964. Dwaj starsi panowie. *Tygodnik Kulturalny* 42: 11.
Kołodyński, Andrzej. 1982. Królik w dyskotece. *Film* 10: 16.
Kończak, Jarosław. 2007. Ewolucja programowa TVP. PhD, Warsaw University.

Krawczyk, Ryszard. 1980. '30 lat Ogólnopolskiej Akcji Zbierania Folkloru Muzycznego. *Ruch Muzyczny* 14: 3–4.
Kydryński, Juliusz. 1964. Upał. *Życie Literackie* 44: 8.
Landau, Zbigniew, and Jerzy Tomaszewski. 1985. *The Polish Economy in the Twentieth Century*, trans. Wojciech Roszkowski. London: Croom Helm.
Lech, A. 1970. Czekając na komedię. *Szpilki* 12: 9.
Lubelski, Tadeusz. 2009. *Historia kina polskiego: Twórcy, filmy, konteksty.* Katowice: Videograf II.
Mazierska, Ewa. 2009. Polish Martial Law of 1981 in Polish Post-Communist Films: Between Romanticism and Postmodernism. *Communist and Post-Communist Studies* 2: 289–304.
Mazierska, Ewa. 2017. *Poland Daily: Economy, Work, Consumption and Social Class in Polish Cinema.* Oxford: Berghahn.
Mazierska, Ewa, and Michael Goddard. 2014. Introduction: Polish Cinema Beyond Polish Borders. In *Polish Cinema in a Transnational Context*, ed. Ewa Mazierska and Michael Goddard, 1–20. Rochester, NY: University of Rochester Press.
Michalski, Dariusz. 2009. *Piosenka przypomni ci... Historia polskiej muzyki rozrywkowej. Lata 1945–1958.* Warszawa: Iskry.
Michałek, Bolesław, and Frank Turaj. 1988. *The Modern Cinema of Poland.* Bloomington and Indianapolis: Indiana University Press.
Milewski, Barbara. 2020. Hidden in Plain View: The Music of Holocaust Survival in Poland's First Post-war Film. In *Music, Collective Memory, Trauma and Nostalgia in European Cinema after the Second World War*, ed. Michael Baumgarten and Ewelina Boczkowska, 111–137. London: Routledge.
Müller, Sven Oliver. 2010. Analysing Musical Culture in Nineteenth-Century Europe: Towards a Musical Turn? *European Review of History* 17: 835–859.
Otto, Wojciech. 2011. Śmiech i piosenka – małżeństwo z rozsądku. O polskiej komedii muzycznej lat 60. In *Polskie kino popularne*, ed. Piotr Zwierzchowski and Daria Mazur, 68–81. Bydgoszcz: Wydawnictwo Uniwersytetu Kazimierza Wielkiego.
Patton, Raymond A. 2011. Screamed Poetry: Rock in Poland's Last Decade of Communism. PhD dissertation, Department of History, University of Michigan.
Płażewski, Jerzy. 1953. Inflacja piosenki. *Film* 38: 18.
Shore, Michael. 1984. *The Rolling Stone Book of Rock Video.* New York: Quill.
Shuker, Roy. 2016. *Understanding Popular Music Culture*, 5th ed. London: Routledge.
Skąpski, Mieczysław. 1967. Pierwszy polski musical. *Głos Wielkopolski* 76: 12.
Skwara, Anita. 1992. Film Stars Do Not Shine in the Sky Over Poland: The Absence of Popular Cinema in Poland. In *Popular European Cinema*, ed. Richard Dyer and Ginette Vincendeau, 220–231. London: Routledge.

Smith, Jeff. 2003. Banking on Film Music: Structural Interactions of the Film and Record Industries. In *Movie Music, the Film Reader*, ed. Kay Dickinson, 63–81. London: Routledge.
Talarczyk-Gubała, Monika. 2007. *PRL się śmieje! Polska komedia filmowa lat 1945–1989*. Warszawa: Trio.
Talarczyk-Gubała, Monika. 2011. Poszukiwana, poszukiwany… Krytyka wobec polskiej komedii filmowej lat 1945–1989. In *Polskie kino popularne*, ed. Piotr Zwierzchowski and Daria Mazur, 82–93. Bydgoszcz: Wydawnictwo Uniwersytetu Kazimierza Wielkiego.
Taylor, Richard. 2012. Soviet Union. In *The International Film Musical*, ed. Corey K. Creekmur and Linda Y. Mokdad, 105–118. Edinburgh: Edinburgh University Press.
Tompkins, David G. 2013. *Composing the Party Line: Music and Politics in Early Cold War Poland and East Germany*. West Lafayette: Purdue University Press.
'Uchwała Sekretariatu KC w sprawie kinematografii'. 1994. In *Syndrom konformizmu: Kino polskie lat sześćdziesiątych*, ed. Tadeusz Miczka and Alina Madej, 27–34. Katowice: Wydawnictwo Uniwersytetu Śląskiego.
Wachowicz, Barbara. 1966. Mocne udrzenie. *Ekran* 30: 16.
Walicki, Franciszek. 1995. *Szukaj, burz, buduj*. Warszawa: TRZ.
Wang, Ning. 2000. *Tourism and Modernity: A Sociological Analysis*. Amsterdam: Pergamon.
Winiarczyk, Mirosław. 1987. To tylko rock. *Ekran* 39: 12.
Wiśniewski, Cezary. 1978. Ramotka ma wdzięk. *Sztandar Młodych* 24 (10): 10.
Wojnach, Andrzej. 1979. Może warto? *Film* 6: 8–9.
Woroszylski, Witold. 1964. O imprezie nader ucieszej traktacik powagi pełen. *Film* 42: 4.
Zajiček, Edward. 1992. *Poza ekranem: Kinematografia Polska 1918–1991*. Warsaw: Filmoteka Narodowa.
ZeD. 1971. Pastwię się nad Laurą. *Trybuna Robotnicza* 142: 16.
Zieliński, Przemysław. 2005. *Scena rockowa w PRL-u: Historia, organizacja znaczenie*. Warszawa: Trio.
Zwierzchowski, Piotr. 2000. *Zapomniani bohaterowie: O bohaterach filmowych polskiego socralizmu*. Warsaw: Trio.
Zwierzchowski, Piotr. 2017. Socialist Content, Hollywood Form: Crime Films and Musicals in the Polish Cinema of the 1960s. *Panoptikum* 17: 198–206.

CHAPTER 4

Recycling Without Nostalgia: Postcommunist Musicals

In the previous two chapters I mentioned the low status of Polish musicals among critics, despite their unwavering popularity among ordinary viewers. Indeed, this popularity was in part to blame for the scorn poured on them by critics. This situation changed after the fall of the Iron Curtain. The main reason was that economic criteria gained in importance when assessing the value of films, in relation to purely aesthetic criteria. Although Polish cinema is still generously subsided by the state, films are now privately produced and need to show their commercial potential to receive a subsidy and, of course, attract viewers. Moreover, the availability of box office results on the internet puts extra pressure on filmmakers to respond to viewers' demands. Another factor is the global trend of dissolving the boundary between arthouse and popular films.

How did these changes affect the production of musicals in Poland? At first sight, the proportion of musical films in the entire film production in Poland is relatively modest, as it was during the state socialist period. However, they offer a greater variety in terms of subgenres and themes. Among them we find musical comedies, musical dramas and a musical horror; rock, folk and disco polo musicals. This differentiation of musicals, as reflected by the fact that some of them are not classified as musicals, is in line with the global trend of an increase in films such as *Kill Bill: Volume I* by Quentin Tarantino, which till recently were not considered as musicals and which K. J. Donnelly and Beth Carroll describe as 'musicals by another name' (Donnelly and Carroll 2017: 8). Moreover, Polish musicals are no longer the preserve of second-class directors, but those with high artistic ambitions, such as the Oscar winner Paweł Pawlikowski. Again, this is no different from the global picture, where this genre attracts many arthouse and independent directors, such as Tarantino, the Coen Brothers and Danny Boyle (ibid.: 5–8).

An upsurge of musicals has occurred in the 2010s and this chapter will focus on this decade. Although it will be difficult to explain why this decade proved so conducive to musical production, possible reasons are the global 'return to musical', as illustrated by the success of films such as *Les Misérables* (2012), directed by Tom Hooper and *La La Land* (2016) by Daniel Chazelle. Another factor is the founding of the Polish Film Institute in 2005, whose support allows for shooting films with higher budgets. An additional reason is that by this point Polish cinema acquired a large crop of actors who feel comfortable singing and dancing on stage, in part thanks to television, which created its own versions of such popular programmes as 'Dancing with Stars'. They include Joanna Kulig, Patricia Kazadi, Dawid Ogrodnik and Tomasz Schuchardt, to name just a few. Finally, I shall mention YouTube, which significantly affected the way films are watched: as decontextualized fragments. New Polish musicals are in reality multimedia phenomena, whose life as a collection of clips available on YouTube often overshadows their 'proper' cinematic life.

The need to be 'heard' on multiple platforms also applies to films from the 2010s which are not musicals. Halina Jasonek observes that the use of popular music in Polish films is often a factor dividing memorable and forgettable films and makes a genre film such as a criminal film or a romantic comedy stand out from the crowd of similar films. Examples are *Facet (nie)potrzebny od zaraz* (*Man Immediately Not Needed*, 2014) by Weronika Migoń and *Hardkor Disko* (2004) by Krzysztof Skonieczny (Jasonek 2015/2016: 94). Here it is also worth mentioning Andrzej Wajda's *Wałęsa. Człowiek z nadziei* (*Wałęsa. Man of Hope*, 2013), which uses as its soundtrack Polish rock songs from the 1980s, much more extensively and effectively than any Polish film from the 1980s. Before I move to discussing the films, I will sketch the political and economic situation in Poland after 1989.

Poland After the Fall of the Berlin Wall

In the late 1980s–early 1990s the system of state socialism was overturned in the whole of Eastern Europe, as symbolised by the fall of the Berlin Wall in 1989. In Poland, the first semi-democratic parliamentary elections took place in the same year. Since then, neoliberal capitalism dominated Polish politics and economy. Although the last three decades saw numerous changes of government and political leaders, in reality it is more homogeneous than the period of state socialism. Postcommunist political elites, be they from the centre-right or centre-left, led by anti-communist Lech Wałęsa, postcommunist Aleksander Kwaśniewski or conservative politicians from the Law and Justice party follow the same political agenda of neoliberalisation, which in the first decade or so was presented as 'economic reform'.

Neoliberalism is defined by several principles, of which the two most important in this context are: (1) privatisation and the commodification of public assets; (2) financialisation, so that any commodity can become an instrument of economic speculation (Harvey 2005: 160–162). Nowadays neoliberalism is almost universally equated with a prolonged austerity, especially following the 2008 crisis, worsening standards of living, deregulation in employment and high unemployment among the young, as well as climate crisis. It is seen as a failed system, which has made a narrow part of society very rich, while making the income of the middle-class stagnate and impoverishing the working class. However, neoliberalism introduced in Poland in the 1990 was widely welcomed, being seen as a perfect cure to the political, economic and social malaise the country suffered from the late 1970s. It released entrepreneurial spirit, thwarted by decades of regulations which were meant to introduce and reinforce the socialist economy and gave the impression of everybody getting wealthier without making anybody poorer. This was mostly due to the fact that in 1989 the vast majority of the country's economy belonged to the state, therefore there was plenty to privatise. Moreover, the fall of the Berlin Wall resulted in an easing of restrictions for travel to the West. Since 2004, when Poland joined the European Union, Poles were also allowed to seek legal employment in the EU, which resulted in almost one million of them moving to Britain.

Early neoliberalisation in Poland was also marked by a large growth of an informal, 'grey' economy, epitomised by the market on Stadion Dziesięciolecia (10th-Anniversary Stadium) in Warsaw, which was illegal, yet tolerated by the city's authorities for many years. Here customers could buy commodities from all over the world, including guns and pirated music cassettes. In this early phase there were also strong links between business and organised crime. In many cities, such as Warsaw, small businesses could survive by paying bribes to gangs, allegedly for protection. There were also some informal monopolies such as 'taxi mafias' in many cities which kept the prices for their services artificially high. Such arrangements pointed to the weakness of the state and its institutions; a problem, which although it did not disappear altogether, became contained in the following decades.

Neoliberalisation also affected the Polish film industry. It began even before state socialism collapsed, in the late 1980s, but this process accelerated in the 1990s. By 1991 the old institutions, through which Polish cinema was financed, were dismantled and new ones created. Among them were Film Studios (Studia Filmowe), which replaced the old Film Units (Zespoły Filmowe). They continued to receive funds from the government, via the Committee of Cinema, albeit relatively smaller sums. At the same time, unlike the old Film Units which only managed the property of the state, the Film Studios became the owners of this property.

The initial economic consequences of the neoliberalisation of the film industry in Poland were the same as across the rest of Eastern Europe: reduced budgets, layoffs of workers, and a fall in the number of feature films produced, in combination with increased ticket prices, lower audience figures and a falling market share for domestic productions, which faced massive competition from Hollywood imports. However, in the first half of the 1990s the state of film production in Poland was relatively healthy. Between 1991 and 1994 on average thirty films were produced and distributed per year and in 1995 the number even rose to thirty-nine. The vast majority of them were made thanks to government subsidy, and about a quarter were co-productions with foreign firms. In the second half of the decade production dropped to below twenty films produced/distributed per year. For example, in 1999 only sixteen new Polish films were shown in cinemas. Although fewer films were produced, they were relatively more expensive than the films of earlier periods, with many of them being lavish heritage films such as *Ogniem i mieczem* (*With Fire and Sword*, 1999), directed by Jerzy Hoffman and *Quo Vadis* (2001) by Jerzy Kawalerowicz. The need to respond to market demands was eased in the next decade and especially after 2005, following the setting up of the Polish Film Institute (Polski Instytut Sztuki Filmowej, the

PISF), which was meant to support the production of films of a high artistic standard. Since then, the Polish film industry recovered from the crisis, which is reflected in an increase of film production, from 20 to 25 films per year at the beginning of the 2000s till 40–50 by the end of the 2010s. Another sign of the health of Polish film production is the fact that Polish audiences enjoy watching Polish films. In 2017 Polish films were watched in cinemas by 57,500,000 viewers, which means that a quarter of them chose Polish films. The two most popular films in Polish cinemas were Polish productions (Wróblewska 2018). Since the early 2000s, Polish films also do well on the festival circuit, with the productions of Paweł Pawlikowski, *Ida* (2013) and *Zimna wojna* (*Cold War*, 2018), collecting most awards, including an Oscar for *Ida*.

From Documenting to Erasing Culture: Disco Polo Musicals

Neoliberalism also affected institutions responsible for the development of popular music in Poland. Under state socialism there was only state television, state radio, state record companies and state press. This situation was conducive to the interests of insiders and those who would be described today as 'metropolitan cultural elites', which were hostile to certain artists and genres of popular music. Neoliberalism broke their monopoly, affording market forces a greater say in deciding who will have access to recording facilities and the media. The genre which benefited most from the new situation was disco polo, a type of dance music, based on beats, with an extensive use of electronic instruments and patriotic, erotic or humorous lyrics. It is also marked by 'soft' singing, contrasting with the rock manner of performance. In the 1990s disco polo was the most popular music in Poland, despite the scorn poured on it by cultural elites. The renowned film critic, Tadeusz Sobolewski, in an article, published in 1996, presented disco polo as a disease which contaminated and displaced the dissident culture of artists such as Wajda, Kieślowski and Zanussi, who during state socialism offered its consumers both a utopian moment and a deeper engagement with social reality (Sobolewski 1996: 5). Another respected critic, Bartosz Żurawiecki, described disco polo as an epitome of kitsch and confessed his fear of this music as an anxiety about reducing Polish society to the lowest common denominator (Żurawiecki 1998: 19–20). As these and similar opinions show, in the

1990s disco polo stirred strong emotions (Borys 2019: 74–77), stronger than big beat in the 1960s.

Not surprisingly, the first Polish musical of the postcommunist period, *Kochaj i rób co chcesz* (*Love Me and Do Whatever You Want*, 1998), directed by Robert Gliński, is devoted to this music. It was followed by *Disco Polo* (2015), directed by Maciej Bochniak and several documentary films. When I'm writing these words, apparently a third one is in production—a biopic about one of the greatest disco polo stars, Zenon Martyniuk, making it the most screened music genre which gained popularity in 'free Poland'.

Love Me and Do Whatever You Want was not only the first fiction film about disco polo, but also the only Polish musical made before the new millennium. The fact that it had its premiere almost ten years after the fall of the Iron Curtain suggests that in the first decade after this momentous event other types of films were favoured by Polish filmmakers. Indeed, as I argued elsewhere, it was a period which privileged gangster and heritage films: genres which were best suited either to capture the rapid transformation which happened in Poland in this decade or attempted to recreate Polish history and national identity suppressed by state socialist rule (Mazierska 2007: 43–89). Musicals, seen as a 'light' genre, were not regarded as the best vehicle to tell the story of privatisation of state assets or of a need to rebuild Polish national identity after 34 years of a rule which was hostile to Catholicism. Moreover, as I argued earlier in this book, the difficulty of producing a good musical and limited critical recognition even in the case of success, disincentivised potential filmmakers. Why, thus, did Robert Gliński decide to take the risk? One factor was the immense popularity of disco polo, which by the middle of the 1990s became regarded not just as a popular genre, but an important social phenomenon in its own right. In a documentary shot on occasion of making *Love Me and Do Whatever You Want* Gliński confessed that disco polo attracted his attention because he wanted to make a contemporary film. By this point he was an eclectic director, who, however, in the second part of his career specialised in realistic films, culminating in his greatest achievement *Cześć Tereska* (*Hello Tereska*, 2001), made in Dogme style. Moreover, he was fascinated by the documentary *Bara bara* (*Hanky Panky*, 1996) (discussed in Chapter 7) and proposed its co-director Michał Arabudzki to write a script for him (quoted in Kaplińska 1998: 83).

Although in the 1990s disco polo was immensely popular, it was seen as a culture of the Polish province: Poland of villages and small towns, especially of the eastern region. This Poland was always of interest to Polish filmmakers, yet there are not many films which show provincial Poland realistically. Usually the province is seen through the trope of nostalgia—as a place which ceased to exist and has to be resurrected by the power of memory. Such a take on the Polish province is offered in the films by Andrzej Wajda, Andrzej Barański, Jacek Bromski and, to some extent, Jan Jakub Kolski. Making a film about disco polo offered a chance to break this trend. However, as some critics observed, Gliński fell into the trap of constructing his province, a (fictitious) village of Kaliszew in the eastern part of Poland, from the building blocks of many earlier films and soap operas about the province. They include a priest, who is not impartial to the pleasures of good food and alcohol, a local millionaire with a beautiful daughter, who falls for the 'wrong guy' and a small crowd of drunkards who play the role of a Greek chorus (Pietrasik 1998: 38), all characters represented in a positive light.

Centre stage is given to Sławek Wiśnik, a young man from Kaliszew from the East of Poland, who becomes a disco polo star. This sounds like a typical story of real disco polo stars, given that many of them came from this part of Poland, often described as Poland B: rural and premodern (second-class) Poland, which during partitions belonged to the Russian Empire. However, there is a twist to Sławek's fate, as we meet him for the first time during a competition to receive a studentship in Germany as an organist. He blows this chance because instead of playing Bach, he performs his own composition, proving that he is a rebel. His subsequent career as a disco polo artist can thus be seen as a revenge on those who didn't recognise his talent as a serious artist. One wonders, however, why Sławek did not choose rock, which seems like a more suitable genre for a renegade. The answer might lie in his thinking that if he cannot be a high-art artist, it is best to choose something completely different, given that rock also has high-art pretentions. Moreover, in his village everybody is listening to disco polo; there is practically no other option, if one wants to monetise one's musical talent.

Sławek's subsequent trials and tribulations concern him establishing himself as a disco polo star, beginning with playing keyboard in the band of female disco polo star Samanti, through playing in a club and finally making a record. This reveals how the disco polo business works: the road from recording to releasing is very short, because songs are recorded on cassettes, which are distributed by small entrepreneurs, selling them at the bazaars, most importantly 10th-Anniversary Stadium, rather than in proper shops. This reduces the cost and increases the profit margin of producers and traders. If the record sells well, the artists record more; if it is a flop, s/he is dropped by the label. To increase their visibility and earnings, the performers give many concerts, often at events, where music is just one of many attractions, such as religious festivals or political rallies. The disco polo business can thus be regarded as an epitome of the stage of early capitalism, pertaining to Poland of the 1990s, marked by selling a simple, hastily prepared product either directly to consumers or using a small number of intermediaries. Due to the short 'chain' of production and distribution, the market is very sensitive to consumers' demands, in contrast to the music market of state socialism, where performers often made records once their heyday was behind them.

Because of its orientation towards profit, disco polo musicians are presented not as authors of their work, but rather as business people and labourers: cogs in the machine. We can thus see a parallel between their work and the Tin Pan Alley model of production of popular music, which was essentially a Fordist institution. In Poland, however, despite the widespread admiration of western popular music, this model was treated with suspicion, because music was meant to be a fruit of personal expression. The openness with which disco polo positioned itself as a business was an important reason why it was scorned by cultural elites, hostile to operating in a market economy.

Gliński shows that, contrary to the widespread opinion that penning disco polo songs is easy, making a career in this genre is difficult. There are some dishonest people working in the business, stealing the songs of competitors and blocking their access to the media; this applies to Samanti and her manager-cum-boyfriend. However, this is not an unusual situation in popular music, as shown in earlier Polish musicals, such as *This Is Only Rock*. Ultimately, Gliński avoids demonising disco polo as a 'murderer of Polish culture' or an epitome of what was worst in Poland during the early years of capitalism. He also presents it as a genre which flourishes in its own space, without suffocating other music genres and cultures.

The story of Sławek's maturation is set against a wide panorama of the early years of postcommunist Poland, when everybody tried to take advantage of the political transformation and get rich. This includes the family of Sławek's girlfriend, who live in the province, as well as people from Warsaw, who try to capitalise on the new fashion. It also shows

Polish politicians trying to take advantage of disco polo's popularity by using it at political rallies. Such a practice was indeed common in the 1990s and several of the country's leading politicians, including Prime Minister Pawlak and Presidents Kwaśniewski and Wałęsa used disco polo music in their campaigns.

Although the story concerns contemporary reality, the visual style gives it a nostalgic tint, resulting from shooting it on Kodak print, which was meant to imitate the ORWO print, used in films made during the state socialist period. In Gliński's own words, his main inspiration was Czech New Wave films, due to the warmth with which they show the Czech province (ibid.: 64). This connection is traceable, yet Gliński's film lacks the fly-on-the-wall quality characteristic of the films by Forman and Passer, which resulted in capturing the characters when they behaved in their most embarrassing way. One upshot of using the 'socialist-style' is the lack of eye-catching spectacles. This can be explained by Gliński's lack of experience in making musicals or his ambition to be true to disco polo's culture, which places emphasis not on creating grandiose events but offering an environment for the communal enjoyment of music during smaller events, such as weddings and country picnics.

The main characters in *Love Me and Do Whatever You Want* are fictitious, but the film makes reference to some authentic people working in the disco polo business. The partner of Sławek's producer and manager is played by Sławomir Świerzyński, at the time probably the greatest star of disco polo and owner of the first professional studio producing disco polo records, 'Blue Star' (featured in the film). Giving the main character the name 'Sławek', which is a diminutive of 'Sławomir', might be in recognition of Świerzyński's role in building up disco polo's infrastructure. In one episode we also see a performance by the band Boys, one of the most famous disco polo acts of the early period. Samanti, with her exotic Gypsy name, can be regarded as a younger and sexier version of Shazza (Magdalena Pańkowska), who was at the time the greatest female star of disco polo.

Sławek is played by Rafał Olbrychski, son of the great star of Polish cinema, Daniel Olbrychski and at the time leader of the rock band Reds. According to Gliński, Olbrychski was full of aggression towards his character because he hated disco polo (quoted in Kaplińska 1998: 64). The actor's dislike of this music emerges through the film, rendering his transformation from serious musician to disco polo star unconvincing. This transformation is also not believable because the type of music he records is not really in disco polo style, but rather pop and very bland at that. As a side note I shall mention that Olbrychski's band failed to make a mark on the Polish rock scene. One can regret that if he was not so aloof towards disco polo, maybe he would be more successful in this genre.

The soundtrack of the film is a mixture of disco polo hits and some songs in this style written specially for the film. While 'real' disco polo hits are captivating, the new songs, especially those which made Sławek Wiśnik a disco polo star, come across as flat.[1] Similarly, in any competition between 'proper' disco polo and other types of music, disco polo wins. Irrespective of Gliński's intention, the film demonstrates that, contrary to widespread opinion that making disco polo music requires minimum talent and effort, the opposite is the case—making music for the masses is at least as difficult as creating serious or experimental music.

Disco Polo was made almost two decades after Gliński's film and the heyday of the first generation of disco polo artists.[2] Such temporal distance allows for a re-evaluation of the given musical phenomenon, often leading to an outpouring of nostalgia. However, my argument is that *Disco Polo* is not a nostalgic film, because it does not express a yearning for the lost past and a desire to recreate and embellish it. Maciej Bochniak, prior to directing *Disco Polo*, which was his full-length fiction debut, like Gliński, had no experience in making musicals. He was mainly shooting short films on different topics. However, subsequently he made a 70-minute long documentary about Ethiopian jazz, *Ethiopiques. Muzyka duszy* (*Ethiopiques: Music of the Soul*, 2017), suggesting more than a passing interest in music. The script of *Disco Polo* was written by Bochniak and the actor Mateusz Kościukiewicz, who also plays in the film. As far as I am aware, neither of them had any extensive knowledge of disco polo and given their age (Bochniak was born in 1984 and Kościukiewicz in 1986), even first-hand experience of this phenomenon in the 1990s, when the action of their film is set. It suggests that they assumed that such knowledge was not essential for their project. Indeed, while Gliński's goal was to root disco polo in a specific culture: that of the Polish province and entrepreneurial culture of early capitalism in Poland, Bochniak's idea was to embed disco polo in the culture of cinema. On this occasion disco polo is merely a pretext to conjure up an autonomous world. From this perspective, *Disco Polo* belongs to a subgenre of musical, which Altman describes as the fairy tale musical (Altman 129–199; Friedman et al. 2014:

221: 23). In such musicals both mundane and exotic locations are transformed into a fairy tale universe, through the use of props, setting and colour.

The film has a thin plot about a young man called Tomek, who tries to make a career in disco polo. On the way to fulfilling his dreams, he comes in contact with a number of eccentric, sinister and grotesque characters. Among them is a disco polo diva, Anka 'Gensonina', with whom Tomek falls in love, mighty music producer Daniel Polak and two young people, who try to frustrate Tomek's efforts. As is often the case in fairy tale musicals, they are cartoonish, rather than presented realistically. Their gestures are exaggerated and they are shown from unusual angles which adds to their strangeness.

Tomek's trials and tribulations are presented in a series of loosely connected episodes. Their purpose is to be visually and aurally exciting in their own right. The entire narrative logic of the film is governed by intertextuality, rather than causality. The main cinematic reference point are films by Wes Anderson (Raczek 2015), a filmmaker with immense appeal to the younger generation of Polish filmmakers, probably due to succeeding commercially without compromising his arthouse ambitions. For example, Kościukiewicz's short cameos bring to mind Anderson's *The Grand Budapest Hotel* (2014). They are also allusions to other arthouse productions, such as two white-clad thugs 'borrowed' from Michael Haneke's *Funny Games* (1997). Viewers who are less well versed in arthouse productions, might enjoy a quotation from *Titanic* (1997) by James Cameron, when Tomek and his beloved Anka stand on top of the yacht in the famous pose of Kate Winslet and Leonardo DiCaprio. While there are many references to western films, I was not able to identify any citation from Polish films. Although *Disco Polo* is nominally set in Poland, it shies away from Polish landscape. Its action begins in an oil field, which looks like a scene from a Western. In another scene the characters ride horses, wearing cowboy costumes. We also see a boat moving through a desert. The roads are wide and almost empty, as in American road movies and the only vehicles are American cars and trucks. By contrast, there are no images of any Polish towns or villages; at best we see buildings taken out of their context, such as a small provincial railway station, a trailer or a prison. The scenes are shot in saturated colour, bringing to mind Technicolor musicals of classical Hollywood era.

When the action moves indoors, we get brightly lit clubs, decorated with objects taken from all possible places and epochs, in Las Vegas style.

The same applies to costumes, whose origins are spectacles created in Las Vegas or on Broadway, rather than those sported by real Polish disco polo stars. Editing reinforces the film's surreal style, by taking us rapidly to different places of action, as in a dream. Disco polo music becomes twisted and decontextualised by placing it in a fake American landscape and contaminating it with other styles. For example, the first time we hear Anka-Gensonina, she does not sing any disco polo song, but an old Russian romantic song 'Oczi cziornyje' (Black Eyes), in Poland known best from the version performed by Violetta Villas, arguably the greatest Polish diva (see Chapter 8). Gensonina's appearance and stage behaviour, with her penchant for long dresses and elaborate hats, renders her more a star of opera or musical theatre, an updated version of Villas, than a typical disco polo star.

Tomek's band Laser mainly sings songs from the 1990s, such as 'Wolność' (Freedom) and 'Jesteś szalona' (You Are Crazy) by Boys and 'Bo wszyscy Polacy to jedna rodzina' (Because All Poles Are One Family) by Bayer Full. Using these songs was a way to attract a 'typical' disco polo fan, while the other aspects of the films were meant to appeal to a more sophisticated audience. Yet, all these songs are performed in a rather dull style, giving the impression that all disco polo songs are the same—an opinion held by those who have little knowledge about the genre. We can conjecture that Bochniak and Kościukiewicz themselves belong to this category. Most of the songs are presented as video clips, watched by somebody on a television screen or from behind the camera in a television studio. On such occasions the spectacle is mainly visual— the baroque design and costumes thwart music, confirming my earlier point that the principal frame of reference for creators of *Disco Polo* are foreign films. There are no images of typical disco polo concerts in open air, in which listeners perform together with artists, creating a community of happy people. The only time we see a larger audience is at the end of the film when 'Because All Poles Are One Family', performed by Tomek and Gensonina, wins a large international festival, which stands for the Eurovision Song Contest. This can be regarded as a sign of appreciation of disco polo, but also, again, the sign of an unwillingness to engage with it as a specifically Polish phenomenon (Fig. 4.1).

Although *Disco Polo* tells next to nothing about disco polo as a genre or cultural phenomenon, ultimately it reveals something about the attitudes of elites towards this phenomenon, namely their unwillingness to engage with it on disco polo's terms. Such a condescending attitude has

Fig. 4.1 Tomek (Dawid Ogrodnik) and Gensonina (Joanna Kulig) perform 'Because All Poles Are One Family' at the end of *Disco Polo* (2015), directed by Maciej Bochniak

lasted practically throughout the genre's entire existence. The only difference between the early 'metropolitan critics' of disco polo and those of Bochniak's generation lies in their regarding it as innocuous and neutral, something which does not pose any danger to Polish culture, but neither does it add anything to it, rather than being horrified by its successes.

Although Bochniak's project of using disco polo as a pretext to make a camp film in the vein of a Wes Anderson production was criticised for its failure to capture the disco polo phenomenon, with flat, uninteresting characters, an unimaginative imitation of Hollywood cinema (Duda 2015; Pietrasik 2015; Raczek 2015), the film was a box office success (Zwoliński 2019), most likely due to attracting two types of audiences: those eager to hear disco polo hits, and those attracted to the film's visual style, unusual in the Polish context.

To conclude this part, it is fair to say that disco polo still awaits appraisal. I will welcome if this is done by an insider, given that disco polo artists, like the eponymous 'subaltern' from Gayatri Chakravorty Spivak's essay or the orientalist subjects from Edward Said's *Orientalism*, in the 1990s were not allowed to speak or at least their power of speaking was curtailed by a hostile media.

Satire Without a Vantage Point

The majority of the remaining Polish musicals produced after 1989 do not present any new music in the sense of music which became fashionable at the time of these films' production. They are thus about music of the past. The main reason is that they are set in earlier periods of Polish history, principally between the end of the Second World War and the end of state socialism. However, even if they are set in a later period, as is the case of *Polskie gówno* (*Polish Crap*, 2015), directed by Grzegorz Jankowski, musically their point of reference are earlier styles and phenomena. Thus, paradoxically, in them the period when popular music was thwarted by political, economic and technological constraints, receives a new lease of life. However, this does not necessarily mean cloaking the music in a nostalgic glow. Often the opposite is the case.

I begin my investigation with *Polish Crap* because this film, like the two previously discussed, is nominally set in the period concurrent with its production, although its principal point of reference is the 1980s. This can be explained by the fact that Tymon Tymański (b. 1968), the author of the script, the actor playing the main role and the author of the score, started his career as a musician in the 1980s and appeared to be well positioned to compare Polish music from the late state socialist period with that from postcommunist times.

The triple role played by Tymański, overshadowing that of the director for whom it was his debut in full-length fiction cinema, points to the difference between this film and films about rock music produced during the period of state socialism. In the 1960s and the 1980s, rockers were not trusted with writing scripts and playing main roles in them. They were made mostly by filmmakers who wanted to capitalise on the popularity of big beat or Music of the Young Generation, but felt little connection with or sympathy towards rock music and its stars. For the same reason, in these films real musicians were relegated to secondary roles or reduced to extras. *Polish Crap* represents the opposite: a film in which the director is so much in awe of the rockers, that they practically have a free hand and just shoot their exploits. Moreover, it is based on the premise that rock is cinematic in itself—it is enough to put a camera in front of the band and it will mesmerise the audience. Such an effect is sometimes achieved in fiction films, but is easier to accomplish in smaller forms, such as short documentaries. Indeed, the initial premise of *Polish Crap* was making a short film. The origins of the film are in 2007, when Tymański and Jankowski were working together in the television programme titled *Łossskot*. Then Tymański confessed to Jankowski his ambition to make a mockumentary about the fictitious band Tranzystory (Transistors). Jankowski, however, convinced Tymański to produce a full-length musical, based on the same idea (Świąder 2015). The original idea can be discerned in *Polish Crap*'s visual style. Shots are often taken with a hand-held, shaky camera; the images are out of focus and underlit, bringing to mind Dogme-95 aesthetics, fresh in the 1990s, but dated in 2015.

The film tells the story of an ageing rocker, named Jerzy Bydgoszcz, whose finances are in a perilous state. This is due to the bankruptcy of a Czech music company, which was meant to release the last record of his band Tranzystory, as well as his general incompetence. The solution to his problem is offered by a bailiff named Czesław Skandal (Scandal), who rather than stripping Bydgoszcz of his remaining assets, suggests that Tranzystory go on tour, from the Baltic Coast to the South, which he promises to finance, adopting the role of the band's manager. This is an unrealistic plot device, as no real bailiff would risk investing his private money in a second-league rock band, especially during a period of crisis in popular music. We can find its justification in the fact that *Polish Crap* was designed as a satirical comedy, a genre which is allowed to take liberties with realism. The object of the satire is Polish show business in postcommunist Poland, presented as corrupt and amateurish. Both of these aspects are embodied by Tranzystory's manager Skandal, who does not miss any opportunity to make Tranzystory a success, but continually fails. On one occasion this is because the audience does not materialise—the band plays for only one listener; on another they fail because they play songs with obscene lyrics at a gig organised by a priest; later their CD is released with the wrong cover. Consequently, the manager merely pays the musicians pocket money and makes them travel in a battered old van and sleep in substandard accommodation, to make ends meet, bringing to mind the adventures of the band Leningrad Cowboys from the films of Aki Kaurismäki. This situation is probably meant to demonstrate the exploitation of the rockers by the postcommunist music industry. However, given that before Skandal's arrival on the scene Bydgoszcz was not able to make money from his music, it is difficult to believe that he is worse off under Skandal's wing than if he was managing his own affairs. Moreover, irrespective of how little money the band earns, it is always enough to buy alcohol and make Tranzystory's drummer completely drunk and sick during the band's performance, which further diminishes the band's value in the eyes of the audience.

The Polish popular music establishment is presented in the film as smug, fake and corrupt. Its representatives come across as enemies of the artists rather than facilitators of their careers. Ironically, such an approach betrays the 'socialist' mindset, with its contempt for 'unproductive' people. The second target of *Polish Crap*'s satire is music presented in the private television station Polsat (here renamed Polwsat), which for many years was the 'home' of disco polo, accused by the cultural elites of lowering the taste of Polish music fans. Again, in contrast to such profit-ridden institution, the filmmakers present themselves as defenders of 'true' art. An 'Idol'-like, televised competition, filling the last part of the film, in which we see musicians representing different genres, yet all abysmally bad, is meant to demonstrate the depth of the decline of popular music in market-oriented Poland. However, to denounce something as substandard requires adopting a certain vantage point, from which one can make such judgments. Tranzystory hardly fit the bill, lacking any interesting repertoire or enthusiasm and being themselves locked in their past. Rather than being a yardstick with which to measure the eponymous 'crap', they are part of 'Polish crap'.

Not surprisingly, the film flirts with the idea that the best time for Polish music was the 1980s. This is suggested by flashbacks, featuring the driver of Tranzystory, Stan Gudeyko, in his youth. This role is played by Robert Brylewski, the real-life leader of two popular bands from the 1980s, Kryzys and Brygada Kryzys. The young Gudeyko-Brylewski with bleached hair looks very attractive; the one from 2015 aged badly—he seems to be older than his real age. The idea that it was better to be a rock musician in the 1980s than in the 2010s is difficult to defend, given that in the 1980s Polish rockers seemed to utterly hate the political and social reality in which they operated. *Polish Crap* also makes reference to the darkest aspects of the 1980s by Gudeyko reminiscing on the times he was beaten up by the police and repeatedly screening General Jaruzelski's announcing martial law on television. Ultimately, denouncing the past and the present furnishes the film with a nihilistic aura and watching it one wonders if it won't be better to emigrate if Poland is so despicable—a conclusion accepted by millions of Poles who left their country after the fall of the Iron Curtain. This idea is referred to by the title of the film, which is taken from a poem by Kazimierz Przerwa-Termajer, 'Patryota' (The Patriot), from 1898, which includes the passage:

Wolę polskie gówno w polu
Niźli fiołki w Neapolu!

(I prefer Polish crap in the field
Than violets in Neapol)

The poem is satirical—it mocks Polish exalting of patriotism over other virtues. It is difficult, however, to establish where *Polish Crap* stands in relation to patriotism, given its negative attitude to the Polish past and present, and showing no optimism for the future. If it promotes patriotism, it is only of the type mocked by Przerwa-Termajer—as irrational love towards one country, not related to any real values espoused by people living there.

Polish Crap is a musical not only because it presents the band singing on stage, but also includes song and dance numbers performed by other characters, such as Bydgoszcz's father and Skandal. They are in different styles than that adopted by Tranzystory. Skandal typically sings and dances in the style of estrada or disco polo, surrounded by a group of young women. Such performances have a clear satirical character, as the movements of the dancers are exaggerated and the colours of their costumes are garish. Moreover, he is presented as somebody who favours female company over male bonding. Thus, the film perpetuates the stereotype of rock as male style (and more arty for that) and other popular styles of popular music as feminine and less worthy than rock. Rock in *Polish Crap* functions as a static genre, musically based on guitar riffs and rebellious lyrics, visually rooted in leather jackets, heavy boots and a scruffy look, culturally showing a penchant to strong alcohol and gratuitous swearing. Times might be changing, as stated by Bob Dylan in his old song, but if we are to believe *Polish Crap*, in Poland the (rock) song and rock culture remain the same.

Female-Friendly Musicals for the YouTube Generation

Unlike the films discussed so far, which focused on male characters, *#WszystkoGra* (*Game On*, 2016), directed by Agnieszka Glińska and *Córki dancingu* (*The Lure*, 2015), directed by Agnieszka Smoczyńska, can be classified as women's cinema, on account of being directed by women, casting women in the main roles and focusing on their problems. What is also important from my perspective, is feminisation of the music presented in these films. The specificity of these two films also lies in their awareness that a large proportion of viewers would watch them in fragments, as clips on YouTube. Their authors encourage such reception, making them easy to adapt to different media, such as stage, television or music video. Their textual characteristics and reception reflect the fact that contemporary musicals are intermedial phenomena (Donnelly and Carroll 2017: 2).

For Agnieszka Glińska (b. 1968) *Game On* was a full-length fiction debut. Yet she was not a real newcomer, as earlier she directed many plays, including in a television theatre, a genre which has a special prestige in Poland. Many of her plays focused on the lives of women, especially from the Polish prewar intelligentsia. In this sense, *Game On* is a continuation of Glińska's previous work, albeit in a different medium. The film is set in contemporary Warsaw and casts in main parts women of three generations: grandmother Helena, mother Roma and granddaughter Zosia, who are about to lose their opulent house because they lack the deed proving that it belongs to them. Such a document was produced during the Second World War, when the great grandmother of the youngest of Glińska's heroines won the house in a game of cards from an officer who subsequently perished in the war. In the present day, Zosia learns about this history and tries to repeat what her grandmother did, by engaging in a game with the officer's great-grandson, although this is no longer a game of cards, but a version of Monopoly.

Two periods are of importance for the film's narrative: the interwar period and contemporary times. They are linked not only through the story of the house, but also some visual references. For example, at some point Roma and Zosia attend an exhibition of postcards showing prewar Warsaw, where Zosia discovers some postcards of her grandmother with the gambling officer. The urban space where most of the film is set brings association either with Poland of the interbellum or the time after 1989. The first is represented mainly by the old house, where Helena, Roma and Zosia live. It is furnished with antique furniture and old books which most likely belonged to Helena's mother or the officer from whom she won the house. We also see a very modern, sparsely furnished apartment inhabited by Staszek, a football star who falls in love with Roma after briefly meeting her at a postcards exhibition. There are also many large buildings and skyscrapers, some unfinished—a sign that Warsaw is still under construction. In contrast, there are no images of the large housing estates which were constantly present in Polish cinema of the 1960s, the 1970s and the 1980s, due to the simple fact that the majority of Warsawians were living in them. The only landmark from the communist period is the Palace of Culture which, however, due to its frequent use in Polish cinema, lost its connection with the circumstances of its erection and original cultural function. In terms of narrative and design, the years 1945–1989 are erased from the film.

Yet, the songs used in *Game On* are all from the state socialist period, mostly the 1970s and the 1980s. They range from estrada songs, such as 'Radość o poranku' (Joy in the Morning), the greatest hit of Grupa I, to 'Ale wkoło jest wesoło' (There Is Fun Around Us), a hit from the repertoire of the rock band Perfect. They are performed by the film characters in a very different arrangement than the originals and typically their function is to explain the situation or the mood of the character. Thus 'Joy in the Morning' is sung by Zosia when she is riding a bicycle and it is conveying her joy and optimism, which can be compared to Curly's opening solo 'Oh, What a Beautiful Mornin' in *Oklahoma!* (1955), directed by Fred Zinnemann (Fig. 4.2).

'There Is Fun Around Us' is performed by a band of footballers. The songs of the state socialist era are not only updated by being taken from

Fig. 4.2 Zosia (Eliza Rycembel) sings 'Joy in the Morning' in *#WszystkoGra* (*Game On*, 2016), directed by Agnieszka Glińska

the original context to the contemporary Warsaw, but also moved backwards, becoming the soundtrack to the episodes set during the Second World War.

Anahid Kassabian argues that compiled scores operate differently than composed scores: 'they bring the immediate threat of history… Airplay for the songs may serve as good advertising for the film, but it means that perceivers bring external associations with the songs into their engagements with the film' (Kassabian 2001: 3). In a nutshell, it means that when listening to compiled scores, we are at risk to 'wander off' from the narrative into the world in which the songs originally functioned. This is also how I reacted to them (and presumably many more viewers who remembered them from their original performances)—they brought the memory of 'innocuous' pop of the 1970s and rebellious and ironic rock of the 1980s, and the respective political contexts of these styles. Such associations, however, are not encouraged in the film. On the contrary, *Game On* comes across as a *game* of associations, whose main rule is 'not to mention state socialism'. It appears that the film's author acknowledges the artistic value and functionality of these old songs, but not the culture in which they were born; this culture is spirited away, as if it was too embarrassing to mention in the polite company of Helena, Roma, Zosia and their friends. A possible reason for this erasure might be the perception that it was a patriarchal culture and hence needs to be reclaimed by women. This reclaiming also happens through changing the character of the songs covered in the film. For example, the romantic song 'Jej Portret' (Her Portrait), originally performed by Bogusław Mec, which is about man's inability to penetrate the mystery of the beloved woman, in *Game On* is sung by Helena, Roma and Zosia who refer to the secrets which they keep from each other.

Reviewers of *Game On* were critical about the way songs were integrated into the narrative, arguing that they hinder the action and that the entire film is a collection of random songs joined together by a thin and unconvincing plot (Pietrzyk 2016). Such a structure suggests that the film is targeted at YouTube viewers who would gladly dissect the film into clips and focus on them rather than the narrative which they see merely as a 'filler'. This is indeed the case and even on one occasion a special video clip was produced, based on 'There Is Fun Around Us', which underscores female agency—in the clip men start to sing the song on the football pitch, while women continue its performance. Moreover, in this clip men are reduced to being objects of the gaze, while women are doers, painting graffiti on the walls and in the last scene carrying a drunken footballer in a wheelbarrow. The clip was watched on YouTube by over 300,000 viewers in a year after it was published—a significant number, suggesting that it played an important role as an advert for the film and extended its afterlife.

Agnieszka Smoczyńska (b. 1978), who directed *The Lure*, belongs to the youngest generation of Polish filmmakers. *The Lure* was her full-length fiction debut; prior to it she directed several shorter, documentary and fiction films, as well as episodes of popular television series. Such a portfolio is typical for Polish filmmakers making their debuts after 1989. What is less typical is Smoczyńska's penchant for making films in which music plays an important role, as well as focusing on women who are either independent or strive to become liberated from the shackles of domesticity and patriarchy through friendship with fellow females. Her *Viva Maria!* (2010) is dedicated to Maria Fołtyn, a renowned Polish opera singer, who excelled in singing in Stanisław Moniuszko's *Halka*. *Aria Diva* (2007) tells the story of a friendship between a well-off housewife and an opera diva living in the same tenement block. A similar theme was previously explored by Věra Chytilová in *O něčem jiném* (*Something Different*, 1963), the director whose work also seems to be a source of inspiration for Smoczyńska's full-length fiction debut. Another connection between *Game On* and *The Lure* are songs which are recycled, yet without embedding them in a wider (national and social) culture from which they are transported.

The Lure is set in Poland of the 1980s. In the words of the director, the more precise setting is 1983 or 1984. Together with the 1950s, the 1980s is the most political period in Polish history, when conflict between political authorities and the society as a whole was most acute and overt, as demonstrated by a series of strikes and the imposition of martial law in 1981. Not surprisingly, Polish films set in this period tend to have a serious tone and even those which do not, like the comedy *Rozmowy kontrolowane* (*Tapped Conversations*, 1991) by Sylwester Chęciński, put politics at the centre of the narrative. The tacit agreement of Polish filmmakers was that setting a film in the 1980s means tackling the politics of this period. Smoczyńska broke with this rule by making a film, which is set in the 1980s, yet is not really about the 1980s as Poles remember it, in the same way *Disco Polo* is set in the 1990s, yet not about the 1990s. However, most likely in her view this was merely a side-effect of breaking a more important Polish cinematic tradition of making 'serious films' by producing a hybrid between musical and horror. When I attended an audience meeting with her during the Wiesbaden Film Festival in 2016, where this film was in competition, she introduced it by saying that until recently it was almost impossible to make such a film in Poland 'because of Krzysztof Kieślowski'. Although she didn't elaborate on this claim, I assumed that she did not argue that Kieślowski personally forbade making musical-horror hybrids, but rather that his cinema represented a certain brand, which acted as a yardstick, against which the other cinematic productions were measured. 'Kieślowski' stands for serious films, engaged with politics or metaphysics, favouring a coherent storyline and focusing on man's plight. For better or worse, *The Lure* is the antithesis of 'Kieślowski's cinema'.

The Lure was inspired by life and music of the Wrońskie sisters (Barbara and Zuzanna), who in 2007 set up the electronic pop band Ballady i Romanse (Ballads and Romances). The film apparently derived from the sisters and Smoczyńska's fascination with the Polish culture of *dancingi*, which consisted of dancing and eating to the accompaniment of live music, mostly of disco and estrada type.[3] For the international viewer, however, the more obvious source of inspiration or 'hypotext', to use Gérard Genette's phrase (Stam 2000: 65–66), is Hans Christian Andersen's fairy tale *Little Mermaid*, whose heroine is severely punished for falling in love with a man. This is because at the centre of the story are two blood-thirsty mermaids, Silver and Gold (admittedly based on the Wrońskie sisters), who reached Warsaw by swimming the Vistula river and find themselves in the Adria, which in the 1980s was the poshest *dancing* in Warsaw. Thanks to their youth and beauty, they find employment in the band Figi and Daktyle (Figs and Dates) and move in with Krysia, the female leader of the band. Silver falls in love with its bass player and is prepared to sacrifice her tail for the female form, but is betrayed by the beloved man and, as in the tale by Andersen, ends as foam disappearing in the water. Her sister revenges the death of Silver by making her lover die a gruesome death. In a contemporary, feminist reading, the moral of the story is for women not to invest in relationships with men, because it only brings pain and danger of self-annihilation. Given that the director of *The Lure* is a woman, who proved herself to be interested in women's stories, one might expect that this message would be accentuated in her film. However, the connections between episodes in *The Lure* are so tenuous that it is almost impossible to extract any message from the film. As one reviewer put it, '*The Lure*'s premise alone will turn heads but once the novelty wears off the question will remain: where's the story?' (Bakare 2016).

Visually, it is difficult to pinpoint the film to a specific period. Apart from the brief image of a queue, we are spared the typical iconography of postmartial law Poland, with obligatory tanks on the streets, neverending winter, shortages of food and greyness. Moreover, all the scenes are drowned in heavy light, giving the impression that the characters move in a colourful fog. Both the topic of the film and its iconography points to the fact that *The Lure* is a fairy tale musical. However, there is no consistency in lighting, adding to the sense that the film is made of separate clips, hastily joined to make a film.

The thinness and fragmentation of the narrative draw attention to the spectacular dimension of the film, most importantly singing, dancing and striptease. Given that feminist authors criticise mainstream patriarchal cinema for its exploitation of female performers exposed to the male gaze, one might be surprised that Smoczyńska follows in the footsteps of such patriarchal, objectifying cinema, only becoming more extreme. The film is full of nudity, most importantly of the two young mermaids who parade without clothes most of the time, as well as of Magda Cielecka, a popular actress who only appears on-screen once to sing and perform striptease, and who plays no role in the mermaid's plot. During this act, the camera shows parts of her body, especially her bottom, in close-up, in a way characteristic of pornography.

There are three types of songs used in *The Lure*, all recorded by actors playing in the film. One is 'I Feel Love', cover of the 1977 hit by Donna Summer, produced by Giorgio Moroder, performed by Krysia. Including this song in the film can be regarded as recognition of the debt of Polish dance music to the American disco. Like Summer in her 1970s performance, Krysia's costume is very shiny and she wears heavy make-up, but her demeanour is playfully demure, as if she was recognising that she is merely adopting someone else's song, rather than singing her own repertoire. The second type are covers of some Polish songs from the 1980s, such as 'Bananowy song' (Banana Song), originally sung by Vox, 'Byłaś serca biciem' (You Were the Beat of My Heart), sung by Andrzej Zaucha and 'Daj mi tę noc' (Give Me This Night), from the repertoire of the band Bolter. In the 1980s these songs were very popular, but derided by cultural elites on the ground of being inauthentic and pandering to the lowest taste (Fig. 4.3).

Fig. 4.3 Krysia (Kinga Preis) and the mermaids (Michalina Olszańska and Marta Mazurek) perform 'You Were the Beat of My Heart' in *Córki dancingu* (*The Lure*, 2015), directed by Agnieszka Smoczyńska

This criticism was especially directed at Bolter's hit, not least because the band's creator, Sławomir Sokołowski, was also a producer of disco polo songs. During its heyday disco music also had a bad press in the West. It was accused of being trivial, inauthentic and irredeemably capitalistic. One of the first critical interventions in defence of disco was an essay of this title published by gay critic and activist Richard Dyer in 1979. In it, Dyer argues that disco is no less capitalist than rock (Dyer 1992: 150–152), while it has certain advantages over rock. In particular, 'rock's eroticism is thrusting, grinding—it is not whole body, but phallic' (ibid.: 153); disco, by contrast, 'indicates an openness to a sexuality that is not defined in terms of cock' (ibid.: 154). By the same token, disco music and culture are more friendly towards gay men and women, both straight and lesbians. The inclusion of disco hits in *The Lure* can be seen as a sign of the recognition of both their musical and social value, namely their suitability to express gay and female desire. The authors of the films further enhance the link between these songs and their femininity and queerness by covering them in a specific way. This is especially the case of 'You Were a Beat of My Heart', which from a male romantic song (a song verging on 'cock sexuality', to use Dyer's terms), changes into a song sung by three women: Krysia and her 'daughters': Gold and Silver, who are connected by familial and erotic love. Finally, the film uses the original productions of the band Ballady i Romanse. They come across as the least catchy of the songs played in the film; and their function is to fill some gaps in the narrative. One can conjecture that if Smoczyńska in her film relied on an original repertoire, the overall result will be less satisfactory. The fact that 1980s pop songs sound so good in the film points to their lasting charm and malleability, which has much to do with their apolitical character. If 'Banana Song' and 'You Were a Beat of My Heart', were replaced by rock hits, it would be difficult to preserve the bubble effect which Smoczyńska tried to create in her film.

The Lure did not spark any discussion about the film's content, either in relation to representation of the 1980s or its sexual politics. Reviewers discussing the film on YouTube admitted that people were leaving the film when watching it in the cinema. I observed the same reaction during its screening in Wiesbaden and I would probably have stopped watching *The Lure* if not for the fact that I was a member of the jury. Subsequently, however, I caught myself rewatching with pleasure the songs from the film on YouTube. *The Lure* can be described as a film made for the YouTube generation, who prefer consuming 'dismembered' films; for such viewing the lack of proper story or even consistent visual style is not a problem. The question arises of why to produce such films at all, as opposed to several music videos. The answer lies in the different cultural status of films and music videos; as a producer of music videos Glińska and Smoczyńska would remain anonymous; as directors of shallow, unbelievable and incoherent films, they were feted as original filmmakers and in the case of Smoczyńska rewarded by numerous awards for technical aspects of her creation.

Cold War Forever

Zimna wojna (*Cold War*, 2018) was directed by Paweł Pawlikowski, who is currently the most acclaimed Polish director, thanks to receiving an Oscar for his previous film, *Ida* (2013). *Cold War* bears many similarities to *Ida* such as setting most of the action during the Stalinist period, using black and white print and casting Joanna Kulig in one of the roles, although in *Ada* she had only a small role as a provincial singer, while in *Cold War* she is cast in the main part.

Ida was a film which connected Poland's war past, marked by the extermination of Jews, with the postwar period, painting both in, literally and figuratively, dark colours. *Cold War* also takes a longer look at Polish history. Its action spans about twenty years, from the end of the Second World War till the end of the 1960s and tells the story of two people, Zula and Wiktor, who are both musicians. At the end of the film we learn that the film is dedicated to Pawlikowski's parents and in various interviews the director emphasised that the main characters were based on his parents, who could not live either together or separately (Hollender 2019). Such declarations inevitably increase the trust of the viewer in the history told on-screen, similarly as when reading 'memoir' or 'non-fiction' we assume that what we read is more truthful than that which presents itself as 'fiction'. However, each memoir gives a partial story, suppressing another part and the same applies to *Cold War*.

The film begins with Wiktor and Irena, a musician and a music coach, as well as Wiktor's friend and possibly lover, recording songs performed by people in different corners of God-forsaken postwar Poland. Initially we believe that Wiktor and Irena scour the Polish countryside for the sake of preserving folk art, which otherwise would be lost, in the same way that early ethnomusicologists preserved the music of exotic tribes. The act of recording places the ethnomusicologists in a position of power over the folk artists, who seem unaware of the purpose of this exercise. This impression is strengthened by the speed with which the film shows Wiktor and Irena's trips. Each recording appears to last less than half a minute and then they move on, paying little attention to the artists.

In due course we learn that the couple have a more pragmatic reason to collect these gems of folk art—to use them to create a 'new Polish folklore': one which would be appreciated not so much by people from the countryside, but by those living in the cities, as well as beyond Poland's borders. Wiktor and Irena's goal is thus changing folklore into what in Poland was described as folklorism: an 'arbitrary, artificial, spectacular representation of folk culture fabricated for a mass audience' (Burszta 1974: 299). One can also see a parallel between folklorism and world music: both types of music draw on folklore, but repackage them for the 'world' (Bohlman 2002: 27). This idea of folklorism is behind creating the Ensemble Mazurek, based on the real band Mazowsze, which, as I mentioned in the previous chapters, featured in several Polish films, such as Bareja's *Wife for an Australian*.

Pawlikowski shows how folklorist project is executed. The strategy to build up Mazurek's line-up and repertoire is similar to that of a tourist guide, because it is based on selection, beautification and homogenisation, a strategy which I discussed first when examining *An Adventure at Marienstadt*, which also referred to Mazowsze. The first means that only certain songs and dances are used; those deemed most catchy and palatable for a non-specialist audience. These songs are not presented in their original form and not by their original performers, but by a specially selected group of the most attractive artists, who had to audition to get a place in the band. It does not even matter whether they are from the countryside or not, if they are able to demonstrate that they sing and dance as the audience imagine the folk ensemble should sing and dance. It is during such an audition that Zula and Wiktor meet. She appears to be an ordinary country girl with a good voice and looks, although as it transpires later, she had a criminal conviction and most likely uses the audition as a way to run away from her past. He is a composer and pianist whose job is to create an attractive repertoire for Mazurek. This group of artists is beautified by putting them in costumes which, although inspired by clothes worn by people in the countryside, are different from those Mazurek's singers and dancers normally wear, as proved by the fact that they come to audition in a different attire. The homogenisation is accomplished by a training regime for the young artists, through which they learn how to sing and dance in the same rhythm and present themselves to the audience in the most attractive way. Due to being manufactured, Mazurek's art can be accused of lacking authenticity, in the same way tourist experience is regarded as inauthentic. With the passage of time Mazurek gets even more inauthentic due to including in its repertoire songs which are openly propagandist by praising communist leaders. However, despite being removed from the true peasant culture and in part thanks to it, Mazurek is successful, as Mazowsze was successful in reality, which was proved by its enthusiastic reception by audiences in many different countries. Its popularity among the Polish diaspora in the United States deserves a special mention, where it awakened nostalgia for their lost country among those unable to return to their homeland. This enthusiasm of the audience points to the fact that lack of authenticity and spontaneity can be made up for by professionalism. The way *Cold War*'s cinematographer films the dancing and singing, presenting the acrobatics from the most flattering angles, adds to the attractiveness of Mazurek's shows (Fig. 4.4).

The scenes showing performances of Mazurek might bring to mind singing and dancing scenes from two Polish musicals of the state socialist period: *An Adventure at Marienstadt* and *Wife for an Australian*. In Buczkowski's film the inhabitants of Warsaw admire performances of apparently numerous folk ensembles, whose members work on state farms. We are to believe that these are amateur performers, but the high

Fig. 4.4 Mazurek's performance in *Zimna wojna* (*Cold War*, 2018), directed by Paweł Pawlikowski

quality of their singing and dancing suggests that they are in fact professionals. *Wife for an Australian* does not pretend any longer that folklorist ensembles are amateur: the heroine of the film, again named Hanka, has no other job than playing in Mazowsze. However, Bareja does not reveal the touristy status of Mazowsze's performance; he embraces it and uses it to strengthen the spectacular character of his film. Pawlikowski, on the other hand, denounces it, while still taking advantage of it, as Mazurek's performances in his film come across as very attractive.

Unlike the audience, which seems not to care about the manufactured and openly political character of Mazurek's spectacles, Wiktor is unhappy about it, because it curtails his artistic freedom. Consequently, he decides to flee Poland during Mazurek's performance in East Berlin, in order to move to France. He assumes that Zula would join him, but she decides to stay in Poland. Her decision is based on her identification with Polish culture. For Zula the fake folk music performed by Mazurek is more authentic than any songs she can sing in France. Moreover (although this is never spelt out in the film), in Poland Zula is a star. However, she eventually changes her mind and follows Wiktor to France. Wiktor and Zula's shared existence allows the director to look at the question of what strategy the Easterner had to use to achieve success in the West—a question which Pawlikowski himself faced, when making films in the UK and France. He points to two possibilities, which I describe as 'mimicry' and 'orientalisation'. The first strategy applies to Wiktor. This is reflected in his dispassionate, almost mechanical playing with a jazz band in a club and writing the score to a film he watches on-screen. These episodes show him being subordinated to somebody's else's art rather than following his own ideas and sensitivity. By contrast, we never see him playing 'his own' music, even to himself, which seemed to be the main reason why he decided to leave Mazurek and Poland. Although Wiktor's social and economic status is higher than that of most Eastern European émigrés to the West (who were typically condemned to manual work), ultimately he suffers from a sense of displacement, a lack of fulfilment and even emasculation. This is noticed by Zula, who tells him: 'In Poland you were a man, and here you are somebody else'.

While in Paris Wiktor tries to be like everybody else, he wants Zula to impress her hosts with her otherness. As Agnieszka Morstin puts it, Wiktor created for Zula the image of an 'untamed Slavic beauty, who killed her father, danced for Stalin and eventually married an Italian prince. All of this is made according to the superficial expectations of the Parisian salon, belonging to which Wiktor aspires, without realising that this very ambition reveals his inferiority complex' (Morstin 2018: 81). Zula initially gives into Wiktor's ambitions for her, but with her vitality and openness, she feels out of place among the Parisian *culturati* who favour more reserved behaviour. She realises that she is unable either to translate her Polish experience into French songs or to identify with French culture so that she can express it the way French singers do, such as Edith Piaf, with whom she shares her untamed nature. Although Zula manages to make a record in France, she feels that it has no value and smashes it on the way from the studio to the apartment she shares with Wiktor. Even if she had a more positive attitude to her work and tried to promote it, most likely it would be just one of many records made by aspiring artists, which would fail to ensure her star status, comparable to what she enjoyed in her homeland. Eventually Zula returns to Poland and makes a career as a star of estrada, which reflects the trajectory of many real stars of Polish folklorist ensembles, such as Irena Santor, who made the transition from folklorist songs performed with Mazowsze to more contemporary 'popular music'.

> As a musical, *Cold War*, as Leslie Felperin observes, is
>   a musicologist's delight, featuring an eclectic swathe of songs that range from traditional 'mountain' tunes and Soviet-era hymns to agricultural reform, classical pieces to snatches of George Gershwin (phrases from the song 'I Loves You, Porgy' play a particularly key role) and other jazz numbers up to Bill Haley & His Comets' 'Rock Around the Clock', the last as much a metonym for the end of a certain era as the death of Stalin or the fall of the Berlin Wall. Hopefully, someone will find a way to release an official film soundtrack for this, or at the very least a Spotify playlist. (Felperin 2018)

To this list we can also add a song inspired by South American music, which Zula sings, after she ended her career in Mazurek, to the applause of an enthusiastic audience. This points to the fact that many members of Mazowsze and Śląsk ensembles managed a successful transition to other types of popular music, most likely because they were professionals, rather than typical folk artists. The career of Lidia Korsakówna, who played in *An Adventure at Marienstadt*, as well as the other singer of Mazowsze, Irena Santor, proves the point. The former became a popular actress; the latter one of the greatest Polish female music stars, specialising in estrada music.

All the examples of popular music used in the film can be described as inauthentic in the Polish context, because either folklorist, propagandist or foreign. However, Pawlikowski shows that songs can be made authentic through connections with personal or group histories. This is demonstrated by different versions of the song 'Dwa serduszka, cztery oczy' (Two Hearts, Four Eyes), which is played in important moments in the film narrative, being a crystal-song (Powrie 2017: 1–2; see Chapter 1). First a young peasant girl sings this song to be recorded by Irena and Wiktor. Next we see it introduced into the repertoire of Mazurek, where it makes Zula the star of the ensemble. Finally, the song, in a jazzy version, is performed by her in a Paris club. Given that the first version is performed in circumstances most similar to the original rendition, we can conjecture that this version is most natural. However, as this version is not related to anybody's story in the film, including the girl who performs it, it probably hardly affects the viewers and most of them probably forgot this version by the time they hear it performed by Zula. Only when Zula adopts it, does it come across as authentic, because it connects to the story of her love for Wiktor. Her singing this song in Paris comes across as authentic again, because in France she continues to suffer from unrequited love. In reality 'Two Hearts, Four Eyes' was not a folk song, but was written in folklorist style by Mazowsze's managers, Mira Zimińska and Tadeusz Sygietyński. Its hit potential was recognised by filmmakers and performers before Pawlikowski put it in front of his camera. It was presented in *Wife for an Australian* in Mazowsze's version and recorded in a jazzy style by Anna Maria Jopek, one of the most popular Polish singers, who in her repertoire draws both on jazz and folk music, and whose father performed in Mazowsze ensemble.

Although songs from *Cold War*, in common with songs from the films previously discussed, also got a second life on YouTube, especially 'Two Hearts, Four Eyes', *Cold War* is not a collection of clips joined by a thin narrative. Rather the various aspects of the film, such as cinematography and soundtrack, are mobilised to tell a compelling story.

Cold War is remarkable not only for the music which it included in its soundtrack, but also for that which it omits. Of that, the most significant omission is rock music, which was born in Poland in the late 1950s as big beat and became the most important genre of popular music in the 1960s, as previously stated. By not including rock music in his film Pawlikowski gives the impression that Poles had little agency in what they chose to play and listen to. By the same token, he also underplays the transition between the 1950s and the 1960s in Poland, which marked not only the end of Stalinism, but also an eruption of youth culture, largely thanks to the government's less 'evangelic', softer stance towards citizens' free time. This unwillingness to differentiate between different periods of Polish postwar history is also reflected in the title of the film. 'Cold war' covers the entire period of Polish postwar history, as opposed to such terms as 'Stalinism', 'Gomułka's thaw', 'small stabilisation' etc., which emphasise the specificity of each postwar period. By giving his film the title *Cold War*, Pawlikowski renders the whole postwar period in Polish history as a long unhappy continuum, where people were locked in their country, governed by a totalitarian regime, living in the shadow of tanks and not being able to create their own culture.

Although Pawlikowski's film covers two decades or so of Polish history and several countries—a scope normally associated with epic films, it comes across as the opposite of an epic, an intimate, 'chamber' story. This effect is achieved by focusing on the main couple with almost all scenes showing them in the centre of the frame, employing tight framing and frequently using close-ups, which present the characters as if they were posing for a portrait. Inevitably, such framing cuts out the 'edges': other people, not closely connected to the protagonists. It does not allow the viewer to see wider circumstances of living in Poland during the said period, most importantly the political and cultural liberalisation brought about by the change in the leadership of the PZPR: the death of Bolesław Bierut in 1956 and the ascent of Władysław Gomułka in the same year. Similarly, the use of black and white print renders the whole period, including the 1960s, black and white. Such stylisation distances Pawlikowski's film from the Polish cinematic production of the 1960s when the majority of Polish films were shot in colour, rendering this period more versatile and cheerful, as in the musicals by Bareja. By making the whole period covered in the film look so homogenous, *Cold War* conforms to its representation which dominated in the political discourse of the 2010s, when under the rule of the Law and Justice Party, the entire period of Polish state socialism has been painted with a wide brush, as times of a continuous period of misery and crimes against humanity. The fact that the central couple decide to commit suicide in the end underscores this opinion, suggesting that there was no way to escape from this dread reality—death was the only solution.

The promotion of folk songs from a position of local art, to popular music, appreciated nation-wide, can be regarded as a metonymy of the promotion of ordinary people, from a position of the underdog to that of political power. This promotion occurred after the Second World War throughout the whole period of Stalinism and, to a lesser extent, in the 1960s, affecting especially people living in the countryside who migrated to large cities and other centres of industrial production. At the time in Poland it was presented as a way to make up for historical injustices, resulting from maintaining an almost feudal system in the large chunks of partitioned Poland, as well as Poland of the interwar period. However, this promotion was seen as taking place at the expense of prewar upper classes, and rewarding such qualities, as obedience and loyalty to the system, as opposed to education, talent and intelligence, what Pierre Bourdieu would call 'high cultural capital'. In *Cold War*, Pawlikowski, who himself is of the intelligentsia background, sides with those who in the late 1940s and 1950s were displaced by 'comrades with only four years of primary school' (Władyka 2009: 116), but eager and able to introduce state socialism in Poland at any cost. This happens through comparing two characters: Wiktor and Kaczmarek, who starts his cinematic life as Wiktor and Irena's driver and finishes as a Party dignitary and Zula's husband. The first is a trained musician and a sophisticated man, most likely with the roots in prewar Polish urban intelligentsia, who, as previously mentioned, cannot stand the philistine atmosphere of postwar Poland. Kaczmarek, whose manner of speaking betrays his peasant's background, is a simpleton, a spy and a philistine, who is unable to connect to music at any deeper level, seeing it merely as a tool of propaganda or cheap entertainment. The fate of these characters is connected—while Wiktor sinks, becoming a victim of destructive love, alcoholism and the rigidity of the Iron Curtain, Kaczmarek moves up the social ladder.

One reviewer described *Cold War* as *Casablanca* or *La La Land* as reimagined by Andrzej Wajda or Agnieszka Holland (Kermode 2018). I find this comparison very apt, not so much because of the textual similarities between *Cold War* and *La La Land* as because both directors and especially Wajda, in common with Pawlikowski, prioritise the plight of the intelligentsia characters, showing distaste and hostility for ambitious provincials (Mazierska 2002). In this sense *Cold War* also belongs to the cluster of films made in the 2010s, such as *Katyń* (2007) by Andrzej Wajda or *Rewers* (*The Reverse*, 2009) by Borys Lankosz, which overtly or covertly pronounce the interwar social order as superior over that which replaced it after the Second World War.

Conclusions

The majority of musicals produced in Poland after the fall of the Iron Curtain recycle songs, created during the state socialist period and give them new life, by presenting their new versions or putting them in new contexts. We thus hear old songs, but they do not remain the same. Different films have different reasons for including them, but two of them played a role in more than one film. One is the ease of accessing old hits in comparison with creating new ones, whose success cannot be guaranteed. The second are the new ways of watching musical films, as a collection of musical clips on YouTube, which requires from the filmmaker to make these clips particularly captivating. Creating new versions of old hits seems like the best recipe for success, as it offers both familiarity and novelty. Another reason why old songs are used in these films, particularly in the films directed by and addressed to women, is creating these songs' alternative history, by aligning them with female experience. The care with which songs are staged in most of these films is not accompanied by attention to narrative coherence and character development. Characters and plots are sketchy, being merely a pretext to play catchy songs. Neither are the songs used to evoke nostalgia—the period of state socialism is either bracketed off as if irrelevant or painted in dark colours, reflecting the dominant narrative of 'communism' in Poland, which is very negative.

While acknowledging the prevalence of old songs in the films made in the 'YouTube era' one can ask why Polish musicals do not use new songs and do not reflect on new fashions in Polish popular music, as was the case with big beat films of the 1960s and rock films in the 1980s. My hypothesis concerns the fragmentation and ephemeral nature of contemporary popular music. The current stars tend to shine for a short time and rarely experience popularity on the scale enjoyed by Czesław Niemen, Skaldowie and Maanam. Using them in films thus brings a risk of rapid obsolescence, which the new generation of filmmakers is unwilling to take.

Notes

1. As the author of the soundtrack is credited Krzesimir Dębski, but I am not sure if he composed these songs or 'collected' them.
2. In the early 2000s one can encounter the opinion that disco polo was in a state of decline (Orliński 2004). However, what happened was rather a generational change and transformation of the genre by hybridisation with other genres, such as hip hop and adopting a more urban outlook.
3. The importance of *dancingi* is conveyed by the Polish title of the film, which translates into 'The Daughters of *Dancingi*'.

Works Cited

Bakare, Lanre. 2016. *The Lure*: Mermaid Musical a Splashy Distraction Until Lack of Story Seems Fishy. *The Guardian*, January 24. https://www.theguardian.com/film/2016/jan/24/the-lure-mermaid-musical-a-splashy-distraction-until-lack-of-story-seems-fishy. Accessed 12 November 2018.

Bohlman, Philip V. 2002. *World Music: A Very Short Introduction*. Oxford: Oxford University Press.

Borys, Monika. 2019. *Polski Bajer: Disco polo i lata 90*. Warszawa: W.A.B.

Burszta, Józef. 1974. *Kultura ludowa kultura narodowa*. Warszawa: Ludowa Spółdzielnia Wydawnicza.

Donnelly, K.J., and Beth Carroll. 2017. Introduction: Reimagining the Contemporary Musical in the Twenty-first Century. In *Contemporary Musical Film*,

ed. K.J. Donnelly and Beth Carroll, 1–9. Edinburgh: Edinburgh University Press.
Duda, Paulina. 2015. Another Polish Complex? Maciej Bochniak's *Disco Polo* (2015). *East European Film Bulletin*, April 2. https://eefb.org/perspectives/maciej-bochniaks-disco-polo-2015/. Accessed 2 March 2019.
Dyer, Richard. 1992. *Only Entertainment*. London: Routledge.
Felperin, Leslie. 2018. Cold War (Zimna Wojna): Film Review | Cannes 2018. The Hollywood Reporter, October 5. https://www.hollywoodreporter.com/review/cold-war-film-review-1110299. Accessed 2 October 2018.
Friedman, Lester, David Desser, Sarah Kozloff, Martha P. Nochimson, and Stephen Prince. 2014. *An Introduction to Film Genres*. New York: W. W. Norton & Company.
Harvey, David. 2005. *A Brief History of Neoliberalism*. Oxford: Oxford University Press.
Hollender, Barbara. 2019. Jeśli "Zimna wojna" spodobała się Nuriemu, rzeczywiście musi być spoko. *Rzeczpospolita*, January 22, https://www.rp.pl/Oscary/306079871-Pawel-Pawlikowski-Jesli-Zimna-wojna-spodobala-sie-Nuriemu-rzeczywiscie-musi-byc-spoko.html. Accessed 20 March 2019.
Jasonek, Halina (2015/2016). Dozwolone piosenki. *Gazeta Magnetofonowa* 1: 94–95.
Kaplińska, Anna. 1998. A to Polska właśnie. *Film* 4: 63–64.
Kassabian, Anahid. 2001. *Hearing Film: Tracking Identifications in Contemporary Hollywood Film Music*. London: Routledge.
Kermode, Mark. 2018. Cold War Review—Love in a Communist Climate. *The Guardian*, September 2. https://www.theguardian.com/film/2018/sep/02/cold-war-pawel-pawlikowski-review-mark-kermode. Accessed 2 October 2018.
Mazierska, Ewa. 2002. The Exclusive Pleasures of Being a Second Generation Inteligent: Representation of Social Class in the Films of Andrzej Wajda. *Canadian Slavonic Papers* 3/4: 233–249.
Mazierska, Ewa. 2007. *Polish Postcommunist Cinema: From Pavement Level*. Bern: Peter Lang.
Morstin, Agnieszka. 2018. 'Kieślowski versus Pawlikowski. Podwójne życie Weroniki i Zimna wojna jako opowieści o świecie dwudzielnym. *Kwartalnik Filmowy* 103: 79–90.
Orliński, Wojciech. 2004. Śmierć disco polo. *Gazeta Wyborcza*, August 12, p. 10.
Pietrasik, Zdzisław. 1998. Majteczki w kropeczki. *Polityka* 56: 38.
Pietrasik, Zdzisław. 2015. Disco Texas. Polityka, February 24. https://www.polityka.pl/tygodnikpolityka/kultura/film/1610021,1,recenzja-filmu-disco-polo-rez-maciej-bochniak.read. Accessed 10 February 2019.

Pietrzyk, Marcin. 2016. Zakładniczki pomysłu. Filmweb, May 9. https://www.fil mweb.pl/review/Zak%C5%82adniczki+pomys%C5%82u-18661. Accessed 15 February 2019.

Powrie, Phil. 2017. *Music in Contemporary French Cinema: The Crystal Song*. London: Palgrave.

Raczek, Tomasz. 2015. Moja recenzja: *Disco Polo*. *Tomasz Raczek blog*, March 9. http://tomaszraczek.pl/blog/id,1778/Moja-recenzja-Disco-Polo. html. Accessed 24 February 2019.

Sobolewski, Tadeusz. 1996. Pusta plaża. *Tygodnik Powszechny* 31: pp. 1 and 5.

Stam, Robert. 2000. Beyond Fidelity: The Dialogics of Adaptation. In *Film Adaptation*, ed. James Naremore, 54–76. London: The Athlone Press.

Świąder, Jacek. 2015. Polskie gówno. Gdy Skandal pieści Szoł-Biza. *Gazeta Wyborcza*, February 6. http://wyborcza.pl/piatekekstra/1,129155,173657 39,_Polskie_gowno___Gdy_Skandal_piesci_Szol_Biza__RECENZJA_.html. Accessed 24 February 2019.

Władyka, Władysław. 2009. Śmierć ideologii (lata 1957–1966). In *Lekcje historii PRL w rozmowach*, ed. Andrzej Brzeziecki, 106–131. Warszawa: W.A.B.

Wróblewska, Anna. 2018. 2017 w kinach: dane i podsumowanie. Pisf.Org.pl, January 28. https://www.sfp.org.pl/wydarzenia,5,26530,1,1,2017-w-kinach-dane-i-podsumowanie.html. Accessed 20 June 2019.

Żurawiecki, Bartosz. 1998. Gęba z disco polo. *Tygodnik Powszechny* 22: 19–20.

Zwoliński, Paweł. 2019. Sukces frekwencyjny Disko Polo. SFP.pl, March 4. https://www.sfp.org.pl/box_office?b=187. Accessed 14 March 2019.

PART II

Biopics on Large and Small Screen

CHAPTER 5

From Socio to Psycho-Biographies: Biographical Films About Popular Musicians

Biographical film or biopic is a fairly well-researched topic in the English literature, but the bulk of existing studies focus on Hollywood films (Custen 1992; France and St. Clair 2004; Tibbets 2005; Bingham 2010). Even those publications which try to move away from equating biopic with Hollywood, omit films from Eastern Europe (Brown and Vidal 2014). At the same time, this subject has attracted little attention from researchers of Eastern European and specifically Polish cinema, with only one edited collection published since the fall of the Berlin Wall (Szczepański and Kołos 2007). This neglect can be explained more by the low reputation of biopic among Eastern European film historians than by a lack of suitable material. For example, the Wikipedia category 'Polish biographical films' lists almost one hundred films, certainly enough to merit a monograph devoted to this topic. However, as I argued earlier, Polish film critics and historians were reluctant to engage with the history of genre films, especially those produced in their own country.

Biopic has also traditionally had a low status in western film criticism. According to Steve Neale, it 'lacks critical rather than industrial esteem' (Neale 2000: 60). In the words of Dennis Bingham, it is 'a respectable genre of very low repute' (Bingham 2010: 3). The bulk of criticism concerns its alleged predictability and the lack of wit of biopics. However, the recent successes of Anglo-American and European biopics about popular musicians from the last decade and a half, including *Walk the Line* (2005), directed by James Mangold, *La Vie en Rose* (2007), directed

© The Author(s) 2020
E. Mazierska, *Polish Popular Music on Screen*,
https://doi.org/10.1007/978-3-030-42779-5_5

by Olivier Dahan, *Nowhere Boy* (2009), directed by Sam Taylor-Wood, *Dalida* (2016), directed by Lisa Azuelos and *Bohemian Rhapsody* (2018), directed by Bryan Singer, are changing the reputation of biopics by showing that they can be both spectacular and convincing as melodramas.

My task here is to examine Polish biopics about popular musicians, produced after the Second World War, in the context of the dominant ways Western and Eastern European filmmakers depicted famous people.

WESTERN AND EASTERN EUROPEAN BIOPICS

According to George Custen, 'a biographical film is one that depicts the life of a historical person, past or present' (Custen 1992: 5). Belén Vidal develops this concept, writing:

> The term 'biopic' is used to refer to a fiction film that deals with a figure whose existence is documented in history, and whose claims to fame or notoriety warrant the uniqueness of his or her story. Like other sub genres within the historical film, the biopic is underpinned by reenactment or, as Robert Burgoyne puts it, 'the act of imaginative recreation that allows the spectator to imagine they are "witnessing again" the events of the past.' Regardless of the audience's degree of prior knowledge about the subject portrayed, it is the fundamental link to historical fact that seals the generic contract between producers and audiences of biographical film fictions, with the attendant pleasures of recognition. (Vidal 2014: 3)

Ian Inglis offers a similar definition, yet narrowed down to one category of represented historical figures: musicians, writing that it is a 'film which purports to tell, in part or in full, the biography of a musical performer (living or dead) and which contains a significant amount of his or her music' (Inglis 2007: 77).

Roy Shuker adds that biopic is a 'biography presented as a film or television feature, but differing from a documentary in that it is aimed at a popular audience and will balance reliability and accuracy against other considerations and the need to entertain' (Shuker 2016: 148).

These definitions suggest that at the 'heart' of every biopic is a pact between the filmmakers and viewers that the film presents a real person. The authors (principally the scriptwriter and director) are permitted to take certain liberties and diverge from the historical truth for a greater dramatic effect or to condense the story, but they should not undermine the overall impression that actor A plays the real person B. Biopics are also expected to reveal something important about the historical figure. Hence, for Custen, hiding the fact that the film is about a historical person precludes classifying a given film as a biopic. 'In biopics', he writes, 'real names are used... [This suggests] an openness to historical scrutiny and an attempt to present the film as the official story of a life' (Custen 1992: 8).

Polish critic and historian, Bolesław Michałek, in a short but perceptive article mentions three types of conflicts in which the protagonists of biopics are engaged: between their personal happiness and their call or mission, between their call and external world and between the character and nature. Michałek mentions that the second type of conflict is typical for artists, who are ahead of their times (Michałek 1976: 18–23).

Authors considering western and especially Hollywood biopics draw attention to the fact that they emphasise exceptional qualities of their protagonists, as well as their conflict with the external world and misfortune, as opposed to the historical circumstances under which they developed their art (Pollock 1980; Custen 1992; Tibbets 2005; Vidal 2014). This is also an observation made by Michałek, based on watching western films, chiefly American, German, Austrian and French (Michałek 1976: 18–19). Griselda Pollock summarises this approach as 'psycho-biography' and mentions films about Vincent van Gogh as their model (Pollock 1980). Ken Russell's films about classical composers also perfectly fit this trend (Tibbets 2005: 155–216). Pollock is critical of psycho-biographies and advocates a greater emphasis on the social, economic and political context in which the artist operates, what can be regarded as a call to produce socio-biographies. George Custen notices a gap between an emphasis on the uniqueness of a great man or woman and the standardised form of films about these unique people: the irony of a 'mass-tailored contour for fame in which greatness is generic and difference has controllable boundaries' (Custen 1992: 25–26), a gap which presumably can be filled by changing the balance between psycho- and socio-biography.

Hollywood biopics are also marked by teleology. 'Through a necessarily selective account of a life, often constructed at the end point through the framing structure of the flashback, linearity and factuality led to a "natural" collapse of the future into the past' (Vidal 2014: 5).

Psycho-biography and teleology dominate in western films about popular musicians and especially rock stars. Lee Marshall and Isabel Kongsaard argue that:

rather than being seen as mere entertainers, or as one of a collective, rock stars became understood as highly individualised, self-expressive artists. A particular kind of rock-star persona began to emerge that reflected many of the characteristics of nineteenth-century bohemians: defying conventions, excessively engaging with sex and drugs to open the 'doors of perception', demonstrating an unusual sensitivity and fragility, disdainful of those who 'sell out', and so on. This bohemian stereotype has been a staple of popular music stardom ever since, right up to contemporary artists such as Amy Winehouse. (Marshall and Kongsgaard 2012: 348)

Moreover, musicians are typically presented as being 'cursed' from an early age, both by their talent and family problems, especially difficult relations with their parents. In the case of Hollywood biopics, this can be linked to the influence of psychoanalysis on the country's popular culture. Inevitably, this approach also affects the choice of stars portrayed. Similarly as in films about painters, where the unhappy and misunderstood van Gogh is a model, films about musicians are more likely to be about Mozart, Chopin, John Lennon, Freddie Mercury and Amy Winehouse than Johann Sebastian Bach or Paul McCartney.

However, if we consider the representation of artists in films made under the conditions of state socialism, we observe a different approach, as if the filmmakers responded to Pollock's call to move away from psycho-biography into the realm of socio-biography. In Eastern European socio-biographical films artists are not severed from history but fully integrated into it. This is especially the case in films made during the hegemony of socialist realism, when filmmakers were required to focus on a typical (wo)man. Yet, 'typical' in this context does not mean 'average', as put by Georgii Malenkov:

> The typical is not that which is encountered most often, but that which most persuasively expresses the essence of a given social force. From the Marxist-Leninist standpoint, the typical does not signify some sort of statistical mean… The typical is the vital sphere in which is manifested the party spirit of realistic art. The question of the typical is always a political question. (quoted in Groys 1992: 51–52)

In practice, the typical character of socialist realist art was expected to be above average and synthesise the most salient aspects of his/her times, like a perfect prism, refracting the significant features of the current political and social situation.

S/he was also meant to show others a new direction either through military struggle or work, undertaken for the benefit of the collective. Such views were presented in the seminal book about biography in the Soviet Union, Rostislav Yureniev's *Soviet Biographical Film*, published in 1949. Its author suggested that the protagonist of a biopic should be a great man and progressive activist, whose achievements the audience would like to imitate. Furthermore, the screen biography should foreground the historical meaning of the work and life of the famous individual, and therefore its author should concentrate on their social dimension, at the expense of depicting his/her private life (quoted in Toeplitz 1952: 118). If we want to summarise the main difference between psycho-biography and socialist realist socio-biography, then we can say that in the former paradigm the heroes create history, while in the latter history creates the heroes. The focus on the typical and grand narrative also means that socialist realist socio-biographies were dismissive about details. Excessive preoccupation with factual detail led to the criticism of naturalism, which could be understood precisely as focusing on details at the expense of seeing a larger picture, what Polish communist official and writer, Włodzimierz Sokorski, described as a 'soulless photograph of reality' (quoted in Tompkins 2013: 78).

Although socialist realism was promoted, even enforced in all European countries which adopted state socialism, this ideology was coloured by or blended with some local specificities. In Poland it was (Polish) Romanticism. This artistic current, arguably the most important paradigm in Polish culture, was born at the end of the eighteenth century, when Poland ceased to exist as an independent state, being partitioned between its mightier neighbours: Russia, Prussia and the Habsburg Empire. During this period artists were endowed with a mission to preserve Polish language, culture and national identity and encouraged their countrymen to fight by military and peaceful means to regain their statehood. A Polish Romantic artist (in contrast to most of his foreign counterparts) was less concerned with self-expression and more with giving a voice to the community and engendering recipients of his work with a sense of responsibility for their homeland. This also affected the understanding of an artist's 'authenticity'—it was measured less by his or her resistance towards the commercial culture industry, and more by his or her opposition towards oppressive political authorities. The socialist realist and Polish Romantic approaches to artists have much in common, as both prioritise artists' service to the community. The difference is that in the

Romantic discourse the privileged community is that of the nation, in socialist realism it is the proletariat.

A seminal example of a Polish biopic which followed the precepts of socialist realism, while also trying to incorporate Romantic ideas was *Młodość Chopina* (*The Youth of Chopin*, 1952) by Aleksander Ford, the most prestigious film about a musician made in Poland during the state socialist period. Ford depicts Chopin as a young revolutionary, who fights against the Tsarist rule, which is both colonial and class oppression, and revolutionises music (Mazierska 2004: 257–261).

Other Polish and Eastern European biopics of musicians, made in the 1950s, when socialist realism had a hegemonic position, followed a similar formula, for example *Warszawska premiera* (*Warsaw's Premiere*, 1950), directed by Jan Rybkowski, about Stanisław Moniuszko, arguably the second greatest Polish composer of the pre-modern epoch, after Chopin. These films, although we would not regard them as films about popular musicians, because the music of Chopin and Moniuszko is now seen as classical or even elitist, present their characters as creating popular music both in the sense of being listened to and loved by the masses of people and being able to capture the essence of the nation in their music.

Western biopics try to convince viewers that they present the real life of artists. Marshall and Kongsgaard draw attention to various techniques, which are meant to produce the effect of verisimilitude, such as voiceovers or involving the artists themselves, their families or close collaborators in their production (Marshall and Kongsgaard 2012: 354–355). In Poland such authenticating techniques were of less importance during the state socialist period because the truth was understood not as sticking to the facts, but as revealing a deeper meaning of the artist's place in the history of his community, which might require neglecting or circumventing historical accuracy.

While biopics flourished under socialist realism, both in terms of their quantity and the resources put into them, they declined in the subsequent period. In the second half of the 1950s, 1960s and the 1970s there are few biographical films and none of them is devoted to popular musicians. This might reflect the polarisation of Polish cinema between the auteurist films, epitomised by productions of the Polish School and the Cinema of the Moral Concern on one hand and the popular films on the other, most importantly comedies and crime films, as mentioned in the previous chapters. Biopics, being somewhat 'serious' and 'educational', hence seen as tedious and pedestrian (Bingham 2010: 11), did not come across as pure entertainment and, at the same time, did not fit comfortably with the idea of authorship, according to which the director ultimately expresses him/herself in the film rather than drawing on the life of somebody more important or famous.

This situation started to change in the 1980s, when two, albeit atypical, biopics of popular musicians were produced. This small wave can be attributed to two factors. One of them was the flourishing of Polish rock. Another reason was the pressure to produce popular cinema which, unlike in the previous decade, couldn't be ignored any longer by the filmmaking community due to the crisis of finances, both factors mentioned by me when discussing musicals.

The fall of state socialism and subsequent changes in the organisation of the Polish film industry, most importantly the privatisation of film studios (even though most of them retained state subsidy), forced filmmakers to be more receptive to the viewers' demands than in the period of state socialism. This meant turning to genre cinema, as previously discussed, but also drawing on the interest of potential viewers in the history of certain public personas, especially those whose life was eventful and tragic. However, as is always the case with cinema, it did not react immediately to this demand, but with a significant delay, usually caused by a need to secure financial back-up for a given project. Moreover, only when certain biopics proved successful, did more filmmakers decide to try their hand in them, following the rule that success breeds success (a rule which summarises the history of genre cinema). The 2010s can be described as a decade of biopics, with twenty or so Polish films fitting this category (Staszczyszyn 2017), some of them, such as *Bogowie* (*Gods*, 2014), directed by Łukasz Palkowski and *Ostatnia rodzina* (*The Last Family*, 2016), directed by Jan P. Matuszyński, receiving the highest accolades awarded to Polish films, such as Golden Lions at the Festival of Polish Films in Gdynia. Only a small proportion of them concern popular musicians. Nevertheless, they can be regarded as the fruit of the Polish industry's recognition that biopics can be both lively and complex.

BIOPICS IN QUOTATION MARKS

The 1980s saw the production of two biopics, *Miłość ci wszystko wybaczy* (*Love Can Take Everything*, 1981), directed by Janusz Rzeszewski, about a prewar singer and actress Hanka Ordonówna and *Czuję się świetnie* (*I Feel Great*, 1984), directed by Waldemar Szarek about the band Maanam.

I label them biopics in quotation marks, because, rather than wearing their biographism on their sleeves by using authentication techniques, they apply what can be described as 'de-authentication techniques' which are meant to seed doubt in the viewer whether s/he is watching a biopic. Refraining from biopic conventions has reasons specific to each film, but also one, which is more general—a lack of a relevant Polish tradition, on which the filmmakers could draw, combined with the assumption that one could not measure up to biopics produced in Hollywood. Hence the question why these two directors decided to make biopics after all, even if only half-heartedly.

In the case of *Love Can Take Everything* the likely reason was the success of Rzeszewski's *Fred the Beard* and the pressure to make another film along the same lines, set in prewar Poland and presenting show business of this period, from front and backstage. The life of the interwar singer and actress Hanka Ordonówna lent itself to such treatment, given that she, like an eponymous chorus girl, came from the bottom and climbed to the top, becoming the greatest Polish singing star of the interbellum. However, Ordonówna's surname is not mentioned in the film, the character is referred to only as 'Hanka' and the film begins with the standard warning that any similarity to the real people is accidental, while at the same time admitting that the film is about a 'woman who became famous'.

The reason not to reveal the true identity of the protagonist was, according to Rzeszewski, a need to avoid any accusation of not adhering closely enough to a specific version of her life, a risk often taken when presenting the life of somebody who died relatively recently and might have relatives objecting to a specific representation of the person. This idea was in fact not Rzeszewski's, but that of the scriptwriter, Krzysztof Teodor Toeplitz, journalist and co-author of the script of a popular television series *Czterdziestolatek* (*Forty Years-Old*, 1974–77) (Rzeszewski, quoted in Zarębski 1981: 7). It appears that the strategy of the film's creators was to enjoy all the advantages of making a biopic without suffering from any accompanying obligations.

Before moving to the film, some information about its main character. Ordonówna was born in 1902 in Warsaw as Maria Anna Pietruszyńska. She came from a working-class family and started her career as a cabaret singer in Warsaw theatres at the age of sixteen. She continued in Lublin, where she adopted the pseudonym Hanka Ordonówna, often shortened to Ordonka, before returning to Warsaw where she continued working in revues and cabaret. Ordonka was noticed by Fryderyk Jarosy (Fryderyk Járosy), a well-known presenter of Hungarian Jewish origin and artistic director of the most famous Warsaw cabaret Qui Pro Quo. Under his tutelage she became a star and recorded her greatest hits, such as 'Miłość ci wszystko wybaczy' (Love Can Take Everything), used in the film *Spy* (1933), discussed in Chapter 2, which also provided the title of Rzeszewski's film. In 1931 Ordonówna married the Polish aristocrat, Count Michał Tyszkiewicz, who worked in the Ministry of Foreign Affairs and wrote songs in his spare time, many of which the singer included in her repertoire. The marriage did not prevent her from having affairs, including with a fellow actor Juliusz Osterwa. Ordonówna was arrested during the Second World War and after spending a short time in the Pawiak prison in Warsaw, was moved east, first to Vilnius and then deeper into the Soviet Union, to Uzbekistan and Tashkent, and then to India. On the way she started to look after the orphaned children of Polish exiles. She ended up in Beirut, where she died of tuberculosis in 1950.

As this description demonstrates, although Ordonówna's life was not particularly long, it was very dramatic: perfect material for a film. Moreover, it was strongly intertwined with Polish history. The beginning of her career coincided with Poland's regaining independence after 120 years of partitions. Her pseudonym was taken from the poem 'Reduta Ordona', written by the Polish Romantic poet, Adam Mickiewicz, about the defence of Warsaw against Russian forces during the November Uprising of 1931. In the twenty years between the two world wars she benefitted from the rise of patriotic feelings and cosmopolitanism of Polish culture, not in a small measure resulting from close contact with the countries which previously ruled over the Polish territory, such as Austria and Germany, performing there on numerous occasions, as well as travelling to Jerusalem and the United States. During the Second World War she was a victim of Poland's being invaded from both sides, west and east, first being imprisoned by the Germans and then the Russians.

Rzeszewski deals with all these aspects of Ordonówna's life, but in an uneven and somewhat sketchy way. This can be explained in part by the parameters of the cine-film, which risks to explode under the weight of a life so rich in events, therefore it requires its makers to edit the life, risking major gaps. Another reason for this sketchiness was self-censorship, in anticipation of problems which might arise if, as in this case, Russia would be presented as Poland's enemy rather than its friend. I will also suggest that a deeper problem might be the lack of a clear vision for *Love Can Take Everything* in terms of deciding which of the three types of conflict, listed by Michałek, was most important in her life and choosing between socio- and psycho-biography. The Polish social realist tradition, still lingering on at the time the film was made, encouraged to make a socio-biography and ultimately it prevails in the film. However, Rzeszewski's own instinct, as revealed in his musicals, pushed him towards psycho-biography.

The film is framed as Hanka's flashback, in which she looks back at her career, living in a camp somewhere in a desert, probably in Libya, during the Second World War. This is a common structure in biopics, as Vidal observes, giving the impression of inevitability of events presented on-screen (Vidal 2014: 5); such structure was used recently, for example, in Piaf's biopic, *La Vie en Rose*. In this case using a flashback also allows the filmmakers to occlude the thorny issue of explaining how Ordonówna ended up in the desert, suggesting that in a teleological scenario, it was simply her 'fate'.

The proper narrative starts with Hanka visiting her dying mother, when the future star is more preoccupied with the political situation than the state of her mother's health. She ecstatically tells her friend Aniela, whom she meets at her mother's deathbed that from now on there will be a free Poland in which she won't suffer poverty. This prediction is somewhat false, given that Poland between the two world wars turned out to be one of the poorest countries in Europe. But Hanka is right that in this Poland she would do very well. How she achieved stardom, we do not really learn from the film, as professional success, similarly to love, comes to Rzeszewski's heroine easily. Love or at least sex helps Hanka in her career. This aspect of Hanka's portrayal was criticised by some reviewers, who pointed to the fact that Ordonówna largely created herself, by writing some of her most popular songs and designing her own clothes, facts omitted from the film (Bobecka 1982: 17).

Of the men with whom Hanka was erotically involved, three: Igo, Fryderyk and Miś, are most important. Like Hanka, they have no surnames in the film, but it is not difficult to identify them as Igo Sym, Fryderyk Jarosy and Michał Tyszkiewicz. Each of them has a specific value for Hanka—Igo is her early-stage partner; Fryderyk is her mentor in the Qui Pro Quo theatre; Miś, who is an object of her mature love and an aristocrat, lifts Hanka to the level of nobility. These three men also stand for different visions of Poland. Igo, who has an Austrian mother, is uncomfortable when witnessing expressions of Polish patriotism. He prefers to talk about Europe and Poland being part of Europe as it was during partitions. Fryderyk, a Jew born in Hungary, admits that he is not a 'true' Pole, but embraces Polish language and culture, in a way often attributed to the supposedly chameleonic Jews. Finally, Miś represents Poland of patriotic nobility.

The three visions of Poland come into sharp relief during the war. At that time Igo becomes a Nazi collaborator and is executed by the Polish resistance. Fryderyk is forced to wear a star of David, which symbolises the failure of his efforts to assimilate into Polish and western culture. Miś joins the Polish army and in the last scene of the film is reunited with Hanka. Not only do these three men meet a very different fate during the war, but the war also makes Hanka lose her flamboyance and promiscuity and choose the pure-blooded Pole, because maintaining a relationship with the semi-Poles are no longer an option.

Rzeszewski shows that Hanka's performance attracts all types of audiences, but does not delve into its character or how it was created. In reality, Ordonówna collaborated with some of the best poets and lyricists of this period, some of them Jewish, such as Julian Tuwim and Emanuel Schlechter. The issue of the contribution of Jewish artists to Polish popular culture of this period is occluded till it is revealed that Jarosy is a Jew. Jews, however, as in the remaining films of Rzeszewski, provide a focus of jokes, most importantly a sketch, highlighting Jewish excessive preoccupation with money. Such jokes, as I mentioned earlier, when analysing Rzeszewski's musicals, remained a staple diet of Polish postwar cabarets and Jan Kobuszewski made a career largely by performing in them. Thus, while condemning the 'hard anti-Semitism' of the Nazis, *Love Can Take Everything* makes capital on the 'soft anti-Semitism' of Poles.

As reviews of the film noticed, there is a certain mismatch between 'the real' Ordonówna and Hanka in Rzeszewski's film. Ordonówna's singing and acting was marked by restraint, ambiguity and a certain melancholia, best conveyed by her performance of 'Love Can Take Everything'. For this reason she could pass as an upper-class woman, despite her humble background. In the film Hanka is played by Dorota Stalińska, who in her heyday resembled Anna Magnani due to her physique (except that she had blonde hair), hoarse voice and expressive acting (Fig. 5.1).

She presented these qualities in Barbara Sass' *Bez miłości* (*Without Love*, 1980), where she played an ambitious and ruthless female journalist Ewa. Stalińska's Ordonka is also ambitious and, if not ruthless, then at

Fig. 5.1 Dorota Stalińska as Hanka Ordonówna with her penchant to luxurious clothes in *Miłość ci wszystko wybaczy* (*Love Can Take Everything*, 1981), directed by Janusz Rzeszewski

least self-centred, although she did not betray her friends or family. She is also shown as indulging in luxury, which perhaps, against the director's intention, renders her as a provincial nouveau riche, rather than a lady. This is reflected most conspicuously in her fashion choices and taste for food. During her trip to Switzerland she is shown in three different fur coats in the space of a couple of minutes and in a restaurant she orders lobster in mayonnaise, a dish which could hardly be spotted in Poland. There is no lyricism, melancholia or ambiguity in Hanka. For this reason, the least convincing is the part when she is shown looking after orphaned children, as it feels like Hanks is not really interested in them. Also, given that Stalińska looks very healthy and athletic, it is difficult to believe that her character suffers from tuberculosis.

In the singing parts Stalińska lip-synchs songs recorded by Hanna Banaszak, a singer with a very feminine, jazzy, melancholic voice. As one reviewer observed, in such scenes it is better to close one's eyes and just listen to the songs (Janicka 1982: 16). Consequently, despite including many true episodes, Ordonówka from Rzeszewski's film remains a palimpsest, on which three different women left a mark: the historical Ordonka, Stalińska and Banaszak. It is worth mentioning that Stalińska was not Rzeszewski's first choice for the role of Hanka; he wanted to cast in it Krystyna Janda, probably the greatest Polish star of the 1980s, to whom Stalińska was often compared. However, most likely if Janda played Hanka, the same problems would appear or even be exacerbated, as melancholy and ambiguity were not Janda's specialism either.

While Rzeszewski's decision to make a biopic was prompted by his experience in making musicals, in the case of Waldemar Szarek, the director of *I Feel Great*, the crucial factor was working in an institution which encouraged experimentation. This institution was the Karol Irzykowski Film Studio, which was set up in 1981 to allow recent graduates from the Łódź and Katowice Film Schools to make experimental films. This was seen as an alternative to the bulk of Polish cinema of this period which took a turn towards more commercial production. Then Szarek was a recent graduate who subsequently became a prolific, yet unremarkable director, oscillating between different genres. Another unique selling point of the Irzykowski Studio was youth—it was dominated by the then young filmmakers and was meant to make films for the young audience. What could be a better subject to fulfil this requirement than making a film about a popular rock band? However, most likely Szarek was encouraged to make a film which would be out of the box, hence not a biopic, but a 'biopic'.

Maanam, the band at the centre of the story, was one of the most popular Polish rock bands of the 1980s. It occupied this position along with Perfect, Republika and Lady Pank. However, unlike these other three bands, which had all-male line-up, Maanam had a charismatic female lead singer, Kora (1951–2018). A testimony to Maanam's renown is the attention devoted to them by other filmmakers. They took part in several fiction and documentary films and their music was used in the soundtracks of more than ten films, such as *Sezon na bażanty* (*Pheasent-shooting Season*, 1986), directed by Wiesław Saniewski and *Bohater roku* (*Hero of the Year*, 1987), directed by Feliks Falk, as well as *Wielka majówka* (*The Big Picnic*, 1981), discussed in Chapter 3.

The band was set up in 1976 as Maanam Elektryczny Prysznic (Maanam Electric Shower) by Marek Jackowski and a Greek musician settled in Poland, Milo Kurtis. Both had significant experience as backing instrumentalists in other bands. Soon Kurtis left to set up his own band

and Maanam was joined by Englishman John Porter. In 1979 Porter left and in the same year Jackowski's wife, Olga, under the pseudonym Kora, started to perform in Maanam as a singer, which ensured its breakthrough. Their appearance at the festival of Polish Songs in Opole in 1980, where they performed 'Boskie Buenos' (Divine Buenos), was a great success. It brought dynamism to Polish rock, which to this point had felt timid and conservative. The Jackowskis became the main authors of Maanam's songs: Marek composed music, Kora wrote lyrics. Maanam's musical style can broadly be defined as punk and it was also a style with which Kora identified herself, due to forming a close relationship with the audience and promoting an alternative lifestyle (Butrym 1985: 56–57). However, this closeness took place only during their concerts. In their private lives the Jackowskis cultivated a certain mystique, particularly around its singer. The fans felt close to Kora not because she was like them, but rather because she projected their dreams, like a diva rather than a typical punk star. The band was most successful in the first half of the 1980s, which is also regarded as the golden age of Polish rock. Back then almost every song written by the Jackowskis became a hit and their records sold hundreds of thousands of copies. The band was also constantly touring, giving as many as 300–400 concerts per year. In the mid-1980s, when at the peak of its popularity, it disbanded. This was caused by alcoholism of its members, and the breakdown of the Jackowskis' marriage in 1985. Subsequently Maanam reassembled and then broke up again and in the meantime its lead members, Kora and Marek Jackowski, pursued different projects, although with less success than they enjoyed as Maanam.

As I mentioned earlier, biopics are fiction films. The clearest sign of their fictionality is casting actors in the roles of characters. Usually this is a historical necessity—the bulk of biopics are made about deceased figures. However, even if they are still alive, actors are used to impersonate them, simply because they act better than non-actors. This is, however, not the case with *I Feel Great* where Maanam is cast in the role of Maanam, which suggests that Szarek's film is a documentary. However, the director included material which is clearly fictional, so disqualifies it as a documentary. But neither does it come across as a mockumentary. Rather it remains suspended between different genres. If we use the effect of verisimilitude as a criterion of categorising the material used in a biopic then we can divide *I Feel Great* into three parts.

One consists of fragments of Maanam's concerts; which look like a straightforward documentary. The film begins with the image of a crowd of young people smashing a gate, most likely to go to Maanam's concert, despite the police trying to prevent them. This impression is confirmed by an image of the feet of a drummer, probably Paweł Markowski, playing the beginning of one of the band's songs. Such an image captures two important aspects of Poland in the first half of the 1980s: the great popularity of rock, as demonstrated by the proliferation of large rock festivals and the omnipresence and impotence of the police. Here policemen not only ensure that order is maintained during the events, but also stand for the 'police state', as Poland was regarded during this period. We also overhear a conversation between the fans, in which one young man asks another, tackled by the police, how he feels and gets the answer 'I feel great'. This response provides the title of the film. The other source of the film's title is Maanam's song, 'Stoję, stoję, czuję się świetnie' (I Stand Up, I Stand Up, I Feel Great). Having the same words uttered both by the band and the fans creates a connection between musicians and audience. At the same time, these words are imbued with irony, given that the first half of the 1980s was marred by food rationing, long queues for basic commodities and political turmoil. But such a 'political rollercoaster' has always been favoured by punk. The remaining scenes from the concerts are made to the formula of a 'rock film', of which *Woodstock* (1970), directed by Michael Wadleigh, is an early example, and which was recently used in *Bohemian Rhapsody*. The camera oscillates between the performance of the band, shown in close-up and the audience, behaving in an unruly way, overcoming the barriers separating them from the stage.

In the documentary category I will also include the early shots when we hear voices off-screen reading fragments of Maanam's fans letters, first against images of the skyline of an indistinct city, dominated by skyscrapers. Then the camera visits some hotel rooms with sleeping people, finishing with Kora and her husband Marek in bed. Voiceover and quotations from letters are one of the devices which give the impression of verisimilitude (Marshall and Kongsgaard 2012: 354–355) in this case read by members of the band. The fans reveal their love of the band and Kora especially, based on the perceived difference between the lives of these young people and that, which in their imagination, Kora leads. Their lives are provincial, monotonous and empty, Kora's life is metropolitan and full of adventure. Listening to Maanam's music allows their fans to transcend their situation and feel as if they are in a different place, not unlike in

The Big Picnic, discussed in Chapter 3, where the music of Maanam also signified adventure and utopia.

The second type of material shows Maanam in private or semi-private situations. The first episode belonging to this category presents Kora with another member of Maanam in a funfair, on a rollercoaster. The metaphorical meaning of this image is easy to decipher: the band lives a fast, exciting and possibly dangerous life. We also see the Jackowskis talking directly to camera about their lives, giving a press conference and travelling in a bus on their concert tour. We expect that these episodes will also show the truth, but they were staged and the members of the band and Kora especially, played to the camera. We get a sense that Maanam lead a fast, but not necessarily a colourful or affluent life. For example, during a press conference, when asked about Maanam's foreign trips to cities such as West Berlin and Copenhagen, Kora admits that she had no time to see them or buy presents for her children because her time was taken up by work. We also see the band crossing a provincial rather than metropolitan Poland. The hotels where the musicians stay are shabby and they travel in a hired bus, which is spacious and quite comfortable, but also brings to mind the way the majority of Poles travelled in the 1980s. There are no images of Maanam on the planes or performing abroad. Such a depiction of 'working musicians' is common in biopics as they often point to the contrast between their on-stage appearance and the less glamorous reality of their life offstage.

In Poland of the first half of the 1980s this motif had an additional context, resulting from the special position of rock in this period, the widespread rejection of the ideological tenets of state socialism and the early neoliberalisation of the Polish economy. All these factors led to an opinion, expressed by rock stars and their fans, that they get less than they deserve. Maanam was no different from this perspective. The juxtaposition of the shabby hotels and thousands of young people attending their concerts could thus be interpreted as a way to expose the injustice of the state socialist culture industry and economy.

Some reviewers argued that Szarek tried to expose Maanam's banality and pomposity, as when we hear Kora saying that she had an unhappy childhood and turned to books to isolate herself from her environment or that their music gives meaning to the lives of their fans (Klimczak 1985). Another possible means to undermine Maanam's intellectualism was including Kora's lyrics, read by her off-screen. Inevitably, devoid of music, they lose much of their poetry and sound fake. If it was indeed

Szarek's intention to prove that rock stars do not deserve their fans' devotion, he followed in the footsteps of probably the most famous Polish film about a rock star prior to *I Feel Great*, *Sukces* (*Success*, 1968) by Marek Piwowski, about Czesław Niemen (which I will discuss in Chapter 7). However, while Piwowski succeeded in undermining Niemen's pretensions to greatness, Szarek failed. This happened either because, unlike Piwowski, Szarek was unable to capture on camera effectively any embarrassing moments, being outsmarted by the Jackowskis, who came across as more natural and modest than Niemen in Piwowski's documentary. Another possible explanation is that, as one reviewer suggested, Szarek tried to appeal to two types of audiences: Maanam's fans and those allegedly more mature and sophisticated viewers who looked with a caustic eye at the Polish rock phenomenon (Pawlicki 1985). It is also possible that he was unsure whether he wanted to offer a eulogy or a satire on Maanam or changed his mind in the course of assembling the material.

The third type of material used in *I Feel Great* is clearly fictional. One example is the extended episode of a ceremony of naming a school after Kora and a Polish literature lesson when teenagers are asked to analyse the lyrics of *I Feel Great*. These episodes suggest a connection between Maanam and Polish Romantic poets as they, most importantly Adam Mickiewicz and Juliusz Słowacki, used to be the most frequent patrons of Polish schools. Moreover, in one part of the lesson the teacher claims that Kora, like these poets, puts herself above the crowd, being the one who is standing, while the crowd is lying down, lazy and passive. Such a comparison is far-fetched and most likely was meant to deride those who saw in the Polish rockers the descendants of Mickiewicz and Słowacki. However, if Szarek's intention was to mock Maanam, it backfired, because it is not the members of Maanam who attribute themselves the position of the 'new (Polish) Romantics', but the authorities who in the film try to integrate them into the Romantic discourse and most likely render Polish rock innocuous. It is possible that this part is a satire on the authorities who attempted to 'make peace' with the rebellious rockers. Again, the reviewers noticed that the result of these fragments were ambiguous and they did not work well, not being funny (Lenard 1985; M.D. 1985; Pawlicki 1985).

The fictional inserts suggest that Szarek attempted to make a mockumentary.[1] However, filmmakers using this genre tend to preserve a consistent tone in their films, which are fictional, but give the impression of being documentaries (Hight 2008). The purpose of making mockumentaries is to ridicule a specific person or social phenomenon and, as its name suggests, to mock-documentary (and documentarists) by demonstrating that the documentary effect is a matter of using specific conventions (such as voiceover or camerawork) rather than representing reality truthfully. By contrast, Szarek's film lacks a consistent tone, oscillating between a serious documentary, fake documentary and a fictional film and it is not obvious what Szarek intended to mock in his film: the band itself, the 'Maanam phenomenon', Polish rock culture or obsession with Romanticism. Whatever was the ultimate motive of shooting *I Feel Great* this way, Szarek's film testifies to the problem of trying to merge socio- with psycho-biography. It also reflects a somewhat schizophrenic attitude of the political authorities and the part of cultural elites towards rock music in the 1980s by, on the one hand, acknowledging the role it played in the lives of young people and willing to support it for the sake of educating and pacifying the youth, and, on the other hand, expressing frustration at its dislocating high art from its privileged position in the country's culture.

Destined for Blues or Condemned to Drugs?

Biopics started to be produced in large numbers in Poland after 2000, when Polish cinema stabilised after the transitional decade of the 1990s and when certain genres which dominated the previous decade, such as gangster cinema and historical epics, became exhausted, leaving space for other genres, most importantly those which do not try to create allegories, but focus on individual fate. In my earlier book I located the turn to biopics in the context of dislodging of grand by smaller narratives (Mazierska 2007: 117).

One such film is *Skazany na bluesa* (*Destined for Blues*, 2004), directed by Jan Kidawa-Błoński, who is also the co-author of the script. Kidawa-Błoński (b. 1953) has enjoyed a versatile, yet unremarkable career in film and television, directing historical films, soap operas and talking-heads type documentaries. *Destined for Blues* is his best-known film and one which is treated as his most personal project, due to the fact that he came from the Silesia region, in common with the protagonist of the film, Ryszard Riedel (1956–1994) and was related to him. The idea of making a film about Riedel, who was a singer and leader of the blues band Dżem, appeared soon after Riedel's death, but it took Kidawa-Błoński ten years to get funding for his project, adding to the perception that it was his personal endeavour for which he was prepared to fight tooth and nail.

Dżem was founded in 1974 as Jam and initially had no professional ambitions, playing for pleasure in one of the youth clubs in Tychy, a middle-size Silesian town. The original name well captures this attitude. It was the manager of this club, who Polonised the band's name, changing it into Dżem, which the band embraced (Majewski 1988: 18). In 1979 Dżem changed its line-up, taking a more professional turn. Consequently, it achieved an enthusiastic reception at the Jarocin Festival in 1980, the largest rock festival in Poland of state socialist period. The next year Dżem was an official star of this festival. National recognition led to the band getting professional managers, first Barbara Horodecka and from 1984 Marcin Jacobson, one of the most versatile and successful personalities on the Polish popular music scene. From that moment the band went from strength to strength, recording many hits and giving concerts practically continuously throughout the 1980s, in Poland and abroad, in countries such as Germany, Switzerland and Yugoslavia (ibid.: 19). The band was praised for its professionalism and authenticity (ibid.: 19). It did not follow fashions, but was rooted in the blues tradition, represented by bands such as the Allman Bros. and Derek and the Dominoes. There was also a sense that there was no difference between the band's leader, Ryszard Riedel's true self and his stage persona. His songs were about himself and he sang them with a strong voice, marked by melismatic techniques, which was frequently compared to the voice of Czesław Niemen. The only serious problems the band encountered were to do with Riedel's heroin addiction. With the passage of time, the drug incapacitated the singer, leading him to miss gigs and spending extended periods in rehabilitation clinics. This affliction eventually led to his death at the age of 37, ten years too late to be included in the famous 27 Club, but rather early as for the average lifespan of a Polish rocker.

The mixture of success and personal problems which Riedel was unable to overcome, which Michałek described as a conflict with one's nature, made the bluesman perfect material for a biopic. *Destined for Blues* lies firmly in the psycho-biography category and in a way which is typical of contemporary biopics, it links genius to pathology and abjection (Codell 2014). Its model is *The Doors* (1991) by Oliver Stone, which emphasises the importance of alcohol and drug abuse in Jim Morrison's life and the character of his artistic output. This similarity between *The Doors* and *Destined for Blues* is even suggested within diegesis, by presenting Riedel as somebody who feels a special affinity to Jim Morrison. This is not far from the truth, given that in Poland Riedel was labelled the 'last hippie'.

Conversely, the wider social and political landscape in which Riedel and Dżem operated is practically excluded from the picture. Kidawa-Błoński did so despite the fact that the peak of Dżem's popularity was in the 1980s, the time of the rise of Solidarity, martial law, when Polish rock became a powerful tool of articulating dissatisfaction with the political authorities. Despite focusing on 'Riedel as Riedel', the singer remains an enigma and his most important decisions go unexplained in the film. Moreover, the film is really about Riedel's life as a drug addict, rather than his life as an artist. It seems as if from twenty or so years which Riedel spent making music Kidawa-Błoński chose those periods when he was most at the mercy of addiction. One wonders when Riedel was able to compose, record and give concerts, if he was always barely conscious. Although concerts and recordings feature in the film, these are aborted recordings and concerts, as an intoxicated Riedel is unable to sing or falls sick in the middle of the performance, vomiting straight onto the prominent guests, who came to offer Dżem a lucrative record contract. I am unable to think of any western biopic in which the life of a musician is so devoid of artistic success as in *Destined for Blues*. In comparison with Kidawa-Błoński's film, even *The Doors* comes across as an optimistic movie. Moreover, although it is a known fact that Riedel tried to get help for his drug problem, in the film he is shown as being completely at the mercy of heroin. His only way of dealing with his drug problem is getting more of drugs. There is also practically no attempt on the part of his family or friends to help him to kick the habit. The only two moments when Riedel's wife Gola intervenes in his life as a junkie, can be described as negative. On one occasion, when he has no money to buy heroin and is humiliated by a drug dealer, who asks him to get on his knees and beg for a portion, she yells at the dealer to give Ryszard the coveted drug. On another occasion, when sitting next to her barely conscious husband, she attempts to inject herself with the drug, but is interrupted by some members of the band who arrive and force the singer to go with them to the recording studio (Fig. 5.2).

John C. Tibbots mentions two types of representations concerning musical geniuses: the 'possessor' and the 'possessed'. The first type is an active genius, epitomised by Beethoven: an active artist who breaks with conventions and moulds others into his image. The 'possessed' is a passive genius, who is detached from worldly affairs and lets the muse or the

Fig. 5.2 Riedel's wife Gola with her drugged husband in *Skazany na bluesa* (*Destined for Blues*, 2004), directed by Jan Kidawa-Błoński

God speak through himself. Mozart, as represented in Milos Forman's *Amadeus* (1984), best fits the 'possessed' type (Tibbetts 2005: 8–9). Notwithstanding the difference of talent and prestige between Mozart on the one hand and Riedel on the other, Riedel can be seen as an extreme case of a 'possessed' musician—an artist who seems to have no influence on his creative output, who does not need to work hard because nothing can stand in the way of his fate. Such a representation can be regarded as reflecting Polish Romantic culture, in which hard work was of little importance.

The role of other members of Dżem, as well as of the Polish music business, in making and breaking Riedel's career, is hidden. We do not learn what role fellow band members played in the creative process and how Dżem gained and maintained their popularity. Apart from an early episode showing a rehearsal of the then amateur Jam, it appears that it needed no effort to become one of the most popular bands of the 1980s and early 1990s. The Polish music business is reduced to a couple from a record company, who sit mute at the concert and look menacing as if they were enemies of the musicians. The time which otherwise could be devoted to the 'backstage', is filled with Riedel's hallucinations, mostly of white horses. Such visions can be regarded as a reference to Polish Romanticism and its reincarnation in Polish cinema (white horses are common in Andrzej Wajda's films), but mainly they point to Riedel's affinity to play an 'Indian', when he was a child and his inability to grow up. Although the director's likely intention in using such symbolism was to show Riedel as incorruptible, the result is banalisation of the star (Żurawiecki 2005: 18).

Destined for Blues proves how difficult it is to make psycho-biography in Poland, where the tradition of seeing the value of an artist in relation to the community looms large. Not surprisingly, the reviews from the film were critical and the film is now practically forgotten. Its only redeeming feature is Tomasz Kot playing the main character. The then young actor, in a manner reminiscent of such American stars as Robert DeNiro, prepared himself for the role of Riedel by immersing himself in 'Riedel's world' or what remained of it. For several weeks he lived in his room and listened to his records, travelled with Dżem and learnt about the work of Monar, an institution helping Polish drug addicts with which Riedel was in contact (Radecki 2017). Ultimately, Kot comes across as not only very similar to Riedel, but in fact more convincing than the real singer. This effect of upstaging the real artist is visible at the end of the film, when the director interweaves in the end titles documentary footage from Dżem's concerts. In years to come, Kot would become a major star of Polish cinema, playing, among other films, in *Cold War*, directed by Paweł Pawlikowski, discussed in the previous chapter. Another strong point of the film is the generous use of Dżem's music in the soundtrack. The well-chosen songs, such as 'Czerwony jak cegła' (Red Like a Brick), 'Złoty paw' (Golden Peacock) and 'Whisky', manage at least partially to solve Riedel's enigma, by describing his anguish and foretelling his downfall. Riedel on stage can be compared to a choir in an ancient play, except that on this occasion the choir and the protagonist are two incarnations of the same man.

A Synthesis of Psycho and Socio-Biography

Jesteś Bogiem (*You Are God*, 2012), directed by Leszek Dawid is a biopic about the hip hop band Paktofonika (often written PKF) from Silesia, charting its history from the beginning in 1998 till the death by suicide of its member and informal leader, Piotr 'Magik' (Magician) Łuszcz, in 2000, at the early age of 22. The fact that Paktofonika was regarded as a worthy subject of a fiction film testifies to the changing taste in popular music in Poland. By the time this biopic was made, rock in Poland had lost its dominant position as an expression of youth culture and hip hop took its place. This shift was by no means exclusive to Poland; in this respect Poland followed global trends. Paktofonika seems the right material for the biopic because of its immense popularity during its short existence and in subsequent years and the tragic fate of Magik. Its director, Leszek Dawid (b. 1971), was only a decade older than the characters in his film and not only remembered the events shown in his films, but participated in them.

You Are God also alludes to the changing relationship between the producers of music and their consumers. In *Destined for Blues* there was a huge gap between them, encapsulated by the band playing above the audience and not seeking any contact with their fans. *You Are God*, by contrast, shows musicians who not only perform mostly in small clubs, surrounded by fans their own age and dressed similarly to them, but they appear to be willing to reach them and invade their space. This is conveyed by musicians' gestures—hands moving towards the audience, as opposed to the aloof posture of the rocker, focused on his guitar or a fellow player. Also, it points to the end of the hegemony of Anglo-American music as the model for Polish musicians. Polish hip hop artists, as presented in Dawid's film, are less in awe of their foreign predecessors and, if they seek inspiration, it comes from Germany, rather than in the USA or UK.

Dawid presents Paktofonika's story against a rich backdrop of the early history of capitalism in Poland, following the fall of the Berlin Wall and shows how this history impacted on Paktofonika's music. This anchoring of an individual biography in the country's history was appreciated by critics, who compared Dawid's film to *Człowiek z marmuru* (*Man of Marble*, 1976) by Andrzej Wajda (Chaciński 2012; Jamrozik 2016: 215). The value of this compliment lies in the fact that *Man of Marble* is regarded as a perfect synthesis of psycho- and socio-biography. It focuses on the individual life of the titular character named Mateusz Birkut, who is fictitious, although inspired by the life of a real shock worker Bernard Bugdol, yet shows it in the context of Polish postwar history. Moreover, Wajda's film underscores the two-way relationship between individual life and the history of the country—the history affects an individual, but individuals shape history. Dawid seemed to have a similar ambition—to synthesise these two types of biography. This task was facilitated by the fact that hip hop music (more than rock and other types of popular music) is rooted in everyday reality.

You Are God begins with the setting up of the band. By this point, Magik already has some local credibility, being a frontman of the band Kaliber 44, while his future partners, Fokus and Rahim, only aspire to be hip hop musicians. They start to rehearse at their homes and play in the local clubs. Dawid shows remarkably well the effort put in by the musicians to achieve proficiency in rapping, a skill acquired after much practice. By this point he is the only Polish filmmaker who represents music as *labour*. As I mentioned earlier, he shows that these three young men are inspired by German rap and it is not so much the music itself which affects them as the fact that the German musicians rap in their own language, encouraging the trio to rap in Polish. Music for the three young men is both a form of self-expression and a means to escape from ordinary life. Their life is not so much marked by poverty, as by tedium, a lack of perspectives and the heavy weight of tradition. One of them is attending the technical college, where he learns throughout a whole semester how to make simple metal tools. Such education is in poignant contrast to the technical knowledge one needs to possess to produce one's own music and which the friends eventually master.

The intertwining of personal story and a wider history, as Żaneta Jamrozik observes, is conveyed through the three characters' interaction with space (Jamrozik 2016: 217–219). They are always on the move, walking through Katowice, the home town of two of them, once famous for being a mining town, which in the new millennium, following the closing down of mines, rebranded itself as a 'city of culture'. Often we see the characters walking through a high-rise estate, living monument of the state socialist era, where the majority of the city's inhabitants still live. Their movements allow the filmmakers to document the changes Poland experienced in the 1990s, the early period of capitalism, most importantly the setting up of shopping centres and proliferation of supermarkets. Much of the action develops in such places and the first large concert of Paktofonika takes place to celebrate the opening of the mall. One can conjecture that the gig is sponsored by the owners of this enterprise, There is a poignant mismatch between the rebellious posturing of Magik, Fokus and Rahim on one hand and the 'god of consumption' whom they serve, on the other. The topic of money, which was practically non-existent in *Destined to Blues*, is foregrounded in *You Are God*, especially for Magik, who, unlike Rahim and Fokus, has family obligations:

a wife and a young child. We constantly see him asking his manager for money and on one occasion even throwing himself onto his car, to force him to give him more. The place where the three characters live and the people with whom they interact provide Paktofonika with topics for their songs and it can be argued that their rhythm reflects the rhythm of the city. At the same time, as Jamrozik observes, music also serves them as a 'protective tool, enabling distanced, "casual" walking through the city. Especially for Fokus music seems to act like armour against the roughness and coldness of the city, letting him keep his "cool" demeanour, which becomes his trademark in the film, in every situation' (ibid.: 218). Poland of the 1990s comes across as an industrious, but also cold and alienating place. This is conveyed by the limited colour, with blue and grey dominating the palette, making the image almost monochromatic at times. Moreover, when shot in the 'temples of consumption', the characters appear to be lost and always something unfortunate happens to Magik. When he is in the supermarket with his manager, Magik is accused of stealing headphones. When he goes to a shopping mall, a shopping assistant asks him to hug her and the image is seen by Magik's wife on multiple screens, convincing her that Magik betrayed her. Subsequently she asks him for a divorce. Not surprisingly, alienation is a favourite topic of Paktofonika's songs. Another is the position of an artist. The title of the film is taken from the song of almost the same title 'Jestem Bogiem' (I'm God), which Magik insisted to include on the band's record when it was officially completed, which pointed to the importance of this song for him. In this song he proclaims that an artist is God; he can conjure up words which make the hair of the listener stand on end and cannot be defeated. It is a matter of opinion whether the lyrics should be taken at face value, as Tadeusz Sobolewski argues (Sobolewski 2012) or read ironically.

Looked at from a contemporary perspective, it is difficult not to see a similarity between Magik's statement and that offered by Eminem in his song 'Rap God'. The songs are also similar in conveying both the power and vulnerability of a star. The death of the protagonist can be regarded as proof that the artist wasn't a god after all, but the posthumous fame Paktofonika achieved, no doubt in part thanks to the death of its leader, suggests that the musician can exert god-like power over his fans.

For the actor who played Magik, Marcin Kowalczyk, it was a debut film. Like Kot playing Riedel, he tried to identify with the rapper entirely, 'become him for a short while' (quoted in Krantz 2010: 61). Kowalczyk's

Fig. 5.3 Marcin Kowalczyk as Magik in *Jesteś Bogiem* (*You Are God*, 2012), directed by Leszek Dawid

unfamiliar face combined with his talent, added significantly to the value of the film as a biopic (Fig. 5.3).

Dawid's film wears its biographism on its sleeve, by using authenticating techniques. At the beginning, it announces that it is based on true events and in the end it juxtaposes the scenes shot with actors with the documentary footage presenting the real members of Paktofonika, as was also the case with Riedel's biopic and which became almost a norm in western biographical films. However, what makes this feel 'authentic' and, in my view, the most successful biopic of a Polish popular musician, is using a visual and aural style which is similar to that used by Paktofonika in its videos. The film feels like an extended version to the clip of their song 'You Are God' (which I will discuss in the last chapter of this book). As Sobolewski observes, 'townscape in this film correlates with music, life and rap intermingle. We have an impression that we look at the characters' apartments, school and workplace without taking off the headphones' (Sobolewski 2012). In other words, Dawid put faith in music as a narrative tool, as opposed to seeing it only as an embellishment or an addition to the narrative.

THE LAST CULT MUSIC JOURNALIST

The bulk of protagonists of popular music biopics are singers and frontmen of rock bands. This situation, as Roy Shuker observes in relation to western films, started to change in the last decade or so, as exemplified by *Good Vibrations* (2012), directed by Lisa Barros D'Sa and

Glenn Leyburn, which is a biopic of Terri Hooley, who ran a record shop (Shuker 2016: 149) and *24 Hour Party People* (2002), directed by Michael Winterbottom, about the record label head and media personality Tony Wilson. *Ostatnia rodzina* (*The Last Family*, 2016), directed by Jan P. Matuszyński, adds to this trend, as its main character is a well-known Polish music journalist, Tomasz Beksiński, who committed suicide in 1999, at the age of 41. Beksiński started working in radio in the early 1980s. He is known mostly for presenting his own programmes: *Romantycy muzyki rockowej* (*Rock Romantics*) and *Wieczór płytowy* (*An Evening with a Record*). In them he educated the audience about British rock: the classics of the late 1960s and 1970s and later trends, post-punk and synth-pop, represented by bands such as the Cure, Depeche Mode and Ultravox. The title of his programme, *Rock Romantics*, referred both to romanticism in rock and to the style of new romantic, fashionable in the 1980s. Beksiński was also a translator of dialogues of English-speaking films, most importantly James Bond and Monty Python productions and occasionally wrote English lyrics to songs of Polish bands, such as Omni. Despite his successes, including being regarded as a cult personality of Polish radio, he suffered from depression and tried to commit suicide several times, before finally succeeding on Christmas Eve 1999, just days before the end of the first decade of 'free Poland' and the old millennium.

Although Tomasz Beksiński was an interesting character with a significant contribution to Polish music journalism, most likely he would not receive the honour of being the subject of a biopic, if not for the fact that he was also the son of a man more famous than himself—the painter Zdzisław Beksiński, who is one of the most renowned Polish artists of the twentieth century. Zdzisław Beksiński specialised in painting skeletons and emasculated bodies with naturalistic precision, often against the backdrop made of plants with overgrown roots which look like animals or deserted cities, as if remnants of a war or an ecological apocalypse. Zdzisław Beksiński's work is not only widely admired by ordinary art-lovers, but also inspires other artists. In Poland, his paintings influenced the creators of the point-and-click adventure video game Tormentum. The noted Mexican filmmaker Guillermo del Toro is also an admirer of Beksiński's works (Blair 2018).

The Last Family was made 16 years after a documentary about Tomasz Beksiński, *Dziennik zapowiedzianej śmierci* (*A Diary of a Death Foretold*, 2000), directed by Daniel Światły. I will use this 24-minute film to illustrate certain aspects of Tomasz's portrayal in *The Last Family*, not least because *The Last Family* belongs to those biopics which do not hide but, on the contrary, show with pride their closeness to historical reality, announcing in the initial titles that the films are based on authentic events—as was also the case with *You Are God*. Authentication also happens through putting dates in the corner of the frame, indicating the time when specific events took place and, at the end of the film, including several fragments from the video-archive of the Beksińskis.

The narrative begins in 1976, when the entire Beksiński family, consisting of Zdzisław, his wife Zofia, their son Tomasz and his two grandmothers, move from Sanok in the South of Poland to Warsaw, to a newly built estate Służew nad Dolinką. They move into a rather spacious, albeit standardised and low-quality apartment in a block made of concrete, with a small, smelly and vandalised lift. From their block they have a view onto an identically looking block. The parents and grandmothers seem not to mind being uprooted, getting on with their new lives. Zdzisław immediately takes over one room to use as a studio. It is filled with books, records and huge tape recorders, which in due course give way to more modern equipment.

The Beksiński family is in some way a traditional family—the father is the breadwinner and the mother looks after the household and the elderly women. Tomasz adopts the role of a rebellious son, except that he has little to rebel against, as he is a loved and pampered child, whose parents try to help him in any way possible. This aspect is emphasised by Tomasz's friends, interviewed in the documentary films, who mention that Tomasz had a very easy life, but did not appreciate it. His rebellion is thus ultimately without a cause and its main result is upsetting his parents. Two situations recur in *The Last Family*. One shows Tomasz during outbursts of anger which change into a performance of self-pity, finishing with him crying like a helpless child. The second is during his suicide attempts. In between, he is shown in his work as a DJ, introducing the audience to contemporary English pop-rock. This focus might reflect Tomasz Beksiński's taste, but also his elevated position of somebody with access to expensive records, to which the film alludes on several occasions. We learn that this collection was acquired largely thanks to his father who, when selling his paintings abroad, demanded that, instead of money, he was paid in records. Off-screen Tomasz Beksiński was known for generously lending his records to fellow music journalists and musicians.

There is little revealed about Beksiński's work as a journalist, for example, how he found out about new performers and records, what he liked about them or how he prepared himself for radio shows. Moreover, we practically do not see him in the company of people with whom he shared his passion for music, such as fellow music journalists, or his peers, where he apparently often shone with his wit. Music plays a surprisingly small role in the film and it seems as if it is the father who is more of a music lover, always painting when listening to something, than his son. There are several scenes with women, all leaving Tomasz, disappointed with their lovemaking, possibly because of his impotence or penchant for voyeurism (in one scene they perform in front of the camera). Ultimately, Tomasz Beksiński comes across as an unsympathetic and uninteresting character.

The first song we hear in the film is 'Don't Go' from the band Yazoo's first record. The words 'don't go' can be regarded as a call to Beksiński junior, uttered by his family and friends, till the exasperated father changes his tack and starts to wish that his son leaves his 'mortal coil'. When he eventually dies and his father says 'at last', it sounds as not only Zdzisław freed himself from an unpleasant individual, but also the viewers from the tedium of observing Tomasz's antics.

The impression that there is little depth to Tomasz is reinforced by casting Dawid Ogrodnik in the role of Tomasz Beksiński. Ogrodnik, who was probably chosen for the film due to his physical resemblance to the young Beksiński, wears one angry expression throughout the film and makes no effort to gain sympathy for his character. This one-dimensionality contrasts with the complexity of Tomasz's father and mother. Zdzisław Beksiński, played by Andrzej Seweryn, is most remarkable for his lust for life, down-to-earth attitude to his career and fame, and acceptance of fate, contrasting with the morbid figures he paints. His appetite for life is revealed most poignantly in a scene where he eats his dinner, licking a bowl in appreciation of the food his wife prepared for him. By contrast, Tomasz often complains about the food and once throws it away, making havoc in the kitchen, just to show his temper. Zdzisław Beksiński also does not mind the landscape outside, most likely because he paints from his imagination and he is modest, both in terms of his material and spiritual needs. At one point Zdzisław says that one shouldn't expect anything from life—every pleasure or reward should be taken as a bonus.

Presenting two creative people living in practically identical circumstances, but reacting in contrasting ways to what life brings them, not only renders *The Last Family* a psycho-biography, but validates this take to biography, by showing that environment cannot explain how people live and create. Yet, the film also attempts to place the lives of the Beksińskis in a wider social context and is remarkable for capturing the lifestyle of the Polish intelligentsia. It shows that despite living in a standard block made from prefabricated material, which in due course Vaclav Havel would contemptuously describe as 'rabbit hutches', the Beksińskis managed to have access to the world of culture and the most advanced technological equipment. The film suggests that the standardisation and anonymity of their abode actually acted as a protection, at least for the father. Of course, the Beksińskis can be regarded as an unusual case, as an average Polish intelligentsia family did not include a famous painter, but such observations, in my opinion, are still valid. Moreover, the culturally rich family which is slowly shrinking and dying without producing an heir, can be regarded as capturing the fate of the Polish nation after the fall of the Berlin Wall, when many Poles emigrated to the West and the intelligentsia lost its privileged position, giving way to a more entrepreneurial 'middle class'. Such a shift did not substantially change the status of those at the very top of the cultural hierarchy, such as Zdzisław Beksiński, possibly even enhanced it, because nowadays his work is validated both by public appreciation and the free market, where his paintings sell for tens of thousands of dollars. However, it affected negatively many other professions, such as music producers and journalists, who lost their exclusive status, following reduction of costs of music production and access to specialised knowledge, facilitated by the internet and social media. In Eastern Europe the loss following the democratisation of means of production and dissemination of knowledge about popular music is particularly acute, because under state socialism possessing a large collection of records and knowing English well, two conditions which needed to be fulfilled to become a radio DJ, were much more difficult to meet than in the West.

This sense of the actual or approaching loss of status and the obsolescence of one's work is captured in both *The Last Family* and *A Diary of a Death Foretold*, by showing Tomasz Beksiński's huge collection of CDs and DVDs. Inevitably, since his death, they lost practically all their value, becoming the detritus of a by-gone era. Although it was not yet the case in 1999, when Tomasz Beksiński took his life, this process of democratisation had already started, threatening the position of 'cult journalists' like him. Nowadays, it is fair to say, Poland does not have any cult journalists, not because the new generation of journalists is less talented, but because the gap between an expert and an ordinary listener has shrunk. In *A Diary of a Death Foretold*, Tomasz's friend, Grzegorz Gajewski, talks about him 'switching off the lights one by one': a metaphor of the shrinking of his professional and social world. It is a pity that Matuszyński decided to focus on the pathological personality of Tomasz as a sole source of his demise, rather than paying attention to some external factors in his tragic fate.

Conclusions

The examples discussed in this chapter demonstrate that although biopics of popular musicians are still relatively rare in Poland, their frequency has increased in the last decade, reflecting global trends. They also show that Polish filmmakers are moving away from the socio-biographic model towards creating psycho-biography, but struggle to convincingly 'psycho-biographise' the lives of stars. Yet, the most accomplished biographical film about popular musician, *You Are God*, combines both approaches. The choice of characters is also in line with the western trends. Not only are the most popular and renowned artists selected, but also those who died young and in tragic circumstances, often by their own hand. This might explain the fact that up to this point there are no biopics about Czesław Niemen, the greatest Polish rock star and no biopics about disco polo stars, arguably the greatest music stars of the postcommunist period.

Note

1. Szarek was probably the first Polish filmmaker to dabble with mockumentary while making films about rock music. However, before him, in 1983, Polish Radio Three programme broadcast a mockumentary about band Republika, titled *Odlot (Trip)*, produced by Zbigniew Ostrowski in cooperation with the band's leader, Grzegorz Ciechowski, which proved very successful (Fortuna 2016). Possibly Szarek was inspired by this programme.

Works Cited

Bingham, Dennis. 2010. *Whose Lives Are They Anyway? The Biopic As Contemporary Film Genre*. New Brunswick: NJ Rutgers University Press.

Blair, Jonny. 2018. The Tragic Story of Zdzisław Beksiński, the Artist Who Inspired Guillermo del Toro. *Culture Trip*, June 10. https://theculturetrip.

com/europe/poland/articles/the-tragic-story-of-zdzislaw-beksinski-the-artist-who-inspired-guillermo-del-toro/. Accessed 23 November 2018.

Bobecka, Barbara. 1982. Miłość nie wszystko wybaczy. *Tygodnik Demokratyczny* 3: 17.

Brown, Tom, and Belén Vidal (eds.). 2014. *The Biopic in Contemporary Film Culture*. London: Routledge.

Butrym, Marian. 1985. *Dola idola*. Warszawa: Młodzieżowa Agencja Wydawnicza.

Chaciński, Bartek. 2012. Jesteś legendą. *Polityka* 38: 82–83.

Codell, Julie F. 2014. Gender, Genius, and Abjection in Artist Biopics. In *The Biopic in Contemporary Film Culture*, ed. Tom Brown and Belén Vidal, 151–175. London: Routledge.

Custen, George F. 1992. *Bio/pics: How Hollywood Constructed Public History*. New Brunswick: Rutgers University Press.

Dolińska, Elżbieta. 1981. Konsumowanie cudzego nawisu. *Film* 48: 12.

Fortuna, Piotr. 2016. Perverse Imperialism: Republika's Phenomenon in the 1980s. In *Popular Music in Eastern Europe: Breaking the Cold War Paradigm*, ed. Ewa Mazierska, 283–301. London: Palgrave.

France, Peter, and William St. Clair (eds.). 2004. *Mapping Lives: The Uses of Biography*. Oxford: Oxford University Press.

Groys, Boris. 1992. *The Total Art of Stalinism: Avant-Garde, Aesthetic Dictatorship, and Beyond*, trans. Charles Rougle. Princeton: Princeton University Press.

Hight, Craig. 2008. Mockumentary: A Call to Play. In *Rethinking Documentary: New Perspectives, New Practices*, ed. Thomas Austin and Wilma de Jong, 204–216. Berkshire: Open University Press.

Inglis, Ian. 2007. Popular Music History on Screen: The Pop/Rock Biopic. *Popular Music History* 2 (1): 77–93.

Jackowska, Olga, and Kamil Sipowicz. 1992. *Kora: Podwójna linia życia*. Warszawa: Agencja Piękna.

Jamrozik, Żaneta. 2016. Everything I love: Sensuous Homelands as a Way of Experiencing History Through Hip-Hop Films. *Studies in Eastern European Cinema* 3: 208–224.

Janicka, Bożena. 1982. Hanka. *Film* 11: 16.

Klimczak, Lidia. 1985. Kora, Kora, Kora…. *Ekran* 8: 16.

Krantz, Małgorzata. 2010. Randka z Magikiem. *Laif* 4: 1–6.

Lemańska, Magdalena. 2016. Nadawcy zwiększają inwestycje w seriale. *Rzeczpospolita*, 18/11. https://www.rp.pl/Media-i-internet/311179841-Nadawcy-zwiekszaja-inwestycje-w-seriale.html. Accessed 12 January 2019.

Lenard, Jolanta. 1985. Maanam Story? *Stolica* 18: 18.

Majewski, Piotr. 1988. Dżem. *Jazz Forum* 4: 18–19.

Marshall, Lee, and Isabel Kongsgaard. 2012. Representing Popular Music Stardom on Screen: The Popular Music Biopic. *Celebrity Studies* 3 (3): 346–361.
Mazierska, Ewa. 2004. Multifunctional Chopin: The Representation of Fryderyk Chopin in Polish Films. *Historical Journal of Film, Radio and Television* 2 (24): 253–268.
Mazierska, Ewa. 2007. *Polish Postcommunist Cinema: From Pavement Level.* Oxford: Peter Lang.
M.D. 1985. Kapłanka rocka w podróży. *Kamena* 6: 10.
Michałek, Bolesław. 1976. *Ćwiczenia z anatomii kina*. Warszawa: Wydawnictwa Artystyczne i Filmowe.
Neale, Steve. 2000. *Genre and Hollywood*. London: Routledge.
Pawlicki, Maciej. 1985. Piłowanie gałęzi. *Film* 12: 9.
Pollock, Griselda. 1980. Artists, Mythologies and Media—Genius, Madness and Art History. *Screen* 3: 57–96.
Radecki, Piotr. 2017. "Skazany na bluesa". Aktorski popis Tomasza Kota w biografii wielkiego polskiego muzyka. *Tele Magazyn*, June 21. https://www.telemagazyn.pl/artykuly/skazany-na-bluesa-aktorski-popis-tomasza-kota-w-biografii-wielkiego-polskiego-muzyka-recenzja-16926.html. Accessed 3 February 2019.
Shuker, Roy. 2016. *Understanding Popular Music Culture*, 5th ed. London: Routledge.
Sobolewski. Tadeusz. 2012. *Jesteś bogiem* - więcej niż film o legendzie hip-hopu. *Gazeta Wyborcza*, September 21. http://wyborcza.pl/1,75410,12524295,_Jestes_bogiem____wiecej_niz_film_o_legendzie_hip_hopu.html. Accessed 15 September 2018.
Staszczyszyn, Bartosz. 2017. A Lust for Life: Making Sense of Biopic Cinema in Poland. *Culture.pl*, June 29. https://culture.pl/en/article/a-lust-for-life-making-sense-of-biopic-cinema-in-poland. Accessed 17 October 2018.
Szczepański, Tadeusz, and Sylwia Kołos (eds.). 2007. *Biografistyka filmowa: Ekranowe interpretacje losów i faktów*. Warszawa: Wydawnictwo Adam Marszałek.
Tibbets, John C. 2005. *Composers in the Movies: Studies in Musical Biography*. New Haven: Yale University Press.
Toeplitz, Jerzy. 1952. Młodość Chopina. *Kwartalnik Filmowy* 5–6: 102–115.
Tompkins, David G. 2013. *Composing the Party Line: Music and Politics in Early Cold War Poland and East Germany*. West Lafayette, IN: Purdue University Press.
Vidal, Belén. 2014. Introduction: The Biopic and Its Critical Contexts. In *The Biopic in Contemporary Film Culture*, ed. Tom Brown and Belén Vidal, 1–32. London: Routledge.
Zarębski, Konrad. 1981. Miłość ci wszystko wybaczy. *Filmowy Serwis Prasowy* 14: 4–8.
Żurawiecki, Bartosz. 2005. Skazany na bluesa. *Film* 8: 18.

CHAPTER 6

Epic Biopics: Biographies of Polish Music Stars on Television

In a piece about biographical films by Bolesław Michałek, which I mentioned in the previous chapter, the author suggests that the best medium to present biographies is television, in particular, television series (Michałek 1976: 18–23). Although the author does not elaborate on this point, we can conjecture that he has two reasons in mind. One is their length, which allows the makers to include more detail from the life of the person represented and show his or her maturation over a long period of time. This offers the viewer an opportunity to get closer to the character than is normally possible and enjoy the psychological aspect of a biopic. Such an intimate relationship is further facilitated by the television format. Television audiences watch the series in their private space and on a small screen. At the same time, due to their length, in common with epic films, they have the means to present the life of a famous person against a wide canvass of historical events: to produce socio-biographies.

Despite these advantages, during state socialist period Polish television produced few biographical series and neither of them concerned a musician. Almost all of those which were produced, concerned transnational figures, such as Ewelina Hańska, supposedly the greatest love of Honoré de Balzac in *Wielka miłość Balzaka* (*Balzac's Great Love*; *Un Grand Amour de Balzac*, 1973), directed by Jacqueline Audry and Wojciech Solarz and the Italian Bona Sforza, who became a Polish queen, in the series *Królowa Bona* (*Queen Bona*, 1980–1981), directed by Janusz Majewski.

The situation changed after the fall of state socialism, when we observe an eruption of multi-episode programmes, seen as a way to ensure high audience figures and a means to attract advertisers. The vast majority of them were soap operas, presenting everyday life in different parts of Poland, often emphasising the centrality of the Catholic Church for the social and cultural identity of ordinary Poles. They gave value for money because they were relatively cheap to produce due to their everyday settings. Over the years, however, more prestigious series went into production, to meet the expectations of Polish audiences, 'spoilt' by foreign series which they could watch on Netflix or HBO (Lemańska 2016). These 'high-end' productions included *Bodo* (2016), a 13-episodes series about the famous interwar singing and dancing actor Eugeniusz Bodo, whose films I presented in Chapter 2. I will examine this series, along with *Anna German* (2013), a ten-episodes series about a Polish singer popular in the 1960s and 1970s. which was produced by Russian television, but co-directed by a Polish director and with a Polish actress in the main role.

Why were these artists chosen for such prestigious productions? There were reasons specific to each series, but they have one factor in common: the lives of both of them were closely affected by Polish-Russian relations. For better or for worse, these productions testify to the importance of Russia to Polish history and national identity and a need to look at Polish-Russian neighbourhood afresh.

Authenticity and Suffering

Anna German (2013) is a production of Star Media, the leading producer of Russian television series, as well as musicals, for the Russian state television channel. Its head is Ukraine-born Vlad Ryashin (b. 1970), who is also credited as the producer of the series. His co-producer was Russian Galina Bałan-Timkina, whose origins are also in Ukraine. There are no Poles among the producers. According to the Polish director of the series, Waldemar Krzystek, this is due to the lack of the interest on the Polish side. In his own words: 'Polish television was given an opportunity to get involved and if they agreed, [*Anna German*] would be a co-production. However, [Polish television] did not reply to the official letters sent by the Russian side' (quoted in Bernat 2013).

Given that the series is Russian, it raises the question why its co-director is Polish and if we are to believe Krzystek, the main director (the second is Ukrainian Aleksandr Timienko). According to Krzystek, it was a condition of Russian television to employ him (ibid.). The reason was the immense popularity of Krzystek's film *Mała Moskwa* (*Little Moscow*, 2008), in Russia. The film is the story of a Russian woman named Vera who moved to Poland after the Second World War with her officer husband, fell in love with Polish culture and the Polish man, and was severely punished for that by the Soviet authorities.

In Poland *Little Moscow* was seen as being patronising towards Russia by suggesting a superiority of Polish culture over that of Russia. It appears that in Russia this facet of Krzystek's film was overlooked and it was seen more as a tribute to the Russian-Polish affinity and even love, which continued despite the authorities on both sides trying to prevent it. It is also possible that the film was appreciated in Russia due to avoiding some negative stereotypes of Russians. True, the NKVD (secret police) types are not embellished, but ordinary Russians, represented by Vera and her husband, come across as decent. In addition, Vera, played by Svetlana Khodchenkova, is very beautiful. I in *Little Moscow* Vera's enchantment with Poland is expressed through her use of Polish language and Polish songs, which she learns by heart. Songs are thus presented as a bridge connecting people and cultures. The same idea is proposed in *Anna German*.

The series' main language is Russian, which suggests that its target was Russian and Ukrainian audiences, rather than Polish. However, the dialogue was recorded in three languages: Russian, Polish and Italian, according to the place where the action is set and who participates in the conversations. That said, the authors privileged Russian by showing that Russian trumps other languages in multinational conversations. For example, when Anna's mother talks to her Polish fiancé, they communicate in Russian, which is unlikely given that it happens after the German's family spending many years in Poland. Russian is also spoken between Anna, her mother and grandmother, although according to witnesses, they used archaic Dutch. This 'Russian bias' is also revealed by extending the part of Anna German's childhood, which took place in the Soviet Union, at the expense of the Polish part of her life. Normally it would take no more than one-tenth of the overall series, but on this occasion three out of ten episodes are devoted to it.

Before I turn to the series, an introduction to the protagonist is in order. Anna German (1936–1982) was born in Uzbekistan in a family, whose original name was Hörmann (Russian German). The Hörmanns' roots were in Germany and Holland. Anna's mother, Irma Martens, was a teacher of German; her father was an accountant in a local bakery. Such an occupation was regarded as 'bourgeois' in the Soviet Russia and merely tolerated by the authorities. However, it was mostly the ethnic background of the Hörmanns-Germans and the decisions made by their ancestors, namely the fact that Anna's grandfather was a priest, that did not bode well for the family under Stalin, particularly once war broke out between Germany and the Soviet Union. The grandfather was sent to a gulag in 1929, her father Eugen tried to escape to Germany, but eventually was arrested and executed in 1938. During the Second World War Irma married a Polish soldier of Jewish origin named Herman Gerner, which allowed her to be repatriated to Poland. Irma, Anna and her grandmother settled in Wrocław, where Anna became a student of geology. During this period her singing career began. Her pure, vibrating voice and type of beauty rendered her similar to the Italian singer Dalida. She was a popular singer in Poland, particularly in the 1960s and 1970s. She also had some success abroad, most importantly in the Soviet Union, where she toured many times and made numerous records. She was also the first artist from behind the Iron Curtain to take part in the San Remo Festival, in 1967, where she received 'Oscar Simpatico': an award recognising her positive effect on the audience. German's style can be described as 'timeless'; it did not change over time, as was the case with other popular female singers, such as Maryla Rodowicz and Urszula Sipińska. For some listeners, this consistency was proof of her artistic integrity; for others a sign that she did not develop. Some sections of the audience viewed her unfavourably on the grounds of catering to the taste of older listeners: those who liked estrada singers. This perception was reinforced by German's style in clothes. She had a preference for long black or colourful dresses, which in Poland were associated with 'Russian style', shunned by younger people.

Anna German begins in Uzbekistan in 1938, shortly after the birth of Anna German's brother Friedrich. He is born into a loving family, consisting of parents, Irma and Eugen and a grandmother, and Anna, who is then five or six years old. The only problem is Irma's Russian former suitor, Lavrishin, who cannot come to terms with Irma choosing another man over him. Jealous of Eugen, he arranges his arrest and internment in a camp—or at least this is what Irma is told. During the subsequent three episodes Irma tries to find her husband, while also escaping Lavrishin's grip. Eventually she gives up hope and marries a Polish man, whom little

Anna mistakes for her father, when she looks for him at the railway station. It is thanks to him that the family eventually relocates to Poland.

Although in this early part Irma is the main character, Anna plays a major role. She is presented as a musical prodigy, whose voice enchants listeners. The film begins with her father leaving her with some women working in a bakery, who ask her to sing and in her presence they forget about their work. Later Irma, instead of being arrested by a Party apparatchik, gains his support and this is because he sees from his window his functionaries enjoying Anna's impromptu performance. These are clearly fictitious scenes, whose point is to demonstrate the power of music to overcome political division and soften cruel hearts. One can think about *The Pianist* (2002) by Roman Polanski, where music was also attributed such quasi-magical power.

Once in Poland, Anna stops singing in public, most likely because of her mother's view that singing is a trivial pursuit and her daughter needs to prove herself in a technical profession. She chooses to study geology. This subject can be regarded as in part reflecting her Russian/Soviet heritage, as in this country women were encouraged to devote their life to science and technology. This also can be regarded as a reflection of her romanticism, love of nature and her desire to return to the Earth, to find the roots, of which she was deprived by the Stalinist oppressors. During her study she starts her musical career, first playing in variety shows and later becoming a solo singer. Her promotion to singing solo is presented as proof of her authenticity. This happens when she goes to the director and manager of the troupe, telling him that she cannot play a 'role'; it is 'not her'. He is first outraged by her behaviour which he interprets as a sign of her posturing as a diva, an attitude at odds with the humble position she occupies in his team, but he changes his mind after hearing her sing. He falls in love with her clear voice and gives her the best slot in their programme.

At this time German sings in Russian, most likely due to the lack of an original repertoire. One might guess that this fact would put the audience off from her performance, but nothing like that happens—they are very enthusiastic. From that point she begins her proper career, of which the first milestone is recording 'Tańczące Eurydyki' (Dancing Euridices), for which she received Second Prize at the Festival of the Polish Songs in Opole in 1964 and the Grand Prix at the Sopot Music Festival the next year. In the series we see how this song is given to the singer by the composer Katarzyna Gaertner. In reality, however, its first performer was another Polish singer, Helena Majdaniec.

Much of the remaining part of the series shows Anna's difficulty in combining career as a musician with having a family. For popular artists working under the state socialist regime touring rather than recording was the main source of income. It was practically impossible for them to earn a living without giving concerts, often as many as over hundred per year, as income from records was small and practically did not depend on the number of records sold. Although Anna's touring receives a somewhat romantic spin by suggesting that she gives concerts to meet the demands of her devoted fans, it also on occasion brings home the truth that without touring she would not be able to put bread on the table. Yet, Anna's husband, Zbigniew, is resentful of her constant absence, partly because he misses her and partly because he finds this arrangement emasculating, with him waiting for his wife at home when she supposedly has a good time.

Each episode begins with a fragment of the Italian 'chapter' in German's life. In 1966 the singer signed a three-year deal with the Italian label, Company Discografica Italiana. She made a record and performed at the San Remo Festival, which she did not win, but received the 'Oscar Simpatico'. Her Italian manager was determined to make her an international star, by arranging performances for her at festivals in Rio de Janeiro, Tokyo, Philadelphia and Majorca. However, these plans were destroyed by a serious accident, when her manager fell asleep at the wheel while driving a car, resulting in German being catapulted from the car and suffering multiple injuries. As a result, she was in a coma for two weeks and convalesced for three years. After that German's dream about making a career in the West was practically over.

Car crashes are common in the lives of pop stars, as exemplified by those of Falco, Cliff Burton, Gloria Estefan and in Poland Ludmiła Jakubczak and Krzysztof Klenczon, who both died in car accidents and Urszula Sipińska, who was seriously injured when travelling in East Germany. They reflect the fact that musicians travel by car more than average citizens, often at night, in unsocial hours or after drinking alcohol. However, privileging this tragic episode in German's life plays two additional functions in the series. First, it presents the protagonist's life as leading to her crash. Such a teleological take on the character's life, as I mentioned in the previous chapter, is typical for Hollywood biopics. As Vidal writes, 'Through a necessarily selective account of a life, often constructed at the end point through the framing structure of the flashback, linearity and factuality led to a "natural" collapse of the future into the past' (Vidal 2014: 5). This device is also symptomatic of the Polish (meta)narrative about the careers of Polish stars in the West, which did not materialise due to a freak accident, as opposed to any failure on the part of the star or structural problems of the Polish popular music industry. Such narratives are perpetuated in their biographies. Although ultimately German survived the accident, the authors of the series suggest that in a deeper sense it killed her, as she subsequently developed cancer which started in the leg which she injured in the crash.

German is presented in the series as flawless. She follows a simple moral code—being loyal, helpful and selfless. She also remains optimistic in the face of adversity. Her integrity is best revealed in situations when she can further her career by using her sexuality, but refuses to do so. This happens first when the director of an Estrada ensemble demands that she has sex with him to repay him for the favour of offering her a solo performance. Not only does she refuse the request, but threatens the man with a lamp, which ultimately makes him respect her. She behaves in the same way when a man helps her to find the way to her hotel in Opole where the festival is about to happen and he then proposes sex on the grounds that he sits on the festival jury. Again, Anna rebukes him and she still manages to win an award at the festival. German also resists the pressure to sexualise her image exerted by the Italian company with which she signed a deal, insisting that she is a singer, not a model (Fig. 6.1).

In *Anna German* we also frequently hear people saying that German had an 'angel's voice'. It is her voice rather than any other aspect of her performance, which made her a star. In the light of such a statement it is understandable that the authors of the film decided to use German's original performances, lip-synched by Joanna Moro, playing the main character, similarly as the authors of *La Vie en Rose* decided to use Piaf's original recordings. One advantage of such inclusion is that it also makes up for the substantial diversion from the principal hypotext of the series—German's biography.

The scriptwriters decided to include only the most famous songs by German, while also choosing those sung in three languages: Russian, Polish and Italian, to demonstrate her linguistic versatility. German was probably the most multilingual of Polish popular singers, singing in seven languages, somewhat undermining the common opinion that Polish culture of state socialism was parochial and inward-looking. The three

Fig. 6.1 Italian hosts try to sexualise Anna German's image in *Anna German* (2013), directed by Waldemar Krzystek

languages also illustrate three chapters in German's career: Russian, Polish and Italian. Another function of the songs is to illustrate German's mindset when she performed the song. 'Dancing Euridices', German's first original song, about careless young women, seeking fun and possibly love (the eponymous nymphs Euridices), can be regarded as a song about the young, single and (relatively) careless German. One of the last songs in the film, 'Nadyezdha' (Hope), is sung at the time when the singer was diagnosed with cancer and, naturally, transmits her hope to overcome the illness. On balance, the songs in Russian prevail over those in Polish. They dominate in the early and late part of the series, as if suggesting that deep down German had a 'Russian soul' which was expressed in her singing. Such privileging of Russian repertoire reflects the fact that *Anna German* is a Russian production, addressed primarily to Russian fans of the singer.

Irrespective, however, of the language German sings, in *Anna German* she always sings for the audience, who is deeply moved by her performance (Fig. 6.2).

We see theatre audiences giving her a standing ovation and fellow female professionals shedding tears when playing with her during a recording session. Her success is the more remarkable as she wins against the odds, for example performing last during the contest. There seems

Fig. 6.2 Anna German (Joanna Moro) performs for the grateful audience in *Anna German* (2013), directed by Waldemar Krzystek

always to be a rapport between the artist and her audience. German sings for them and to express herself, as opposed to doing her job or earning money. The authors of the series placed special emphasis on German's relationship with the Russian audience. Not only she was most admired and loved by the Russians, but she also had a special relationship with another Anna, her Russian songwriter. By contrast, we do not see her forging any lasting links with Polish collaborators; her meeting with Katarzyna Geartner is just a one-off.

A strong point of the series is revealing the unglamorous character of working in the socialist culture industry, especially in the episodes showing the times, when German was working in Estrada. This involved carrying and packing decorations into vans and showing obedience to rude, powerful bosses. This part of the series demonstrates the attraction to Poles of what I termed elsewhere 'banal exoticism' (Mazierska 2016: 49–52). The term points to the superficial engagement with exotic places, using musical and visual clichés, as we see in the scenes where German, with her face painted black, plays a black woman jumping out of cauldron or appropriating the character of a Japanese geisha.

Anna German proved an immensely popular series in Poland, attracting over 6 million viewers for each episode. Its success has largely to do with the script, which sacrificed historical truth for dramatic effect. It humanised all the main characters and managed to present all nations in a good light, even the officer of the NKVD, whose persistence to win the love of Irma and Anna ultimately renders him tragic rather than sinister. Nevertheless, the portrayal of different nations, as in *Little Moscow*, is very flattering to Poles, because it shows Polish culture as very attractive to foreigners from the East.

The series was also praised for good acting, especially of the two main female characters, Irma, played by Mariya Poroshina and Anna German, played by Joanna Moro. Moro was born in Vilnius to a Polish family, but relocated to Poland to study there. In this respect she is similar to German and this renders her more credible as somebody who is neither completely Polish nor Russian, but embracing both cultures and identities. Like German, Moro is also multilingual, speaking five languages, including Russian and Italian. Her portrait of German gained her much sympathy in both countries, as demonstrated by the fact that she received an award of Polish and Russian foreign ministers for her contribution to understanding between the countries as well as a 'Wiktor', an award for the most popular television actress.

Living as a Pole, Dying as a Swiss

Most likely the success of *Anna German* was a factor in the decision of Polish television to produce its own series devoted to a music star. The choice fell on Eugeniusz Bodo, perhaps because, with the exception of German, one could not find a Polish popular star with a more colourful and tragic life than him. Moreover, while the story of German shows Russia in a good light, Bodo's life and especially his death, renders Russia as Poland's enemy and Russian people as hostile to their western neighbours.

The series, titled simply *Bodo*, was produced by Akson Studio, operating since 1992 and specialising in high-budget films and television series. Its owner is Michał Kwieciński, who is also one of the directors of the series. It belongs to the most expensive television productions; each episode cost about 1.5 million Zloties (about 400,000 Euro), which was three times the cost of an average episode in a Polish television series (Ufniarz 2016). Much of the budget was spent on costumes, made abroad and decorations (ibid.). This was to be expected, as historical productions tend to be more expensive than contemporary ones. Moreover, the way the series was scripted required employing a crowd of actors and extras or, to be more precise, over 340 actors and 4000 extras (Połaski 2016).

Bodo has two scriptwriters, Piotr Derewenda and Doman Nowakowski, two directors, Michał Rosa and the previously mentioned Michał Kwieciński and two actors playing the titular character, Antoni Królikowski, cast as a teenage Bohdan and Tomasz Schuchardt as his older version, when he adopted the pseudonym Bodo. Such doubling, as I argued previously, was not uncommon in Polish musicals, reflecting the difficulty of producing this genre. Of course, when the length of the product exceeds ten hours, the difficulties multiply, requiring a larger cast and crew. Both directors of *Bodo* had a long experience of working in television, including co-directing the series *Czas Honoru* (*The Times of Honour*, 2008–2016), about Polish soldiers fighting in Britain during the Second World War and their post-war fate. They can be described as 'professionals': competent, yet lacking a distinct authorial stamp, which is probably a good way to ensure that the final product comes across as made by the same hand.

Bodo's social milieu of interwar cabaret, musical theatre and the Polish film industry can be regarded as the Polish miniature version of Broadway and Hollywood—a perfect setting for a Polish version of a backstage musical (Kosecka 2016). This was also a reason why three decades earlier Janusz Rzeszewski decided to set his musicals during the interbellum. Another reason why Bodo was seen as good material for an extended biopic is a post-communist tendency to idealise interwar Poland as a sovereign and colourful country, in contrast to postwar Poland which was authoritarian and remained under the (semi)colonial rule of the Soviets. The authors of *Bodo* did not subscribe to such a simplistic representation, but showing colour, both literally and metaphorically, was an important goal of their project.

The series' main character, Eugeniusz Bodo (true name Bohdan Eugène Junod), was the greatest male movie star of the interwar Poland and one of its greatest singing and dancing stars, hence can be regarded as the male version of Ordonówna, who was 'snatched' by Rzeszewski before other Polish directors could use her story as biopic material. Bodo played in over thirty films and recorded many songs, some of which are popular to this day (see Chapter 2). He was also an accomplished director, scriptwriter and film producer, despite lacking any formal education. Bodo's ability to extract monetary value from his artistic work did not have any equal in Poland. As Anna Mieszkowska observes, he was a pioneer of using a famous name and face in advertising; he advertised, among other things, Old England suits, Chojnacki's neckties, Młodkowski's hats, Kielman shoes and Wedel chocolates. He was also paid several hundred Zloties per month by the owner of Café Bodo on the current Foksal Street, for using his name (Mieszkowska 2016: 78).

Although Bodo is closely identified with Polish popular culture, he is one of Poland's most international and cosmopolitan stars. He was born in 1899, in Geneva from Swiss father and Polish mother. His father, Teodor Junod, was an early cinema entrepreneur, who travelled in the Russian Empire and beyond, showing the invention of the cinematograph to those who never before witnessed it working, before settling in Łódź. There he set up a revue-cinema Urania, the first permanent cinema theatre in that city. Throughout his life Bodo retained his Swiss citizenship, which most likely was a major factor in his tragic death in the Soviet Gulag. Moreover, his best known affair was with a woman from Tahiti, Anne Chevalier, known as Reri. His career, in many ways, represents what many Polish film professionals today aspire to—staying in Poland, but travelling widely, literally and metaphorically.

The authors of the series admitted that they needed to add fiction to the facts, both for stronger dramatic effect, as well as to fill gaps in the historical knowledge about Bodo, which were significantly larger than those in Anna German's history. The series begins in 1916, when Bohdan Junod, called Bodzio by his mother, is still at school and prepares himself for his final exams (*matura*), while his parents live separate lives. His mother wants Bodzio to become a lawyer and asks her friend-cum-lover to arrange an internship for him in his legal firm. Bodzio, however, prefers to spend his time in his father's Urania. There the boy becomes enchanted by the moving images projected by his father and learns to tap dance. When his mother, regarding her son's truancy as a result of the corrupting influence of his father, forbids him to visit Urania, he moves to Warsaw, trying to make a career there. Despite many setbacks, he remains undeterred. The only time when he tries his hand in a different job, Bohdan chooses to collect dead bodies for a living. This is a sought-after job, following the outbreak of a flu epidemic in some parts of Poland. However, the job is sufficiently off-putting not only for Bohdan, but also to his parents, who give him their blessing to try his luck in acting. Of course, he succeeds. The series thus adheres to the typical scenario about a talented and determined individual, who follows his dreams and after overcoming numerous obstacles, receives his award. One advantage of using a television series, as opposed to a cine-film, lies in extending the period of apprenticeship, hence shifting the balance from success to labour (normally neglected in Polish musicals), and presenting the fate of the protagonist in conjunction with the fortunes of his friends, his social class and his country.

The theatres and cabarets, where Bohdan, now using the pseudonym Bodo, tries his luck, are presented as a precarious and exploitative business, bringing to mind *The Ghosts* (discussed in Chapter 2), where Bodo, fittingly, also played. We see numerous theatres and music halls being closed down, including Urania, mostly due to debt, exacerbated by the war economy. In reality, even the most popular entertainment business, such as Qui Pro Quo, at some point filed for bankruptcy (Wolański 2012: 22). Still, this did not put off aspiring artists from trying their luck. Inevitably, some tried to get a competitive edge through offering sexual services to people in power or acquiescing to their advances. In the series it is the strategy of many chorus girls as Bodo learns when he discovers that Nina, with whom he fell in love, has an affair with a leading actor in the show. He is also offered help in his career, respectively by the wife of a theatre director, where he auditions, a gay friend and eventually by a female journalist. He resists the wife of the director and also the gay friend, but acquiesces to the journalist, in recognition of the power of the media. He himself also learns how to use his relationships with women to further his career, kissing his fellow star and one-time lover Zula Pogorzelska in front of the cameras, when he is told that as a couple on and off-screen Bodo and Zula would increase their 'market value' than if they were seen as not being romantically involved with each other.

Despite numerous problems, music theatre and cabaret are presented in *Bodo* as a thriving industry, at least in large cities. At some stage they are joined by cinema. The power of cinema does not lie in its artistic quality, but in its value for money. This is because, once the equipment is fitted in the cinema, it costs little to show films, while the costs of live spectacle remain high. Indeed, cinema in interwar Poland was practically the cheapest entertainment on offer (Madej 1994: 52) and hence attracted even the lowest social strata: 'cooks, maids and shop assistants'. In *Bodo* cinema is presented as being in a symbiotic relationship with live entertainment (see Chapter 2). This is conveyed by showing the transfer of personnel between these two media: the stars of Polish cabaret and musical theatres, such as Bodo, Adolf Dymsza and Pogorzelska, are also film stars. Equally, theatre directors, such as Pogorzelska's husband,

Konrad Tom, became successful film directors. In reality, this rule also applied to songwriters but, unfortunately, this profession is neglected by the authors of *Bodo*. In both types of spectacle the actors are expected to sing and dance well; other skills and talents are secondary. The closeness of these two media is emphasised during film premieres, when the performers sing and dance for the audience on stage, before the film is shown on screen. However, the makers of *Bodo* also hint that at some point these two forms of entertainment might go their separate ways. This happens in one of the last episodes, when Bodo is approached by Eugeniusz Cękalski, the director of *The Ghosts*, who tells him to eschew his star persona, stop 'playing Bodo' and identify with the character he is meant to play. Meaningfully, although in *The Ghosts* Bodo plays an actor, it is a role in which he does little singing or dancing.

Biopics are, inevitably, tales of maturation, By the same token, they are stories of gaining and changing identities or, to use Stuart Halls's phrase, 'identification'. This is also how Bodo's life is presented in *Bodo*—as a series of events, which make the character identify with a certain group or idea. In this sense *Bodo* is different from *Anna German*, where German's cultural identity, her sense of belonging to any ethnic group is played down and her individual identity is emphasised, which can be explained by the multinational cast and crew of the film, representing countries with a history of conflict. Of those identities which Bodo embodies, national identity is of greatest importance. In Łódź, where Bohdan spent his formative years, his best friends are a young Jewish tailor Moritz, German Hans and Polish Ada. These are fictional characters, whose presence indicates that Bodo spent his youth in a cosmopolitan town where cultural differences were tolerated and members of different ethnic groups lived in relative harmony. However, his relationship with each of these three friends is different. Moritz is completely devoted to Bohdan and wants to follow him everywhere; Hans is presented more as a rival, especially for the heart of the beautiful Ada. Such a dynamic reminds one *Ziemia Obiecana* (*Promised Land*, 1975) by Andrzej Wajda, at the centre of the story of which was a Polish industrialist who had Jewish and German friends and partners. Of the three friends the most important for Bohdan is Ada, with whom he is in love. This love can be regarded as a metaphor for his love of Poland. Yet, Ada, keeps rejecting Bohdan and marries Hans, who becomes a doctor, leaving the aspiring actor heart-broken. Only when WWII is in sight and Hans joins the SS, the couple come together, but then it is too late—Ada remains in Berlin and Bodo travels from Warsaw to Lviv, where he is arrested by the NKVD. The relationship between Bodo and the two non-ethnically Polish characters can be regarded as metonymy of the position of Jews and Germans in interwar Poland, with the former being humble and loyal and the latter arrogant and disloyal, trying to snatch from Poles what was most precious to them—their country.

However, throughout the film Bodo remains apolitical and even ignorant of Polish history and geography, as shown during his school lessons. For him wars are merely an obstacle to the pursuit of his career, rather than an opportunity to prove his love for his homeland. This is exemplified by his willingness to switch languages—in Poznań he plays in German in the German theatre; in Lviv, when the city is captured by the Soviet army, he performs in Russian, to an audience made largely of Soviet officers and their wives. Only on one occasion does Bodo show his patriotism, during the Polish-Bolshevik war of 1919–1921, when he joins a queue to be drafted into the Polish army. He makes this decision, however, not out of his true concern for Poland, but because some people accuse him of indulging in frivolities when other young Polish men are dying as heroes and martyrs. However, in the end his contribution to the war effort is limited to taking part in a patriotic film. Significantly, even then his small role is cut out, as if nullifying any pretence he might have to being considered a Polish patriot. Bodo's cosmopolitan taste is also revealed in his choice of women. Apart from the (fictitious) Ada, his greatest love is (real) Reri, a feisty woman from Tahiti, who came to Poland to promote *Tabu* (1931) by Friedrich Wilhelm Murnau, in which she played the main female role. It appears that her very exotic beauty and temperament were the reason why Bodo fell for her (Fig. 6.3).

Throughout his life Bodo is also surrounded by Polish Jews, beginning with Moritz and finishing with the director Konrad Tom, with whom he leaves Warsaw for Lviv, to avoid the approaching Nazis, through his one-time lover and screen partner Nora Ney and Michał Waszyński, who directed many of his films. With the exception of Moritz, the Jewishness of these people is never considered an issue, pointing to the fact that the Polish film business in the interwar years was dominated by Polonised Jews. This might also explain the fact that Bodo, despite being ethnically only half-Polish, felt at home in the company of fellow actors, movie producers and directors.

Bodo's cosmopolitanism is also examined in the context of his possible emigration to make a career abroad. It is broached for the first time when

Fig. 6.3 Eugeniusz Bodo (Tomasz Schuchardt) with Reri (Patricia Kazadi) in *Bodo* (2016), directed by Michał Rosa and Michał Kwieciński

he meets briefly in Warsaw Pola Negri, the then greatest Polish film star. She advises the young actor to go to Berlin because the cinema business there is thriving, while Poland remains a cinematic backwater. In the end, Bodo does not follow her advice because, after trying his hand in Warsaw and Poznań, he does not want to start afresh in an unfamiliar environment. Using the language of Bourdieu, we can say that what keeps Bodo in Poland is his cultural capital. With the passage of time and as he accumulates success, the argument for staying in Poland gets stronger. He prefers to be a large fish in a small pond, 'the king of Polish cinema', as he is described, than a small fish in a large pond, one of many foreign actors fighting for the attention of Hollywood producers. The status he achieves and the luxury and freedom to shape his career commensurate with it, gives the impression that Bodo's life in Warsaw during the peak of his career in the second half of the 1930s, was as good as that of the greatest Hollywood stars. It is only shortly before the Second World War that he makes the decision to emigrate to the USA, but this is not prompted by professional considerations, but by romantic factors—a desire to find a safe place for himself, Ada and her two children.

There are several moments in the film when the issue of Bodo's Swiss citizenship is broached. It happens for first time when his father tells him that a 'Swiss passport is the best in the world, therefore he should stick to it no matter what.' The explanation is not so much patriotic, as pragmatic, pointing to Switzerland's status as a neutral country. The second time when his Swiss citizenship helps Bodo is when he causes a car crash, in which another actor dies, and subsequently has a court trial and avoids harsh punishment because, as he is told, the Polish authorities do not want any conflict with a foreign country. The last time, however, the Swiss passport becomes a liability, when he is arrested by the Soviet secret service and imprisoned. Then he is considered a Swiss spy, tortured, sent to different prisons and gulags and eventually executed, in 1943. The authors of *Bodo* suggest that if the actor had Polish citizenship, he would have avoided such a fate. This is because, following the outbreak of the Soviet-German war, there was an amnesty for Polish citizens imprisoned by the Soviets. However, this did not refer to people like Bodo, whose 'neutral' status rendered them suspicious in the eyes of their captors.

The circumstances of Bodo's death, like those of the Polish officers murdered in Katyń, were kept secret by the Soviet authorities. According to their version, he was shot by Germans. Only the fall of state socialism allowed the truth about Bodo's death to be rendered, and the erecting in 2011 of his monument at the cemetery in Kotlas, where he died, which is also his symbolic grave (Mieszkowska 2016: 76). By the same token, Bodo's 'honest' biopic could not have been made before 1989, similarly as any film about Katyń could not have been produced before this period. *Bodo* not only blames the Soviet state for the death of 'king of the Polish (interwar) cinema', but adds a fictitious story to implicate the Russians more in Bodo's death than one can gather from historical documents. When performing in Lviv, singing in Russian, Bodo is 'befriended' by a Soviet officer and his wife. The wife, named Tamara, is infatuated by the singing actor and he agrees to have sex with her, assuming that refusing her might cause him problems. Bodo asks Tamara's husband to facilitate his escape to the USA via Berlin. However, Tamara becomes angry, when she finds Bodo and Ada's photo on his desk and realises that he is in love with another woman. Consequently, she persuades her husband to plot Bodo's demise. The Russian couple encapsulate the worst traits of Russians, according to the Polish stereotype of their eastern neighbour: they are vulgar, selfish, treacherous and cruel. The entire 'Soviet' chapter in Bodo's life brings to mind some earlier films about Polish-Soviet relations, made after the fall of the Berlin Wall, especially *1920 Bitwa Warszawska* (*Battle of Warsaw 1920*, 2011) by Jerzy Hoffman. In these films Russians do not merely lack culture, but are anti-culture: they make a virtue of hating culture. In *Battle of Warsaw* this is epitomised by Russian characters drinking alcohol from chamber-pots; in *Bodo* by Russian secret services treating Bodo particularly harshly because he has talent. It feels like the Soviet oppressors need to reduce the actor to an animal existence and destroy him, in order to be on an equal footing with him; moving up to achieve his level is beyond their reach. Such a negative portrayal of Russians poignantly contrasts with the representation of Russians in Polish cinema of state socialism and post-communist depictions of the second nation, which played the role of Polish enemy—Germans. Indeed, *Bodo* is remarkably subdued in this respect. For example, Hans, Ada's husband, despite ending as an ardent Hitler supporter, ultimately comes across as an honest man, who helps diagnose Zula's illness, is a good husband to Ada and in the end lets her go, probably in part because he loves her and wants her to be happy. Needless to add, such a negative portrayal of Russians is very different from that offered in *Anna German*, where even the biggest Russian villain had some redeeming features. The cruelty of Russians is magnified by the way the series is narrated, with every episode beginning by revealing a fragment of Bodo's ordeal in the Soviet prison, for example in one episode showing his head being shaved; in another being beaten by his oppressors. It feels like the Russians killed Bodo over and over again. As I mentioned earlier, such structuring of biopics, effectively as an extended flashback, suggests a '"natural" collapse of the future into the past' (Vidal 2014: 5), a fatalistic reading of the protagonist's life. Such a fatalistic scenario, on this occasion, contains a nationalistic message: if you live in Poland, live like a Pole and are not ashamed to show it to the world. Ultimately, Bodo's travails, as represented by Kwieciński and Rosa, validated the agenda of the then ruling Party, Prawo i Sprawiedliwość (Law and Justice), which is fervently nationalistic and anti-Russian. The latter was in part explained by the Smolensk catastrophe of 2010, when the Polish President Lech Kaczyński and many other prominent Polish politicians, originating from the Law and Justice Party lost their lives, significantly worsening already tense, Polish-Russian relations.

The cinematic Bodo has to define himself not only in relation to nationality, but also sexuality. While, as I mentioned, he is prepared to prostitute himself with women to further his career or buy his safety, he refuses the advances of another upcoming, yet better-to-do gay actor. However, he is not a homophobe and is happy to perform in drag, first in a seedy cabaret-cum-brothel and later in the film *Upstairs* (examined in Chapter 2), where he sings 'Sex-appeal', one of his most famous songs, adopting the identity of Mae West. That said, he experiences his greatest crisis when Ada sees him performing in drag and decides that he is demeaning himself. This, however, tells more about her conventionality than his 'deficient manhood'.

I mentioned earlier that musicals can be divided into singer's musicals and dancer's musicals. Given that biopics of musicians are also usually musicals, and that Bodo was known for both his singing and dancing talent, it is worth asking which of the two types are foregrounded in the series. The answer is that it changes over the course of the thirteen episodes. The young Bodzio comes across as a dancer—the series begins with him learning tap dance. Once he becomes famous, his singing is more in demand. We see Bodo singing in three places, theatre, cinema and in the recording studio, representing three media. This promotion from dancer to singer can be interpreted as him finding his own voice. To make this point, he is shown changing lyrics in songs written by professional lyricists and it is suggested in the diegesis that he wrote lyrics to some songs which in fact were written by other authors. Such enrichment of Bodo's artistic portfolio can be regarded as a legacy of the auteurist paradigm in the Polish moving image, according to which the performer is not the author of his or her performance, unless s/he is also a composer, lyricist or choreographer. Significantly, the role of the true composers and lyricists of Bodo's songs, such as Henryk Wars and Emanuel Schlechter, is subdued in *Bodo*, in line with the rule of Jewish invisibility or 'ob-scenity', as discussed in Chapter 2.

The musical-dance aspect of the series is also international in its production. The catchy soundtrack of the film was written by Bulgarian composer, Atanas Valkov and the main choreographer is the Polish-Cuban dancer, Agustin Egurrolla. The scale and quality of dancing numbers, especially in the music theatre, is a crucial reason why *Bodo* represents 'quality tv'. In each episode we see several such numbers with dozens of dancers and typically they finish the episode, which adds to their importance. However, while the choreography is spotless, the cinematography is less so, as dancing scenes are always shown from the same, frontal perspective of the viewer sitting in the front row, which gives a sense of repetition. Given that it is always a place, occupied by Bodo's mother, we can assume that the filmmakers tried to adopt her position—that of an utterly devoted fan.

The series proved a moderate success. It was watched on average by 2.7 million viewers. The most popular was the first episode, which was watched by 3.8 million viewers, suggesting that it caused some disappointment, given that it in subsequent weeks it lost over a million viewers (Kurdupski 2016). In the Polish media it was compared negatively to the series *Ranczo* (*The Ranch*), which was broadcast in the same slot (Sunday 8.25 p.m.) the previous year, yet was watched by 3 million viewers more. Another obvious comparator is *Anna German*, which attracted an audience of more than twice that of *Bodo*.

The reviews were moderately positive, praising the spectacular side of the series, yet criticising its narrative and especially its failure to raise strong emotions (Podczarska 2016). This shortcoming is in part a reflection of the fact that Bodo is not an obvious positive character, which admittedly television audiences want to see on screen to a larger extent than their cinematic counterparts. In many ways, Bodo was an anti-hero: he caused another actor's death and mistreated women. This contrasts with Anna German who is remembered by everybody as an 'angel in a female body'. Moreover, the attempts to romanticise Bodo and render him tragic, were rather unsuccessful. In particular, his continuous attachment to Ada, who for most of the film is scornful of the actor, is unconvincing. There are also no sparks, no 'sexual energy' between the actors playing these characters, Tomasz Schuchardt and Anna Pijanowska. Similarly, Bodo's affair with a Russian woman comes across as heavy-handed and too obviously Russophobic. The actors playing the titular character received mixed reviews. This contrasted with enthusiasm about the performance of Joanna Moro in the role of German. In my opinion, however, both Antoni Królikowski and Tomasz Schuchardt did a good job, especially Schuchardt, who had a difficult task to mimic Bodo's unique screen persona, well known from his films and, at the same time, build his off-screen persona practically from scratch.

During the production of *Bodo* there were rumours of plans to produce more biographical television series and the most likely protagonist mentioned was Violetta Villas, the ultimate Polish diva of state socialism (see Chapter 8), with Katarzyna Figura, the main sex symbol of the late state socialist period, cast in her role. Given, however, that *Bodo* performed below expectations, it looks like this project was shelved.

Works Cited

Bernat, Anna. 2013. Waldemar Krzystek: Rosjanie mówią o German "nasza Anna". Dzieje.pl, February 21. https://dzieje.pl/film/waldemar-krzystek-rosjanie-mowia-o-german-nasza-anna. Accessed 15 January 2018.

Kosecka, Barbara. 2016. Umiarkowany sukces. *Dwutygodnik*, 5. https://www.dwutygodnik.com/artykul/6550-umiarkowany-sukces.html. Accessed 17 October 2018.

Kurdupski, Michał. 2016. Bodo oglądało o 3,30 mln widzów mniej niż Ranczo. 7 mln zł z reklam. Wirtualnemedia.pl, May 31. https://www.wirtualnemedia.pl/artykul/bodo-ogladalo-o-3-30-mln-widzow-mniej-niz-ranczo-7-mln-zl-z-reklam. Accessed 15 January 2019.

Lemańska, Magdalena. 2016. Nadawcy zwiększają inwestycje w seriale. *Rzeczpospolita*, November 18. https://www.rp.pl/Media-i-internet/311179841-Nadawcy-zwiekszaja-inwestycje-w-seriale.html. Accessed 12 January 2019.

Madej, Alina. 1994. *Mitologie i konwencje. O polskim kinie fabularnym dwudziestolecia międzywojennego*. Kraków: Universitas.

Mazierska, Ewa. 2016. From South to East: Exoticism in Polish Popular Music of the State Socialist Period. *Popular Music History* 11 (1): 46–60.

Michałek, Bolesław. 1976. *Ćwiczenia z anatomii kina*. Warszawa: Wydawnictwa Artystyczne i Filmowe.

Mieszkowska, Anna. 2016. *Bodo wśród Gwiazd: Opowieść o losach twórców przedwojennych kabaretów*. Warszawa: Marginesy.

Podczarska, Marta. 2016. Bodo: Uśmiercona legenda. Światseriali.pl, March 4. https://swiatseriali.interia.pl/newsy/seriale/bodo-1143/news-bodo-usmiercona-legenda,nId,2156652. Accessed 12 January 2019.

Połaski, Krzysztof. 2016. *Bodo*: Materiał na przebój. Telemagazyn.pl, March 6. https://www.telemagazyn.pl/artykuly/bodo-material-na-przeboj-recenzja-49052.html. Accessed 15 December 2018.

Ufniarz, Bartek. 2016. *Bodo* ma dwa razy mniej widzów niż *Ranczo*. Za to jeden odcinek kosztuje… To fortuna! Party.pl, April 8. http://party.pl/seriale/wyniki-ogladalnosci-bodo-ile-kosztuje-produkcja-odcinka-101455-r1/. Accessed 17 October 2018.

Vidal, Belén. 2014. Introduction: The Biopic and Its Critical Contexts. In *The Biopic in Contemporary Film Culture*, ed. Tom Brown and Belén Vidal, 1–32. London: Routledge.

Wolański, Ryszard. 2012. *Eugeniusz Bodo: 'Już taki jestem zimny drań'*. Poznań: Rebis.

PART III

Music Documentaries

CHAPTER 7

From Reporting to Analysing: Documentaries About Musical Events and Phenomena

As with other genres examined in this book, we know intuitively what a music documentary is, but defining it is not easy. There are problems with capturing the specificity of a documentary film and deciding how much music there should be, to qualify it as a music documentary. In regards to the first problem, the consensus is that documentaries differ from fiction films by representing reality or purporting to do so. The first definition of a documentary, by John Grierson, states that it is 'the creative treatment of actuality' (Rotha 1952: 70). The addition of 'creative' subsequently led to doubts whether documentaries can indeed represent reality. This conundrum, as Stella Bruzzi notes, is reflected in the frequent use of inverted commas with terms such as 'reality', 'the real' or 'truth', which documentaries purport to capture and represent, suggesting that 'the real can never be authentically represented and that any film, whether documentary or fiction, attempting to capture it will inevitably fail' (Bruzzi 2000: 2). In common with Bruzzi, however, I maintain that documentaries capture reality, even if they cannot be reality itself, but 'negotiations between reality on the one hand and image, interpretation and bias on the other' (ibid.: 4). For practical purposes, Jack Ellis and Betsy McLane provide a useful guide to how to differentiate documentaries from other types of films: (1) The subject is generally specific and factual, more often public than private; (2) The purpose is informative. The documentary serves to increase our understanding of, or our interest in, the subject; (3) Documentaries consist of material and situations that already exist (rather than creating situations in fiction); (4) They use non-actors (real people) and shoot on location rather than on set; (5) The main goal of a documentary is to communicate information (rather than express feeling) (Ellis and McLane 2006: 1–3).

The problem with 'creative' also refers to the difference between proper documentaries and lesser forms of non-fiction film. On this topic Jack Ellis and Michael Saffle argue that we cannot equate documentary with broadcasting something which happens in reality. Documentaries have to be retrospective and compiled from various sources, with each documentary representing its compiler's purpose/point of view/approach (Ellis 1989: 1–3; Saffle 2013: 42). There are exceptions to this rule, such as recordings of concerts (Saffle 2013: 42), but such recordings also tend to be carefully planned. Nevertheless, the similarity between concert films and live broadcasts affects the unspoken hierarchy of music documentaries, with Thomas Cohen noticing that concert films have the lowest status of all music documentaries and being seen as 'marginal to cinema proper' (Cohen 2012: 10). However, he refutes such an opinion. In a Polish context the difference between a music documentary and other non-fiction films about music is reflected in using terms such as 'music programme' (*program muzyczny*) or 'transmission' (*transmisja*), to describe the latter. Such terms were typically used to describe television broadcasts from music events and interviews with musicians, which were treated as utilitarian and ephemeral forms without pretensions to artistry.

The second issue is the place of music in a documentary to merit the use of the term 'music documentary'. Does the film have to include diegetic music to qualify for such a label and is this a sufficient condition? I will answer 'no' to both parts of this question, because there can be much music in a documentary, and still its topic might be something other than music and conversely, a documentary film might contain little or no music and still say much about a specific 'music world': its producers and fans, as well as its relation to politics, social life and a wider culture.

There are no global histories of music documentaries in English and the existing histories of documentary cinema tend to ignore or marginalise this subgenre. I will not attempt to write one here either, due to both space constraints and because it is not essential to understanding the Polish take on music documentary. However, it is worth mentioning several milestones in this history, recurring in literature. One of them is the premiere of *Woodstock* (1970), directed by Michael Wadleigh, a documentary about the famous countercultural Woodstock Festival (Kitts 2009; Grant 2012: 116–130; Edgar et al. 2013: 3), which took place in 1969 near Bethel, New York. Its importance lay in its novelty and artistic quality, and the insight it gave into a specific music world, namely the relationship between the music presented at the Woodstock Festival and the counterculture of the 1960s (Grant 2012: 121–130). Wadleigh's film drew attention to and dignified music documentaries as a specific subgenre of documentary film. Another music documentary worth mentioning is *All You Need Is Love: The Story of Popular Music* (1977) by Tony Palmer—its significance lies in demonstrating that filmic history of popular music can compete with its written history in terms of scope and depth, as well as offering a distinct perspective (Long and Wall 2013). Finally, there are several documentary films about musicians which became classics, such as *Johnny Cash! The Man, His World, His Music* (1969), directed by Robert Elfstrom and in the later period *Madonna: Truth or Dare* (1991), directed by Alek Keshishian, which took issue with the nature of celebrity.

Because of the relatively low status of music documentaries, there are few film directors whose work in this genre is recognised as an auteurist pursuit. Probably the most celebrated of them is Tony Palmer, although this might be more to do with his achievements as a maker of documentaries about classical than pop musicians. Other examples include Martin Scorsese and Jean-Luc Godard. They are mainly known for their fiction films, but Scorsese's *The Last Waltz* (1978) about the final concert of The Band and *Shine a Light* (2008) about the performance of the Rolling Stones, and Godard's *Sympathy for the Devil* (1968) about the Rolling Stones are regarded as works of exceptionally high quality.

Poland does not have an equivalent of Palmer, who dedicated his life to documenting serious and popular music. Neither does it have director-stars like Scorsese or Godard, who from time to time directed their camera to important musical events and personalities. The 'national directors', such as Andrzej Wajda, Krzysztof Kieślowski and Krzysztof Zanussi, on occasions used popular music and musicians in their films, but never showed interest in popular music as a phenomenon in its own right, probably regarding it as too frivolous a topic. Consequently, making documentaries about popular music was left to less well-known directors and newcomers, contributing to the relatively low status of their productions. Nevertheless, the body of such documentaries is significant and I will present them in two chapters. The first is devoted to events and phenomena; the second to stars. Such a division in a sense mirrors the first two parts of this book, devoted to musicals, which tackle musical genres and fashions (folklorism, big beat, rock) and biopics, which tell stories about music stars.

Polish Documentaries About Popular Music

Poland produced thousands of documentary films and it has a sizeable number of documentaries about popular music. However, up to the 1980s, their proportion in relation to the entire documentary production was relatively low and they rarely offered a deeper insight into this phenomenon (Pławuszewski 2015), which can be seen as a reflection of the specific bias of Polish documentary cinema, which regarded high art as a worthier subject of filmmaker's investigation than popular culture. Initially, the films were reports from large music events, in a few minutes trying to introduce the artists and their audience, sometimes commenting in a humorous or patronising manner about the event presented, as was the case with the new fashion of big beat in the 1960s (ibid.: 105–109). Films of this type, which can be described as 'reportages', functioned as stand-alone short films, shown on television, but more often they were part of newsreels, screened in cinemas before the main show. The history of Polish music documentary is thus not very different from that in the USA or the UK, as till the 1970s filmmakers usually limited themselves to shooting live events. As Robert Edgar, Kirsty Fairclough-Isaacs and Benjamin Halligan argue, on such occasions 'the camera engaged in reportage, the musicians primarily engaged in the live delivery of their music' (Edgar et al. 2013: 3).

With the passage of time, the range of topics covered by Polish music documentaries increased, incorporating longer transmissions from musical events and portrayals of the artists, and analyses of certain music phenomena. A real explosion of music documentaries took place in the 1980s, when Polish rock enjoyed a period of renaissance (Hučkova 2015: 405). Some music documentaries from this period were full-length, to allow them to be screened in cinemas not as an addition to the main feature, but as the main programme. Still, throughout the whole period of state socialism, television was the main platform for music documentaries. Either it produced documentaries using their own facilities or, more often, commissioned them from Wytwórnia Filmów Dokumentalnych (Documentary Film Studio). Most of these films were directed and scripted by filmmakers working on permanent contracts there, such as Jerzy Gruza (b. 1932), Janusz Rzeszewski (1930–2007), Grzegorz Lasota (1929–2014) and Józef Gębski (b. 1939), whom I interviewed for the purpose of writing this chapter. They specialised in all types of music-centred productions, including music videos, and often their documentaries were a by-product of the television broadcasts from large events and an opportunity to earn extra money.

The fall of state socialism led to a break-up of the monopoly of television and the mushrooming of private film and video production companies offering their services to whoever wanted to pay for it, for example regional television channels or recording companies. Moreover, changes in the technology, resulting from the use of video and digital cameras, led to a situation when documentaries could be made cheaply by people with little or no professional training, using as little of equipment as mobile phones. The main platform where they can be accessed today is YouTube. It is also the main archive of older music documentaries.

It will be impossible here to provide a comprehensive history of Polish documentaries about popular music, therefore my approach in this chapter is to examine the most important or typical documentaries in Polish history, beginning with festival reportages and finishing with a film attempting to capture the state of the popular music business after the fall of the Iron Curtain.

From Festival Reportages to Festival Impressions

The first Polish popular music documentaries were about public performances during popular events, such as large music festivals. They were made for Polish television which broadcast them or rather they were events set up mainly for a television audience who watched them in the most attractive slots. For this reason they started in the 1960s, when television sets stopped being a luxury and started to be an essential piece of furniture. We can appreciate how the popularity of television grew, by comparing the situation from 1960 to 1963. In 1960 there were 50,000 television sets in Poland; in 1963 there were 1,000,000 television subscribers (Kończak 2007: 30).[1]

The early festivalisation in Poland began with the International Music Festival in Sopot, in 1960 (in the years 1977–1980 the Intervision Music Festival), the Festival of Polish Songs in Opole, existing officially from 1963, the Festival of Soviet Songs in Zielona Góra, from 1965 and the

Festival of Army Songs, first in Połczyn-Zdrój and then Kołobrzeg, from 1967. Their emergence in this decade can be explained by a change in the approach and style of governing by the political authorities: from highly ideological to technocratic. According to the new approach, the main goal of the authorities was not so much to turn the masses into a community of socialist 'new men and women', but to make them content enough not to question the system openly and accept their place in it. Providing entertainment, which could be tightly planned and monitored, was an important means to this end and popular music festivals fulfilled this requirement (Kienzler 2015: 317; Sankowski 2016). Therefore, the audience *watched* these state socialist festivals, either in person, sitting on benches in large amphitheatres rather than participating in them more actively by, for example, dancing to the rhythm of the music. Not surprisingly, the festivals were criticised by Polish intellectual elites for their low quality and diverting people away from political activities (Kisielewski, quoted in Bittner 2017: 143). However, they were truly popular; almost everybody who lived in Poland during their existence, myself included, was familiar with their format and knew their winners.

The festivals were organised by regional authorities with the support of national institutions, most importantly television and the ministry of culture which, in effect, were accountable to the Party's executive. They took place on one stage, as usually a given town or city only had one stage suitable for the festival and because this ensured that they were easier to plan and monitor. Such a format was also most convenient for television transmission. Popular television presenters, such as Lucjan Kydryński, Krystyna Loska and Grażyna Torbicka, were employed to present these events and they became festival stars in their own right. The peak of their popularity was in the 1970s, which coincided with investment into Polish television under the chairman of the Television Committee Maciej Szczepański. Szczepański was into pomp and spectacle, and music festivals, especially the Sopot Festival, were a perfect outlet for his grandiose ambitions (Krajewski 2018).

These festivals were theme rather than genre-oriented, as conveyed by their names: festivals of Polish, Soviet and Army songs. Although, in principle, representatives of different genres could participate in them, in practice they favoured estrada singers over rockers. By the same token, they were friendly towards female performers, as women dominated this type of music, such as Maryla Rodowicz, Urszula Sipińska and Izabela Trojanowska, and to older audiences and families.

The Sopot and Opole festivals were directed, respectively by Janusz Rzeszewski and Jerzy Gruza, who were also in charge of many other television programmes centred on music, as well as directing films, with the former being the leading director of Polish film musicals of the state socialist era, along with Stanisław Bareja (see Chapters 3 and 5). Most of their broadcasts did not survive or are difficult to access. However, there are some films made from the material used in the broadcasts. One of them, titled *Sopot 68* (1968), directed by Janusz Rzeszewski, gives a good insight into the Sopot Festival, as seen by a television audience. The film has no external commentary; the only information about performers and awards is from the festival presenter Lucjan Kydryński. Most of the film is filled with shots of performing artists in medium-close shots and close-ups. They are juxtaposed with images of the audience, which is always respectful, giving applause to the artists, but rarely becoming rapturous. A viewer unfamiliar with the format of the festival might be surprised by the large number of artists from non-socialist countries, such as Spain (whose representatives won the Grand Prix in 1968), Italy, Denmark, Japan and the USA, along with performers from socialist countries, such as Romania and, of course, Poland.

Despite the technical poverty of Polish television in this period, about which both Rzeszewski and Gruza complained in the previously mentioned documentary by Adam Wyżyński, the film does not come across as inferior to those produced on the occasion of a Eurovision Song Contest. It is difficult to identify in it an authorial stamp, reflecting the fact that Rzeszewski did not perceive himself as an *auteur* or an artist, but rather as a television functionary, following its ethos, which means promoting what is popular.

A different approach to documenting the Sopot Festival was taken by Józef Gębski and Antoni Halor in *Sopot 70* (1970). Gębski, better known of the two directors, who was the leading force on this film, is primarily a documentarist with well over one hundred films in his portfolio. He also directed several fiction films, mostly comedies and many music videos. Many of his productions show penchant for paradox, irony, incongruent juxtaposition and non-verbal, slapstick humour. In Gębski's own words, he was a big admirer of the films of Jacques Tati, whom he visited in Paris, in order to learn how he makes his films (Gębski 2009a: 59–60), Richard Lester and the Polish creator of the absurdist theatre, Sławomir Mrożek (Gębski 2009a: 70). These inspirations are not difficult to identify in *Sopot 70*, but we can also find here a similarity to the films by Stanisław

Kokesz, which I will discuss in the part about music videos. They also testify to Gębski's temperament of somebody who is not only able to switch from genre to genre, but transcend genre boundaries. In an essay he wrote about documentary art, he mirrors the views of pioneers such as Grierson, saying that 'fiction and documentary films are like Siamese twins' (Gębski 2009b: 49) and 'documentary is creative' (ibid.: 55).

Sopot 70 juxtaposes fragments of concerts of the stars of the festival with still images illustrating their songs, subtitles written in elaborate font and humorous scenes taking place in Sopot. The most interesting are shots of Karel Gott, who is shown pretending to be a cameraman. We also see the greatest Polish singer of 'singing poetry', Ewa Demarczyk, the folk-rock band No To Co and Maryla Rodowicz, at the time a new star of Polish pop (Fig. 7.1).

We also get snapshots of the previously mentioned Lucjan Kydryński and Jerzy Gruza, respectively the main presenter and director of the Festival. Of the performers, the most screen time is given to Rodowicz

Fig. 7.1 Ewa Demarczyk performing in *Sopot 70* (1970), directed by Józef Gębski and Antoni Halor

(for whom Gębski also shot some music videos). She sings one of her greatest hits, 'Jadą woozy kolorowe' (Colourful Waggons Are Passing), a song about Gypsy Life. Gębski and Halor create a story about it, a kind of music video in a music documentary, playing on the double meaning of 'wozy', which in Polish can mean a waggon or a motorcar. The protagonist of the 'fictional' part is played by Jacek Gmoch, a footballer and trainer of the Polish national football team, with a distinctive face and a very long chin. Gmoch, wearing old-fashioned gentleman's attire, is looking for a lost Cinderella on the Sopot streets, beaches and at the open air theatre (Opera Leśna), where the festival takes place. In the end he collects plenty of shoes and other female garments, yet he finds no Cinderella, perhaps because Sopot is full of beautiful women and he is spoilt for choice. Like a character from Tati's films, he remains silent and the humour of his behaviour lies in him being oblivious to what happens around him.

Together with *Success* by Marek Piwowski (which I discuss in the next chapter), Sopot 70 is, in my view, the most inventive music documentary made before the 'rock wave' of the 1980s. However, the tradition of making films on music in such a way, namely using whimsical humour and mixing music documentary with comedy, disappeared in the subsequent period.

ALL YOU NEED IS ROCK

The 1980s was the decade of the 'second coming' of rock music in Poland, as I argued in Chapter 3. This was reflected in the upsurge of fiction films about rock music and even more so, documentaries on this topic, The bulk of them showed the concerts of the most popular bands and several were devoted to rock festivals, including Jarocin Festival,[2] founded in 1980, which in this decade was not only the leading festival of rock music in Poland, but probably the most important event in young people's calendar in this country. Another important rock festival was Rockowisko, held in Łódź.

These festivals featured the most important Polish rock bands of the period and allowed its participants, both artists and audience, to forge countercultural identities. Jarocin in particular was seen as a political event, expressing opposition to the (by then declining) state socialist regime. However, it could also be seen as a sign of the state's acceptance of youth culture, as shown by the fact that it was an official festival, supported by the local authorities of Jarocin (a small town in the Wielkopolska region with a population of twenty thousand people) and that its director, Walter Chełstowski, was part of the official music establishment in Poland. It can thus be construed as a safety valve, allowing disgruntled youth to express their grievances in the limited time and space of a 'carnival', according to the scenario described by Mikhail Bakhtin. It can also be regarded as a sign of the early neoliberalisation of Poland—the authorities' recognition of the need to monetise popular music and youth culture as a way to plug a gap in the national and local economies. In the Polish context, the Jarocin Festival was also a festival of a new type, which would provide a blueprint for the music festivals of the post-communist period. In contrast to the festivals like those in Opole and Sopot, the focus there was not on winning a coveted award, but on creating a space where the audience can meet and bond with like-minded people, and create a specific subculture. Jarocin's audience was also much younger than the Opole and Sopot crowds and they lived on the festival camp, hence could experience the festival for a much longer and more intense period, having an opportunity to meet fellow fans on the way to the showers or the morning cigarette, as well as at the concerts. The bulk of visitors were standing and dancing rather than sitting, which also facilitated a closer interaction with fellow festival-goers.

Two of the rock festivals films were made by the Irzykowski Studio, an outlet for young directors, eager to experiment and react to the needs of younger audiences, and they had cinema distribution. The first of them, *Koncert* (*Concert*, 1982) was about Rockowisko 81, directed by Michał Tarkowski (b. 1946), for whom it was his diploma film. The director of *Concert* is better known as an actor, including in the celebrated *Wodzirej* (*Top Dog*, 1977) by Feliks Falk, where he stands as an opposite of the careerist Lutek Danielak. Tarkowski was also involved in student culture, which explains such a 'youthful' topic as his debut. He described himself as being 'fascinated by music' (quoted in Jóźwiak 1984: 12). *Concert* was meant to be a typical short documentary, but during its production the authors realised that there was commercial potential in the project and decided to extend it to a full-length format. *Concert's* history is protracted, as the final stages of its production coincided with the imposition of martial law. To finish his film, Tarkowski added scenes shot elsewhere and its premiere was delayed—hence its first reviews come from 1984, three years after the event which was at the centre of the film.

True to its title, the film focuses on performances given by the leading bands of this period, such as TSA, Maanam, Republika and Dezerter. The scenes from the concerts are juxtaposed with shots of the audience—faces covered in paint, often frozen, so that one can contemplate the difference in their appearance from how people looked on an average Polish street. There are also shots showing the visitors first sleeping in bags, in order to reach their destination and then dancing ecstatically and swimming naked in the lake. Such scenes imply the closeness of the visitors to nature that informed the counterculture of the 1960s (Roszak 1995) and were also intensively used in *Woodstock* (Grant 2012: 121–122), which was clearly the main inspiration for Tarkowski's film.

There is no off-screen commentary or interviews with the artists. The idea behind the film is that the sound and image should speak for themselves. This was Tarkowski's intention—he confessed that he was scornful about films which tried to present the music of young people from the perspective of some older sociologists or psychologists; instead, he wanted young people to speak with their own voice (Jóźwiak 1984: 12). However, what they say is mostly predictable—that they go to the festival to enjoy freedom, which is what one expects to hear at rock festivals, be it Woodstock or Glastonbury. Moreover, probably against the intentions of the filmmakers, we get a sense of a cultural lag, as such images of freedom seeking hippies were more suitable to the 1960s that the 1980s.

The strongest point of the film is its music. It comes across as very versatile, reflecting the wealth of subgenres of rock music which were tried at the time by Polish bands. The bands represent such styles as metal (TSA), new wave (Republika), post-punk (Maanam), as well as blues (Krzak, Kasa Chorych), reggae (Brygada Kryzys) and mainstream rock (Perfect). Of them, Republika and Maanam sounded the most original in the 1980s and fared best during the time which has passed since the film's premiere, and the fact that Tarkowski decided to present them at length testify to his good judgement about what would survive from this period. Not only did he document the performance of these bands, but attempted to find its visual equivalent. Hence, the music of Republika, which comes across as static, is shot in a static way; during the performance the camera focuses on the band's leader, Grzegorz Ciechowski, standing behind the keyboard, as if oblivious to the surrounding reality, focused only on his music. By contrast, the performance of TSA, which is very dynamic, is rendered even more dynamic through the use of handheld cameras. Tarkowski also uses animation and changes the speed of action, as often happened in music videos of this period, which prompted reviewers to compare his film to a music video (Bratkowski 1985: 11; Pawlicki 1985: 9). What is lacking in the film, as one reviewer noted, is an overall authorial concept, maybe because the director was too preoccupied with showing each band in its glory (Bratkowski 1985: 11) and using all possible artistic means, like a child who received all available toys at once—a problem often encountered by inexperienced directors. It might also be that, by this point, filmmakers, as well as popular music historians, were unable to provide a synthesis of Polish rock of the 1980s.

The second rock festival film made by the Irzykowski Studio was *Fala* (*Wave*) by Piotr Łazarkiewicz. Made in 1986, it concerns the 1985 festival in Jarocin. Łazarkiewicz (1994–2008), like Tarkowski, was then a young director 'full of promise'. However, this promise was never fulfilled. After *Wave* Łazarkiewicz produced many cine and television films, both fiction and documentary, which by now are practically forgotten. *Wave* remains his best known film, but this is probably more due to the then fashionable subject than the way the director handled it. Unlike Tarkowski, who focused on the rock festival as a large-scale concert, Łazarkiewicz, as the title of his film suggests, is more interested in the festival as a social phenomenon—as a 'wave of people' coming to Jarocin. We get many shots showing crowds of people: the tent city, the crowds listening to the concert, dancing in front of the stage, etc. A large part of the film is filled by interviews with its participants: the audience and the musicians, as well as representatives of Jarocin's authorities, such as a council leader, the head of the local police and an elderly woman from a women's organisation. It appears that Łazarkiewicz tries to show the clash between the views of these older people and that of the youth coming to Jarocin, which can be regarded as a metonymy of generational conflict. However, there is no real clash of opinions, only a difference of perspective on the value of the event. The young say that the festival allows them to escape the mundane reality and express themselves. For Jarocin's political establishment, on the other hand, the festival is an opportunity to put their town on the map, increase tourism and to earn extra revenue. Although the lady from the women's league is two generations removed from the guests, she lists the advantages of the festival, such as bringing together youth from different parts of the country which facilitates their understanding of each other. While her language is different from those used by the young people, they also claim that the main attraction of Jarocin for them is not music, but being together. The attitude of all these people testifies to the change of mindset of the authorities, which consisted of sidelining the ideological principles of socialism and focusing on generating income, even through exploiting initiatives which might be critical of this ideology. This is also how capitalism works—it will be happy to sell revolution, if it brings income. In this context it is worth returning to *Woodstock*, as in this film, as Barry Keith Grant observes, 'more than one local merchant speaks of the potential significant boost to the county's economy from the event' (Grant 2012: 126).

The musicians and visitors who are interviewed in the film are asked about the future. This question was probably meant to elicit deeper responses, but the result is that the answers are banal. Some people say that they don't think about the future or that the future will be good, because music in Jarocin is getting better and better. However, the film captures the last 'golden years' of rock music in Poland. The sense of an approaching exhaustion is reflected in the quality of the filmed performances—the bands, mostly representing punk, lack the charisma and energy of those included in Tarkowski's film, such as Republika and Maanam. The lyrics of the songs are crude—there is much anger in them, but each band appears to express them in the same way. Łazarkiewicz also lacks Tarkowski's talent in accentuating the specificity of styles of the Polish bands. With the exception of Aya RL, the bands captured by Łazarkiewicz's camera, are by this point forgotten. In this way, Łazarkiewicz's film foreshadows the crisis of Polish rock music after the end of state socialism, being taken over by new genres, most importantly hip hop and disco polo.

Polish rock documentaries of the 1980s received their second and third lives, due to their fragments being reused in documentary and fiction films. For example, footage from *Jarocin 82* (1982), a 20-minute documentary by Paweł Karpiński, was recycled by him in his fiction film *Only Rock* (discussed in Chapter 3) and *Beats of Freedom*, which I will examine in the next section. They also adorned various commemorative events, such as, in the case of *Concert*, in 2001, during the Music and Film Festival. The journalist Robert Leszczyński, writing about its re-release, noted that the film's shortcomings, pointed out by the reviewers in the 1980s, were irrelevant; what mattered was its documentary function, such as capturing the performance of bands which soon after ceased to exist (Leszczyński 2001).

Beats of Freedom When There Was No Freedom

The fall of the Iron Curtain saw the production of a large number of 'historical documentaries', whose purpose was to present Polish history, especially of the years 1945–1989, in a way which could not be shown earlier due to censorship. They included films about the Katyń massacre, workers' strikes and the activities of the secret services. Mirosław Przylipiak argues that 'historical documents', are characterised by the use of archival photos and found footage, opinions of witnesses and experts, which are connected by the author's commentary: all means mobilised to give an impression of presenting an objective, historical truth (Przylipiak 1998: 70). We find all these elements in the 72-minute *Beats of Freedom—Zew wolności* (2010), directed by Wojciech Gnoiński and Leszek Słota, which Justyna Czaja and Katarzyna Mąka-Malatyńska include in the subgenre of historical documentaries (Czaja and Mąka-Malatyńska 2015: 608). The reason is that this film also intends to present a fragment of Polish history, on this occasion Polish rock music, in an objective way. It can be regarded as the Polish equivalent of Tony Palmer's *All You Need Is Love: The Story of Popular Music*.

The title of Gnoiński and Słota's film includes an English and Polish phrase—the Polish one being a loose translation of 'beats of freedom'. Such a title suggests that the film is addressed to two constituencies: foreign and Polish viewers. This intention can also be deduced from the fact that its co-producer was the Adam Mickiewicz Institute, an institution, whose mission is to promote Polish culture abroad. Another sign of the film's international ambition is the use of Chris Salewicz in the role of narrator, a London-based music journalist of Polish ancestry, who narrates the film in English and talks in English to his interviewees, on occasion correcting their clumsy expressions. Such a take on Polish documentary, which brings to mind BBC documentaries about foreign lands, would come across as natural, if the topic was music in a foreign land, but strikes me as strange when it is meant to speak to Poles. It gives the impression that they are unable to construct their own history; somebody from outside, with a deeper insight, has to do it for them. In other words, *Beats of Freedom* can be seen as a product of western cultural imperialism (Laing 1986) and self-colonisation, given that Polish institutions invited a British journalist to tell them a story, or even *the* story of their music, as the film has the aura of a definitive work. This impression is reinforced by Salewicz, who presents himself as an experienced journalist who wrote many books about popular music. Covers of his books are included in the film, acting as conveyors of his authority and, at the same time, give him free publicity.

Salewicz presents the history of Polish rock from the 1960s till the end of state socialism, using all these elements identified by Przylipiak, including archival footage originating from the Documentary Film Studio and the Military Film Studio (Czołówka), as well as films about the Jarocin Festival, examined in the previous section. The documentary footage is focused on the state's totalitarian character and the hopelessness of life under the 'communist' regime. We repeatedly see May Day parades in front of the Palace of Culture, military vehicles on the streets, crushing protesters, and empty shelves in the shops. There are also interviews with prominent musicians and music journalists and a politician from the Solidarity camp, Arkadiusz Rybicki. In doing so, Salewicz emphasises certain characteristics of Polish rock: its lagging behind western rock, derivative character and, finally, maturation through politicisation. We can also find such an approach in one of the first books about Eastern European popular music, written by another author of Polish ancestry, Timothy Ryback (1990), which in my own work I criticised it as colonial and crude (Mazierska 2016a).

Salewicz begins by saying that in the mid-1950s, when Elvis Presley was changing the history of popular music and youth culture in the Anglo-American world, Poland was still in the thralls of Stalinism, a kind of cultural middle-ages. He admits that in the 1960s this started to change, A crucial factor was the 1967 Rolling Stones concert in Warsaw. After that Poland had its first rock star—Czesław Niemen and we see Niemen singing 'Dziwny jest ten świat' (Strange Is This World), which Salewicz describes as a protest song, in this way presenting Niemen as a Polish response to Bob Dylan. In reality, as I argued elsewhere, 'Strange Is This World' was not an ordinary protest song, because it did not take issue with any political event; Niemen himself described it as a 'protest song against protest songs' (Mazierska 2016b: 249), a genre which the Polish singer treated with scorn.

Niemen is the only Polish star from the 1960s who is featured in *Beats of Freedom*, and there are no artists from this period whose interviews are included in Gnoiński and Słota's film, despite the fact that the 1960s are regarded as the first 'golden age' of Polish rock. The 1970s, when some Polish rock musicians started to experiment with electronic instruments, is skipped. The largest part of the film is devoted to the 1980s because at that time Polish rock became overtly political, delivering the eponymous beats of freedom to the audience. This is conveyed in interviews with musicians, as well as the images from the Jarocin Festival, which Salewicz describes as an 'enclave of freedom', a unique place not only in Poland, but in the entire Soviet bloc. Salewicz's main informant on this topic is Tomasz Lipiński, a rock musician best known from the bands Brygada Kryzys and Tilt, popular in the 1980s. Lipiński's main thesis is that at the time everything was hopeless, there was 'no future'. Such a claim, however, poses a conundrum to the authors of the film, because it is difficult to square with an assertion that at the time Polish rock reached its apex. Salewicz is aware of this tension and asks his interviewees how this could happen. The answers he receives is that the authorities were ultimately too weak and foolish to be able to control Polish rock. For example, in one anecdote Lipiński states that his band was asked to test equipment in a newly opened music studio which allowed him and his friends to record an 'oppositional' record. Even though the 1980s are presented as the peak of Polish rock and youth culture, still the music and culture of this period is presented as merely a delayed response to the western phenomena—a Polish version of the hippie culture of the 1960s and British punk productions of the 1970s.

The focus on politics affects the choice of music played in the film. Apart from Niemen, we hear the most political songs by bands such as Brygada Kryzys, Perfect, Maanam and Republika. By contrast, there are no signs of other popular bands, such as Czerwone Gitary, Skaldowie, Karin Stanek, Ludmiła Jakubczak, Marek Grechuta or Exodus, whose productions endured the passage of time better than some of Salewicz's favourites. We can guess that they were not included, because they did not shout about their need to be free as did Perfect or Brygada Kryzys. The film also alludes to the fact that attitudes to politics had affected the tacit hierarchy of Polish popular music and perpetuates this hierarchy itself. This happens, most conspicuously, when one of Salewicz's interviewees says that people like Edward Gierek (the leader of the Party in the 1970s) did not like rock and favoured Boney M. Such a claim suggests that disco music (both western and Polish) must be of a lower value than rock, which was political. There are also some scornful comments about pop, albeit without pointing to any specific performers. Despite its narrow focus, political bias and western imperialist attitude, *Beats of Freedom* is a valuable introduction to Polish pop-rock. However, it is unfortunate that the film is not followed by a more comprehensive film history (or, indeed, a written history) of Polish popular music.

THE SOUNDTRACKS TO LIFE
AMONG THE CONCRETE BLOCKS

Although the documentaries from the 1980s tried to capture musical phenomena as social phenomena, they still focused on performing musicians and distinct events, such as festivals, presented as special occasions allowing subcultural identities to be activated. In such films artists are separated from the audience, who treat them as their idols. The films also attempted to preserve the mystique of music production and performance, presenting the singers as being metaphorically and literally above the audience.

This situation changed after the fall of the Berlin Wall, when we find more documentaries which focus on the subcultures which gave birth to specific musical genres and use music as a means to investigate this subculture. One of the first films which adopted such a perspective is *Blokersi* (*Blockers*, 2001) about the hip hop phenomenon in Poland, principally in Poznań and Warsaw. Its director, Sylwester Latkowski, in the first half of the 2000s shot several documentary films about different aspects of popular music in Poland, including one about pop star Michał Wiśniewski, which will be discussed in the next chapter. In the later part of his career he made mostly films about scandals in Polish politics.

Hip hop in *Blockers* is presented as music which stems from a specific place and culture: concrete block estates (*blokowiska*). There we find the leading producers of hip hop music and its consumers. In *Blockers* the difference between them is blurred; both types come from the same social milieu and it is difficult to say who in the film is a musician and who is merely a fan. Moreover, musicians self-identify themselves as amateurs, because they haven't yet made any money from music. Together, we can describe them as 'musickers' (Small **1998**). Hip hop music is a soundtrack to their lives, rather than something which takes them away from their ordinary existence.

The main characters in the film are Peja (Ryszard Andrzejewski) from Poznań and Eldo (Leszek Kaźmierczak) from Warsaw, who at the time were upcoming hip hop musicians. They talk about their lives and introduce us to their friends from the estates, who are DJs, rappers, as well as graffiti artists and break-dancers, which constitute the four pillars of hip hop subculture (de Paor-Evans 2018: 1). They all present the same narrative about their involvement in this subculture: it allows them to express themselves, as well as provides an alternative to criminal behaviour, such as stealing or abusing drugs. Although painting on trains is illegal in Poland, the man interviewed in the film does not regard his behaviour as criminal and distances himself from the gangs who destroy property. Similarly, hip hop musickers do not see themselves as poor, but only suffering from boredom and a lack of attractive opportunities.

Apart from artists and fans of hip hop, some journalists are interviewed in the film. Talking to them reveals the conservatism of the Polish popular music establishment, namely a long-held view in Poland that hip hop is a solely American phenomenon, hence by definition its Polish version must be inferior and even fake. The only person who has a different view (and the only woman featured in the film) is Bogna Świątkowska, editor in chief of the music magazine *Machina*. Świątkowska admits that she started to champion hip hop music because she lived in the UK where she familiarised herself with productions of this type and upon returning to Poland missed them. Her comments testify to the fact that hip hop music flourished in post-communist Poland despite a lack of promotion in the media and endorsement by cultural elites. This situation would change in due course, in part thanks to YouTube, where Polish rappers could compete with representatives of other genres on an equal footing. Hip hop artists featured in the film take poetic revenge on the journalists who denigrated their music without listening to it, by reading aloud and deconstructing an article about hip hop published in the influential (and culturally rather conservative) magazine *Polityka*.

The material used in *Blockers* is very versatile. It includes shots from the housing estates, interviews with hip hop artists, journalists and fans, footage from concerts and breakdance competitions, shots of graffiti artists in action, and recordings and rehearsals in 'bedroom studios'. Such a method demonstrates the richness of the hip hop phenomenon, as well as adding dynamism to the film. Unlike in *Beats of Freedom*, which relied heavily on high-quality archival footage, shot by state-owned studios, *Blockers* favours low-quality material, shot by the insiders. There is a fit between hip hop as a genre which captures the 'pulse of the city' and is always on the move and Latkowski's film which tries to do the same—capture the life of the estate.

Latkowski's film was not only concerned with the birth of hip hop in Poland, but also affected its development, affording Peja the status of a hip hop star. As Artur Szarecki observes, 'Peja became the real beneficiary of the film's massive success, as its premiere coincided with the release of *Na legalu?* (2001), his fifth full-length album with Slums Attack. *Na legalu?* sold almost one hundred thousand copies and turned platinum, which has never since been repeated by a Polish hip-hop album. It also won Peja his only Fryderyk, an annual music industry award. However, despite all of his commercial success, Peja remained the voice of the "subaltern", speaking on behalf of those afflicted by poverty, struggling with addictions, and suffering from lack of social acceptance' (Szarecki 2020: 157). Until now, it is probably the only film which not only represented popular music, but affected its development.

DISCO POLO AND TECHNO THROUGH THE LENS OF MARIA ZMARZ-KOCZANOWICZ

Along with hip hop, disco polo and club music became the two main music phenomena in Poland of the 1990s and 2000s. Consequently, they attracted the attention of the Polish documentarists. This included Maria Zmarz-Koczanowicz (b. 1954), one of the most renowned documentary filmmakers in Poland, who started her career in the 1980s, largely thanks to her use of irony. In a booklet, accompanying the DVD box set of her films, we find an essay, written by Tadeusz Sobolewski entitled 'A Liberal Ironist'. Irony in Zmarz-Koczanowicz's earlier films could be seen as a means to express a position critical of the government, without being censored. After 1989 there was no longer a need to use irony for this purpose, but Zmarz-Koczanowicz retained it when presenting phenomena which clash with her taste, including disco polo, which gained huge popularity in the 1990s, as well as scorn of Polish cultural elites, as mentioned in Chapter 4.

To disco polo Zmarz-Koczanowicz devoted one of her best known films, *Bara bara* (*Hanky Panky*, 1996). *Hanky Panky* lasts 65 minutes and consists of interviews with leading representatives of the disco polo industry and fragments of their performances. One of the interviewees is Sławomir Skręta, who set up the record studio Blue Star, the first to specialise in producing cassettes and CDs with this music. He is also credited with inventing the term in 1993 (Filar 2014). Two other principal interviewees are Sławomir Świerzyński, leader of the band Bayer Full and Marlena Magdalena Pańkowska, performing under the artistic pseudonym Shazza (Fig. 7.2).

Fig. 7.2 Shazza recording in *Bara bara* (*Hanky Panky*, 1996), directed by Maria Zmarz-Koczanowicz

Throughout the film disco polo is presented as a lucrative business. Skręta explains the rationale for setting up Blue Star in terms of filling a gap in the market, rather than promoting music which he particularly enjoys and neither of the performers mentions their emotional attachment to this music. Its importance is explained by its value to their audiences rather than the artists themselves. The musicians talk with pride about the letters which they receive from their fans, including children, who confess that disco polo accompanied them in happy moments, for example when an unemployed father got a job. We learn that prisoners tend to be disco polo fans. 'Wolność' (Freedom) by Boys is presented as an absolute favourite of the radio station in the Białołęka prison. We also see a secretary working in Blue Star, negotiating a deal with a customer, wanting to book a band for a wedding. The discussion can be compared to that negotiating the sale of any other commodity. The artists, most importantly Shazza and Świerzyński, reveal how making disco polo music saved them from performing mundane jobs, such as in the case of Shazza entering data onto a computer, and Świerzyński working as a gardener in the USA, cutting grass in the houses of rich people. It is not mentioned that both

Pańkowska and Świerzyński have a musical education to the college level. A disco polo musician comes across an amateur, who makes up for deficiencies in his talent and education with his smartness. This happens by projecting an image of success irrespective of one's actual situation, rather than creating one's own unique path to attainment. This point is reinforced by the film's mise-en-scene. The camera focuses on images of success achieved by the people linked to disco polo. On numerous occasions we see a villa where Blue Star studio is located and the background of one of the interviews is most likely a car showroom, with several expensive cars behind the interviewee. Zmarz-Koczanowicz also suggests that the money generated by disco polo is of a nouveau riche type. This point is most conspicuously made by showing in close-up garden ornaments in front of the Blue Star studio, which include clay gnomes, traditionally associated with bad taste and large clay dogs which can be seen as bad taste multiplied. By contrast, there are no images showing disco polo artists in their private, domestic space, which might soften their image as shrewd entrepreneurs.

Producing disco polo music consists of filling the same formula. As Świerzyński explains in the film, musically disco polo is based on polka, with an emphasis on 'snare drum and pedals' and 'janizary clinking and clanking'. Lyrically, the songs draw on the uhlan (Polish light cavalry) imagery and evoke traditional ideals of Polish femininity and masculinity, harking back to the period of Poland's partitions. The female protagonist of a typical disco polo song is beautiful, tender and devoted to her family, not unlike the Polish Mother. The man is ready for battle (a sabre is a common motif of disco polo songs and videos) and has a penchant for strong alcohol. Disco polo makes reference to the tradition of the Polish nobility, but suggests that all Poles (or all listeners to disco polo songs) are descendants of this culture. The lyrics of disco polo songs have to be simple and easy to repeat so that the audience can sing along with the musicians, as disco polo is meant to be consumed by people dancing and enjoying themselves.

The success of the early Beatles had to do partly with the simplicity of their lyrics, and lines such as 'Bara bara, riki tiki tak, If you love me, give me a sign' are not miles away from 'She loves you, Yeah, yeah, yeah, and you know that can't be bad'. However, the simplicity of disco polo in Zmarz-Koczanowicz's film is explained by crude exploitation of naive fans by its producers and stars, as Adorno argued in relation to all popular music. This connection is shown by images from a bazaar where we see many traders from the East, some looking Oriental, playing disco polo songs on the keyboard which reduces the music to a few badly performed cords. Those who trade in disco polo, not unlike the musicians themselves, lack emotional attachment to their fare and are ignorant about what it contains, as shown in an episode where a woman selling cassettes on a stall, reads in a monotonous voice the titles from the cover, without making any suggestions as to which ones are most suitable for her customer.

Disco polo is presented as music which accompanies communal events rather than existing for and by itself; it is used for weddings, family picnics and political rallies. It helps to achieve extra-musical objectives, such as celebrating a family gathering or presenting a politician in a positive light. The only exception is the concert in the Congress Hall at the Palace of Culture in Warsaw. However, even this concert has an atmosphere of a picnic, attended by families with children, as children are encouraged to climb onto the stage and perform with the artists.

That disco polo reassures, tranquilises, and unites families and society as a whole, is most conspicuously made in one of the greatest hits of Bayer Full, which includes the line 'All Poles are one family'. Music often plays such a role and it can be seen as its noble aspect. Take Beethoven's *Ode to Joy* with the line 'All men are brothers'. Building communities is also, as Richard Dyer argues, a characteristic of disco; hence the utopian potential of this genre (Dyer 1992: 156). However, in a post-communist context and from the perspective of a neoliberal ironist, it is regarded with suspicion.

Zmarz-Koczanowicz also draws attention to the sexual nature of disco polo performances, especially female singers, on whose legs and bottoms the camera lingers. This aspect is also underscored by the title of the film, taken from a song by the band Milano, which is also a colloquial and semi-vulgar description of a sexual act. Again, eroticism, as Dyer argues, is a crucial characteristic of disco and the author claims that the advantage of disco is that its eroticism focuses on the whole body, rather than being disembodied and cock-oriented, as is the case with rock (Dyer 1992: 152–154; see also Chapter 4). However, the way Zmarz-Koczanowicz draws attention to the eroticism of disco polo spectacles renders them sleazy, most importantly by showing the female artists from their less attractive angles. The director also points to the perceived contradiction between the eroticism of disco polo on one hand and its family-friendliness and Catholicism on the other. It appears that the artists are asked to explain themselves for their readiness to 'serve two gods': sex and the Catholic patria. Świerzyński's answer to this criticism is that disco polo is heterogeneous and different sections of the audience relate to its different facets.

The connection of disco polo to Polish politics receives much attention in the film. It is discussed by Świerzyński and the leader of the main Polish peasants' party, Polskie Stronnictwo Ludowe (the Polish People's Party, the PSL) and the former Prime Minister Waldemar Pawlak. Świerzyński admits that he is himself a member of the PSL and regards it as a natural thing that disco music is used by politicians from this party, given its origin in the province. He also refers to the well-known (and widely criticised) fact that this music was also used in the presidential campaign of Aleksander Kwaśniewski, by this point the most successful Polish politician, representing the old regime and for a while we see Kwaśniewski surrounded by disco polo artists. Świerzyński adds that this is also a favourite music genre of the most famous politician from the Solidarity camp, Lech Wałęsa, but this fact is played down in the media, and it is played down in *Hanky Panky*. We do not see Wałęsa or any other Solidarity politician connected to this music. In my opinion this is because the link of Solidarity politicians with disco polo was embarrassing for cultural elites, who wanted the state to protect what they saw as high culture. Instead, Pawlak talks at length about the value of disco polo, drawing attention to its vernacular character, unlike other genres of popular music in Poland, such as rock, which was merely an imitation of western music. The symbiosis between disco polo and the PSL is made explicit by awarding Pawlak a special medal for popularising this music.

Tracing the genealogy of disco polo takes up a large part of *Hanky Panky*. Although on no occasion is it stated explicitly that its creators plagiarise foreign hits or that this music serves as ersatz of a foreign product of a higher class, such opinions are implied by beginning the film with a group of young people dancing to the sounds of 'Macarena', a hit by Spanish band Los del Rio. Such framing underscores the derivative character of disco polo. The interviewees themselves offer a different genealogy of disco polo, mentioning American blues, country and Elvis Presley, and Polish hits of the 1970s. However, this explanation is cut short, suggesting that Zmarz-Koczanowicz is not interested in such a narrative which might edify this genre.

Several years after completing Hanky Panky, Zmarz-Koczanowicz directed *Miłość do płyty winylowej* (*Love for a Vinyl Record*, 2002), which also takes issue with music which is produced primarily for dancing: techno. However, unlike disco polo, which is vernacular, techno is an international phenomenon, originating in Detroit and then spreading to Europe, with Berlin becoming its main centre. It is an urban music, because it needs infrastructure which can only be found in large cities. Techno favours instrumental music; when it uses human voice, it distorts it, so that it sounds like one of the instruments (Thornton 1995: 75). This renders techno a particularly transnational genre, as not knowing the language of the performers is not an obstacle to understand it. While there is disco polo, there is no 'techno polo' and at no point in Zmarz-Koczanowicz's film is the Polishness of techno discussed. The DJ in techno plays a privileged role, choosing tracks and presenting them in a specific order, often distorting the original sound.

Most likely Zmarz-Koczanowicz made a film about techno in Poland because at the time of its production, namely at the turn of the century, it started to be seen as an important cultural and social phenomenon, in the same way disco polo was seen several years earlier. Moreover, one can observe a certain fit between the promotion of techno as music for young Poles and Polish efforts to join the European Union, which took place about the same time as Zmarz-Koczanowicz's film was made, culminating in 2004, when Poland achieved this goal.

In *Love for a Vinyl Record* the director follows the same formula as in *Hanky Panky*. The film consists of interviews with the principal protagonists of the Polish techno scene, and episodes showing consumption of this music. An important difference in the way Zmarz-Koczanowicz represents these two genres is conveyed in the titles of the films. 'Bara bara', translated into 'hanky panky', is a colloquial expression, verging on vulgarity and referring to sex. It points to disco polo being a low, 'body genre', not unlike disco at large. *Love to a Vinyl Record*, on the other hand, points to a much nobler attitude to music on the part of techno producers and consumers. This difference is confirmed in interviews with three leading Polish DJs, specialising in techno, who use artistic pseudonym Angelo Mike, Insane and Edee Dee. Unlike the stars of disco polo, they hardly talk about their involvement in techno as a form of business, but ponder on it as a form of art and quasi-religious experience. They claim that techno allows them to escape mundane life and access the core of their existence. Thus, paradoxically, although techno uses complex technology, it is a means of regaining lost innocence. The fusion of technology and nature is underscored in an episode where

Angelo Mike says that we decide ourselves what is music and illustrates this fact by mentioning that a bird singing against the background of a moving train creates a perfect sound. Techno is like the bird singing combined with the noise emitted by a train: it has a purity of nature and the intoxicating rhythm of industry.

While production of disco polo was framed by Zmarz-Koczanowicz as a Fordist, conveyor belt industry, undertaken in a studio and leaving little scope for individualism and virtuosity, success in techno is based on combining hard work with a desire for personal expression. This aspect is highlighted by Edee Dee, who mentions that every day he spends long hours practising DJing and other skills required to be a successful techno artist. Virtuosity is accentuated by close-ups of DJs' hands touching the records, especially Edee Dee's. This contrasts with the way the performance of disco polo artists was presented by Zmarz-Koczanowicz, where camera, in a highly objectifying way, focused on the legs and bottoms of female performers. The interviewed DJs also evoke a concept of research, of making music as a form of learning about music, which brings association with Brian Eno's take on a 'studio musician' (Eno 2011). The idea that a DJ is not an artist in the old sense, namely somebody producing artefacts from scratch, is presented as an advantage as it allows him to remain mysterious and at some distance from the audience. The DJs cast by Zmarz-Koczanowicz reject the idea of a pop star, regarding stardom as vulgar and an obstacle of cultivating one's love of music.

The importance of money is played down by the Polish DJs. Edee Dee mentions that techno DJs belong to two categories: those who do it because they have money and those who do it because they want to learn about music. He places himself in the second, higher category. Angelo Mike, somewhat less idealistically, admits that the great popularity of techno in Poland led to interest in this genre by the music establishment and this resulted in its commercialisation. Techno became a business, not unlike disco polo. However, disco polo songs, as presented by Zmarz-Kocznowicz in *Hanky Panky*, were written with the intention of affording their producers and promotors a comfortable life. In the case of techno, profit appears to be an unwelcome by-product of its development.

Similarly as having little to do with money, techno artists are presented as being apolitical. Angelo Mike mentions that he knows nothing about politics and only recently learnt that there was a recession in Poland. He describes fans of techno as new hippies who escape a bourgeois existence marked by pursuit of family and money. At the same time, however, he states with pride that their audience consists mostly of 'serious people employed in serious firms'. He also mentions that techno events have elitist characters; the guests are selected on the spot and the so-called 'track-suit man' (*dresiarz*) is banned. The term *dresiarz* connotes an unruly provincial working-class man, the Polish equivalent of the British 'chav'. The DJ adds with regret that in some cases selection of the audience is not possible. The implicit assumption is that techno events are for representatives of higher classes. The concept of class is also evoked obliquely by mentioning Europe. The clubs where techno is played are described as 'European'. This term is implicitly contrasted with 'Polish', which means provincial and 'chav'. In this way there is a fit between techno artists and their fans. They are also connected by their individualism. Although techno raves gather thousands of people, Angelo Mike claims that the music does not connect the dancers with each other, but with their inner selves. They dance solo and experience music individually.

Love for a Vinyl Record finishes with an image of Polish techno fans attending Love Parade in Berlin, which used to be the largest festival in Europe dedicated to electronic dance music. This image can be read as a symbol of the Polish road to the European Union. The ending can be compared to the beginning of *Hanky Panky*, where we saw some people dancing to the disco hit 'Macarena', as both point to the international connections of the respective phenomena. However, the connotations of these two episodes could not be more different. In *Hanky Panky* foreign music is brought to Poland for Poles to engage in some kind of mimicry. In *Love to a Vinyl Record* Polish techno fans are part of a colourful crowd, engaged in a cosmopolitan event, where there are no 'natives' or 'guests'; everybody is equal in his or her Europeanness.

Polish Music Business as *Szołbiznes*

In 2003 Sylwester Latkowski, who previously made *Blockers*, shot probably his most ambitious film about Polish popular music up to this point, titled *Nakręceni, czyli szołbiznes po polsku*. I'm translating this title as *Wound Up, or Polish Show Business*, but such a translation does not reflect the disdain included in the title, conveyed by the term 'nakręceni', which suggests being agitated without any specific reason and show business spelt phonetically, 'szołbiznes', which suggests that the Polish show business is a distorted or diminutive version of show business proper. Such an idea is also conveyed in the film, which is a collection of interviews with prominent representatives of the Polish popular music business, such as musicians, heads of record companies, music impresarios, journalists, presenters of television programmes combined with fragments of various music events. On occasions the faces of interviewees are blacked out and the recording is stopped to demonstrate that the material was self-censored, because many people were afraid to talk openly about the situation. This, of course, suggests dissatisfaction with the business and this is also the view which prevails in the film. It is first conveyed by the question 'does show business exist in Poland?' posed in the film, to which some interviewees respond negatively. Obviously, this demonstrates a mismatch between the expectations of these actors and the Polish reality. There are several problems mentioned or alluded to in the film. One of them is the record companies cheating the artists, by not paying them the full amount of royalties due and making them sign contracts which bind them to specific labels for many years. Another is the lack of music specialists in positions of power, such as heads of record companies or producers of television programmes. There is also a sense that people making important decisions about music do not communicate effectively with the artists. Finally, there is a sense of widespread corruption, for example recording firms pay employees of radio channels to play 'their' music. We also hear a complaint that large recording companies ('the majors') which entered the Polish music market in the 1990s failed to make the Polish music industry a success, as demonstrated by the fact that the companies which sell records in the largest numbers are local, independent companies, often owned by musicians themselves.

Many of these problems are not exclusive to Poland. Almost as long as the recording industry has existed, artists have complained about being exploited by it. The problem was exacerbated during the period of the acute crisis of the record industry in the 2000s, whose beginning coincided with the production of Latkowski's film. Similarly, many of the problems mentioned by Latkowski's 'talking heads' can be regarded as applying to neoliberalism and specifically neoliberal (neo)colonialism. In this system the colonised country is treated as a source of cheap labour and a dumping ground for surpluses produced in the centre rather than a place to invest and nurture local talent. The complaint that the majors are not interested in Polish artists could also be found elsewhere in Eastern Europe (Elavsky 2011). However, Latkowski seems to be unable or unwilling to locate the Polish artists' predicament in a wider context. On the contrary, *Wound Up* gives the impression of Polish exclusivity.

In this way, the author follows in the footsteps of a certain discourse on Poland as a place which is particularly backward and suffering, which can be traced as far back as Polish Romanticism.

The fact that the film is focused on the popular music business rather than music itself explains why there is little music in the film and we hardly see any Polish musicians in action. The recurring motif is of the veteran Polish rocker and the leader of the band Perfect, Zbigniew Hołdys, preparing for a solo performance at the Opole Music Festival. However, he is unable even to start playing his guitar which can be regarded as a metaphor of the atrophy suffered by the Polish music business at the beginning of the 2000s.

Wound Up, or Polish Show Business was privately produced by Opusnet, which also produced *Blockers*. Like *Blockers*, it also gives an impression of being done quickly, without polishing specific episodes or editing them with care, unlike the previously mentioned films by Zmarz-Koczanowicz. At the time of the film's production, this was an asset, as it afforded it a sense of urgency. However, watched one and a half decades later, Latkowski's film looks shabby and dated.

Conclusions

This chapter shows that music documentaries in Poland underwent significant change during their postwar history. They started as short reports from music events, included in the newsreels, progressed to longer reports, presented on television and finally to full-length films about rock festivals, exhibited in cinemas, during the peak of Polish rock fever in the 1980s. After the fall of the Berlin Wall we also observe the production of films which try to capture specific music phenomena and subcultures, such as hip hop, disco polo and techno. Finally, we get a film about the specificity of the Polish music business in the post-communist period. What is lacking are films about events with estrada stars and the operations of the state socialist music business. These gaps point to the privileging of high art and politically oppositional popular music, at the expense of other types of music, and of favouring music understood as a form of self-expression over the music industry.

Notes

1. 1963 was also a year when my parents bought their first television set.
2. The official name of the Festival changed several times, from Wielkopolskie Rytmy Mlodych (Greater Poland's Rhythms of the Youth), which had been organised in Jarocin since 1971, to Ogolnopolski Przegląd Muzyki Młodej Generacji w Jarocinie (All-Polish Review of Music of Young Generation in Jarocin), to Festiwal Muzyków Rockowych (Rock Musicians' Festival).

Works Cited

Bittner, Karolina. 2017. *Partia z piosenką, piosenka z partią: PZPR wobec muzyki rozrywkowej*. Warszawa: Instytut Pamięci Narodowej.

Bratkowski, Piotr. 1985. Cały ten rock. *Kino* 7: 10–12.

Bruzzi, Stella. 2000. *New Documentary: A Critical Introduction*. London: Routledge.

Cohen, Thomas F. 2012. *Playing to the Camera: Musicians and Musical Performance in Documentary Cinema*. London: Wallflower Press.

Czaja, Justyna, and Katarzyna Mąka-Malatyńska. 2015. Historia oglądana spod spodu. In *Historia polskiego filmu dokumentalnego*, ed. Małgorzata Hendrykowska, 607–614. Poznań: Wydawnictwo Uniwersytetu im. Adama Mickiewicza.

de Paor-Evans, Adam. 2018. The Intertextuality and Translations of Fine Art and Class in Hip-Hop Culture. *Arts*, 1–14.

Dyer, Richard. 1992. In Defence of Disco. In His *Only Entertainment*, 149–58. London: Routledge.

Edgar, Robert, Kirsty Fairclough-Isaacs, and Benjamin Halligan. 2013. The Formats and Functions of the Music Documentary. In *The Music Documentary*, ed. Edgar Robert, Kirsty Fairclough-Isaacs, and Benjamin Halligan, 1–21. London: Routledge.

Elavsky, Michael C. 2011. Musically Mapped: Czech Popular Music as a Second 'World Sound'. *European Journal of Cultural Studies* 1: 3–24.

Ellis, Jack C. 1989. *The Documentary Idea: A Critical History of English-Language Documentary Film and Video*. Englewood Cliffs: Prentice Hall.

Ellis, Jack C., and Betsy A. McLane. 2006. *A New History of Documentary Film*. London: Continuum.

Eno, Brian. 2011. The Studio as Compositional Tool. In *Audio Culture: Readings in Modern Music*, ed. Christoph Cox and Daniel Warner, 127–130. London: Continuum.

Filar, Witold. 2014. Fenomen disco polo w kontekście polskiej kultury popularnej lat 90. *Kultura Popularna*, 1. http://kulturapopularna-online.pl/abstracted.php?level=1&cid_issue=87559 . Accessed 15 June 2016.

Gębski, Józef. 2009a. Jak osiągnąć nonsensus. In *Józef Gębski: Retrospektywa filmowa Kielce 4-5 czerwca 2009*, ed. Barbara Gierszewska, 59–75. Kielce: Kieleckie Towarzystwo Naukowe.

Gębski, Józef. 2009b. Kilka paradoksów o filmie dokumentalnym. In *Józef Gębski: Retrospektywa filmowa Kielce 4-5 czerwca 2009*, ed. Barbara Gierszewska, 49–58. Kielce: Kieleckie Towarzystwo Naukowe.

Grant, Barry Keith. 2012. *The Hollywood Film Musical*. Southern Gate, Chichester: Wiley-Blackwell.

Hučková, Jadwiga. 2015. Opowieści naocznego świadka. Kino pomiędzy wiosnami Solidarności. In *Historia polskiego filmu dokumentalnego*, ed. Małgorzata Hendrykowska, 361–469. Poznań: Wydawnictwo Uniwersytetu im. Adama Mickiewicza.

Jóźwiak, Katarzyna. 1984. Mówi Michał Tarkowski. *Film* 18: 12.

Kienzler, Iwona. 2015. *Życie w PRL: I strasznie, i śmiesznie*. Warszawa: Bellona.

Kitts, Thomas M. 2009. Documenting, Creating, and Interpreting Moments of Definition: *Monterey Pop*, *Woodstock*, and *Gimme Shelter*. *The Journal of Popular Culture* 4: 715–732.

Kończak, Jarosław. 2007. Ewolucja programowa TVP. PhD, Warsaw University.

Krajewski, Andrzej. 2018. Krwawy Maciek z telewizji. Kim był Maciej Szczepański? *Newsweek*, 15/07. http://www.newsweek.pl/wiedza/historia/jak-maciej-szczepanski-krolowal-w-telewizji-w-prl,70368,1,1.html. Accessed 12 August 2018.

Leszczyński, Robert. 2001. Koncert po 20 latach. *Gazeta Wyborcza*, 14-5/07, p. 8.

Laing, Dave. 1986. The Music Industry and the "Cultural Imperialism" Thesis. *Media, Culture and Society* 8: 331–341.

Long, Paul, and Tim Wall. 2013. Tony Palmer's *All You Need Is Love*: Television's First Pop History. In *The Music Documentary*, ed. Edgar Robert, Kirsty Fairclough-Isaacs, and Benjamin Halligan, 25–41. London: Routledge.

Mazierska, Ewa. 2016a. Introduction. In *Popular Music in Eastern Europe: Breaking the Cold War Paradigm*, ed. Ewa Mazierska, 1–27. London: Palgrave Macmillan.

Mazierska, Ewa. 2016b. Czesław Niemen: Between Enigma and Political Pragmatism. In *Popular Music in Eastern Europe: Breaking the Cold War Paradigm*, ed. Ewa Mazierska, 243–264. London: Palgrave Macmillan.

Pawlicki, Maciej. 1985. Być sobą. *Film* 20: 9.

Pławuszewski, Piotr. 2015. Kino mocnego uderzenia: Polska muzyka rockowa w polskim kinie dokumentalnym lat 60. i 70. *Kwartalnik Filmowy* 91: 105–120.

Przylipiak, Mirosław. 1998. Polski film dokumentalny po roku 1989. *Kwartalnik Filmowy* 23: 62–84.

Roszak, Theodore. 1995 [1968]. *The Making of Counter Culture*. Berkeley: University of California Press.

Rotha, Paul. 1952. *The Documentary Film*, 2nd ed. London: Faber.
Ryback, Timothy W. 1990. *Rock Around the Bloc: A History of Rock Music in Eastern Europe and the Soviet Union*. Oxford: Oxford University Press.
Saffle, Michael. 2013. Retrospective Compilations: (Re)defining the Music Documentary. In *The Music Documentary*, ed. Edgar Robert, Kirsty Fairclough-Isaacs, and Benjamin Halligan, 42–54. London: Routledge.
Sankowski, Robert. 2016. Festiwale w PRL-u, czyli więcej niż rozrywka. *Gazeta Wyborcza*, 4/06. http://wyborcza.pl/1,90535,20180028,festiwale-w-prl-u-czyli-wiecej-niz-rozrywka.html. Accessed 15 July 2018.
Small, Christopher. 1998. *Musicking: The Meanings of Performing and Listening*. Middletown, CT: Wesleyan University Press.
Sobolewski, Tadeusz. 'Maria Zmarz-Koczanowicz – A Liberal Ironist', an essay added to a DVD of Zmarz-Koczanowicz's films. Polskie Wydawnictwo Audiowizualne.
Szarecki, Artur. 2020. The Making of Polish Hip-Hop: Music, Nationality, and the Limits of Hegemony. In *Made in Poland*, ed. Patryk Galuszka, 155–164. London: Routledge.
Thornton, Sarah. 1995. *Club Cultures: Music, Media and Subcultural Capital*. London: Polity.

CHAPTER 8

Victims of the System? Documentaries About Popular Musicians

Famous popular musicians are frequent topics of biographical films. The same applies to documentaries. Many of these documentaries are merely reports from their concerts, but there are also some which offer a more in-depth representation of a given artist, trying to capture him or her both as an artist and a private persona. Such films can be described as 'documentary biopics', except that in these biopics artists play themselves, and there is less emphasis on drama. In this chapter I discuss several such films, devoted to some of the greatest stars of Polish popular music, in order to offer a more comprehensive picture of Polish popular music and illuminate the differences between fictional and documentary representations. I will only cover here the period after the Second World War, because in the interwar period Poland did not produce documentaries about popular musicians, only about classical composers, such as Chopin.

Whose Life Gets Documented?

Before I made my choice of documentaries of Polish popular musicians, I had to check if a specific choice could be made. I prepared a list of popular music stars and tried to establish if there were documentary films made about them. What I discovered confirmed my suspicion that great popularity does not guarantee having a documentary film devoted to the artist. Popularity is a necessary, but not a sufficient condition of attracting cameras. The musician also needs to hold the status of a 'true artist', whose work survived or has a realistic chance to survive the passage of time. It is also expected that s/he made an impact not only on popular music, but also popular culture at large. For these reasons, we find more documentary biopics about representatives of rock than about pop music, hip hop, estrada, disco polo and electronic dance music stars, despite the fact that, judging by the chart results and popularity of music videos on YouTube, non-rock genres are currently more popular in Poland than rock music. Tragedy and premature death also help immensely to become immortalised on celluloid and online.

Polish documentary filmmakers working in the post-communist period favour stories of older stars, who began their careers under the state socialist regime or even dead stars. This might be a consequence of their realisation that it is easier to assess one's life from a distance, knowing that the person to whom the filmmaker directs his (as this is usually a male) camera, would not be able to substantially change his narrative, talk back to him or prevent him from finishing his film. Another advantage of focusing on older or deceased stars is the wealth of archival material about them, which is currently easier to access thanks to the internet and especially YouTube, than in pre-internet times, when making films based on archival footage required trips to real archives of television or the Documentary Film Studio, which were difficult to enter (one needed special permission to do so), navigate, as well as costly. Furthermore, unlike in the period of state socialism, when power was almost always on the side of the state and its agents, which included filmmakers employed by state institutions, after 1989 the balance of power shifted and the filmmaker is at risk of being sued by a star. Consequently, the bulk of documentaries made after 1989 show the artist in a positive light, verging on being hagiographic. Still, despite their bias, they offer a wealth of material both about the stars and their public perception.

From the perspective of their style, documentaries about Polish musicians (popular and serious) can be divided into two categories. One type is the 'auteurist documentary'. Such a documentary foregrounds its form and uses various cinematic techniques, such as lighting, framing and editing to convey a specific message. Usually it has a well-defined beginning, middle part and end. It is never just a collection of interviews with the musician and people familiar with his or her work. Interviews are used sparsely or avoided altogether to allow the image and music speak for themselves. One of the first Polish documentaries about musicians and a model of the 'auterist documentary' in the Polish context was *Muzykanci*

(*Musicians* or rather *Musickers*, 1960), directed by Kazimierz Karabasz. This 9-minute film presents the rehearsal of an amateur brass band in Warsaw, made up of men working in a tramway depot: mechanics, drivers and conductors. The goal of the film is to demonstrate the will and ability of common people to create art and, at the same time, capture the dying tradition of amateur brass bands. As we learn from the opening titles of this film, these men are 'the last Mohicans', perhaps because younger people prefer big beat or because the spread of television technology changed workers into passive consumers of culture. In Karabasz's miniature one can detect a desire to make a film which would match the music. Like a piece played by an orchestra which is the product of a joint effort, *Musickers* do not have a dominant protagonist; the camera moves from one character to another and editing allows the appreciation of the effort of each musician, without privileging any of them.

Subsequently we find more Polish documentaries about musicians made in this way. They were typically produced by the Documentary Film Studio and most of them concern serious musicians, such as classical dancers and jazzmen, from films about Krzysztof Komeda to a documentary about rock jazz hybrid yass band *Miłość* (2012), directed by Filip Dzierżawski. By and large, popular musicians have been treated with less care. Perhaps the only Polish film about a popular musician which deserves the label of an auterist documentary is *Sukces* (*Success*, 1968) by Marek Piwowski about Czesław Niemen. Ironically, to this day in Poland it is also the most criticised film about a pop star, due to its supposed dishonesty, even malice.

While *Musicians* and *Success* are labelled 'films', many of the remaining documentaries about popular musicians are downgraded to the status of 'programmes', due to their character as television productions about something topical, yet short-lived, not expected to last beyond the time of their broadcast. However, YouTube gave these 'programmes' a new lease of life and they provided me much of the material used in this chapter.

Two 'Shots' at Czesław Niemen

When writing about biographical films, I mentioned that their makers use various authenticating techniques, to convince the viewer that the portrayed character matches the real persona. Documentary filmmakers do not need to do this because the very fact of using the real musicians and other people from their circle playing themselves authenticates their representation. Paradoxically, this gives them more freedom to manipulate their material, shape it according to their perspective, in the knowledge that the audience will trust these films anyway. It seems like nobody recognised and used this power more effectively than Marek Piwowski (b. 1935), who made one of the first Polish documentaries about Czesław Niemen, giving it the meaningful title: *Success*.

By the time Piwowski made his film, Niemen was already a rock star in Poland, while he was only a young filmmaker, even though with a distinct ironic style, as demonstrated by his 'etudes' *Muchotłuk* (1966) and *Welcome Kirk* (1966), shot when he was still a student at the Lodz Film School. In common with representatives of the Polish School of documentary cinema, such as the previously mentioned Karabasz, Piwowski recognised the importance of understatement and the need of the viewers to draw their own conclusions about the reality represented. However, he went further than Karabasz; as his films typically lack a voice-over, allowing his characters to present themselves and they are less sympathetic towards their protagonists (Mazierska 2016a).

When I asked the director why he decided to make a film about Niemen, he replied that at the time he was a Niemen fan and regarded the singer as an interesting character. Why Niemen agreed to be the protagonist in the film of a newcomer, I can only guess, given that the singer is no longer with us. It is, however, very likely that no other filmmaker at the time was interested in making a film about Niemen and the star was charmed by the young, yet charismatic director, who in due course became a leading Polish documentarist and a major media personality.

Before I move to the film, let's briefly present its protagonist. Niemen's real name was Czesław Wydrzycki. He was born in 1939 in the so-called Kresy (Borderlands) of Poland, currently Belarus, and in 1958 moved to Poland with the last wave of repatriates. Wydrzycki started his career in the early 1960s covering American and Latino songs. Then he changed to singing rock ballads with lyrics penned for him by professional lyricists, such as Marek Gaszyński and Franciszek Walicki. During this period he adopted 'Niemen' as his stage name from a river that passes through Belarus and Lithuania, seen as the cradle of a Polish Romantic culture. In due course Niemen became an *auteur* of his repertoire, created entirely in his studio, full of electronic equipment and a kind of national poet-prophet, drawing on the poetry of the neoclassical poet Cyprian Kamil Norwid and adopted the posture of a reclusive sage indifferent to the trappings of fame (Mazierska 2016b: 250–251; Gradowski 2019: 130–133). After the end of state socialism he produced less and less work and it attracted relatively little critical attention. He died of cancer in 2004.

When Piwowski made his film, Niemen was at the peak of his big beat period; his philosophical ambitions were not yet visible to the public. However, it looks like the director was able to capture something of the 'future Niemen' in *Success*. According to the director, he did not have any ideological agenda when embarking on this project. Instead, he wanted to capture on celluloid how Niemen worked. For this purpose, he sent the musician a list of questions and Niemen chose those he wanted to reply to during the course of the shooting. These responses make up roughly half of the film; the rest is filled by Niemen's rehearsals with his band. It is clear that Piwowski gained the trust of the singer, who allowed his crew to film him and his band for several days without any restrictions. As in other cases of shooting documentaries, after some time the film characters forgot about the presence of the camera and were just 'themselves'. Such an approach would also inform Piwowski's subsequent films, including his cult classic *Rejs* (*Cruise*, 1970).

The result of Piwowski's work is humorous and mildly cruel towards the artist because of the incongruity between different parts of Niemen's answers, as well as between his statements and those of his collaborators. Piwowski's method is revealed by the title of the film, which has a double meaning: it refers to the title of Niemen's song and to the meaning of success according to the singer. Niemen keeps saying that success (understood as fame) does not matter to him. He also dismisses the fans who ask him about tips for breaking into show business. In a romantic fashion, his song 'Success' states that love is the ultimate success. Yet at the same time, Niemen boasts about various privileges he enjoys thanks to being a celebrity, such as being allowed into a high-class restaurant when it officially does not admit any guests, while also claiming that he does not take advantage of these privileges because material goods do not matter to him. In the same vein, he states that everybody is an individual, and he is himself absolutely unique, thanks to having a deeper contact with the essence of life. Subsequently, however, he mocks Poles wearing ties on elastic bands (here epitomising people who follow the prudish, unfashionable and humourless then leader of the Party Władysław Gomułka) and says that everybody should dress like him, that he should be the ultimate trendsetter. His pretensions to uniqueness and his dismissive attitude towards the trappings of fame are also undermined by a member of his band. The attitude of this colleague towards Niemen is mildly ironic because he is well aware that behind the veneer of the blasé and spiritual artist, there is a typical pop star craving popularity.

Niemen's pretensions to originality and spirituality are also undermined by the fragments of music Piwowski chooses for his film, such as the titular song, whose lyrics are banal, and another, sung in English, that sounds like an imitation of English or American pop songs of the period. By shooting the rehearsal, which leads to repeating the same fragments of music, Piwowski strips the performance of some of the magic expected at a concert and draws attention to the fact that Niemen's success is the result of collaborative work, rather than the creation of one person's genius. Critics and Niemen himself also drew attention to Piwowski including an image of Niemen drinking water straight from the soda stream, which apparently ridiculed the artist (Michalski 2009: 110), although for me it rather underscored his sobriety, contrasting with the Polish penchant for alcohol (Fig. 8.1).

In due course *Success* became a frequent topic of discussion among Polish popular music critics; the singer's biographer, Dariusz Michalski, devotes to it a 10-page long chapter in his book (Michalski 2009: 99–110). In it, Michalski suggests that Piwowski wanted to produce a

Fig. 8.1 Niemen drinking water from the soda stream in *Sukces* (*Success*, 1968) by Marek Piwowski

sympathetic portrait of Niemen, but was forced by some Party apparatchiks to re-edit it in a way, which rendered Niemen a buffoon. This is also the view which Niemen himself allegedly held (ibid.: 101). In a conversation with me Piwowski claimed that he made the film the way he wanted; there was no pressure to re-edit it. The most likely scenario was that once the director started to edit it, his penchant for irony won over a desire to build a monument for Niemen—if he had such goal in the first place.

According to the then tradition of showing the best of Polish documentary films in cinemas, before the main programme, *Success* had a cinema release and a large audience, as at that time cinema was still a mass medium in Poland. Despite begrudging the director, Niemen and other critics of the film admitted that it helped to build Niemen's popularity (ibid.: 110), confirming the rule that bad publicity is better than no publicity.

Success is probably the only film about a Polish popular musician, which is known not only because of its topic, but also its director. The remaining films discussed in this chapter circulate as anonymous productions, whose claim to fame is the person presented in them. This is also the case of the most recent documentary about Niemen, *Sen o Warszawie* (*Dream about Warsaw*, 2014), directed by Krzysztof Magowski. Lasting 107 minutes, it is several times longer than Piwowski's film. Moreover, unlike *Success*, which through minute observation of Niemen tries to capture his persona, *Dream about Warsaw* attempts to present Niemen's life from his birth to his death against the larger canvass of Polish politics and culture. It can be described as a documentary bio-epic.

The director of *Dream about Warsaw*, Krzysztof Magowski (b. 1952), is an experienced documentarist and a television executive. Currently he holds the position of vice-chair of the programme board of state television. Such a position, as was also the case during state socialism, suggests being in tune with the 'Party line'. Since 2015, when the socially rightwing Law and Justice party was in power, this means, among other things, adopting a harsh attitude towards the 'communist' past and its relics. Magowski suits this agenda well, because throughout his career he was interested in Polish political history and since the fall of the Iron Curtain proved to be an ardent critic of the old political regime. A good example of his work is *Łóżko Lenina* (*Lenin's Bed*, 1996), in which the author visits the defunct Lenin Museum in Poronin in the South of Poland, to denounce the propaganda concerning Polish-Soviet friendship, perpetuated after 1945. Watching this film one might think that Magowski would approach Niemen's life and work as a vehicle to condemn the communist system and its functionaries for thwarting the talent of the greatest Polish rocker. This is indeed the case. Magowski ensures it by choosing interviewees sympathetic to this position, as well as episodes from Niemen's life which render him as a victim of the communist system and emphasise his 'western orientation'. Structurally, the film brings to mind the documentary *This Is Elvis* (1981) by Andrew Solt and Malcolm Leo, as it is also made up of interviews, fragments of Niemen's performances and archival interviews. It also contains re-enactments, thus conflating fiction with fact.

The title of the film is taken from one of the greatest hits by Niemen, with lyrics by the popular journalist and lyricist Marek Gaszyński. This song became an unofficial anthem of the Legia football club in Warsaw; its matches starting with the fans chanting it. Then the action moves to Stare Wasiliszki, where Niemen was born as Czesław Juliusz Wydrzycki and spent his youth before being repatriated with his family to the North of Poland. There is thus a certain incongruency in presenting Niemen as a Warsaw patriot, while in reality he originated from elsewhere. The early part of his life is described mainly by Niemen's sister and the curator of the Niemen museum in his home village. In this part we also see a boy re-enacting Niemen as a child, singing to the accompaniment of an old record player. Once the action moves to Poland, Niemen's family gets less screen time and more is taken by Niemen's collaborators, such as members of his bands, music journalists and specialists in Niemen's music ('Niemenologists'). Their testimonies are juxtaposed with archival footage, presenting Niemen's concerts and fragments of his interviews. They are meant to illuminate specific stages of the artist's career. However, rather than examining how Niemen's musical style evolved over the decades, Magowski is more interested in his relationship with the political authorities. As I mentioned elsewhere, this relationship was complex. Niemen was both a victim of the political system and its beneficiary (Mazierska 2016b: 246–253). Magowski, however, emphasises the artist's victimhood and plays down any benefits he might have drawn from working in state socialist Poland. This happens by presenting in great detail episodes when the artist suffered injustice or was not adequately rewarded. The injustices are of three categories. The first concerns the insufficient financial rewards for Niemen's work. We hear, for example, about Niemen living in a studio flat in Warsaw, when he was already a star, because he could not afford to buy a larger property. There is also a small fragment of an interview with Niemen when he says that on average he earned an equivalent of 5 USD per concert. Such complaints, which can be reduced to the opinion that the 'state robbed me of my earnings' are very common among stars of the state socialist period, for example filling many pages in the autobiography of Urszula Sipińska (2005). However, they had to be looked at in the context of very low salaries of Poles (and Eastern Europeans) in relation to western currencies. In this context, one cannot claim that popular musicians were singled out for particularly harsh treatment. On the contrary, they enjoyed certain privileges, resulting from the fact that they could work in the West where earnings were much higher.

The second complaint about Niemen's career concerns him not receiving exposure in the Polish media adequate to his popularity and his originality, of which a sign was his dressing style (Fig. 8.2).

The music journalist Roman Rogowiecki regularly mentions certain concerts of Niemen, which were either not recorded or deleted by television. This is presented as a proof of a concerted effort by the media establishment to undermine Niemen. This might indeed be the case, but

Fig. 8.2 The unique dressing style of Czesław Niemen in *Sen o Warszawie* (*Dream about Warsaw*, 2014), directed by Krzysztof Magowski

an equally likely reason was somebody's lack of insight into the future of Polish pop-rock or his or her personal taste. Again, to judge it, we would have to compare the presence of Niemen in the media with that of other popular music stars, such as Maryla Rodowicz or Czerwone Gitary.

Thirdly, the film considers episodes when the authorities tried to tarnish Niemen's reputation. One example is the previously mentioned film by Piwowski, although Magowski's interviewees stop short of accusing the director of being an agent of an anti-Niemen conspiracy, steered by the cultural department of the Party. Another is a newspaper article published in the 1960s, which accused Niemen of taking off his pants on stage and showing his bare bottom to the audience. This article, which most likely was politically motivated, led to a court trial against the journalist which Niemen won. There is also an extended piece about using a fragment of an interview with Niemen recorded before the introduction of martial law in Poland in the television news, which suggested that Niemen supported General Jaruzelski's rule. This broadcast led to Niemen being criticised, even boycotted, by the Solidarity camp, which contributed to his withdrawal from touring and public life. This event, however, should not be placed in the same category as accusing Niemen of disrespecting his audience because it rather pointed to the authorities trusting the rock singer, regarding him as somebody who was on their side.

Conversely, episodes when Niemen could be seen as benefitting from the system or collaborating with the authorities receive very little screen time. Even when they are mentioned, they are presented as a result of Niemen being 'manipulated' or 'badly advised', doing something which was not in accordance with his true outlook on life. In my previous work on Niemen I mention that these incidents of Niemen's open collusion with the system mostly happened in the 1970s, when the Party, under the leadership of Edward Gierek, adopted a more conciliatory tone towards citizens and realised that youth culture can be an asset in the state's attempt to appease the masses (Mazierska 2016b: 250–252). That Niemen was not immune to such friendly gestures from the political establishment can be deduced from his participation in a number of musical events which were overtly political. For example, in 1977 Niemen took part in the Soviet Song Contest in Zielona Góra, regarded as the most pro-regime music event in Poland. The next year he accepted an invitation to participate in the World Youth Festival in Havana, again an event with distinct political connotations. In 1976 he accepted two high state awards for cultural achievements (Zasłużony Działacz Kultury and Złoty Krzyż Zasługi) (Wąs 2014). To that we can add his tours in the Soviet Union. Most of these events are ignored by the makers of *Dream about Warsaw*. There is only a very short shot from the festival in Havana; and Niemen's tours in the Soviet Union are mentioned in relation to his return to his home village. Even when it is impossible to ignore Niemen's official recognition in Poland, such as his winning of the Sopot Festival in 1979, this is presented as an almost worthless honour. We learn that Niemen got a yacht, a very luxurious commodity not only in the Polish context, but it is suggested that this luxury was lost or destroyed before he could use it.

Although Magowski's film is filled with grudges towards the state socialist system, there are also moments when the West is also chastised for obstructing Niemen's international career. Niemen's biographer Dariusz Michalski mentions that Niemen's plan to perform at the San Remo Festival in the 1960s was thwarted by the Italian trade union of musicians, which prioritised domestic musicians and those with whom Italy had reciprocal agreements. Niemen's performance in San Remo after the fall of the Berlin Wall is presented as the West repaying (although only partly) its debt towards the Polish musical genius. There is relatively little time in the film devoted to Niemen's unsuccessful attempts to make career in the West, and this is also clouded by a suggestion of anti-Niemen conspiracy, rather than explained by his inability to adjust to the way the pop-rock business was run there and his squandering of his excellent opportunities, such as a five-year contract with CBS. The accusation of the East and the West of conspiring to prevent Niemen's global successes can be considered as a part of a larger narrative of Polish victimhood and exceptionalism, which was created during the period of Romanticism, principally by the Polish national poet-prophet, Adam Mickiewicz. After the fall of the Iron Curtain this narrative lost its currency, but survived in residual form, especially in texts concerning Polish postwar history.

Despite the unusual length of Magowski's film as for a music documentary, one is also struck by certain absences. The first concerns the period of Niemen's career after the fall of the Iron Curtain. It is only discussed in the context of his failing health and his death, rather than the character of his music and its reception. This lack can be explained by the fact that post-1989 Niemen's productions were scarce and disparaged by the critics. Moreover, focusing on this period would undermine the victimhood discourse, perpetuated by Magowski. Second, despite the significant presence of Niemen's family in the film, there are no interviews with Niemen's second wife Małgorzata or his daughters from his second marriage, while the daughter from his first marriage features prominently, candidly describing the failure of Niemen's marriage to her mother and his infatuation with the Italian singer Farida, described in the film as the love of his life. I suspect that this absence might have something to do with Małgorzata Niemen's refusal to be put in (metaphorically speaking) the same place as Farida, with whom she fought in court over Farida's right to sing a song which Niemen wrote for her. The starkest lack is, however, of Niemen himself. His interviews are truncated and his music is reduced to a handful of his best known songs constantly repeated. Ultimately, it feels like Magowski, following some of his guests who claimed that Niemen was prone to manipulation, did not want to allow his protagonist to say something which might incriminate him, even from beyond the grave or change the frame into which the director wanted to place him—as the ultimate Polish pop star, a 'king after whom there is no king', as Marek Gaszyński, the author of the lyrics to 'Dream about Warsaw' describes Niemen in the film.

Dream about Warsaw was presented in a number of film festivals in Poland, including Dwa Brzegi (Two Coasts) Festival in Kazimierz and had a theatrical release, distributed by the dynamic Gutek Film. It was also shown on Polish state television. As for a documentary film, it had unusually wide exposure, testifying to the unfaltering popularity of Niemen and this film inscribing itself into the dominant narrative of the Polish state socialist past.

When a Band Is Still a Band

Czerwone Gitary (Red Guitars) were the most popular Polish rock band of the 1960s, frequently compared to the Beatles (Królikowski 1986: 15; Michalski 2014: 250; Gradowski 2018: 126–127). Mariusz Gradowski singles it as the most important band in the period of 'Polonisation' of Polish rock, drawing on foreign influences, but adding many innovations in areas such as playing guitar, use of voices and intelligent lyrics, conveying the experiences of the generation (Gradowski 2018: 125–134). Most likely it is also the most popular Polish pop-rock band of all time. According to some estimates it sold more than 10 million records in Poland and many more were pirated. Czerwone Gitary was also one of the best export products of the Polish popular music industry, having a strong fan base in many countries of the old Soviet Bloc, especially in the Soviet Union and Eastern Germany, where it frequently performed and sold several million records.

The band was set up in 1965 by Jerzy Kossela, on the ruins of the amateur band Pięciolinie with some members of the super-band Niebiesko-Czarni (Michalski 2014: 255). Kossela was also the band's first leader. The name was taken from the Czech Jolana guitars the band played, which were only available in red colour (ibid.: 251). Kossela left Czerwone Gitary after three years, after which its best known members became Krzysztof Klenczon and Seweryn Krajewski and, after Klenczon left the band in 1970, Krajewski. Czerwone Gitary have existed to this day, although its only original member is drummer, Jerzy Skrzypczyk. In 2015 the band celebrated its fiftieth anniversary and on this occasion a documentary was made, *Czerwone Gitary... i pół wieku* (*Red Guitars... and Half a Century*), scripted and directed by Maciej Wróbel and produced by TVP Olsztyn (regional channel of the Polish state television). The film lasts about fifty minutes and includes interviews with the band's current members and other people connected to it, fragments of their recent concerts and their old performances.

Before I look at the film in detail, it is worth asking why, given Czerwone Gitary's popularity, there are no more substantial documentary films about their career, especially those made during the heyday of their popularity in the 1960s and 1970s. It seems to me that one reason was the scarcity of folk motifs in their productions.[1] This might explain the fact that in the 'big beat films' it is Skaldowie or No To Co rather than Czerwone Gitary, which provide the background to the stories which unfold on screen. Another possible reason was, paradoxically, the immense photogenic qualities of its two leaders, Krzysztof Klenczon and Seweryn Krajewski, frequently, albeit wrongly in my view, compared to John Lennon and Paul McCartney. This means that it was difficult to reduce Czerwone Gitary to the background. When placed next to Krajewski and Klenczon, the majority of male Polish stars of the 1960s and 1970s would most likely lose their allure. Not only were Krajewski and Klenczon very attractive, but they complemented each other. The former had delicate features, well groomed hair, dark eyes covered by thick dark eyebrows and rarely smiled on stage. In his appearance, he represented a 'romantic type' with a small touch of Mediterranean beauty. He was also introverted and taciturn.

Klenczon, on the other hand, came across as macho and unruly, fitting the idea of a rocker. The songs, composed by these two musicians, reflected their different personalities. Krajewski's songs were gentler, they often concerned unrequited love or yearning for something, as in 'Anna Maria' or 'Płoną góry, płoną lasy' (Hills Are Burning, Forests Are Burning). Klenczon's works were more dynamic, typically 'rock', as in 'Powiedz stary, gdzieś ty był' (Where Have You Been, My Old Man?). It is possible that the band, made up of four people, could not accommodate two such strong personalities, as the gossip had it. However, it is more likely that Klenczon's departure reflected his difficulty to conform to a band's discipline, as well as his problems with reconciling the life of a rocker with having a family—he was the first member of Czerwone Gitary who got married and had children. After leaving the band, Klenczon set up a new band Trzy Korony (Three Crowns), which was short-lived. In 1973 he emigrated to the USA, where he died in a car crash in 1981. Klenczon's emigration and tragic death could be regarded as a reason for the filmmakers to turn the camera on Czerwone Gitary and explore the band's career and self-perception after such a momentous loss, but it was difficult, given Krajewski's overall discretion and unwillingness to discuss his relation with the man widely seen as his rival.

As a long-lasting fan of Czerwone Gitary I regretted my inability to find out about the private lives of its members, their team dynamics and the way they created their numerous hits, many of which were for me much more than catchy pieces—miniature masterpieces, conveying in three-four minutes my deepest longing. I even saw the label the 'Polish Beatles' as demeaning of Czerwone Gitary, as the Polish band lasted longer and its style developed more than that of the Beatles. Moreover, if we regard Krajewski as the Polish Paul McCartney, then we can conjecture that his career developed in a more interesting way than McCartney's, as he became not only a solo performer, but also wrote numerous hits for other singers, as well as film music. At the same time as regretting the scarcity of audiovisual material about my favourite band, I appreciate the fact that thanks to this lack Czerwone Gitary preserved a certain mystique and to this day are seen as old style stars, whose position was based on their musical talent and professionalism, rather than their celebrity status.

Red Guitars... and Half a Century comes across as a modest film: a report from the band's concert tours enriched by some archival material. However, at the same time it provides an unusual insight into the story of a famous band, because it is told not by its central, but by its peripheral members. On this occasion this is Jerzy Skrzypczyk, the band's drummer (hence the Polish Ringo Starr) and its only constant member from the moment of its inception, its first leader Jerzy (Juras) Kossela and the new members of the band who replaced Klenczon, Krajewski and the guitarist and bassist Bernard Dornowski. Thanks to their testimonies we learn that Kossela left the band because he could not stand Klenczon's antics and that the band found out about Krajewski's departure from a newspaper's article. The new members present themselves as fans of the old line-up of the band who feel honoured to carry its torch and quench the nostalgic yearning of the old fans and the appetite of the new ones. Among them is Marcin Niewęgłowski, who as a 12-year old child won a competition for the best performance of Czerwone Gitary's songs performed by children. This very fact makes Niewęgłowski feel justified to take the place of Krajewski, to whom he is even slightly similar and whose romantic sensitivity he shares.

The film also includes a familiar trope of the failure of the Polish recording industry to fully exploit the popularity of Czerwone Gitary. Kossela mentions that the band received many letters from fans complaining about their difficulty to purchase their records and asked them to direct their complaints to the Polskie Nagrania record company, which possibly worked, given that the band released many records in Poland which received the status of 'golden records'. However, Skrzypczyk and Kossela do not present themselves as being cheated by the state socialist culture industry. They rather, quite humbly, acknowledge their immense popularity in this period and their freedom to produce music which pleased their fans and themselves.

The film encourages the question of when does a band lose its identity, in this case—is Czerwone Gitary on its 50th anniversary still Czerwone Gitary? For Skrzypczyk this is the case, ensured by his presence in the band and the fact that they still play the old songs in a way which brings tears to their audience's eyes. Moreover, since Krajewski's departure, the band enjoyed significant successes. It recorded four LPs, of which three were certified gold. New songs such as 'Jeszcze gra muzyka' (Music Still Plays), 'Senny szept' (Sleepy Whisper) and 'Tańczyła jedno lato' (She Danced One Summer) did well at various festivals and radio playlists, were voted 'songs of the year' and received millions of views on YouTube. Despite these successes, the other members, understandably, are not sure if they fully earned their place in the band. This uncertainty is conveyed by Mieczysław Wądołowski, who admits that he is 'covering' Klenczon rather than being a new, fully fledged member of the band.

The view that the recent line-up of Czerwone Gitary is substantially different from the original can also be found among the comments about the documentary, published on YouTube, with some fans stating that the band was essentially about Klenczon and Krajewski—without them, it is, as one commentator put it, 'the wheel on a Mercedes, rather than a Mercedes'. On the other hand, the story of the band's perseverance points to the truth in the saying that drummers are the most important members of rock bands—when they go, the band disintegrates, as was the case with Led Zcppelin. Conversely, if he stays, the band has a greater chance to survive.

The Ultimate Polish Diva

Women and representatives of other genres than rock, especially estrada music, are marginalised in the histories of Polish popular music. This situation reflects the received notions of cultural hierarchy which music historians apply to popular music. As rock was regarded as a more high-brow genre than estrada music, historians privileged rock.[2] Another reason why there is less interest in estrada stars is a perception that they were politically more conformist or at least less engaged in anti-government conspiracy than their fellow rockers; such a view is presented, for instance in the film *Beats of Freedom*, discussed in the previous chapter. What applies to the written histories, is also true of filmic history. There are few biographical films about Polish estrada stars and they tend to be rather short. The only exception known to me is a film about Violetta Villas, titled simply *Violetta Villas* (1988) and directed by Zbigniew Kowalewski, which lasts 72 minutes. This was not the only film in which Villas appeared. Along with Czesław Niemen, she was probably the most 'cinematic' Polish popular singer of all times and her presence in films (again, as with Niemen), was varied. In 1970 she was the protagonist of the film *Śpiewa Violetta Villas* (*Violetta Villas Sings*), directed by Konstanty Ciciszwili, which presented a montage of her revue numbers. Villas also played in several fiction films, such as *Dzięcioł* (*The Woodpecker*, 1970), directed by Jerzy Gruza and *Sen o Violetcie* (*Dream about Violetta*, 1983), directed by Paweł Pitera. Essentially, in these films she played herself as an object of desire of men who could only dream about her. Her songs were used in numerous films, especially after 2000, such as

Bellissima (2000), directed by Artur Urbański, *Mój Nikifor* (*My Nikifor*, 2004), directed by Krzysztof Krauze and *Aria Diva* (2007), directed by Agnieszka Smoczyńska. To that we can add many shorter films and 'reportages', following her somewhat mysterious death in 2011. This upsurge of interest by a younger generation of Polish filmmakers can be regarded as a sign of the weakening of the 'rock paradigm' in the Polish popular music history and growing fashion for camp.

Villas (b. 1938) shares several characteristics with Niemen. In common with the 'king of Polish rock', she was born abroad, in Liège province in Belgium, in the family of Polish miner Bolesław Cieślak. The Cieślaks returned to Poland in 1948, when the future star was ten and they settled in the tiny village of Lewin Kłodzki in the South of Poland. Like Niemen, Villas also used an artistic pseudonym; her true name was Czesława Cieślak. Of course, using pseudonyms is a common practice among popular music artists, but it was not the case in Poland of state socialism, when people were expected not to hide their true identities. Moreover, of all artistic pseudonyms of Polish stars hers was the most conspicuous—it sounded foreign and connoted a certain flamboyance and exoticism. Both characteristics were frowned upon in the ascetic Poland of the 1960s, when she began her career. Yet, as Marek Krajewski observes, at the same time, in the grey Polish reality she 'provided audiences with highly desirable yet simultaneously safe culture shock' (Krajewski 2018: 758). Furthermore, there is a sense that, again like Niemen, Villas was one of a kind. This has to do both with her artistic style, including her unique voice, apparently spanning four octaves, hence suitable both for opera and popular music and her demeanour and lifestyle which was at odds with mainstream Poland. Finally, as with Niemen, there is a perception that Villas had a chance to make a great international career, but her talent was squandered.

In interviews, Villas used to say that she wanted to be a singer from an early age, aware of the power of her voice. Once she moved to Poland, she tried to get a musical education and in 1956 travelled from Lewin to the opposite corner of Poland, Szczecin, where her sister lived, to go to the music school, and later continued her musical education in Wrocław and Warsaw. Once she recorded her first album in 1962 and started to appear at festivals in Opole and Sopot, she gained country-wide fame and started to be invited abroad. She toured in many countries in Europe, such as Germany, Belgium, Switzerland, Spain, the Soviet Union and Czechoslovakia, as well as the USA, Canada and Israel. Thanks to attracting the interest of French impresario, Bruno Coquatrix, she was also invited to perform in the famous Olympia in Paris. In the second half of the 1960s her successes became even more spectacular as for somebody coming from the 'wrong side' of the Iron Curtain. In Paris she performed with such stars as Frank Sinatra, Paul Anka, Barbra Streisand and Charles Aznavour and got a lucrative contract to perform in Las Vegas, where she travelled in 1968 and 1969 (Michalewicz and Danilewicz 2011: 101–118). She was also approached by producers from Hollywood. Why she did not take advantage of these opportunities, remains a matter of contention. According to the version of her biographers, Iza Michalewicz and Jerzy Danilewicz, this had to do with the fact that in 1968 she agreed to collaborate with the Polish secret service (SB) under the pseudonym Gabriella, in order to enjoy freedom of movement and make an international career (ibid.: 101). However, the lack of her usefulness to the SB and her erratic behaviour both in Poland and abroad, including her disclosure of her connection to the SB to her friends, led to severing her contact with this institution in the early 1970s (ibid.: 124). In the version of Paweł Pitera, director of one of the films in which she played, Villas was not allowed to leave Poland because she did not agree to collaborate with the Polish secret service, and was punished by having her passport confiscated.

Whatever the truth, in the next decade and a half Villas was confined to Poland. Only in the second half of the 1980s, following the end of martial law and the effective dissolution of the state socialist system did she resume her international career and went on tour in the USA and Canada, performing, among other places, in New York, Las Vegas and Chicago, where she met her second husband, millionaire businessman of Polish origin, Ted Kowalczyk, whom she married in 1988. It was around this time when Kowalewski made his film, no doubt to take advantage of Villas rebooting her career and achieving a financial status commensurate with her talent. *Violetta Villas* tries to capture this moment, but also to present Villas's entire biography, largely using the singer's perspective. It includes archival footage, her interviews with the director, as well as fragments of her concerts and scenes from her private life, including her lavish wedding to Kowalczyk, which lasted five days, apparently costing 300,000 USD. Despite this huge investment, the marriage lasted only one year. However, this fact the film is unable to show, as it finishes before the roads of Kowalczyk and Villas parted.

What we get in *Violetta Villas* is in part a Cinderella story of the girl from a disadvantaged background who succeeded despite numerous obstacles and in part of a diva, with an affinity to pomp and garishness. Villas' penchant to extravagance contrasts with the greyness of the last years of socialist Poland. This contrast is achieved through juxtaposing scenes from Villas's performances and her wedding with shots from the Polish streets where we see poorly dressed, mostly older people, perhaps Villas's fans (Fig. 8.3).

To add to the sense of drabness of the world in which Villas became a star, these shots are monochromatic.

In interviews, which fill a large part of the film, the star presents herself as somebody who is lonely and misunderstood. She says that many people dislike her, because they don't know her. This might be seen as the typical posturing of a star, but in hindsight such words capture well Villas's character and her life. Her image, consisting of very long blond hair and a penchant for 'meringue' dresses with puffy sleeves and deep cleavage, projected the image of an 'immodest' and cunning woman, who used her sexuality to ensnare men. Her marriage to the American millionaire can be construed this way as well. However, in a psychological test, in which the singer is meant to finish sentences, Villas presents herself as somebody who appreciates most 'purity of heart', 'does not hate anybody' and sees herself as the humble servant of her audience whom she brings joy.

Fig. 8.3 Violetta Villas performing in *Violetta Villas* (1988), directed by Zbigniew Kowalewski

The contrast between excessive sexuality and innocence brings to mind some of the greatest sex symbols of the twentieth century, such as Marilyn Monroe and Brigitte Bardot. Villas also mentions on several occasions in the film that her greatest love is God and presents herself as somebody who has direct contact with God and who in her performances conveys the energy which she receives from heaven. Paradoxically, such religiosity renders her unusual in the Polish context, where religion is matter of a tradition rather than deep faith and where contact with God is mediated by the clergy. As if to confirm that with her devotion she was out of step with society at large, one of the reasons for her split with her second husband was, in his words, her excessive religiosity, manifested in long prayers.

The visual style emphasises the fact that in the mass consciousness Villas existed as an image, by including her numerous photographs, cut-outs from newspapers and glossy magazines, as well as her other renditions, such as drawings, caricatures and figurines. It is worth mentioning here that one of Villas's most popular songs was titled 'Mechaniczna Lalka' (also known as 'Laleczka'), which means a 'mechanical doll'. The lyrics to this song, written by renowned Polish lyricist and poet, Agnieszka Osiecka, express objection to treating an attractive woman like a doll, on the grounds of her being a living, feeling and dreaming person. It is difficult to find a better portrait and self-portrait of Villas than this song.

The film also draws attention to the fluidity and elusiveness of Villas's image, as if the director wanted to tell us: 'Neither I nor you can capture her'. This impression of elusiveness is achieved through putting Villas's photos in motion, making a small animated film of them. In rendering Villas contradictory and elusive *Violetta Villas* proved prophetic. Subsequent decades saw her increasingly erratic behaviour, which resulted in periods spent in a psychiatric hospital and being unable to cope with her household, including hundreds of animals (cats, dogs and goats) she looked after. The singer was also apparently manipulated by her maid, her manager and her lawyer, who prevented her son and other members of her family from contacting her in the last years of her life. Her death in 2011 in her home village of Lewin led to speculation that she was maltreated and even murdered by her staff, given that, when she was found dead, she had a broken leg and numerous signs of neglect on her body. These mysteries, inevitably, led to an increase of interest in Villas's work, as reflected in many books devoted to her, as well as theatre plays and television programmes. They demonstrate that while during most of her career Villas was seen as an epitome of kitsch, she is seen by the younger generation as a great artist and a tragic heroine.

A BITTER SELF-MADE HERO

At the beginning of the 2000s, Michał Wiśniewski, the leader of pop band Ich Troje, was probably the greatest Polish pop star. Not surprisingly, he became a protagonist of the documentary *Gwiazdor* (*The Star*, 2002), made by Sylwester Latkowski, whose other productions, including *Blockers*, I discussed in the previous chapter.

In his films Latkowski positions himself as a friend of the artists and an investigating journalist, whose purpose is to disclose and denounce the machinations of the system and its institutions. This is also the case in *The Star*, which is about Wiśniewski's stardom and, at the same time, the cold treatment afforded to him by Polish musical and cultural establishment.

As in the previous films, Latkowski shoots in the style of a 'man with a movie camera', who follows his subject and other relevant people, in order to discover truth about his topic. Latkowski's film brings to mind Keshishian's *Madonna: Truth or Dare*, in which Keshishian's crew followed Madonna during her tour. On this occasion, however, the director's ambition is to tell the artist's story from the 'cradle' till the present moment. We learn that when Michał Wiśniewski was three, he was abandoned by his alcoholic mother. Subsequently he spent some years with his father, who committed suicide when Michał was fourteen. The future star also lived in an orphanage and with foster families before moving to Germany, where he lived with his aunt whom he thought to be his biological mother. It seems like his relationship with this woman also broke down, although the reasons for this are unclear. Wiśniewski's mother is shown in the film, but she is hiding from the camera and unwilling to be interviewed. Given that the film lasts over an hour, there are few voices included in the film and almost all of them belong to Wiśniewski's family: his then wife, singer and dancer Mandaryna, his brother Kuba and a fellow member of Ich Troje. Most of the time is given to Wiśniewski himself, who muses on his life and career. The tone of these confessions is that of grievance. The singer feels like all of his life he was at a disadvantage, and succeeded despite numerous obstacles. Even when he is at the top, he does not receive the recognition which he deserves.

There are two main problems to which Wiśniewski alludes, which make him frustrated, despite his records being certified platinum. One is the lack of professionalism of the people with whom he works. He mentions, for example, the lack of fog and fire effects at some of his gigs. The second issue is the hostility of the music establishment to him, as reflected in overlooking him in the Fryderyk awards, the 'Polish Grammy', despite commercial successes of Ich Troje, and denying the band accesses to television programmes which renders Wiśniewski's success even more spectacular. The film also makes a point about the Polish tabloid press, which in order to sell more copies, prints scandalous stories about Polish celebrities.

Given this context, I was expecting to learn more about how Wiśniewski managed to achieve his stardom. This issue, however, is downplayed by Latkowski. The only clues we get are from observing Wiśniewski's behaviour on and off stage. We see that he is very attached to his fans, understanding that his livelihood depends on them. At one point he mentions that his management suggested to him to throw a bunch of signed postcards into a crowd, but he preferred to give them out in person, spending an hour shaking the hands of his most devoted fans. Wiśniewski also shows a penchant for creating lavish spectacles on stage, including entering on a motorcycle and behaving like an actor, rather than a singer, as is the case with his cover of Falco's song 'Jeanny'. His fondness for a masquerade is also testified by his everyday appearance, such as hair dyed in bright red colour, numerous studs adorning his face and a white leather jacket with black cross on the back. Such a conspicuous image was still rare on the Polish popular music scene, when Latkowski's film was made.

Conclusions

In comparison with films about serious musicians, the number of documentaries about Polish popular musicians is rather low. During the period of state socialism, such imbalance reflected the hierarchy of art, with serious art being seen as higher than popular art, and the ethos of Polish cinema and television, which put education over entertainment. However, this topic still failed to take off after 1989 which might come as a surprise in the light of the advances in technology, most importantly the possibility of shooting high-quality material on a low budget, which was impossible during the time of state socialism, and the privatisation and commercialisation of the Polish screen media. There is a particular scarcity of documentary films about new stars. Why is this the case? I will list here two reasons. One is the fragmentation of popular music scene and ephemeral nature of fame in the times of YouTube. This means that while there are Polish songs and music videos which can reach millions of views in the span of several months, its authors and protagonists are seen as niche stars, known to followers of a particular genre, and are expected to lose their star status soon, unlike stars of the 'communist' era, such as Czesław Niemen or Violetta Villas. Second, currently stars have more autonomy and control over their image than those of the state socialist period. Hence, it became difficult to make a documentary presenting them in a negative or ambiguous light, as was the case in *Success*. The sign of their power and autonomy is Latkowski's inability to finish his documentary about Wiśniewski, because at some stage the singer forbade him to continue shooting. Another sign of the popular music stars' insistence on creating their own biographies are frequent rumours about their plans to produce their own biopics or documentaries about them. This refers, for example, to Maryla Rodowicz and Zenon Martyniuk, the stars of disco polo, whose video to 'Przez twe oczy zielone' (*Because of Your Green Eyes*, 2014) is the most viewed Polish video on YouTube. Whether such a film will eventually be produced, time will tell. In the meantime, we should expect more documentaries about deceased stars or those who stopped performing and recording.

NOTES

1. The only exception was 'Hosa-dyna' from the beginning of the band's career, which never achieved popularity.
2. As rock music was dominated by men, while in estrada music women played a more prominent part, the focus in the Polish history of popular music is on male musicians.

WORKS CITED

Gradowski, Mariusz. 2018. *Big Beat: Style i gatunki polskiej muzyki młodzieżowej (1957–1973)*. Warszawa: Oficyna Wydawnicza ASPRA-JR.

Gradowski, Mariusz. 2019. Success, Failure, Splendid Isolation: Czesław Niemen's Career in Europe. In *Eastern European Popular Music in a Transnational Context: Beyond the Borders*, ed. Ewa Mazierska and Zsolt Gyori, 119–136. London: Palgrave Macmillan.

Krajewski, Marek. 2018. Popular Culture in Poland. In *Being Poland: A New History of Polish Literature and Culture Since 1918*, ed. Tamara Trojanowska,

Joanna Niżyńska, and Przemysław Czapliński, 739–761. Toronto: University of Toronto Press.

Królikowski, Wiesław. 1986. Czerwone Gitary: Dozwolone do lat 18, 2: 5.

Mazierska, Ewa. 2016a. Production, Consumption, Power, and Humor in the Films of Marek Piwowski. *Journal of Film and Video* 2: 14–28.

Mazierska, Ewa. 2016b. Czesław Niemen: Between Enigma and Political Pragmatism. In *Popular Music in Eastern Europe: Breaking the Cold War Paradigm*, ed. Ewa Mazierska, 243–264. London: Palgrave Macmillan.

Michalewicz, Iza, and Jerzy Danilewicz. 2011. *Villas: Nic przecież nie mam do ukrycia....* Warszawa: Świat Książki.

Michalski, Dariusz. 2009. *Czesław Niemen: Czy go jeszcze pamiętasz?*. Warszawa: MG.

Michalski, Dariusz. 2014. *Trzysta tysięcy gitar nam gra, czyli historia polskiej muzyki rozrywkowej (Lata 1958–73)*. Warszawa: Iskry.

Sipińska, Urszula. 2005. *Hodowcy lalek*. Poznań: Zysk i S-ka.

Wąs, Marek. 2014. Czesław Niemen: Z podniesionym czołem. Wyborcza.pl, 18 November. http://wyborcza.pl/1,87648,16985749,Czeslaw_Niemen__Z_p odniesionym_czolem__CYKL__WYBORCZEJ_.html. Accessed 16 January 2015.

PART IV

Music Videos

CHAPTER 9

Singing and Dancing Without the Audience: Music Videos of the Interbellum and State Socialist Period

The last part of this book offers a brief history of Polish music video, from its beginning in 1930 to the present day, taking into account its presence in cinema, on television, at festivals and on YouTube. I'm writing it aware that researching Polish music video, in common with music videos in Eastern Europe in general, poses a challenge, which results from the sheer amount of material and the fact that it is not properly catalogued or archived, unlike Polish fiction and documentary films. There are probably tens of thousands of clips, but they are not listed in the most comprehensive database of Polish screen productions, filmpolski.pl. For example, if we search there for information about the most famous Polish producer of music videos, Zbigniew Rybczyński, we will read in his biographical note that he is a 'cinematographer and director of animated and experimental films'. Information about his music videos is buried further in the text and his filmography does not include even one music video. It appears as if between 1981 and 2006 Rybczyński did not make any films, although during this period he actually produced music videos for artists such as John Lennon, Lou Reed, Chuck Mangione and Pet Shop Boys, which are his commercially most successful works. The same applies to Tomasz Bagiński. He is known from his award-winning shorts *Katedra* (*Cathedral*, 2002) and *Sztuka spadania* (*Fallen Art*, 2004) as well as cinematics for *The Witcher* computer game based on the books of Andrzej Sapkowski, as well as for a number of music videos for Polish young stars, such as Dawid Podsiadło and Karolina Czarnecka. Yet, these videos are not acknowledged in his filmography on filmpolski.pl or in a longer biography published on culture.pl (Hałgas 2009). Yach Paszkiewicz, arguably the most prolific Polish producer of music videos (Laskowski 2016), exists on the database filmpolski.pl only thanks to a handful of documentary films, rather than several hundred music videos he produced during his career.

Many Polish music videos are available on YouTube, but one needs to know what one is looking for to find them. Even then, important details are missing in their description, such as the date of production, the name of the director and crew, location and budget. On many occasions it is impossible to establish whether this is an 'official video', commissioned by a television or record company or a fan-made product. Instead, we get the date of uploading a film, the number of views and 'likes' and on occasion fans' comments. This is a valuable source of information, but needs to be contextualised. In particular, the number of views does not reflect true popularity of old songs and videos (made in the predigital age), because they do not capture the number of views and 'likes' the videos enjoyed in their heyday. If anything, it allows us to check how specific artists and genres fared with the passage of time.

These problems are reflected in the scarcity of research on Polish music video. Such an absence can additionally be attributed to the dominance of the auteurist paradigm in scholarship about Polish and Eastern European cinema, as emphasised several times in this book already. As music videos (with few exceptions) are not seen as an auteurist endeavour, they have attracted little attention from Polish film and media scholars, especially those of the older generation. Other factors contributing to this neglect is the semi-professional character of many of them, while in Poland there used to be a cult of professionalism, often measured by the number of certificates brought by the artist and the opinion, transmitted from the West, that a music video is a form of advertising. This can be seen in the context of the hostility towards any form of commercial art, pertaining to the period of state socialism. Music videos are also practically ignored by Polish popular music scholars, who prioritise the analysis of songs and larger musical forms, and treat them from an auteurist perspective, as an emanation of the personality of a specific singer-songwriter. In this context, music video is seen as a secondary product in relation to the music and lyrics of the song, hence not worthy of consideration. Another, connected factor, is a perception that music video is a western or more precisely, an Anglo-American genre.

Consequently, most literature about music video published in Polish, tried to familiarise readers with the history and specificity of this genre, without including any Polish material. This is the case of the only book, published on this topic in Poland, Urszula Jarecka's *Świat wideoklipu* (*The World of the Music Clips* 1999), which includes an eight-page long appendix of titles of music videos used by the author (281–288), about three hundred in total. However, there are no Polish examples among them; suggesting they do not merit consideration. A similar approach is taken by the majority of Polish authors writing popular and (semi)academic articles about this genre (for example Przylipiak 1990; Piątek 1998; Topolski 2013), including one written by myself at the beginning of my journalistic career in Poland (Mazierska 1993). That said, this situation started to change in the last decade or so. For example, the popular magazine 'Kino' has published several reports from the Cameraimage Film Festival, which is in part devoted to this form, as well as a short piece summarising the Polish history of this genre, authored by Iwona Cegiełkówna (2007). Recently the journal *Studies in Eastern European Cinema*, published its first article devoted to Polish music videos by Paulina Duda (2019).

When searching for material for this topic, I also encountered a recent MA thesis devoted to Polish music videos. The author of this thesis, Łukasz Laskowski, also adopts an auteurist approach. His focus is music videos by the leading Polish director of this genre, Krzysztof Skonieczny and he treats his productions the way films directed by Wajda or Kawalerowicz were treated by Polish film scholars—as 'their' films, rather than as a products of collaboration of different agents (Laskowski 2016). Similarly, the previously mentioned Duda devoted her article to the videos of two established film directors, Wojciech Smarzowski and Jan Jakub Kolski and the cinematic character of their music videos (Duda 2019). In this chapter and the next my focus will be more on the representation of music genres and stars in music videos rather than their authors, although I will devote some attention to them as well.

Before I move on to discussing some examples of Polish music video from different periods (interwar and socialist in this chapter, and post-communist in Chapter 10), let's look briefly at the research of this form.

Art, Not Commerce

Western literature about music video emphasises its commercial character. In one of the first essays devoted to music videos, Peter Wollen maintains that it represents the 'breakdown between programme and ad' (Wollen 1986: 168). Carol Vernallis adds: 'the video must sell the song; it is thereflore responsible to the song in the eyes of the artist and record company' (Vernallis 2004: x). Steve Reiss and Neil Feineman begin their book about music videos by saying: 'No art form is as schizophrenic as the music video. In part a commercial and in part a short film, it has flaunted the line between art and commerce, undermined narrative and character development, and shortened an entire generation's attention span' (Reiss and Neil Feineman 2000: 10). Railton and Watson elaborate on these assertions, pointing to a large number of directors of music videos who also made advertisements for other products, for example 'Hype Williams, who has directed music videos for artists such as Beyonce, Ashanti, Janet Jackson and Pharrell, has also made commercials for Nike' (Railton and Watson 2011: 2). Such examples are not meant to undermine the artistry of specific music videos, only to illuminate certain aesthetics of this genre, such as their limited narrative content, rejection of realism and linearity and focus on visual style and mood (Vernallis 2004: x). If anything, they are supposed to prove that their producers work to the highest standard, despite budgetary constraints.

In the Polish context, a different connection is emphasised: between music video and experimental art. The spiritual father of Polish music video is admittedly Józef Robakowski, who is also a pioneer of experimental cinema and video art in Poland. His first film, made in 1962, entitled *6,000,000* (a reference to a number of Jews who perished in death camps during the Second World War), is a compilation of fragments of Holocaust-era documentaries. In due course, such compilations would be widely used in Polish music videos produced in the 1990s, including in the work of Yach Paszkiewicz. In an interview from 1994, Paszkiewicz states explicitly that Robakowski was his artistic father. Robakowski taught Paszkiewicz how camera can be used in an innovative way and organised in his house, together with his then wife, Małgorzatą Potocka, screenings of video art, including the work of the previously mentioned Zbigniew Rybczyński (Paszkiewicz 2014). Rybczyński is celebrated in Poland as a creator of innovative animated films and a multimedia artist (Rutkowska 1992) and his work as a director of music videos is seen in the context of his experiments with digital technologies. By contrast, the commercial value and potential of Polish videos is played down. In an article, published in 2007, Iwona Cegiełkówna explains this lack of interest by the fact that the majority of Polish videos by this point were made on the cheap, because the record companies which paid for their production, did not believe that they add much value to the product (Cegiełkówna 2007: 48). Since then, however, the situation has changed considerably.

It is natural to divide the study of Polish music videos into two parts: music videos produced during the interbellum and the state socialist period, and those produced after the fall of the Iron Curtain. The difference pertains both to the social and political context in which they were made and to the medium in which they were presented: cinema and television in the case of early music videos and (mostly) the internet in the case of videos made during postcommunist period.

Polish Music Videos Before Music Videos

I was unable to establish when the first Polish music video was produced and in order to do so, one needs a robust definition of this form. However, if we agree that it is a recording of a performance of a song without audience, which is meant to serve to promote its musical aspect, then we can argue that more than ten of such clips were produced in 1930, the year Polish cinema acquired sound, putting Poland at the forefront of this medium. They were the product of the collaboration between Wytwórnia Doświadczalna (Experimental Studio), which specialised in producing documentary films and newsreels, and the largest Polish record company, Syrena-Record (discussed in Chapter 2) and directed by Konrad Tom, the leading Polish director of musicals. Typically they presented revue numbers from the Qui Pro Quo theatre, the most successful musical theatre in Warsaw and probably entire Poland. The majority of them presented the popular band of 'revellers' Chór Dana (Choir of Dan), in which sang, among others, Mieczysław Fogg. Among them were song of different genres, such as a folk song 'Hej, idę w las' (Hey, I Go Into the Forrest) with the lyrics by Konrad Tom and several cover version of foreign pieces, included a tango and a cabaret song. There was also a great hit from the repertoire of Zula Pogorzelska, 'Panna Mania gra na mandolinie', which was a Polish version of a German song 'Ich hab' eine kleine braune Mandoline', to which Polish words wrote Marian Hemar.

Unfortunately, these clips did not survive—we can only learn about their existence from the old press.

In the subsequent years Polish singers and bands were often shown singing songs in the newsreels. These performances were recorded in the studio, hence can be regarded as another example of early Polish music videos. Some of them survived and can be accessed on the website of the Polish Film Archive, including a performance of Choir of Dan and a singer from Lviv Marian Rentgen. These clips showed an artist performing in front of the static camera. To add some sparks to the otherwise static performance, Choir of Dan are presented wearing folk costumes and the camera shows Rentgen's guitar in a close-up. Meaningfully, such devices will be also frequently used in early Polish music clips of state socialist period. Of those clips which did not survive, of interest is an aria from *Halka* by Stanisław Moniuszko, recorded by probably the most internationally recognised Polish singer of the interbellum, Jan Kiepura, performing in a mountaineering outfit.

In the category of the interwar music clips we can also include the film *Parada Warszawy* (*Warsaw's Parade*, 1937), directed by Konrad Tom, which includes revue numbers of the greatest stars of the 1930s. The film survived only in a truncated version, lasting slightly more than 20 minutes, which includes performances of Lena Żelichowska, Fryderyk Jarosy, Loda Halama, Helena Grossówna and Choir of Dan. In most cases we just see a singer doing his or her number, but in the case of Grossówna, it includes a longish dialogue between her and her partner, before the singing begins. The question is why such a film was made in the first place and had no successors in pre-war Poland. Most likely it was regarded as a good investment, namely a cheap production which could be promoted as a 'proper film'. However, as one reviewer noted, in Warsaw (where the audience could see their favourite stars performing live) *Warsaw's Parade* was sentenced to a flop, only in the province it had a chance to be a moderate success (Fryd 2012: 262).

Something like a musical clip was also included in the film *Romeo i Julcia* (*Romeo and Julcia*, 1933), directed by Jan Nowina-Przybylski, where at the beginning, before the film titles, we see Henryk Wars' orchestra playing the leitmotiv from the film, the song 'Ho-ho!'. We might guess that such introduction was meant to draw attention to the film's music and encourage buying records with music composed by Wars.

As I mentioned in the chapter about state socialist musicals, after the Second World War the connection between Polish cinema and popular music has weakened and commercial considerations lost its importance in the production of films and popular music. This meant that there was no need to produce clips to sell records.

The situation changed, however, with the development of television. The more television sets were sold, the longer was the period of daily broadcast, the more its programme diversified, encompassing entertainment. Crucial from this perspective was the year 1964, when the executive bodies of the television (TVP) and the cinema (NZK) signed an agreement, according to which cinema studios were obliged to produce a certain number of different genres, including television series, children and animated films, 'estrada films', and music videos (teledyski) (Kończak 2007: 58). This does not preclude production of such films in the earlier period, but most likely by this point they were part of larger programmes, such as the chat show *Tele-Echo*, rather than works in their own right. Thanks to this development viewers could see singers perform for the camera rather than for an audience during concerts. Art design and props were meant to illustrate the content of the songs. Some such clips were shot in the studio; others were set in picturesque locations, most often on the Baltic coast.

These clips did not a have special name, when offered to the viewers; they were typically called 'musical interludes' (*muzyczne przerywniki*). This name reflected their utilitarian function—to fill the time between longer, more important programmes. They functioned as anonymous material—usually they were shown without any introduction by the television presenters and they did not have opening titles and their closing titles were limited to the information that they were produced by Wytwórnia Filmów Dokumentalnych (the Documentary Film Studio). It is impossible to establish with precision how many were produced in each year, only that their numbers were in tens, by whom and who specifically commissioned their production. However, it is plausible to assume that the majority of them were directed by people working in television on permanent contracts and responsible for music in other television programmes and longer music documentaries, such as Józef Gębski, Grzegorz Lasota and Stanisław Kokesz.

It is likely that only a proportion of the early clips survived as it was a common practice in 1960s television to delete broadcast material, in order to recycle print or not to clutter the archives. On the other hand, given that the pieces were short, they might have been left in peace as not much was gained by destroying them and they were always in demand.

When revisiting them on YouTube I realised that I watched some of them on Polish television many times. Some clips were also inserted into cultural or musical programmes, such as the chat show *Tele-Echo*, or *Elderly Gentlemen's Cabaret*, which I mentioned, when discussing musicals from state socialist period. They typically had a different style, with singers appearing in a space looking like a cross between a bourgeois apartment and a television studio, often decorated with heavy vases full of flowers or pseudo-Greek sculptures.

Initially the musicians favoured by the producers of music clips represented estrada music. The favourites of the 1960s were Maria Koterbska, Irena Santor and Zbigniew Kurtycz. Their videos were made on the cheap (as music videos usually are), but were inventive and today are admired by YouTube audiences for their elegance. Take the video to 'Powrócisz tu' (You Will Return Here, 1968), performed by Irena Santon, with lyrics by Janusz Kondratowicz and music by Piotr Figiel, which attracted almost a million viewers on YouTube. The song is about a desire to return to Poland from wherever fate had thrown its protagonist. In a nutshell, it is a patriotic song, although passing its message with subtlety. It starts with a translucent cloth fluttering in the wind, like a banner; a connotation encouraged by the song's lyrics. Later, however, we see that it is not a banner, but the train from the dress of the singer. The rest of the clip shows Santor singing with the dress's train fluttering. Santor's dress is black and long and she has an elaborate hairstyle, with plenty of small braids held together by a shiny head-band, worn in the style of an ancient Egyptian queen. One can gather that Santor's elevated posture is symbolic—she stands for a patria addressing the Pole who left her. Next to Santor there is a white sculpture which looks like a cross between a tree and a woman, bringing to mind Chopin's monument in Warsaw, except that this monument was male while the statue in Santor's video is female. Santor and the statue look like mirror reflections, perhaps pulling the hesitant migrant in different directions.

Near the end of the 1960s the group of artists considered worthy of music clips expanded, including girls' bands and big beat stars. Among the former Filipinki were favoured, perhaps because some of their songs subtly conveyed warm feelings towards Poland's eastern neighbour, such as 'Wala Twist' about Valentina Tereshkova or 'Herbaciane pola Batumi' (Batumi's Tea Fields). Filipinki's videos were usually more dynamic than those of the estrada stars; for example in 'Wala Twist' the girls were shown in an amusement park, enjoying themselves on merry-go-rounds. Even if some songs can be regarded as political, as in the case of Santor's 'You Will Return Here' or Filipinki's 'Wala Twist', the videos softened the political connotations.

A similar tendency pertained to videos to big beat songs; their perceived rebelliousness was neutered and admiration of western music obscured by playing up their roots in Polish folk music. These are tendencies which could be also observed in Polish musicals of this period (see Chapter 3), but in music videos they are easier to capture because they are not obscured by any extraneous material—videos are all about songs, as opposed to musicals which might have a narrative only tenuously related to them.

One of the best known clips to Polish big beat songs from this period, which perfectly illustrates this approach, is to the song 'Gdybyś kochał hej' (If You Loved Me, Hey, 1969), by Breakout. The lyrics were written by Franciszek Walicki, the 'father of big beat', who tried to make the song come across as Polish not only by virtue of using Polish language, but also in view of the topic, lexical choices and rhetorical figures. 'If You Loved Me, Hey' reads:

> If you loved me just a little bit, hey
> If you loved me as much you don't love me,
> If you weren't as you are,
> wanted me as much as you don't want me...
>
> You would be a wind and I would be a field, hey
> You would be a sky and I would be a poplar, hey
> You would be sun and I would be a shadow
> If you just changed yourself...
>
> If you weren't in my dreams at night, hey
> If you finally left me alone, hey
> Maybe I would forgive you,
> Maybe I would forget...

The frequent use of the word 'hey' and the choice of nouns which refer to nature (wind, field, sky and poplar) renders the verse similar to a folk song, although it is performed in a distinctly rock style. The video adds much to the rustic character of the song. It is set somewhere in rural

Poland, whose agricultural methods and way of life look like the interwar or earlier period, rather than pertaining to modern times. We see a windmill, a field covered with stacks of hay and a singer, Mira Kubasińska, drawing water from a well, putting pots on the fence to dry, and feeding chickens some grain from a bucket, while sitting on the steps of a simple farmhouse. Its doors are open, perhaps to signify the openness and hospitality of Polish peasants. Kubasińska has her long hair plaited in braids and wears a waistcoat made of sheepskin on a simple white shirt. She plays a peasant woman and represents nature. In contrast to her, the three male members of the band have a rock outlook, sporting long hair, and are playing their instruments, standing on the stairs of the mill, rather than being engaged in any peasant activities. The conflict and unfulfilled love, as described in the song, is reflected in the position of the male and female members of the band. This opposition can be seen as reflecting the two sides or roots of Polish big beat: Polish folklore and western rock. The lyrics suggest that it can be solved, if there was only good will on both sides; a view that can be attributed to Walicki himself.

An exception to the rule of making short clips was a video to Czesław Niemen's song 'Bema pamięci żałobny rapsod' (Mournful Rhapsody in Memoriam of Bem, 1969), which lasts over sixteen minutes, because the song is so long. On this occasion the clip is not anonymous—it was directed by Janusz Rzeszewski, the same Rzeszewski who in the 1970s and the 1980s specialised in musicals set in interwar Poland. The song is regarded by many critics as Niemen's greatest artistic achievement, on account of both its lyrics and music. For example, Piotr Chlebowski, in an essay entirely devoted to it, argues that recording this piece by Niemen was a breakthrough in Polish popular music, because it 'moved popular music from a song to artwork, from a simple to a complex form… From 1969 in Poland a rock record became a coherent whole, as opposed to being a collection of banal songs' (Chlebowski 2010: 61).

The song is based on a poem by Cyprian Kamil Norwid, a Polish poet typically regarded as a Romantic, but with a strong affinity to the Classical tradition, as demonstrated by the fact that 'Mournful Rhapsody' is written partly in Latin. It concerns the death of the Polish General Józef Bem (1794–1850), a hero of the Polish fight for sovereignty during the time of partitions, who was also a leader of the Hungarian Uprising of 1848–1849. Bem thus epitomised the ideal pairing of patriotism with universalism. Apparently, it was not Niemen himself who discovered Norwid's poem: it was suggested to him by the popular songwriter

Wojciech Młynarski. What is more important, however, from my perspective, is that Niemen choosing such a poem was also in tune with 'turning to the classics', which was the trend in the 1960s in Poland. This change could be explained by the fact that the classics were popular but also seen as innocuous, simply because they were safely embalmed in their graves. I am not suggesting that Niemen used Norwid cunningly, to avoid political controversy, but this was an outcome of his choice. The fact that television decided to produce a video to this song confirms it. Musically, 'Mournful Rhapsody in Memoriam of Bem' bears many similarities with the precursor of progressive rock, 'In-A-Gadda-Da-Vida' (1968) by Iron Butterfly, on account of such characteristics as its excessive length, the long passages of instrumental music, when Niemen plays the organ, and its solemn mood. Rzeszewski's film strengthens these connotations. Its setting is a room filled with burning candles, which looks like a forest. Among them we see a group of people, dressed in black and white with their heads bowed, as if attending a funeral. Against this image we hear a chorus of female voices singing in Latin. Only after their voices are silenced, do we see Niemen singing in Polish and playing an electric organ, which is also decorated with burning candles. The image brings to mind a church, with Niemen as the church organist. Later we see him walking in this 'forest of candles'. He wears a costume similar to a black military uniform with white or silver decorations, with a large medal hanging round his neck. Such attire can be traced back to the cover of the Beatles' 'Sgt. Pepper's'. However, the Beatles' costumes were playful while Niemen's is solemn. Progressive rock was inevitably a subgenre of rock, whose purpose was to legitimise rock as a serious form. In *Mournful Rhapsody in Memoriam of Bem*, however, Niemen took it to a different level, rendering it as the type of music which would fit school curricula, and Rzeszewski's film strengthened this claim to be considered as patriotic high art.

Music Video 'Combines'

Apart from short music videos (*teledyski*), Polish television in the late 1960s produced several films, which are described on the filmpolski.pl website as 'music documentaries', but which in reality are collections of music videos, held together by a thin narrative. In common with the previously discussed clips, they were produced by the Documentary Film Studio for Polish television. I was not able to establish the circumstances of their production, but a possible reason why they were made was to kill two birds with one stone: to have 'proper' films, however short, and a number of clips, which could work as musical interludes.

Two of them, *Kulig* (*Sleigh Ride*, 1968) and *Jak powstali Skaldowie* (*How Skaldowie Were Born*, 1969), were directed by Stanisław Kokesz and lasted, respectively 28 and 22 minutes. *Sleigh Ride* was shown repeatedly on Polish television during the winter season and some songs from it were shown as separate clips. In both films Skaldowie play a prominent role, most likely because the band was the most folk-oriented from the 'first-league' of big beat bands.

During his career, which lasted from 1950 until his emigration to the USA in 1981, Kokesz made a large number of short and medium-length films, many of which were devoted to artists, mostly musicians, and some to tourism. None of them made a lasting mark on Polish documentary cinema and most of them are today forgotten, in part because he stayed away from politics and was perceived merely as a maker of 'useful films'.

Sleigh Ride can be seen as a Polish response to the Beatles films, directed by Richard Lester in the 1960s, and particularly *Help!* (1965). This is suggested by the similarity of certain episodes of these two films. However, *Sleigh Ride* has nothing of the narrative complexity and production values of Lester's film. It is set in practically just one location and its thin plot concerns a professional photographer or a tourist with a high-quality camera, whose car breaks down in the Tatra mountains during winter. The photographer is rescued by joining a sleigh ride, in which some of the most popular performers of the time participate: Skaldowie, Niebiesko-Czarni, Alibabki and Maryla Rodowicz. They sing their hit songs while speeding through the wintry landscape and engaging in winter sports such as skiing, until they reach a large house, where they continue performing. Except for the photographer, all other characters in the film are singing.

As with the examples presented earlier, the rock connotations of Polish big beat are 'softened' in *Sleigh Ride*. This happens in three ways. The first is via a blurring of the division between rock and pop. Although Skaldowie and Niebiesko-Czarni are normally categorised as big beat, while Alibabki and Maryla Rodowicz as pop or estrada, in *Sleigh Ride* they all take part in the same sleigh ride and their performances merge seamlessly. This happens because most of the songs concern winter, and in the outdoor scenes we do not see the main attributes of rockers, their guitars, because their hands are occupied with skis or the reins of horses.

The second way is by linking rock to the mountain folk culture, which the sleigh ride epitomises. This also happens through the costumes of the performers, who wear traditional mountain dress, and the depiction of a party where the attendees, also clad in traditional costumes, dance to the songs of the rockers. The title song, *Sleigh Ride*, is sung by Skaldowie and Alibabki, who begin with high-pitched voices, reminiscent of mountain singing. Finally, stripping rock of its sense of rebellion and the present moment happens through their association with the photographer. This character, played by one of the greatest Polish stars of the 1960s, Bogumił Kobiela, seems to come from a different epoch. His car is from before the Second World War and his clothes are typical of a gentleman from the early twentieth century: he wears breeches and knee-high socks and sports a curled moustache. Although the photographer is presented as an eccentric outsider, in line with the way Kobiela was cast in most films, ultimately the film's message is that rock music and the rock lifestyle are innocuous and can coexist with different cultures: pop, folk and archaic. As well as being influenced by these cultures, big beat manages to update them, rendering mountain folk sexier and more contemporary. Skaldowie's ski acrobatics brings to mind the scene in the Alps in Lester's *Help!*, in which the Beatles show their physical prowess.

In *How Skaldowie Were Born* Kokesz brought the band to the Baltic coast. Again, this film in some way emulates the work of Lester, who in turn followed the first film about the Beatles with another. *How Skaldowie Were Born* is a mockumentary, filled with music clips, presenting the songs of this band. The mockumentary part consists of a voice over belonging to the band's leader, Andrzej Zieliński, who presents the beginnings of the band in a humorous way. He says that the second member was easy to find because it was his own brother, Jacek. However, the next member, a drummer, was playing in a brass band and he was snatched during this performance, using chloroform. In this way the film suggests that Skaldowie's origins lie in part in Polish brass bands with their military tradition. Skaldowie are shown in white mock military costumes with epaulettes, bringing to mind the costumes of the Beatles from the cover of their album, *Sgt. Pepper's Lonely Hearts Club Band*, released two years earlier. The drummer is shown sporting a similar costume. In this way Kokesz shows the continuity between the Polish military tradition and big beat, as well as pointing to the similarity between Polish and western (British) rock. Another member of the band is spotted when singing 'O sole mio' in a mock opera voice, while working as a welder in the shipyard.

Andrzej Zieliński explains in the voice-over that if the guy was able to sing with enthusiasm in such conditions, this means that he will fit into the band. Although this is meant to be a humorous comment, it suggests that there is no conflict between rock and this Neapolitan song. The rest of the film shows the band performing against the background of the Baltic Sea: riding a pedalo, sitting on a boat, jumping from a boat into the sea, juxtaposed with images of attractive female holidaymakers. The film thus acts as an advertisement for the Baltic tourist industry. An exception is a clip to 'Prześliczna wiolonczelistka' (A Super-Beautiful Cellist) performed with a female cellist (played by popular actress, Ewa Szykulska) and a military orchestra. Such a performance evidently suggests that Skaldowie's music fits into such a non-rock context very well.

Another music video 'combine' is *I ty będziesz moją panią* (*And You Will be My Lady*, 1969), directed by Grzegorz Lasota, lasting 20 minutes and made up of clips to the songs of Marek Grechuta (1945–2006). Most likely Grechuta received the honour of being a protagonist of such a film because he was very popular at the time and the type of art he represented was seen as a 'safe bet' from the perspective of television's requirements, similarly as the productions of Skaldowie, although for different reasons. Grechuta's songs represented so-called sung poetry, written to pre-existing poems or lyrics with high poetic quality and performed in a way which foregrounded the lyrical content as opposed to music (Piotrowska 2019: 324–325). His entire demeanour also suited the idea of a singing poet, as opposed to a rocker or an estrada star—he wore elegant, somewhat archaic clothes and his performance was restrained—he did not dance or jump on stage, only smiled shyly. Grechuta also did not use any instruments himself, but performed with the accompaniment of a large band Anawa, whose members played a cello, violins and grand piano, which brought association with a classical concert. Significantly, Grechuta claimed that they never had problems with censorship, because he was never interested in criticising immediate reality: 'I always wanted my poetry to provide a refuge, a shelter from reality, rather than being an attack on the grey everyday… A poem which is concerned with "here and there" and takes issue with a specific problem, tomorrow is outdated' (quoted in Szabłowska 1993: 158). Despite not fitting the idea of big beat, Grechuta had a significant following among young people and some of his songs, such as 'Korowód' (Peagant, 1970), are regarded as early examples of prog rock in Poland.

And You Will be My Lady perfectly reflects these characteristics of Grechuta's artistic persona, as well as bearing witness to the specific stage of his career, when he sung mostly love songs. Love songs also fill the film, including the eponymous song, as well as 'Nie dokazuj' (Don't Frolic or Don't Dare), both written by Grechuta, and 'Niepewność' (Uncertainty) to the poem of Adam Mickiewicz. The music was composed by Jan Kanty Pawluśkiewicz, the leader of Anawa and the composer of the vast majority of songs included on Grechuta's first LP, titled *Marek Grechuta & Anawa* (1970). The film is set in some old castle or mansion which Grechuta passess through, interacting with the female cellist, Anna Wojtowicz (the only woman in his band) and some other women, who are the objects of his romantic attention. In 'Uncertainty', which begins the film, Grechuta descends the stairs with a candlestick in his hand and finds himself in a salon where his band already waits for him. There are only candles lighting the room and the wall is decorated by an old portrait, adding to the gothic aura of the film. In the middle of the song the camera leaves the interior and for a moment we see Grechuta giving a flower and kissing his cellist on a small bridge in a park, surrounding the mansion. The remaining songs follow the same formula. In 'Don't Frolic', which ends the film, the artist again sings in the salon, but this time we see close-ups of many portraits, while he directs his love song to a discreetly smiling Wojtowicz.

Softening big beat by associating it with pop, folk music and culture, Polish Romanticism, military music, tourism and humour and the absence of rebellion in the discussed examples might be regarded as an effect of censorship (mostly in the form of self-censorship), pointing to the fear of rock on the part of the political and cultural establishment. Such an explanation inevitably draws attention to the constraints of working under the state socialist system. These constraints were even more pervasive in television than in cinema where filmmakers had more autonomy, and stronger than in live music, when Polish bands could sing and behave practically how they wanted, because Estrada, which organised live events, was decentralised and thus its operations were more difficult to control, and concerts were rarely visited by the censors (Patton 2012). However, not only in Poland and the socialist Eastern Europe was rock softened when put on screen; it happened in the West too, as exemplified by films with Elvis Presley, and 'audiovisual performances by Pat Boone, Frankie Avalon, Fabian, Bobby Ryddel and other "teen-idols" in the late 1950s and early 1960s which were widely perceived as inappropriate, sanitized and tamed versions of the original, raw and rawdy rock'n'roll stars of the mid-1950s' (Karja 2003: 123).

When discussing Polish musicals prompted by the big beat wave, I mentioned that the songs of the musical stars, such as Skaldowie, never belonged to their greatest films and were forgotten. This fact contributed to these films ageing rather badly. Possible reasons why the authors used such immemorable songs might be their lack of knowledge about the taste of the young audience and privileging narratives over the songs, to discourage what Anahid Kassabian terms 'affiliating identifications' (Kassabian 2001: 2). The choice of songs used by the authors of *Sleigh Ride*, *How Skaldowie Were Born* and *And You Will be My Lady* is different—all three films are built from the greatest hits of their performers. This points to a different strategy, encouraging affiliating identifications by, metaphorically speaking, moving freely between the world conjured up on screen and one existing externally, strengthening previous connotations of the songs. The fact that Kokesz and Lasota used very catchy, well-known songs ensured that their films fared much better with the passage of time.

= = =

Music Videos in the Polish *Top of the Pops*

The framework in which music clips were broadcast changed in October 1982, when Polish television launched *Telewizyjna Lista Przebojów*, a Polish version of *Top of the Pops*, the first Polish television programme made exclusively of Polish music videos. *Telewizyjna Lista Przebojów* was inspired by MTV, which started in 1981 and its first instalment was planned for 13 December 1981, but it did not happen due to the imposition of martial law.

When it was eventually launched, it showed the most popular Polish songs of the week, chosen by the audience. The first song/video which won this poll was 'Co mi panie dasz' (God What Will You Give Me) by the band Bajm. Unlike the clips from the 1960s which were often shot on location, the vast majority of the clips used in this programme and in subsequent versions of the Polish *Top of the Pops* were shot in the studio, with rather modest sets, as was the case with 'God What Will You Give Me'. The overall impression was of a static film, devoid of any narrative, whose only goal was showing the singer at his/her most attractive; somewhat in contrast to western videos, which tend to be dynamic. The only exception from this rule was the video to 'Ten wasz świat' (This World of Yours) by the punk rock band Oddział Zamknięty, which was number two in the first edition of the programme. It was shot on location in Warsaw and showed the band on top of a mound of gravel, against some box-like apartment blocks. This music video broke with the tradition of showing Poland at its most attractive and instead moved towards the aesthetics of 'dark tourism'. Over the next few years videos presented in this programme became more complex. Instead of using one location, it used multiple sets, although typically shot in the studio. Instead of showing one artist performing in the same costume, there were artists appropriating multiple personas. The camera also became more mobile, its angles more versatile, and a continuous shoot was on occasion broken by freeze frames. The artists started to be accompanied by other performers, which suggested an attempt to create a story, but the narratives to Polish 1980s videos remained minimal. Another development was including dissolves and optical illusions. Most of these changes can be observed in the videos to 'Diabelski krąg' (The Devil's Circle) and 'Prorocy świata' (World's Prophets) for Bajm and 'Lipstick on the Glass' for Maanam, all made in 1984. In 'The Devil's Circle' the singer, Beata Kozidrak, is trapped in a huge glass ball; in the second she wanders through rooms with cabinets filled with curiosities. In 'Lipstick on the Glass' the main artistic device is juxtaposing close-ups of lips with that of full bodies. These videos were typically of a lower standard than 'the best of the West' (Laskowski 2016), but the difference was not huge and the aesthetics matched what was fashionable at the time in the UK and the USA.

Near the end of the decade some music videos came across as very developed according to the 'western' criteria. In 1987, the year *Telewizyjna Lista Przebojów* was discontinued, a video to 'Aleja gwiazd' (Stars' Alley) by Zdzisława Sośnicka, one of the greatest hits of the second half of the 1980s, has a very large cast of actors, singers, dancers and extras clad in costumes from different historical periods, with a prevalence of the Middle Ages, moving on a chequered floor, as if they were figures in somebody's game of chess. Among them is Sośnicka, stylised as a queen of this eclectic court. The editing is dynamic, especially in the first part of the video. In the last part there are fireworks; rendering this mini-film literally and metaphorically, flashy. This video epitomises the ambitions of Polish television from the early 1970s onwards, to produce breath-taking spectacles.

The possible consequences of introducing *Top of the Pops* to Polish television were the rise in the status of photogenic (or rather videogenic) female stars and closing the gap between pop and rock, and music for older and younger adults. This confirms the view of Simon Frith that video is 'an empowering medium for female acts, whatever the sexist or "objectifying" visual elements involved' (Frith 1996: 225). For example, the previously mentioned Zdzisława Sośnicka was before 'Stars' Alley' regarded as a parochial estrada singer with little appeal to young audiences. However, in this video, whose music was produced by the leader of rock band Budka Suflera, Romuald Lipko, she reinvented herself as a Polish Mariah Carey of sorts. The success of 'Stars' Alley' was also a factor in casting her in *Pan Kleks w kosmosie* (*Mr Kleks in Space*, 1988), directed by Krzysztof Gradowski, the last part of the popular SF franchise for children, where she looks very much like a queen in the 'Stars' Alley' video.

'Stars' Alley' can be seen as a culmination of a certain style of music and music spectacle, pertaining to Poland of state socialism. The next period will bring a somewhat different type of videos.

Acknowledgements I am grateful to Michał Pieńkowski for helping me to establish the interwar prehistory of Polish music video.

Works Cited

Cegiełkówna, Iwona. 2007. Teledysk.pl. *Kino* 4: 48–49.
Chlebowski, Piotr. 2010. Norwidowy *Rapsod* w interpretacji Niemena. In *Unisono na pomieszane języki: O rocku, jego twórcach i dziełach (w 70-lecie Czesława Niemena)*, ed. Radosław Marcinkiewicz, 60–73. Sosnowiec: Gad Records.
Duda, Paulina. 2019. Transgressing Boundaries Between Film and Music Videos: Smarzowski, Kolski, and Music Videos in Poland. *Studies in Eastern European Cinema* 2: 146–160.
Frith, Simon. 1996. *Performing Rites: Evaluating Popular Music*. Oxford: Oxford University Press.
Fryd, Józef. 2012 [1937]. Parada Warszawy. In *Polski Film Fabularny 1918–1939: Recenzje*, ed. Barbara Lena Gierszewska, 262. Kraków: Księgarnia Akademicka.
Hałgas, Iwona. 2009. Tomasz Bagiński. Culture.pl, November. https://culture.pl/en/artist/tomasz-baginski. Accessed 30 March 2019.
Jarecka, Urszula. 1999. *Świat wideoklipu*. Warszawa: Oficyna Naukowa.

Karja, Antti-Ville. 2003. Ridiculous Infantile Acrobatics, or Why They Never Made Any Rock'n'roll Movies in Finland. In *Popular Music and Film*, ed. Ian Inglis, 117–130. London: Wallflower.
Kassabian, Anahid. 2001. *Hearing Film: Tracking Identifications in Contemporary Hollywood Film Music*. London: Routledge.
Kończak, Jarosław. 2007. Ewolucja programowa TVP. PhD, Warsaw University.
Laskowski, Łukasz. 2016. Niosę dla was bombę: Wideoklipy Krzysztofa Skoniecznego na tle historii gatunku. Masters Thesis, Gdansk University.
Mazierska, Ewa. 1993. Szaleństwo na sekundy. *Film* 9: 8–9.
Paszkiewicz, Yach. 2014. Wideoklip jako sztuka komunikacji: Interview with Yach Paszkiewicz. *Prowincja*. http://prowincja.art.pl/wideoklip-jako-sztuka-komunikacji-yach-paszkiewicz/. Accessed 3 November 2017.
Patton, Raymond. 2012. The Communist Culture Industry: The Music Business in 1980s Poland. *Journal of Contemporary History* 2: 433–437.
Piątek, Tomasz. 1998. Teledysk: nie wszystko jest sieczką. *Film* 9: 116–117.
Piotrowska, Anna G. 2019. The Phenomenon of Marek Grechuta—Not Only Poet and Composer. In *Popular Music in Communist and Post-Communist Europe*, ed. Jan Blüml, Yvetta Kajanova, and Rüdiger Ritter, 321–329. Oxford: Peter Lang.
Przylipiak, Mirosław. 1990. Tam, gdzie rodzą się sny. *Film Na świecie* 10: 3–12.
Railton, Diane, and Paul Watson. 2011. *Music Video and the Politics of Representation*. Edinburgh: Edinburgh University Press.
Reiss, Steve, and Neil Feineman. 2000. *Thirty Frames per Second: The Visionary Art of the Music Video*. New York: Harry N. Abrams.
Rutkowska, Teresa. 1992. Zbigniew Rybczyński – czyli siła techniki, toposów i wyobraźni. In *Między Polską a światem: Kultura emigracyjna po 1939 roku*, ed. Marta Fik, 259–267. Warszawa: Krąg.
Szabłowska, Maria. 1993. *Cały Ten Big Beat*. Łódź: Opus.
Topolski, Jan. 2013. Kino/muzyka. Zbliżenia. Teledysk: bękart kina między reklamówką a filmem. *Ruch Muzyczny* 15: 18–19.
Vernallis, Carol. 2004. *Music Video: Aesthetics and Cultural Context*. New York: Columbia University Press.
Wollen, Peter. 1986. Ways of Thinking About Music Video (and Postmodernism). *Critical Quarterly* 1–2: 167–170.

CHAPTER 10

The Power of YouTube: Music Videos After the Fall of the Iron Curtain

Despite the termination of the Polish *Top of the Pops* in 1987, music videos did not disappear from Polish television. On the contrary, they grew and became more accessible thanks to the break-up of the monopoly of state television on the one hand and changes in technology on the other. Proliferation of satellite channels, which were more commercial than state television allowed Polish viewers to watch more foreign and domestic products. From the perspective of the latter, of special importance is the channel Polsat, which in 1995 started to broadcast the programme *Disco Relax*, devoted to videos of a specifically Polish genre, disco polo. Another important event was the setting up in 1997 of Poland's first channel, broadcasting music videos 24 hours a day, Atomic TV. In 2000, this channel was renamed MTV Polska. Inevitably, creating space for music videos led to an increase in their number. The 1990s can thus be regarded as the decade when this genre matured in Poland, which is reflected in a desire on part of some of the producers to create something like a 'Polish style' of music video.

Cheaper digital cameras were another factor in the increase in the number of music videos. Unlike before 1989, when they were produced by state-owned, professionally equipped studios, such as the Documentary Film Studio, which also ensured their 'right' ideological line, after 1989 music videos have been made in private studios, including 'bedroom' studios and by people with no university qualifications. This does not mean that the division between professional and amateur music videos broke down, but the latter became possible to make and were allowed to compete in the same space as professional productions. A typical approach to making professional videos is by a recording company commissioning it from a film/video company.

In the following decade the main platform for presenting music videos became the internet, especially YouTube, launched in 2005, a 'maxi-television', with millions of channels, devoted to specific genres, artists and tastes. This development dramatically increased the capacity of presenting videos, their audiences and the mode of accessing them, allowing for multiple viewing of each video. It became obvious that videos greatly help songs to become popular. Songs with videos often have many times more views than the same songs which do not have them. The importance of YouTube and social media publishing videos also lies in the fact that it undermined existing hierarchies of taste, because online communities and social networking sites are based on class hierarchies and formal knowledge to a lesser extent than traditional media (de Boise 2016).

Apart from television and the internet, Polish music videos also penetrated a different space: that of festivals. Poland has had a festival devoted to this genre, since 1989, 'Yach Film', set up by Yach Paszkiewicz (1958–2017), first in Bydgoszcz, then Gdańsk and finally Opole. From 1991 it has given awards for the best music video produced in Poland (Laskowski 2016). On top of that, the Camerimage Festival, an international festival devoted to the art of cinematography, since 2008 has had a competition for the best music video. However, in this festival Polish music videos do not fare particularly well. Only once, in 2010, did a Polish video receive the main award—for the song 'Zabawa w chowanego' (Peekaboo) by Kora, directed by Bartek Ignaciuk, which refers in an artistic way to the issue of paedophilia among Polish priests. From 1994 'wideoklip roku' (videoclip of the year) was also added to the Fryderyk music awards, the most important honours, awarded to Polish popular musicians. The first winner was a video to the song 'Zanim zrozumiesz' (Before You Understand) by the band Various Manx. In the main body of this chapter I will present some of the most popular and iconic videos to songs representing specific genres and the work of some important musicians. At the end of the chapter I will take an 'auterist turn' and discuss music clips produced by Tomasz Bagiński, a leading Polish director of short and animated films.

Celebrating Parochialism

As with practically all cultures which can be described as peripheral, in this case in relation to the Anglo-American centre, in Polish popular music and videos we can observe two tendencies, which can be described as localism (or parochialism) and universalism. The first tendency is most widely associated with disco polo, as conveyed in the very name of this genre. In the second half of the 1990s its popularity was recognised and promoted by the private channel Polsat, especially in the programme *Disco Relax*, from 1994 broadcast on Sundays (Borys 2019: 67–68). Later the main platform broadcasting such videos became YouTube. Commercially this has been the most successful genre of Polish music existing on this platform, as demonstrated by the fact that the top three most watched Polish music videos on YouTube represent disco polo (Dark 2017).

There are several motifs which recur in disco polo videos, such as life in the Polish provinces, with a specific focus on celebrating private and public holidays, as well as just having fun, and the difference between dream and reality. The dream typically focuses on exotic travels and finding love. Another factor unifying disco polo songs and videos is their optimistic tone. For example, if they contain a love story, there is a happy ending. Disco polo is not a monolithic genre and it has changed significantly since its early successes in the 1990s and this transformation is reflected in videos to this music. To demonstrate it I look in detail at two videos from the 1990s: 'Bo wszyscy Polacy to jedna rodzina' (Because All Poles Are One Family) by Bayer Full and 'Bierz co chcesz' (Take What You Want) by Shazza and two from the 'You Tube era': 'Przez twe oczy zielone' (Because of Your Green Eyes, 2014) by the band Akcent and 'Ona czuje we mnie piniądz' (She Senses Money on Me, 2015) by Łobuzy.

'Because All Poles Are One Family' combines two types of material. One shows the performers, Bayer Full, singing the song at the Sala Kongresowa in the Palace of Culture, the most prestigious venue in Poland, together with other stars of this genre, such as Shazza. The second is documentary footage presenting crucial personalities and moments from Polish postwar history, such as the Party leaders, Władysław Gomułka and Edward Gierek, and the police crushing political demonstrations. By the same token, the found footage draws on the dichotomy between 'us' and 'them', pertaining to the dominant discourse about this period, according to which the authorities were 'them' and the 'people' were 'us'. However, the combination of lyrics and images leads to ambiguity, as the lyrics state that 'all Poles are one family', irrespective of their political affiliations or whether they live in Poland or abroad. The song encourages one to overcome the old political divisions and celebrate unity.

In the video 'Take What You Want' we see Shazza, who in the 1990s was the greatest female star of disco polo[1] and admittedly also the greatest pop star in Poland, playing a shop assistant in a provincial bakery. Her daily activities are juxtaposed with the performance of a song by Shazza stylised for an Egyptian priestess. At some point we also see her dining in an elegant restaurant with a well-dressed, upper class man. We can gather that this part of the video represents the baker's dream about exotic lands and love. The conflict between dream and reality is resolved when the bakery is visited by a man of humble class, as suggested by his clothes, yet physically attractive, who hands the woman a bunch of flowers. He is played by Norman Kalita, a model and previously a member of the celebrated Mazowsze ensemble (Borys 2019: 219). The last part of the video shows two versions of Shazza leaving the scene. The upper class 'Shazza' does it with a wealthy man, who drives a Mercedes; the bakeress with the man who brought her flowers in an old, battered Skoda, overloaded with junk. It appears that using one's imagination is not the only way to achieve happiness; one can find it in real life, in one's own milieu. This is also the message of the vast majority of disco polo videos. At the same time, as Monika Borys argues, the inspiration for Shazza's video was the Polish classical film *Faraon* (*Pharaoh*, 1966), directed by Jerzy Kawalerowicz and the contemporary Egypt, which in the 1990s was a destination of thousands of Polish tourists (ibid.: 223). Although, from the current perspective Polish music videos from the 1990s look somewhat cheap, the production of this and other Shazza's videos look professional. The author of scripts and director of Shazza's videos was Antoni Kopff, pianist and composer of numerous pop songs for stars such as Andrzej Dąbrowski, Andrzej Zaucha and Anna Jantar. As Borys observes, his collaboration with Shazza was seen as professional misalliance (ibid.: 222), pointing to, on one hand, the desire to ostracise and ghettoise disco polo as an illegitimate part of Polish popular music and culture and, on the hand, a difficulty to do it in a market-driven reality.

'Because of Your Green Eyes' is the most popular disco polo song on You Tube and the most popular Polish music video available on this platform, with over 173,000,000 views reached by October 2019. On this occasion the video tells the story of a man, played by the leader of the band Akcent, Zenon Martyniuk, who falls in love with a woman with the eponymous 'green eyes' in a restaurant, where he is a guest and she works as a barmaid and waitress. He brings her a red rose and writes her a love letter. Subsequently, the couple take a stroll in Warsaw's Old City, get married and disappear in his (western) car. What indicates that this video was made in 2010s rather than 1990s is its visual style which betrays the use of digital technologies. It begins by showing the singer recording the song against a background of cameras and the effect of a rolling film reel. Later the screen is split into several parts to show what happens in the narrative and how this is rendered in the song, which is simultaneously composed by the singer. There are also changes in the colour scheme, from almost black and white into bright colours, to underscore the difference between the story told in the song, presented in colour, and the story of its creation and recording, which is in black and white, indicating that art production consists of reducing reality to its basic elements. In one scene the owner of the green eyes steps from 'reality' into the studio where her suitor sings about her and at the same time her dress changes, from dark into white, which gives the impression that the barmaid turned into a bride. There is also a motif of soap bubbles, which Martyniuk touches in the studio and which are also produced by some street performer in Warsaw's Old City, where part of the story is set. Soap bubbles normally stand for 'pie in the sky': dreams which have no chance to be fulfilled, but their double existence might suggest that these dreams come true. Ultimately, the song can be interpreted both as a story about an affluent man falling in love, and about a musician writing a song and making a video about falling in love in the style of disco polo. Although the video is self-referential, as is the case with many music videos, it does not distance the viewer from the romantic tale, rendering the song optimistic. Martyniuk, who was in his mid-forties when playing in this video, does not look like a rock star, but rather like a provincial businessman, judging by his formal clothes. This adds to the feel-good, optimistic character of the video by suggesting that it is about ordinary people finding happiness.

Finally, this video of 'She Senses Money on Me' is described as a parody of disco polo, but it is rather a parody of hip hop video made in a disco polo style, containing all the typical ingredients of a hip hop piece. Told in the first person, it is the story of the rich man, possibly an Arab[2] (as suggested by the head gear worn by the male singers) who, thanks to his money, has no problem going to fashionable clubs, where he is approached by attractive women who 'sense money on him'. This unsentimental attitude to money and women, who are after a man's money, betrays the hip hop approach, according to which all women are sexual and predatory 'bitches'. Moreover, unlike disco polo videos from the 1990s, which were 'family-friendly' and coy in representing sexuality, on this occasion the sexual images are explicit. This connotation is reinforced by the use of cars; a prop common both in disco polo and hip hop videos, connoting status and ambition. The setting is a car wash, where a group of scantily clad women wash cars and at the same time are covered in foam, adding to the erotic character of the video. At the beginning we see three small Fiats driving to the car wash, but there they change into luxury cars. By the same token, the makers of this work play on a typical trope of disco polo, namely the dichotomy of reality and dream, as in the video for Shazza's song and use cars to present it. The singers employ the gestures of hip hop artists, as if they wanted to invade the space of the listeners, yet they do not rap, but sing in a typical disco polo style. This hip hop—disco polo hybrid, which since 2015 managed to attract over 87,000 000 views on YouTube, demonstrates the vitality of the disco polo genre and inventiveness of its videomakers, which is still rarely acknowledged by the authors writing about this genre.[3]

'She Senses Money on Me' is not the only disco polo-hip hop hybrid, which has attracted millions of YouTube views. Such examples are common, while examples of crossing disco polo with other genres (such as punk) are rare. I will explain this situation by the fact that both genres are seen as somewhat 'underground' and rejected by the metropolitan elites (although disco polo is much more so than hip hop) and for this reason can be regarded as authentic.

Despite their great popularity, music videos to disco polo songs remain anonymous. For example, the only thing we can learn about 'Because of Your Green Eyes' from the description on YouTube is that it was produced by Green Star, a Białystok-based leading label releasing records of disco polo stars, including Akcent, Boys and Milano. Only when I contacted Green Star directly, did I learn that 'Because of Your Green Eyes' was scripted by the music director of Green Star Robert Kiełczewski, produced by Anima Films from Poznań and had a budget of 16 000 Zloties, which is the equivalent of 4000 Euro. Given the tremendous success of the song, it might be the best investment ever made in Polish popular music. Despite the skill with which makers of music video convey ideas and topics pertaining to this genre, no music video to disco polo song has ever received the Fryderyk award or was nominated for one, pointing to the previously mentioned prejudices of the cultural establishment.

OjDADAna

Polish rural landscape and the culture of the Polish province also found its way into the music of Grzegorz Ciechowski (1957–2001), widely regarded as one of the most original Polish popular musicians of all times, as demonstrated by the fact that he won ten Fryderyk Awards, more than any other Polish artist. Ciechowski's work is marked by arthouse sensibility and a penchant for experimentation, on one hand and care for mainstream appeal on the other. Ciechowski was leader of the band Republika and is best known for its productions, but he also recorded under aliases, such as Obywatel G. C. and Grzegorz z Ciechowa. The latter he used on his record *OjDADAna*, recorded in 1996.

OjDADAna reflects Ciechowski's double preoccupation with high art and achieving mainstream popularity. Already the title foretells that the record will be popular and arthouse. 'Oj da da na' is a typical Polish interjection, used especially in the region of Mazovia (Waś 2015: 24). Yet, singling out in this phrase the words 'DADA', is a nod to Dadaism, an artistic current which influenced the artist at the time, most importantly due to its affinity to creating collages from already existing elements. As the artist himself explained, it means juxtaposing elements from different wholes; making one song from three different songs (Brzozowicz 1996: 52). Grzegorz z Ciechowa, the alias which Ciechowski uses on the record, is a reference to the archaic Polish way of identifying people, by using only their first name and their place of origin.

The record is based on sampling the work of Polish folk musicians, taken from the archive of the Radio Centre of Folk Music (Radiowe Centrum Kultury Ludowej) and from a record *Songs and Music From Various Regions*, released by Polskie Nagrania in 1996. Ciechowski focused on folk music from Lubelszczyzna, especially the Biłgoraj region (mentioned in the greatest hit from the record, 'Piejo, kury, piejo'), as well as music from Łowicz and Skierniewice in Central Poland. He used many long samples, which enables one to recognise specific voices and styles of singing and added instruments which bring association with folk music, such as flute, pipe and Pan flute. At the same time, he wanted these folk pieces to sound contemporary, so that they could 'function in mainstream media', as he put it. For this purpose, he harnessed the majority of them to verse-chorus structure and furnished them with a faster tempo. He also added to them rock and electronic instruments, such as drums, bass guitar and electric guitar. In this way he created a dynamic folk club music, what some fans of Ciechowski described as electro-folk.

Four of the songs from *OjDADAna* were enriched by music videos, directed by Jan Jakub Kolski, who by then was the most respected Polish filmmaker specialising in films about Polish countryside. These songs were 'A gdzież moje kare konie' (Where Are My Black Horses), 'Oj zagraj że mi zagraj' (Oh, Play for Me), 'Piejo kury, piejo' (Hens Are Crowing) and 'Polka galopka' (Galloping Polka). This collection of music videos can be described as Polish equivalent of what Eszter Ureczky and Zsolt Győri describe as 'popular music multi-clip movie', when discussing Hungarian 2015 film *Balaton Method* (Ureczky and Győri 2019: 175). Most of these videos tell stories, reflecting the fact that they were directed by a film director, as opposed to music video specialist, and they begin with the camera moving along the row of 'holy pictures', hung on a wooden fence somewhere in the countryside. We also see a priest and an altar boy in the background. Such an image provides the scenery of a 'generic' Polish countryside, where life is marked by observing Catholic rituals which are also foregrounded in Kolski's films.

'Where Are My Black Horses' is about an old peasant woman who is sent to an old people's home in a white Mercedes. She is unhappy there and decides to return to her old house and is given a lift by a man driving a truck, played by Ciechowski, who shares with her his sandwich. Her journey to the old people's home and back is filled with flashbacks, showing her happy marriage to a handsome man and sharing with him a traditional rural life. This flashback structure, juxtaposing a happy past with the unhappy present of an old woman brings to mind Roman Polanski's short film *Gdy spadają anioły* (*When Angels Fell*, 1959). The video underscores the difference between the present and the past by the use of colour. The present is shot in colour; the past in black and white. In the last scene the woman flies in the air in a little wooden booth, which can be regarded as a metaphor of her (happy) death.

The clip to 'Hens Are Crowing' shows a typical country house with a thatched roof. Then the camera moves inside, an old man gets up, most likely woken by the crow of cockerels and has a simple breakfast of bread with milk, before leaving on his bike with a cardboard box. It turns out that the purpose of his journey is to buy a chicken. The clip finishes when the man brings the little bird to his home and places him in a colourful little house. The visual style of this story is based on contrasts. The static shots showing peasants against the background of their houses, reminiscent of the documentaries of Yugoslav filmmaker Karpo Godina (who most likely influenced Kolski's full-length films) are juxtaposed with shots of people and camera moving at the same time. Black and white shots, which look like photographs from old family albums, are interwoven with others shot in colour, showing the multi-coloured clothes of peasants. On two occasions we also see Ciechowski. First he is shot on a train playing the flute, an instrument widely used in Slavic folk music, but also one which Ciechowski learnt early, at a time when he was fascinated by the rock band Jethro Tull and which rendered his production with Republika unusual in Poland. The image of him playing a flute suggests that one can be traditional and avant-garde at the same time. The second time we see him in the end of the clip, when he sits between the old peasant and his wife, as if he was their adopted son. It is difficult to find a more telling image encapsulating Ciechowski's project of immersing himself in an archaic culture and at the same time bringing this culture into the present.

For this reason, I do not agree with Paulina Duda, who claims that 'Kolski does not really try to experiment with the music video genre, nor adjust his characteristic universe to fit this new mode of expression. Rather, he treats music videos as a new platform for the expansion of his already-established "world of Kolski". In short, he does not downplay the significance of music videos, seeing it instead as an extension of his cinematic art. It is the image that matters, music is an afterthought' (Duda 2019: 156–157). For me, these videos as much present the 'world of Kolski', as 'Ciechowski's universe'; seeing them one way rather than another is a matter of perspective, in this case privileging either the director or the star of the video. Instead, to capture the specificity of Ciechowski and Kolski's collaboration, I will repeat Ureczky and Győri's description of *Balaton Method*, only changing Hungarian into Polish: 'an intergeneric and intergenerational audio-visual experiment in mainstreaming Polish alternative music while resignifying through retro memory an iconic site of national heritage' (Ureczky and Győri 2019: 189).

Rocking Intelligently

The next type of music videos I consider here concerns a genre of music which I label, with a hint of irony, as 'intelligent rock' (taking cue from the term 'intelligent dance music'). I refer here to artists who are widely appreciated not so much because of the quality of their music or an attractive stage persona, but because of the quality of their lyrics, which are seen as sophisticated, and engaging with issues of importance to the country. In the 1990s, this description fitted well the band Kult and the solo productions of its leader, Kazik Staszewski. The videos to Kult and Staszewski's songs reinforced the ideas conveyed by their lyrics and added coherence to the band's productions. Many of them were produced by the previously mentioned Yach Paszkiewicz, who during this decade was the best known filmmaker specialising in this genre.

Among Kult's best known videos are 'Hej, czy nie wiecie' (Hey Don't You Know, 1987), 'Polska' (Poland, 1992) and 'Celina', all produced by Paszkiewicz. The song 'Hey Don't You Know' can be seen as a protest song against the Polish authorities, known for their abuses, especially in the context of martial law, imposed in Poland in the early 1980s, but also against everybody who holds political power, as conveyed by the chorus: 'Hey, don't you know, you don't have power over the world'. The video consists of archival footage, showing speeches of political leaders (beginning with a speech by Leonid Brezhnev), military parades, state visits of dignitaries and scenes of the army and police suppressing anti-government demonstrations, as well as images of Polish streets during martial law. The message concerns not only the brutality of state socialist regimes, but also their hypocrisy. Some viewers accessing this video on YouTube, where it has over 6,500,000 views (which is a very good result for a Polish rock video from the 1980s), expressed their surprise that such a work was broadcast in the 1980s, given its message. My response is that it was produced near the end of the decade, when the collapse of the old system was in sight and this reflected the fact that, as a minor genre, music videos were less heavily censored than other screen genres. 'Hey Don't You Know' was most likely inspired by the work of Paszkiewicz's mentor, Józef Robakowski, especially his video to 'Czarna Data' (Black Date) by the band Moskwa, which used found footage of military parades, screened in slow motion. However, while in Robakowski's work form is more important than content, as the artist manipulates the image to show its materiality, in 'Hey Don't You Know' the political content is foregrounded.

The video to 'Poland', also produced by Paszkiewicz, shows the band moving through the coastal town of Gdansk (known worldwide as a cradle of the Solidarity movement), privileging places of neglect, such as those of the railway station and suburban railway. These shots are juxtaposed with Staszewski singing about walking the streets covered in the vomit of drunkards and on a dirty beach smelling the oil-contaminated Baltic sea. The film is shot on a 16 mm camera, which amplifies the message by including grainy discoloured images, changing attractive background into a sea of amorphous greyness. Staszewski's unshaven square face and ordinary clothes complete this picture of Poland as a land of alcohol abuse and neglect. Yet, the chorus of the song stubbornly states 'Polska, mieszkam w Polsce' (Poland, I live in Poland), which announces the band's identification with their country, even patriotism. It is indeed love of one's country which makes the band angry about its decay.

While 'Hey Don't You Know' problematises the political history of Poland, 'Poland' looks at the (then) current Polish social and cultural landscape, 'Celina', as its title suggests, takes issue with the private sphere. The titular Celina is a provincial femme fatale with a penchant for alcohol and fun. The province in this case, however, does not refer to the Polish countryside, but more likely to provincial Poland of districts such as Praga nad Bródno in Warsaw, on the left bank of the Vistula river, as suggested by the pronunciation, especially of the word 'Celina'. The video shows a party, in which people drink heavily, dance, kiss and take off their clothes. The colours are garish and the pace is accelerated, which underscores the lack of moderation on the part of the participants in this event. The band is among these people, clad in bright, old-fashioned attire, as if suggesting that they also belong to this culture. The scene from the party is edited with a fragment taking place outdoors, showing a man chasing a woman and stabbing her. All in all, the video is a critical, yet also humorous take on Polish culture, known for its excessive drinking and violence.

The last video I want to discuss in this section, comes from 2007, 'Koledzy' ('Friends', 2007) to a song by Wojciech Waglewski and Maciej Maleńczuk, two musicians, who are strongly identified with 'intelligent rock'. It presents Waglewski and Maleńczuk as two older singers, dressed in solemn black suits drinking alcohol and musing on their friendship. They are served by a younger woman, who subsequently disappears into the background, where she performs a dance. In the background we also see some musicians with wind instruments. The video has a nostalgic feel thanks to being shot in sepia, and being composed of static shots, which give an impression of browsing through an album with old photographs, suggesting that the film recreates a Poland which belongs to the past. While this video can be complimented for its ascetic elegance, it also illustrates that by this point the type of Polish music and music video art which mocks the Polish penchant for alcohol, its provinciality and mild patriarchalism, had reached its end. By the same token, it acknowledges that the creators of 'intelligent rock' of the 1990s reached a crisis point and had no obvious successors.

Striving for Universalism

While producers of disco polo and 'intelligent rock' videos capitalise on their knowledge about Polish history and national character and their target audience are Polish listeners, creators of videos to Polish electronic music, in common with those of videos to this genre made elsewhere, gravitate towards universalism. This tendency is encapsulated by (most likely) the first Polish video to the electronic piece, 'Ucieczka z tropiku' (Escape from the Tropics, 1984) by Marek Biliński, who is also hailed as the first fully fledged electronic musician in Poland (Szubrycht 2016). The video juxtaposes, on occasions dividing the screen into several parts, shots of a man operating a console (Biliński himself) with footage of vehicles crashing, mostly cars, but also helicopters and space ships, taken from disaster films. The video suggests that the man, later presented as an employee of the Department of Catastrophe, is responsible for these disasters. The video underscores the power of computers which can remotely control the whole universe. As in science fiction films, the reality in this mini-movie is transnational, with English functioning as the lingua franca, and the question of Poland and Polishness excluded from the film.

Despite the tremendous success of this production, electronic videos disappeared from the Polish media till the 2000s. The main reason for this situation was the lack of interest on the part of Polish television, which, as I already indicated, was chiefly interested in 'videogenic' stars. When I contacted Władysław Komendarek, one of the first Polish electronic musicians, who was a solo artist, as well as a member of the alternative band Exodus, to ask him why there are no videos to his music on YouTube up till the 2010s, he responded that there was never any money available to produce them, which confirmed my hypothesis. However, this should also be seen in the context of the posture adopted by veterans of electronic music in Poland (as well as elsewhere), namely as 'pure' musicians, distrustful of showmanship and celebrity.

By the time YouTube became the main platform for music videos, electronic music itself significantly changed in Poland in comparison with the 1980s. The genre fragmented into hundreds of mini-genres and electronic instruments invaded rock productions, raising the question whether a particular band can be labelled electronic or not. Such problems are, however, of little interest to this chapter. What I want to argue, however, is that in the era of YouTube, gravitating towards electronic music in Poland goes hand in hand with the production of many videos whose imagery and message are universal. To illustrate this, let's focus on two videos: 'Colonization of Time' (2014) by Komendarek and 'Town of Strangers' (2013) by Bokka.

The examples which I used so far dealt with specific, social and material reality—they represented real people and events. 'Colonization of Time', by contrast, deals in abstractions. The musical piece is entirely instrumental; it is an ambient piece in the style of 'cosmic music', popular in the 1990s and still produced by many electronic artists all over the world. It begins with images of a pulsating line, piercing the black-green-orange background, which slowly changes. One can think about sound or light travelling through space, which provides a modern concept of time. Subsequently the line is broken into many smaller lines, most likely signifying the birth of galaxies and planets. After that, we see more familiar shapes of objects populating the Earth, including people running to catch a bus and a naked woman, but they are all reduced to contours—abstractions. Louder sounds punctuating the beat-less music are accompanied by changes of images, for example a distinct shape being broken into lines or points. The way 'Colonization of Time' works brings to mind the concept of synaesthesia, as used by Nicholas Cook and in particular the type described by him as 'conformance', namely relations of similarity (Cook 1998: 100). Allan Cameron, drawing on this concept, uses as an example Ryoichi Kurokawa's video for Aoki Takamasa's track 'Mirabeau' (2006), in which the glitchy rhythms are 'mirrored by Kurakowa's abstract black and red shapes, which pulse and contort in time to the music' (Cameron 2013: 757). Cameron argues that such videos show how sound and image converge as data (ibid.: 758). Needless to add that such a project is not nation-specific; it is instead universal.

'Town of Strangers' comes from the self-titled first album by Bokka, recorded in English and released in 2013, to much critical acclaim. Music journalists have defined the record as an 'exciting mixture of synth pop, dream pop, shoegaze and psychedelic electronica' (Świąder 2014). The first single of Bokka's debut album was 'Town of Strangers'. It was mastered in London by Many Parnell, who has been working regularly with artists such as Björk, Sigur Ros, Little Dragon, Depeche Mode and Paul McCartney, among others. The music video reflects these influences. It presents the story of a boy about ten years old who feels a special affinity to birds, as shown by him climbing the roofs and being locked in a dovecote, most likely by an angry parent. In the last part of the video we see the boy making something from pieces of wood and rope which turns out to be wings. The video finishes with him jumping from the roof. Of course, the story of a young man who wants to be a bird is universal, bringing to mind the myth of Icarus. More importantly, the video, although most likely shot on location in Poland, shuns Polish landmarks. Instead, it brings to mind a Scandinavian landscape and the dominant way to present it, which accentuates the vastness. Not surprisingly, many comments on this video, as much from Polish as foreign listeners, expressed surprise that the song and video is Polish, thinking that Bokka is a Scandinavian or Icelandic band.

'Town of Strangers' is one of the few videos discussed in this chapter which includes full credits, including the director Dorota Piskor and scriptwriters Piskor and Tomek Ślesicki. In total, one can learn that about twenty people were involved in its production, testifying to the growing importance of the genre in the Polish media ecology.

From Slums to Pleasure Boats

Hip hop music entered the Polish audioscape in the 1980s, via recordings of hip hop American artists. In the early 1990s some Polish rockers started to include rapping vocal delivery, scratching and sampling in their productions. The best known example of this practice, pertaining to hip hop, was the record *Spalam się* (*I Burn*) from 1991, by the previously mentioned Kazik Staszewski (Szarecki 2020: 155). However, Staszewski did not identify himself as a hip hop musician. Hence, 'proper' hip hop artists surfaced in Poland only in the second half of the 1990s, beginning with Liroy's (true name Piotr Krzysztof Marzec) debut single *Scyzoryk* (*Pen Knife*), inspired by gangsta rap, which catapulted him into stardom.

This led to a backlash from those Polish musicians who were hostile to hip hop becoming mainstream (ibid.), reflecting the idea of hip hop as underground and pure. Subsequently every year brought Poland new hip hop records and new stars of this genre. Of them, one of the greatest was Paktofonika, whose story eventually became the topic of a biopic (discussed in Chapter 5).

The early successes of hip hop music were explained by it being a voice of the generation known as *blokersi* (block dwellers): youngsters trapped in concrete housing estates, disillusioned with Polish style capitalism. Hip hop was a way to express this frustration. The history of Paktofonika demonstrates this trend—the members of the band represented the generation of *blokersi*, yet managed to transcend their predicament. The best known video of Paktofonika is to their song 'Jestem Bogiem' (I Am God), from 2001. It is a video devoid of a story, showing the characters walking through some nondescript city, covered with graffiti. This is in line with the dominant style of hip hop videos, but there are also Polish specificities. One is that 'I Am God' privileges what Marc Augé describes as 'non-places' (Augé 1995): underground passages and the areas where the city finishes and the countryside begins, as demonstrated by the recurring images of a railway track and a hill, which the character climbs. Moreover, rather than showing characters driving cars, in Paktofonika's video the focus is on walking. Not only do we see the characters walking, but the camera often focuses on shoes and the city is presented from the perspective of a walker; hence the walls covered in graffiti, which are almost always visible in American videos, move more slowly. On some occasions we also see musicians driving cars, but such moments are short and there are no visions from the city from the perspective of a driver.

The video is almost monochromatic, in part reflecting the fact that it was shot in winter or autumn. The colours are cold: blue and dark green, giving the impression of the city being inhospitable. If we see any bright colour, it is artificial: the colour of some graffiti or advert on a tram, passed by the character. Here nature is as unwelcoming as civilisation; it is not difficult to mistake naked trees for poles supporting bridges. The images are out of focus and blurred, which gives the impression that the clip is made by amateurs, which in the case of hip hop videos is an asset, being proof of the authenticity of the music.

The video begins with the band giving a rapping version of a fragment from the 1970s hit, 'Tyle słońca w całym mieście' (So Much Sun in the City), sung by Anna Jantar. The use of this fragment is twofold:

it validates Paktofonika's production as hip hop music, according to the rule that citation is the fundamental practice of hip hop and provides a counter-point to the gloomy vision of the city offered in Paktofonika's original work. The song itself is self-referential. It lists the names of members of the band and proclaims hip hop as 'authentic music' ('pure technique, no falseness'), which affords its users divine powers ('unlimited potential') and ability to attract the members of the opposite sex. Claims of this type will reappear in subsequent Polish rap tracks, but Paktofonika's was probably the first one which used them so effectively.

A decade later one of the most iconic hip hop videos was 'Głucha noc' (Silent Night) by Peja and Slums Attack. Peja is the narrator of Latkowski's film *Blokersi*, discussed in Chapter 7, and this video reflects on the themes broached in the film. Unlike the video to 'I Am God', which presented the three main characters, 'Silent Night', in a manner reminiscent of American hip hop videos, underscores the relationship between the main rapper, his crew (Slums Attack) and the audience. Most of the video shows Peja singing supported by his crew, looking very much like him: young men with short hair in track suits (commonly known as *dresiarze*) or jeans. He makes the typical gestures of a rapper, amplified by shooting the film from low angles, which gives the impression of invading the space of the listener. Music videos often question the boundary between the space of the performer and the space of the viewer. The gaze of the performer in music video, unlike cinema, is often directed towards the viewers acknowledging their presence, which sets up a spatiotemporal relation between the spectator and the artist. Laura Frahm calls this kind of video 'photographic' (Frahm 2010: 174) and this term applies especially to hip hop videos.

There are also images of cars, passing through dark streets and tunnels and a scene showing the men sitting at a table, drinking beer. We also see some aggressive dogs barking at each other, which can be regarded as a metaphor of the aggression and danger pervading life on a working-class housing estate. As is almost always the case with hip hop videos, 'Silent Night' is a song about and for young men, with women playing an even smaller role than in their American counterparts. Through the duration of the short film we see only one, scantily clad woman with blonde hair, who is there merely to entertain the men, rather than being a character in her own right.

The background to the performance is a housing estate, with some blocks and nondescript buildings, corresponding to the lyrics of the song, which convey the sense of boredom and danger of living on such an estate, resulting from harassment by the police; a motif which also can be found in *Blokersi*. The title of 'Silent Night' is taken from a 1974 song of pop-rocker Stan Borys, 'Chmurami zatańczy noc' (Night Will Dance with Clouds), sampled by Peja. This addition immensely increased the hit value of 'Silent Night'. However, this borrowing was not officially acknowledged, leading to a lengthy dispute between Peja and Stan Borys, in which Borys accused the rapper of stealing from his hit and presenting his work in a disrespectful way. In the end Peja apologised to Borys and the conflict was resolved (Żytnicki 2011). While Borys felt robbed of his intellectual property, viewers of this video commented that Peja resurrected a forgotten song, drawing the attention of young listeners to the heritage of Polish pop-rock.

My last two examples come from the most recent period. 'Chevy Impala' by O.S.T.R. (Adam Andrzej Ostrowski), a popular rapper from Łódź, uploaded on YouTube in 2018 and by this point boasting about 5,000,000 views represents what I describe as 'nostalgic hip hop'. Such hip hop not only references past achievements of popular music in a given country, but suggests that the past is better than the present. The very title of the song, from Chevrolet Impala, expresses affection for 'classical' things, favoured over what is new. This is confirmed by the first lines of the song where the intellectual standard of Polish rappers is described as if 'being stolen from Zenon Martyniuk', the previously mentioned star of disco polo. Such a comparison, of course, is an indictment of the decline of this genre. The main point of reference is the 1990s, as demonstrated by mentioning the song 'You Are God' by Paktofonika, as well as audio-cassettes which stand for a world free of social media.

Visually, the film brings to mind American hip hop from the West Coast. It is full of old American cars, cruising in slow motion in what looks like a resort, with tasteful wooden villas hidden in a wood. The colours are warm, the opposite of what one could see in the two videos previously discussed. The change can be seen as an acknowledgement that hip hop made rappers such as O.S.T.R. affluent, but at the cost of the genre losing its innocence and authenticity. Unlike in the old videos, we here find all essential information about the video, namely that it was produced and directed by Michał Kawecki and Bartek Jankowski, and was edited and coloured by Ziemowit Jaworski.

My last example comes from 2016—it is the video to 'Błąd' (Mistake) by two musicians from Szczecin, Łona and Webber. Łona (Adam Bogumił

Zieliński) is the lyricist and rapper, while Webber (Andrzej Mikosz) is the music producer. Łona, who is also a lawyer specialising in copyright, is a leading representative of the so-called intelligentsia rap (Grzebałkowska and Karaś 2012). This means that he is well educated, but also that the perspective he adopts in his songs is that of a member of the intelligentsia, who feels superior to the rest of society, albeit expressing it in a subtle and humorous way.

In 'Mistake' Łona presents himself as an intellectual who tries to read in peace, but is continuously interrupted, first by a girl looking for a friend, then tourists searching for historical monuments and finally three quarrelling men on a boat who ask Łona to be an arbiter in their dispute. Łona's status as a representative of the intelligentsia is underscored by his attire—in the first fragment of the video he parades in a civil servant's suit consisting of a black jacket, white shirt and a tie. Later his clothes become more informal, but on no occasion does he look like a typical hip hop musician in loose trousers and a hoodie. Similarly, rather than walking through a high-rise estate, we see him in the historic centre of the city or on a pleasure boat—locations very unusual in hip hop music.

Despite wearing its intelligent ethos on its sleeves or because of it, the video of 'Mistake' proved very popular, attracting almost 9,000,000 since its premiere, a sign of great popularity of Polish hip hop and its growing sophistication.

Between Music Video and Computer Game

I mentioned earlier that music videos brought Polish filmmakers significant international recognition and, conversely, internationally recognised Polish filmmakers dabbled in this genre. In the period of state socialism this phenomenon was epitomised by Zbigniew Rybczyński; in the last decade by Tomasz Bagiński, an author of experimental animated films *Katedra* (*The Cathedral*, 2002) and *Sztuka spadania* (*Fallen Art*, 2004), which received many international awards.

In 2015 Bagiński wrote the script and directed his first video to the song 'Chwytaj ten stan' (Catch This State), performed by Karolina Czarnecka, who is both a singer and actress, with the music by Vitalis Popoff. The song is a cross between hip hop and electro, about an eccentric girl and her friends, who begin their cinematic life basking in an underground passage and, instead of money, receive a mysterious paper ball, thrown into a cap by a man escaping security guards or the police. When unfolded, the ball reveals instructions about building a machine, which looks like a cross between a gun and a huge flashlight, and allows the user to control people's movements from a distance. Its construction brings to mind the complicated movie projector from Bagiński's *Fallen Art*. After a couple of false starts, the constructors climb the highest building in the town and direct their machine towards three young women who jump into the air as if they were marionettes, which again brings to mind *Fallen Art*, where the projector sets in motion a fallen soldier. The short film can thus be regarded as a sunnier version of *Fallen Art*, as in both films the conflict is about controlling the bodies of other people.

The video has some elements typical for Bagiński's style, such as mixing life action with animation, by showing the characters freezing and changing into characters in a comic strip, a motif of defying gravity and super-fast storytelling. The montage is very dynamic, but not for the sake of making as many cuts as possible, but rather to save precious seconds to tell the story economically. The film is shot in Białystok, Bagiński's hometown. Located in the eastern part of Poland, it epitomises 'Poland B'—rural, poor and socially conservative Poland, which Bagiński changed in his film into a funky, dynamic and futuristic city.

Although it is not possible to state precisely how much a song owes its success to the video, on this occasion it appears to me that the video helped the song immensely, given that it is not a catchy song, but at best a 'niche' hit. Despite that, since 2015 it attracted over 6,000,000 views. The importance of the video is also reflected in the viewers' comments, which focus more on the video than the song. The prestige of the video is augmented by a documentary film, also available on YouTube, about its production, in which Bagiński muses on his attachment to Białystok.

The second of Bagiński's videos is to the song 'Małomiasteczkowy' (Small-Town) from the record of the same title, recorded in 2018 by one the greatest Polish pop stars of the 2010s, Dawid Podsiadło, whose career started with winning the television talent show, *X Factor*, in 2012. Since then, Podsiadło released several bestselling records, praised for their modern sound and optimistic tone. In the singer's own words, in Poland 'small-townness' has negative connotations and he wanted to change this, by showing 'small-towness' in a positive light (Świąder 2019). Bagiński's video helped Podsiadło in this task. As usual, he offers us a story. This time it concerns a woodsman from somewhere in the Polish province, who digs out a tree with its roots to bring to the city where it is planted on a newly built housing estate and after fulfilling this task, returns home. The video is based on a dichotomy: the city/civilisation versus the province/nature. The province wins as it is beautified: shown in flattering colours, which makes the trees glow, while the city is presented as a concrete desert, immersed in cold blue light.

Although such praise of nature seems to be very different from what Bagiński offered in his previous productions which were focused on technology, the video to 'Small-Town Boy' also reveals the director's technophilia, by devoting much attention to an excavator used to dig up the tree. Thanks to fast editing and using multiple camera angles, the excavator looks complex and modern, suggesting that people who use such machines, even if they come from small towns, aren't simpletons. The video was watched in less than a year by more than 27,000,000 viewers, testifying to the appeal of the song and the video.

Bagiński videos set a high standard for the subgenre of Polish videos which can be described as 'narrative video'. It remains to be seen whether his successes will lead to creative imitations.

Conclusions

In the earlier parts of this book I often mentioned imbalances, absences and gaps, such as the lack of biographical films about the greatest Polish popular music stars or the scarcity of hits in Polish postwar musicals. This criticism cannot be so easily directed towards Polish music videos of the post-communist period, because almost every important artist or genre is represented in them. They thus act as a litmus test of the state of Polish popular music of the last three decades. Checking their popularity also provides a good insight into the changes which took place in Polish popular music over this period, marked by the declining importance of rock and the growth in popularity of disco polo, hip hop and electronic music.

Do these videos testify to the originality of Polish popular music and videos? This is a difficult question, as demonstrated by the attempts of my predecessors, for example Mariusz Gradowski, who asked such a question in relation to Polish rock. Gradowski points to the difficulty of defining originality and establishing that a certain musician was the first to use a specific technical or stylistic innovation. He maintains that the main claim to originality in relation to Polish rock was its use of Polish language and drawing on Polish folklore (Gradowski 2018: 92–93). He also draws attention to the individual achievements of specific musicians, such as Grzegorz Ciechowski, mentioned in this chapter (ibid.: 97–99). Like Gradowski, I also argue that Polonisation is an original aspect of Polish popular music and music videos, as exemplified by such diverse phenomena, as the productions of Ciechowski, Bayer Full and Dawid Podsiadło. Such Polonisation does not mean uncritically recycling folk motifs, but reworking them, putting them in a new, on some occasions, technophilic context.

Notes

1. Her importance was the genre is recognised by Monika Borys, who dedicate Shazza an entire chapter Borys (2019: 215–234).
2. Such association of Arabs with wealth has been common in Poland of the 1970s and the 1980s, when Poland welcomed guests with petro-dollars and many Arabs could be seen in Polish luxurious hotels, taking advantage of cheap alcohols and prostitutes.
3. Łukasz Laskowski is scathing in his dissertation about disco polo videos Laskowski (2016).

Works Cited

Augé, Marc. 1995. *Non-Places: Introduction to an Anthropology of Supermodernity*, trans. John Howe. London: Verso.

Borys, Monika. 2019. *Polski Bajer: Disco Polo i Lata 90*. Warszawa: WAB.

Brzozowicz, Grzegorz. 1996. Elektryfikacja wsi. *Machina* 7: 50–52.

Cameron, Allan. 2013. Instrumental Visions: Electronica, Music Video, and the Environmental Interface. In *The Oxford Handbook of Sound and Image in Digital Media*, ed. Carol Vernallis, Amy Herzog, and John Richardson, 752–769. Oxford: Oxford University.

Cook, Nicholas. 1998. *Analysing Musical Multimedia*. Oxford: Clarendon Press.

Dark, Martino. 2017. Top 25 – polskie klipy na YouTube. *Popheart*, July 26. http://popheart.pl/2017/07/top-25-najpopularniejsze-polskie-klipy-na-youtube/. Accessed 10 November 2017.

De Boise, Sam. 2016. Post-Bourdieusian Moments and Methods in Music Sociology: Toward a Critical, Practice-Based Approach. *Cultural Sociology* 10: 178–194.

Duda, Paulina. 2019. Transgressing Boundaries Between Film and Music Videos: Smarzowski, Kolski, and Music Videos in Poland. *Studies in Eastern European Cinema* 10 (2): 146–160.

Frahm, Laura. 2010. Liquid Cosmos: Movement and Mediality in Music Video. In *Rewind, Play, Fast Forward: The Past, Present and Future of the Music*

Video, ed. Henry Keazor and Thorsten Vubbena, 155–179. New Brunswick and London: Transaction Publishers.

Gradowski, Mariusz. 2018. Kruszyć kopię? Kilka uwag o oryginalności polskiej muzyki rockowej w czasach PRL. In *Mity PRL-u*, ed. Jerzy Sosnowski, 81–101. Gdynia: Kancelaria Adwokacka Tomasz Kopczyński.

Grzebałkowska, Magdalena, and Dorota Karaś. 2012. Łona - raper wykształciuszny. *Wysokie Obcasy*, April 27. http://www.wysokieobcasy.pl/wysokie-obcasy/1,53668,11576569,Lona__raper_wyksztalciuszny.html. Accessed 3 April 2019.

Laskowski, Łukasz. 2016. Niosę dla was bombę: Wideoklipy Krzysztofa Skoniecznego na tle historii gatunku. Masters Thesis, Gdansk University.

Paszkiewicz, Yach. 2014. Wideoklip jako sztuka komunikacji: Interview with Yach Paszkiewicz. *Prowincja*. http://prowincja.art.pl/wideoklip-jako-sztuka-komunikacji-yach-paszkiewicz/. Accessed 3 November 2017.

Railton, Diane, and Paul Watson. 2011. *Music Video and the Politics of Representation*. Edinburgh: Edinburgh University Press.

Świąder, Jacek. 2014. Bokka, Culture.pl. http://culture.pl/en/artist/bokka. Accessed 3 November 2017.

Świąder, Jacek. 2019. Dawid Podsiadło. Culture.pl, January. https://culture.pl/pl/artist/dawid-podsiadlo. Accessed 27 March 2019.

Szarecki, Artur. 2020. The Making of Polish Hip-Hop: Music, Nationality, and the Limits of Hegemony. In *Made in Poland*, ed. Patryk Gałuszka. London: Routledge.

Szubrycht, Jarek. 2016. Marek Biliński: Między klasyką a kontrolą rzeczywistości. In *Antologia Polskiej Muzyki Elektronicznej*, ed. Marek Horodniczy, 17–23. Warszawa: Narodowe Centrum Kultury.

Ureczky, Eszter, and Zsolt Győri. 2019. Fluid Audio-spatial Aesthetics and the Communalization of Popular Music in the Multi-clip Movie *Balaton Method*. *Studies in Eastern European Cinema* 10 (2): 175–192.

Waś, Natalia. 2015. Folklor w muzyce popularnej na przykładzie płyty OjDADAna Grzegorza z Ciechowa. 1996. Bachelor dissertation, Warsaw University.

Żytnicki, Piotr. 2011. Peja przeprasza Stana Borysa. "Głucha noc" już legalna'. *Gazeta Wyborcza*, September 1. http://poznan.wyborcza.pl/poznan/1,360 01,10213145,Peja_przeprasza_Stana_Borysa__Glucha_noc__juz_legalna. html. Accessed 31 March 2019.

Index

A

Ada, Don't Do It! (Ada to nie wypada!), 27
Ada to nie wypada! (Ada, Don't Do It!), 27
Adorno, Theodor, 7, 8, 26, 229
Adventure at Marienstadt, An (Przygoda na Mariensztacie), 66–70, 74, 75, 86, 138, 139, 142
Adventure with a Song (Przygoda z piosenką), 72, 73, 78, 80
Akcent, 289, 291, 292
'Aleja gwiazd' (Stars' Alley), 283
Alibabki, 278, 279
Alice (Alicja), 99–101
Alicja (Alice), 99
All You Need Is Love: The Story of Popular Music, 211, 222
Amadeus, 171
And All That Jazz (Był jazz), 9
Andersen, Hans Christian, 134
Anderson, Wes, 123, 125
And You Will be My Lady (I ty będziesz moją panią), 280–282
Anna German (series), 186–188, 191–194, 198, 202, 204
Arabudzki, Michał, 118
Astaire, Fred, 26, 81, 101
'At the First Sign' (Na pierwszy znak), 41
Audry, Jacqueline, 185
Aya RL, 221
Aznavour, Charles, 258

B

Bach, Johann Sebastian, 154
Baez, Joan, 79
Bagiński, Tomasz, 288, 304–306
Bajm, 282, 283
Bakhtin, Mikhail, 218
Balzac's Great Love (Wielka miłość Balzaka), 185
Banaszak, Hanna, 162, 163
Bara bara (Hanky Panky), 118, 227, 229
Barański, Andrzej, 119
Bardot, Brigitte, 260

Bareja, Stanisław, 4, 5, 71–76, 78–80, 83, 90, 91, 107, 138, 140, 144, 215
Barjac, Sophie, 100
Battle of Warsaw 1920 (*1920 Bitwa Warszwska*), 201
Bayer Full, 124, 227, 230, 289, 307
Beatles, the, 12, 252, 254
Beats of Freedom—Zew wolności, 221–224, 226, 256
'Because All Poles Are One Family' (Bo wszyscy Polacy to jedna rodzina), 124, 289
'Because of Your Green Eyes' (Przez twe oczy zielone), 263, 289, 290, 292
Będzie lepiej (*Happy Days*), 38
Beethoven, 170, 230
Beksiński, Tomasz, 177–180
Beksiński, Zdzisław, 177–180
'Bema pamięci żałobny rapsod' (Mournful Rhapsody in Memoriam of Bem), 276
Berens, Jadwiga, 82
Berkeley, Busby, 26, 49, 73, 75
Bez miłości (*Without Love*), 161
Bierut, Bolesław, 59, 66, 144
'Bierz co chcesz' (Take What You Want), 289
Big Beat (*Mocne uderzenie*), 6, 83, 85–88
Big Picnic The (*Wielka majówka*), 101–104, 163, 166
Biliński, Marek, 298
Blockers (*Blokersi*), 225, 226, 234, 236, 261
Blokersi (*Blockers*), 225, 301–303
Blonde in Love, A, 77
Bochniak, Maciej, 118, 122, 124, 125
Bodo, Eugeniusz, 30, 31, 35, 36, 42, 43, 45, 51, 81, 186, 194, 195, 198

Bodo (series), 37, 186, 194, 195, 197, 198, 201–204
Bogowie (*Gods*), 157
Bohemian Rhapsody, 152, 165
Bokka, 299, 300
Bolter, 135, 136
Boney M., 224
Borys, Stan, 118, 303
Bourdieu, Pierre, 7, 144, 200
'Bo wszyscy Polacy to jedna rodzina' (Because All Poles Are One Family), 124, 289
Boyle, Danny, 114
Boys (band), 121, 124, 228, 292
Breakout, 93, 275
Bromski, Jacek, 100, 101, 119
Brygada Kryzys, 128, 219, 224
Brylska, Barbara, 78
Buczkowski, Leonard, 62–64, 66, 68, 86, 139
Budka Suflera, 93, 106, 284
Burano, Michaj, 84
Był jazz (*And All That Jazz*), 9

C
Cameron, James, 123
Cassell, Jean-Pierre, 100
Cathedral (*Katedra*), 267, 304
Cękalski, Eugeniusz, 46, 47, 49–51, 198
Chaplin, Charles, 40
Chazelle, Daniel, 114
Chęciński, Sylwester, 133
Chełstowski, Walter, 218
Chevalier, Anne (Reri), 196
Chevalier, Maurice, 26
Chopin, Fryderyk, 8, 64, 65, 154, 156, 241
Chór Dana (Choir of Dan), 271
Chyła, Tadeusz, 76
Chytilová, Věra, 133

INDEX 311

Ciechowski, Grzegorz, 219, 293–295, 307
Clark, James B., 37
Classix Nouveaux, 106
Clinical Death (Śmierć kliniczna), 105
Coen Brothers, the, 114
Cold War (Zimna wojna), 67, 117, 137, 140
Concert (Koncert), 218, 221
Coquatrix, Bruno, 258
Córki dancingu (The Lure), 129
Cruise (Rejs), 245
Cure, the, 177
Cybulski, Zbigniew, 61, 101
Czarnecka, Karolina, 267, 304
Czas Honoru (The Times of Honour), 195
Czerwone Gitary, 84, 85, 224, 250, 252–256
Czerwone Gitary... i pół wieku (Red Guitars... and Half a Century), 253
Czerwono-Czarni, 84
Cześć Tereska (Hello Tereska), 118
Człowiek z marmuru (Man of Marble), 4, 173
Czuję się świetnie (I Feel Great), 157
Czyżewska, Elżbieta, 61, 78

D
Dahan, Olivier, 152
Dalida (film), 152
Dalida (singer), 188
Dames, 49
Dancer in the Dark, 25
'Dancing Euridices' (Tańczące Eurydyki), 189, 192
Dawid, Leszek, 172, 173, 176
Demarczyk, Ewa, 79, 216
Demoiselles de Rochefort, Les (The Young Ladies of Rochefort), 81

Demy, Jacques, 26, 73, 81, 100
Deneuve, Catherine, 81, 100
DeNiro, Robert, 172
Depeche Mode, 177, 300
Destined for Blues (Skazany na bluesa), 168–170, 172, 173
Dezerter (band), 219
Disco Polo, 118, 122–124, 133
Domestic War (Wojna domowa), 72, 100
Donen, Stanley, 81
Doors, The, 169, 170
Dream about Violetta (Sen o Violetcie), 256
Dream about Warsaw (Sen o Warszawie), 247, 249, 251, 252
Drzewiecki, Conrad, 87
Dunayevsky, Isaak, 36
Dvořák, Antonín, 33
'Dwa serduszka, cztery oczy' (Two Hearts, Four Eyes), 142
Dylan, Bob, 12, 129, 223
Dymsza, Adolf, 30, 35, 197
Dżem, 168–172
Dzięcioł (The Woodpecker), 256
'Dziwny jest ten świat' (Strange Is This World), 223

E
Easy, Light and Pleasant Music (Muzyka łatwa, lekka i przyjemna), 81
Edee Dee, 232, 233
Elderly Gentlemen's Cabaret (Kabaret Starszych Panów), 80–83
Elderly Gentlemen's Cabaret (Kabaret Starszych Panów), 274
Eldo (Leszek Kaźmierczak), 225
Elfstrom, Robert, 211
Eminem, 175
Eno, Brian, 233

'Escape from the Tropics' (Ucieczka z tropiku), 298
Exodus, 224, 298

F
Fala (Wave), 220
Falco, 190, 262
Falk, Feliks, 9, 105, 163, 218
Fallen Art (Sztuka spadania), 267, 304, 305
Faraon (Pharaoh), 61, 290
Fedorowicz, Jacek, 88
Femme est une femme, Une, 25, 81
Fethke, Jan, 38
Fields, Gracie, 30
Figura, Katarzyna, 204
Filipinki, 274, 275
Fitelberg, Grzegorz, 29
Flantz, Marta, 39
Flipper, 37
Fogg, Mieczysław, 30, 93, 271
Fołtyn, Maria, 133
Footlight Parade, 49
Forbidden Songs (Zakazane piosenki), 45, 52, 62–66, 68, 70
Ford, Aleksander, 60, 62, 156
Forgotten Melody (Zapomniana melodia), 38, 39
Forman, Milos, 77, 121, 171
Formby, George, 30
Fronczewski, Piotr, 94, 95, 98, 108

G
Gaertner, Katarzyna, 95, 190
Game On (#WszystkoGra), 129–133
Garbo, Greta, 41
Gardan, Juliusz, 29
Gaszyński, Marek, 244, 248, 252
Gębski, Józef, 213, 215–217, 273
German, Anna, 187, 188, 194, 196, 204

Gershwin, George, 142
Ghosts, The (Strachy), 39, 46–51, 197, 198
Gierek, Edward, 59, 60, 91, 96, 97, 99, 224, 250, 289
Glińska, Agnieszka, 129, 130, 137
Gliński, Robert, 118
Gmoch, Jacek, 217
Gnoiński, Wojciech, 222, 223
Godard, Jean-Luc, 25, 36, 81, 211
Godina, Karpo, 295
Gods (Bogowie), 157
Gołas, Wiesław, 74, 100
Gomułka, Władysław, 59, 60, 66, 73, 75, 77, 80, 81, 144, 245, 289
Gott, Karel, 216
Gradowski, Krzysztof, 284
Grand Budapest Hotel, The, 123
Grechuta, Marek, 224, 280, 281
Grierson, John, 209, 216
Grossówna, Helena, 30, 32, 35, 36, 38, 39, 51, 52, 272
Grupa I, 131
Gruza, Jerzy, 100, 101, 213, 215, 216, 256
Gwiazdor (The Star), 261

H
Halama, Loda, 29, 30, 52, 272
Halka, 133, 272
Halor, Antoni, 215, 217
Halo Szpicbródka (Hello, Fred the Beard), 92–94
Hanky Panky (Bara bara), 118, 227, 228, 231–234
Happy Days (Będzie lepiej), 38–40
Hardkor Disko, 114
Has, Wojciech Jerzy, 4
Heat (Upał), 82, 83
Hello, Fred the Beard (Halo Szpicbródka), 92–98, 100, 107, 158

Hello Tereska (Cześć Tereska), 118
Help!, 278, 279
Hemar, Marian, 271
Hertz, Aleksander, 28
Hervé, 27
Hitchcock, Alfred, 41
Hoffman, Jerzy, 116, 201
Holland, Agnieszka, 4, 60, 145, 188
Hołdys, Zbigniew, 236
Hooper, Tom, 114
How Skaldowie Were Born (Jak powstali Skaldowie), 278, 279, 282

I

Ich Troje, 261, 262
Ida, 137
Ida, 117
'If an Adventure, Then Only in Warsaw' (Jak przygoda, to tylko w Warszawie), 70
I Feel Great (Czuję się świetnie), 157, 163, 164, 167, 168
'I Feel Love', 135
'I'm Such a Cold Cad' (Już taki jestem zimny drań), 44, 45, 64
Innocent Sorcerers (Niewinni czarodzieje), 91
Insane (musician), 232
Iron Butterfly, 277
Irzykowski, Karol, 2, 163
Irzykowski Studio, the, 163, 218, 220
'I Stand Up, I Stand Up, I Feel Great' (Stoję, stoję, czuję się świetnie), 165
I ty będziesz moją panią (And You Will be My Lady), 280

J

Jachnina, Anna, 63
Jackowska, Olga (Kora), 102
Jackowski, Marek, 102, 163, 164, 166, 167
Jahoda, Mieczysław, 92, 95
Jail House Rock, 85
'Jak przygoda, to tylko w Warszawie' (If an Adventure, Then Only in Warsaw), 70
Jak powstali Skaldowie (How Skaldowie Were Born), 278
Jakubczak, Ludmiła, 190, 224
Jakubowska, Wanda, 60, 61, 66
Janda, Krystyna, 61, 163
Jantar, Anna, 290, 301
Jarocin (festival), 102, 105, 106, 169, 217, 218, 220, 221, 223, 224
Jarocin 82 (film), 104, 221
Jarosy, Fryderyk, 159–161, 272
Jazz Singer, The, 1
Jędrusik, Kalina, 83
Jesteś Bogiem (You Are God), 172
Jethro Tull, 295
Johnny Cash! The Man, His World, His Music, 211
Jopek, Anna Maria, 143
Jurandot, Jerzy, 80
'Już taki jestem zimny drań' (I'm Such a Cold Cad), 44

K

Kabaret Starszych Panów (Elderly Gentlemen's Cabaret), 80
Kaczyński, Lech, 202
Kaliber 44, 174
Karabasz, Kazimierz, 243, 244
Karpiński, Paweł, 89, 102, 104–107, 221
Katedra (Cathedral), 267, 304
Katyń, 145, 201, 222
Kawalerowicz, Jerzy, 4, 60, 61, 116, 269, 290
Kazadi, Patricia, 114

Kelly, Gene, 26
Keshishian, Alek, 211, 261
Kidawa-Błoński, Jan, 168, 170
Kiepura, Jan, 8, 16, 272
Kieślowski, Krzysztof, 4, 60, 98, 117, 134, 211
Kill Bill: Volume I, 113
Kłamstwo Krystyny (*Krystyna's Lie*), 29
Klenczon, Krzysztof, 190, 253–256
Kobiela, Bogumił, 279
Kobuszewski, Jan, 161
Kochaj i rób co chcesz (*Love Me and Do Whatever You Want*), 118
Kochajmy Syrenki (*Let's Love Mermaids*), 83, 88, 89
Kochaj tylko mnie (*Love Only Me*), 39
Kokesz, Stanisław, 216, 273, 278, 279, 282
Kolski, Jan Jakub, 119, 269, 294, 295
Komeda, Krzysztof, 243
Komendarek, Władysław, 298, 299
Koncert (*Concert*), 218
Kopff, Antoni, 290
Kora (Olga Jackowska), 102–104, 106, 163–167, 288
Korda, Wojciech, 84
Korsakówna, Lidia, 67, 142
Korzyński, Andrzej, 94, 95
Kościukiewicz, Mateusz, 122–124
Kossela, Jerzy, 253, 255
Koterbska, Maria, 274
Kot, Tomasz, 172, 175
Kowalczyk, Marcin, 175, 176, 258
Kowalewski, Zbigniew, 256, 258, 259
Kownacka, Gabriela, 94, 95, 98
Kozidrak, Beata, 283
Krafftówna, Barbara, 80, 83
Krajewski, Seweryn, 253
Krawicz, Mieczysław, 31, 40, 41
Królikowski, Antoni, 195, 204
Królowa Bona (*Queen Bona*), 185

Krystyna's Lie (*Kłamstwo Krystyny*), 29
Krzystek, Waldemar, 186, 187, 192, 193
Krzyżacy (*Teutenic Knights*), 62
Kulig, Joanna, 114, 125, 137
Kulig (*Sleigh Ride*), 278
Kult, 296
Kunicka, Halina, 93
Kurtis, Milo, 163
Kurtycz, Zbigniew, 274
Kutz, Kazimierz, 82, 83, 108
Kwaśniewski, Aleksander, 115, 121, 231
Kwiatkowska, Irena, 94, 98
Kwieciński, Michał, 37, 194, 195, 200, 202
Kydryński, Lucjan, 83, 214–216

L
Lady Pank, 102, 106, 163
La La Land, 114, 145
Lankosz, Borys, 145
Lasota, Grzegorz, 213, 273, 280, 282
Last Family, The (*Ostatnia rodzina*), 157, 177, 178, 180
Last Stage, The (*Ostatni etap*), 66
Lata dwudzieste, lata trzydzieste (*The Twenties, the Thirties*), 92, 93, 98
Latkowski, Sylwester, 225, 226, 234–236, 261–263, 302
Laurel and Hardy, 39
Łazarkiewicz, Piotr, 220, 221
Łazuka, Bohdan, 81, 89
Led Zcppelin, 256
Legrand, Michel, 101
Lenartowicz, Stanisław, 51
Lennon, John, 154, 253, 267
Leper, The (*Trędowata*), 29
Lester, Richard, 215, 278
Let's Love Mermaids (*Kochajmy Syrenki*), 83

Lipiński, Tomasz, 224
Lipko, Romuald, 284
Liroy (Piotr Krzysztof Marzec), 300
Lissa, Zofia, 69
Little Moscow (*Mała Moskwa*), 187, 194
Łobuzy, 88, 289
Łona (Adam Bogumił Zieliński), 303, 304
Love Can Take Everything (*Miłość ci wszystko wybaczy*), 42, 92, 157–162
Love for a Vinyl Record (*Miłość do płyty winylowej*), 231, 232, 234
Love Me and Do Whatever You Want (*Kochaj i rób co chcesz*), 118, 121
Love Only Me (*Kochaj tylko mnie*), 39
Łuszcz, Piotr ('Magik'), 172
Lutosławski, Witold, 69

M
Maanam, 102–104, 107, 146, 157, 163–167, 219, 221, 224, 283
'Macarena', 231, 234
Machulski, Juliusz, 4, 5, 60, 61, 108
Madonna: Truth or Dare, 211, 261
Magnani, Anna, 161
Magowski, Krzysztof, 247–252
Majdaniec, Helena, 84, 190
Majewski, Janusz, 185
Maleńczuk, Maciej, 297
Mała Moskwa (*Little Moscow*), 187
Małżeństwo z rozsądku (*Marriage of Convenience*), 72, 78
Mangione, Chuck, 267
Mangold, James, 151
Mankiewiczówna, Tola, 30, 42
Man of Marble (*Człowiek z marmuru*), 4, 173
Marriage of Convenience (*Małżeństwo z rozsądku*), 72, 76, 78

Martyniuk, Zenon, 118, 263, 291, 303
Matuszkiewicz, Jerzy, 76, 77
Matuszyński, Jan P., 157, 177, 181
Mazowsze (ensemble), 67, 69, 73–76, 138–140, 142, 143, 290
Mazurówna, Krystyna, 81
McCartney, Paul, 154, 253, 254, 300
Mec, Bogusław, 132
Mercury, Freddie, 154
Mickiewicz, Adam, 159, 167, 222, 251, 281
Mike, Angelo, 232–234
Milano, 230, 292
Milion za Laurę (*Million for Laura*), 83, 87, 88
Million for Laura (*Milion za Laurę*), 83
Miłość ci wszystko wybaczy (*Love Can Take Everything*), 42, 92, 157, 159, 162
Miłość do płyty winylowej (*Love for a Vinyl Record*), 231
Misérables, Les, 114
Młynarski, Wojciech, 277
Mocne uderzenie (*Big Beat*), 83
Modern Times, 40
Moniuszko, Stanisław, 8, 133, 156, 272
Monroe, Marilyn, 260
Monterey (festival), 12
Moroder, Giorgio, 135
Moro, Joanna, 191, 193, 194, 204
Morrison, Jim, 169, 170
'Mournful Rhapsody in Memoriam of Bem' (Bema pamięci żałobny rapsod), 276, 277
Mozart, Wolfgang Amadeus, 8, 154, 171
Młodość Chopina (*The Youth of Chopin*), 156

Mr Kleks in Space (*Pan Kleks w kosmosie*), 284
Mrożek, Sławomir, 215
Munk, Andrzej, 60
Murnau, Friedrich Wilhelm, 199
Musicians (*Muzykanci*), 243
Muzyka łatwa, lekka i przyjemna (*Easy, Light and Pleasant Music*), 81
Muzykanci (*Musicians*), 242

N
Nakręceni, czyli szołbiznes po polsku (*Wound Up, or Polish Show Business*), 234
'Na pierwszy znak' (At the First Sign), 41
Nebeski, Andrzej, 84
Negri, Pola, 200
Ney, Nora, 199
Niebiesko-Czarni, 84, 87, 253, 278
Niemen, Czesław, 11, 79, 84, 146, 167, 169, 181, 223, 243, 249, 256, 263, 276, 277
Niewinni czarodzieje (*Innocent Sorcerers*), 91
Norwid, Cyprian Kamil, 244, 276
No To Co, 84, 85, 88, 90, 216, 253
Nowhere Boy, 152
Nowina-Przybylski, Jan, 272

O
Oddział Zamknięty, 283
Ogniem i mieczem (*With Fire and Sword*), 116
Ogrodnik, Dawid, 114, 125, 179
OjDADAna, 293, 294
Oklahoma!, 131
Olbrychski, Rafał, 121
'Ona czuje we mnie piniądz' (*She Senses Money on Me*), 289

On connait la chanson, 26
Ordonówna, Hanka (Maria Anna Pietruszyńska), 41–43, 51, 96, 157–162, 195
Osiecka, Agnieszka, 76, 77, 260
Ostatnia rodzina (*The Last Family*), 157, 177
Ostatni etap (*The Last Stage*), 66
Osterwa, Juliusz, 159
O.S.T.R. (Adam Andrzej Ostrowski), 303

P
Paktofonika (PKF), 172–176, 301–303
Palkowski, Łukasz, 157
Palmer, Tony, 211, 222
Pan Kleks w kosmosie (*Mr Kleks in Space*), 284
Parada Warszawy (*Warsaw's Parade*), 272
Passendorfer, Jerzy, 83, 86
Paszkiewicz, Yach, 268, 270, 288, 296, 297
Paweł i Gaweł (*Poe and Joe*), 31
Pawlak, Waldemar, 121, 231
Pawlikowski, Paweł, 67, 114, 117, 137, 138, 140–145, 172
Pawluśkiewicz, Jan Kanty, 281
Peja (Ryszard Andrzejewski), 225–227, 302, 303
Perfect (band), 102, 104, 107, 131, 163, 219, 224, 236
Pet Shop Boys, 267
Pharoah (*Faraon*), 61, 290
Piaf, Edith, 141, 160, 191
Pianist, The, 37, 69, 189, 290
Pieśniarz Warszawy (*Singing Fool of Warsaw*), 43, 44
Piestrak, Marek, 101
Piętro wyżej (*Upstairs*), 31, 34
Piłsudski, Józef, 28

'Piosenka jest dobra na wszystko' (Song Is Good For Everything), 82
Pitera, Paweł, 256, 258
Piwowski, Marek, 167, 217, 243–247, 250
Podsiadło, Dawid, 267, 305, 307
Poe and Joe (*Paweł i Gaweł*), 31, 35, 36, 41, 52
Pogorzelska, Zula, 42, 197, 271
Polanski, Roman, 69, 189, 294
Poroshina, Mariya, 194
Porter, John, 164
Preis, Kinga, 136
Presley, Elvis, 12, 85, 90, 223, 231, 281
Promised Land, The (*Ziemia obiecana*), 61, 198
Przekładaniec (*Rolly-Polly*), 80
'Przez twe oczy zielone' (Because of Your Green Eyes), 263, 289
Przybora, Jeremi, 82
Przybył, Hieronim, 83
Przygoda na Marienszłacie (*An Adventure at Marienstadt*), 66, 68
Przygoda z piosenką (*Adventure with a Song*), 72

Q
Queen Bona (*Królowa Bona*), 185
Quo Vadis, 116

R
Raksa, Pola, 79, 81
Red Guitars... and Half a Century (*Czerwone Gitary... i pół wieku*), 252–254
Reed, Lou, 267
Rejs (*Cruise*), 245

Rękopis znaleziony w Saragossie (*The Saragossa Manuscript*), 61
Republika, 102, 104, 107, 163, 219, 221, 224, 293, 295
Resnais, Alain, 26
Reverse The (*Rewers*), 145
Rewers (*The Reverse*), 145
Rhythm and Blues, 84
Riedel, Ryszard, 168–172, 175, 176
Robakowski, Józef, 270, 296
Rock Around the Clock, 85, 142
Rodowicz, Maryla, 79, 93, 106, 188, 214, 216, 250, 263, 278
Rogers, Ginger, 26
Rogulski, Krzysztof, 102–104
Rolling Stones, the, 12, 211, 223
Rolly-Polly (*Przekładaniec*), 80
Romeo and Julcia (*Romeo i Julcia*), 272
Rosa, Michał, 37, 195, 200, 202
Royal Wedding, 81
Rozmowy kontrolowane (*Tapped Conversations*), 133
Różycki, Ludomir, 29, 76, 78, 88, 90
Rusowicz, Ada, 84
Russell, Ken, 153
Russolo, Luigi, 35
Rutkiewicz, Jan, 83
Rybczyński, Zbigniew, 267, 270, 304
Rybkowski, Jan, 156
Rzeszewski, Janusz, 43, 70, 81, 92–98, 100, 101, 107, 157–163, 195, 213, 215, 276, 277

S
Said, Edward, 125, 269
Salewicz, Chris, 222–224
Santor, Irena, 70, 81, 141, 142, 274
Saragossa Manuscript, The (*Rękopis znaleziony w Saragossie*), 61
Sass, Barbara, 161

Schlechter, Emanuel, 37, 40, 161, 203
Schuchardt, Tomasz, 114, 195, 200, 204
Scorsese, Martin, 211
Sears, Fred, 85
Seksmisja (*Sex Mission*), 4, 108
Sen o Violetcie (*Dream about Violetta*), 256
Sen o Warszawie (*Dream about Warsaw*), 247, 249
Seroka, Henri, 99
Seweryn, Andrzej, 179
Sex Mission (*Seksmisja*), 4, 108
Sfinks, 28
Shazza (Marlena Magdalena Pańkowska), 121, 227, 228, 289, 290, 292
'She Senses Money on Me' (Ona czuje we mnie piniądz), 291, 292
Sinatra, Frank, 258
Singing Fool of Warsaw (*Pieśniarz Warszawy*), 43–46, 64
Sipińska, Urszula, 79, 188, 190, 214, 249
Skaldowie, 84, 86, 87, 90, 146, 224, 253, 278–280, 282
Skazany na bluesa (*Destined for Blues*), 168, 171
Skonieczny, Krzysztof, 114, 269
Skorupka, Adam, 94
Skręta, Sławomir, 227, 228
Skrzypczyk, Jerzy, 253, 255
Sleigh Ride (*Kulig*), 278, 279, 282
Śląsk, 67, 142
Słota, Leszek, 222, 223
Słowacki, Juliusz, 167
Smarzowski, Wojciech, 269
Śmierć kliniczna (*Clinical Death*), 105
Smoczyńska, Agnieszka, 129, 133–137, 257

Sobczuk, Bogusław, 105
Solarz, Wojciech, 185
'Song Is Good For Everything' (Piosenka jest dobra na wszystko), 82
Sopot (festival), 92, 106, 189, 213–215, 251
Sopot 70, 215–217
Sośnicka, Zdzisława, 93, 106, 283, 284
Spy, The (*Szpieg w masce*), 40–43
Stalin, Josef, 66, 141, 142, 188
Stalińska, Dorota, 161–163
Stanek, Karin, 224
Starr, Ringo, 255
'Stars' Alley' (Aleja gwiazd), 284
Starski, Ludwik, 37, 44, 45, 62, 69, 86, 94, 97
Star, The (*Gwiazdor*), 261
START (Society of the Devotees of Artistic Film), 46, 49
Staszewski, Kazik, 296, 297, 300
'Stoję, stoję, czuję się świetnie' (I Stand Up, I Stand Up, I Feel Great), 165
Stone, Oliver, 169
Strachy (*The Ghosts*), 46, 48
'Strange Is This World' (Dziwny jest ten świat), 223
Success (*Sukces*), 167, 243, 246
Sukces (*Success*), 167, 243, 246
Summer, Donna, 135
Światły, Daniel, 177
Świątkowska, Bogna, 226
Świerzyński, Sławomir, 121, 227–229, 231
Sygietyński, Tadeusz, 69, 143
Sym, Igo, 160
Sympathy for the Devil, 211
Szapołowska, Grażyna, 98
Szarek, Waldemar, 157, 163, 164, 166–168

Szaro, Henryk, 29
Szczepańska, Lucyna, 8
Szczepański, Maciej, 91, 99, 214
Szołowski, Karol, 46–50
Szpieg w masce (*The Spy*), 40
Szpilman, Władysław, 36, 69
Sztuka spadania (*Fallen Art*), 267, 304

T
Tabu, 199
Tacjanki, 39, 48, 49
Tajfuny, 89
'Take What You Want' (Bierz co chcesz), 290
'Tańczące Eurydyki' (Dancing Euridices), 189
Tapped Conversations (*Rozmowy kontrolowane*), 133
Tarantino, Quentin, 113, 114
Tarkowski, Michał, 218
Tati, Jacques, 215, 217
Taylor-Wood, Sam, 152
Test of Pilot Pirx, The (*Test pilota Pirxa*), 101
Test pilota Pirxa (*The Test of Pilot Pirx*), 101
Teutenic Knights (*Krzyżacy*), 62
This Is Elvis, 248
This Is Only Rock (*To tylko rock*), 89, 102, 104–106, 120
Thorpe, Richard, 85
Times of Honour, The (*Czas Honoru*), 195
Timienko, Aleksandr, 187
Tin Pan Alley, 30, 120
Titanic, 123
'To idzie młodość' (The Youth Is Marching), 69
Tom, Konrad, 27, 30, 38, 80, 198, 199, 271, 272

Top Dog (*Wodzirej*), 105, 218
To tylko rock (*This Is Only Rock*), 89, 102, 104
Trędowata (*The Leper*), 29
Trojanowska, Izabela, 51, 106, 214
Trubadurzy, 84
Trystan, Leon, 31, 34
Trzciński, Wojciech, 94
TSA, 219
Turek, Jerzy, 86
Tuszyńska, Teresa, 78
Tuwim, Julian, 42, 161
Twenties, the Thirties, The (*Lata dwudzieste, lata trzydzieste*), 92, 93, 96–100
24 Hour Party People, 177
'Two Hearts, Four Eyes' (Dwa serduszka, cztery oczy), 143
1920 Bitwa Warszwska (*Battle of Warsaw 1920*), 201
Tyszkiewicz, Beata, 78
Tyszkiewicz, Michał, 159, 160

U
'Ucieczka z tropiku' (Escape from the Tropics), 298
Ukniewska, Maria, 46, 47, 51
Ultravox, 177
Umbrellas of Cherbourg, The, 100
'Umówiłem się z nią na dziewiątą' (I Have a Date with Her at Nine), 37
Upał (*Heat*), 82
Upstairs (*Piętro wyżej*), 31–36, 203

V
Vabank, 4, 108
Valkov, Atanas, 203
van Gogh, Vincent, 153, 154
Various Manx, 288
Vie en Rose, La, 151, 160, 191

Villas, Violetta, 124, 204, 256–261, 263
Violetta Villas (film), 256, 258–260
Viva Maria!, 133
Vogelfänger, Henryk, 39
von Trier, Lars, 25
Vox (band), 135

W

Wadleigh, Michael, 165, 210, 211
Waglewski, Wojciech, 297
Wajda, Andrzej, 4, 5, 60, 61, 80, 91, 114, 119, 145, 172, 173, 198, 211
Wajda, Kazimierz, 69
Walicki, Franciszek, 84, 90, 244, 275
Walk the Line, 151
Wałęsa. Człowiek z nadziei (*Wałęsa. Man of Hope*), 114
Wałęsa, Lech, 115, 121, 231
Wałęsa. Man of Hope (*Wałęsa. Człowiek z nadziei*), 114
Warsaw's Parade (*Parada Warszawy*), 272
Wars, Henryk, 33, 34, 36–40, 42, 44, 203, 272
Warszawska premiera (*Warsaw's Premiere*), 156
Wasowski, Jerzy, 82
Waszyński, Michał, 38, 40, 43, 44, 199
Wave (*Fala*), 220
Webber (Andrzej Mikosz), 304
West, Mae, 203
West Side Story, 87
Wielka majówka (*The Big Picnic*), 101, 163
Wielka miłość Balzaka (*Balzac's Great Love*), 185
Wife for an Australian (*Żona dla Australijczyka*), 72–75, 78, 138–140, 143

Wilk, Gerard, 77, 81
Wilson, Tony, 177
Winehouse, Amy, 154
Winterbottom, Michael, 177
Wiśniewski, Michał, 225, 261–263
Withcher, The, 267
With Fire and Sword (*Ogniem i mieczem*), 116
Without Love (*Bez miłości*), 161
Wodzirej (*Top Dog*), 218
Wohl, Stanisław, 46, 50
Wojna domowa (*Domestic War*), 72, 100
Wojnicki, Mieczysław, 89
Woodpecker, The (*Dzięcioł*), 256
Woodstock (festival), 12, 211, 219
Woodstock (film), 165, 210, 219, 221
Wound Up, or Polish Show Business (*Nakręceni, czyli szołbiznes po polsku*), 234, 236
Wróbel, Maciej, 253
Wrońskie sisters, 134
#WszystkoGra (*Game On*), 129, 131
Wysocka, Tacjanna, 39, 48

Y

Yazoo, 179
You Are God (*Jesteś Bogiem*), 172–174, 176, 178, 181
Young Ladies of Rochefort, The (*Les Demoiselles de Rochefort*), 81
'Youth Is Marching, The' ('To idzie młodość'), 69, 70
Youth of Chopin, The (*Młodość Chopina*), 156

Z

Żabczyński, Aleksander, 38, 40
Zakazane piosenki (*Forbidden Songs*), 62
Zanussi, Krzysztof, 60, 211